In association with MasterCard

KEY TO SYMBOLS

13 rms	Total number of rooms
	MasterCard accepted
VISA	Visa accepted
	American Express accepted
	Diners Club accepted
	Quiet location (not situated on road)
	Access for wheelchairs to at least one bedroom and public rooms
	Chef-patron
40	Theatre-style conference facilities with maximum number of delegates
20	Boardroom-style conference facilities with maximum number of delegates
	Children welcome, with minimum age where applicable
	Dogs accommodated in rooms or kennels
	At least one room has a four-poster bed
	Colour television in all bedrooms
	Direct-dial telephone in all bedrooms
	No-smoking rooms (at least 1 no-smoking bedroom)
	Lift available for guests' use
	Indoor swimming pool
	Outdoor swimming pool
	Tennis court at hotel
	Croquet lawn at hotel
	Fishing can be arranged
	Golf course on site or nearby, which has an arrangement with hotel allowing guests to play
	Shooting can be arranged
(H)	Hotel has a helicopter landing pad

HOW TO ORDER YOUR JOHANSENS GUIDES

Our 24-hour FREEPHONE number may be used to place an order for copies of Johansens Recommended Guides.

FREEPHONE 0800 269397

CONTENTS

D1471604

HOW TO USE THIS GUIDE

If you want to read all about a Hotel whose name you already know, look in the national alphabetical indexes on pages 466–472.

If you want to find a Hotel in a particular area there are three ways of doing it:

You can turn to the Maps on page 10 and pages 458–464

You can search the County Indexes on pages 466–472

You can look for the Town where you wish to stay in the main section of the Guide. This is divided into Countries. Place names are in alphabetical order at the top of each page.

Not all Towns feature so it may be helpful to consult the Maps and Indexes. The Indexes list the Hotels not only by Counties, they also identify Hotels with special facilities such as golf courses, wheelchair access, conference centres, swimming pools, etc.

The Maps cover seven different regions, including London. Each Hotel symbol relates to a hotel in this guide situated in or near the location shown.

The Inns, Private Country Houses and Small Hotels appearing on the Maps are listed in order of place names and divided nationally so that, if you cannot find a Hotel locally, you may be able to find a smaller Johansens Recommendation. Copies of this guide and of the Guides in which the Inns, Private Country Houses and Small Hotels appear in full are obtainable in bookshops, by Johansens Freephone (see below left) or by using the mail coupons on pages 473–477.

The prices refer to the inclusive cost of one night's accommodation, with breakfast, for two people in a double or twin room or suite, and prices are also shown for a single occupancy. These rates are correct at time of going to press but we advise you to check them prior to booking.

Facilities: *Before making a reservation guests should make certain that facilities described in this guide will be suitable and fully available.*

Published by
Johansens, Astley House, 33 Notting Hill Gate, London W11 3JQ

Editor:	Rodney Exton
Publisher:	Andrew Warren
Associate Publisher:	Peter Hancock
P.A. to Associate Publisher:	Carol Sweeney
Regional Inspectors:	Christopher Bond, Geraldine Bromley, Susan Harangozo, Joan Henderson, Marie Iversen, Sarah Macpherson, Pauline Mason, Mary O'Neill
Production Manager:	Daniel Barnett
Production Controller:	Kevin Bradbrook
Page Layout:	Matthew Davis
Copywriter:	Elizabeth Hubbard
Sales and Marketing Manager:	Mike Schwarz
Marketing Assistant:	Leonora Tonkinson
Managing Director:	Martin Morgan

Front cover:
Cliveden, Taplow, Berkshire. Winner of the 1993 Johansens Recommended Luxury Hotel Award for Excellence.

Member of Association of British Directory Publishers

Copyright © 1993 Johansens
a division of Hobsons Publishing plc,
a subsidiary of the Daily Mail and General Trust plc

ISBN 1 85324 750 2

Printed in England by St Ives plc

Colour origination by Lithospeed

Distributed in the UK and Europe by Biblios PDS Ltd, Partridge Green, West Sussex, RH13 8LD
and in the USA by Worlwide Media Service, INC. 30 Montgomery Street, Jersey City, New Jersey 07302

No matter where you are, cash is always at hand...

...from Austria to Venezuela, whenever you need cash in the local currency you can rely on the MasterCard®/CIRRUS® ATM Network. With over 135,000 cash machines in 49 countries and territories worldwide, your cash is always at hand.

Simply match the symbols on your card and cash machine and tap in the same personal identification number you use at home.

And remember, when you use your MasterCard or CIRRUS card for cash, you'll receive an excellent foreign exchange rate. So no matter where you are, trust MasterCard and CIRRUS for cash at the touch of a button.

OFFICIAL CARD
WorldCupUSA94™

Ask your bank for further details.

JOHANSENS AWARDS FOR EXCELLENCE

Every Hotel, Inn and Country House which has received a Nomination for the 1994 Award is denoted by our special symbol on its page. The names of the Winners of the Awards will be published in our 1995 edition of Johansens Guides.

The winners of the 1993 Award are shown in the photograph below after receiving their certificates from Sir David English, Chairman of Associated Newspapers, at the Johansens Annual Awards lunch held at The Dorchester in November 1992.

From left to right: *Jonathan Thompson (Hartwell House), Trevor and Christine Forecast (Congham Hall), Geoffrey and Patricia Noble (Langshott Manor), Michael and Annette Royce (The Kingshead), Rick and Jill Stein (The Seafood Restaurant), Jeffrey Carey and Kate Hewlett (Cliveden)*

WINNERS OF THE 1993 JOHANSENS AWARDS

Johansens Luxury Hotel Award for Excellence
Cliveden, Taplow, Berkshire

Johansens Hotel Award for Excellence
Congham Hall, King's Lynn, Norfolk

Johansens Country House Award for Excellence
Langshott Manor, Horley, Surrey

Johansens Inn Award for Excellence
The Kingshead, Bledington, Oxfordshire

Johansens Restaurant Award for Excellence
The Seafood Restaurant, Padstow, Cornwall

Johansens Most Excellent Value for Money
Hartwell House, Aylesbury, Buckinghamshire

...AND THE 1993 JOHANSENS AWARDS RUNNERS UP

The Luxury Hotel Award
Hartwell House, Aylesbury, Buckinghamshire

Kinnaird, Dunkeld, Perthshire

The Hotel Award
Ballathie House, Kinclaven, Perth

Buckland Manor, Buckland, Gloucestershire

The Country House Award
Sedgeford Hall, Sedgeford, Norfolk

The Steppes, Herefordshire

The Inn Award
The Lamb, Shipton-under-Wychwood, Oxfordshire

The Wheatsheaf, Onneley, Staffordshire

The Restaurant Award
Knockinaam Lodge, Portpatrick, Wigtownshire

The Leatherne Bottel, Goring-on-Thames, Berkshire

Candidates for Nominations come from three sources, from all Johansens guide users who send us guest survey reports commending Hotels, Inns and Country Houses in which they have stayed, from our own regional inspectors and from various members of the hotel and catering industry. Guest Survey Reports can be found on pages 473–478. They are a vital part of our continuous process of assessment.

The Judges each year are recruited from among the winners of the previous year's awards. For that reason, although a Nomination may carry forward from one year to the next, the winner of an award is ineligible for the following two years.

The Judges for the 1993 Awards were:-

The Baron of Portlethen, Owner of Thornbury Castle, Winner of the 1992 Johansens Most Excellent Value for Money Award.

Mr Nicholas Dickinson, Managing Director of Le Manoir Aux Quat' Saisons, Winner of the 1992 Johansens Recommended Luxury Hotel Award for Excellence.

Mrs Janette Bland, Owner of St Tudno Hotel, Llandudno, Winner of the 1992 Johansens Recommended Hotel Award for Excellence.

Ms Jan Davies, Owner of Tanyard, Boughton Monchelsea, Winner of the 1992 Johansens Recommended Country House Award for Excellence.

Mr Neil Rusbridger, Chef and Partner of the White Horse at Chilgrove, Winner of the 1992 Johansens Recommended Restaurant Award for Excellence.

Mrs Tina Mussell, Owner of The Wild Duck Inn, Winner of the 1992 Johansens Recommended Inn Award for Excellence.

INTRODUCTION

By Trevor Forecast, Proprietor of Congham Hall, Winner of the Johansens 1993 Hotel of the Year Award.

1992 was a year of mixed emotions for Christine and me, and for all our staff at Congham Hall. It was our tenth year here and it was a year when we were thrilled to receive many accolades, awards and favourable press comments. Not least amongst these were the Catey Award - the industry's Oscar - for the Best Individual Hotel's marketing campaign, and then culminating in November our presentation at the Johansens Annual lunch at The Dorchester of their Recommended Hotel Award for Excellence 1993.

However, like many other hotels and restaurants we have suffered from the recession which limited our scope for celebrations after the awards! What it did do was focus our minds on retaining our commitment to high standards whilst at the same time looking to ways of improving our efficiency, and, most important of all, continuing to offer guests value for money.

We purchased our first hotel in West Norfolk in 1972, convinced that not only was West Norfolk a lovely county, but it had great potential to become an area of growing interest from the points of view of both tourism and business. In 1982 we felt that the time was right to achieve our final ambition of opening a country house hotel. We eventually found and purchased Congham Hall from a private family in April 1982, converted it and opened the doors in November 1982. As early members of the Pride of Britain marketing consortium we have always enjoyed a high percentage of repeat business and personal recommendations from friends. However, since first appearing in the early editions of the Johansens Guide we have received a steadily increasing amount of new business, both from the business community and from guests who come for a quiet weekend break or a few days away from it all.

A word of thanks here to all our guests. We and our fellow hoteliers have all noticed how appreciative you are of our efforts in these times. On behalf of us all thank you for your kind letters and comments, they are very encouraging. You also tell us that Johansens' inspectors seem to have the knack of finding hotels which are maintaining their standards, their warmth of welcome, their friendly skilled staff and all other little things that make up a happy stay in a hotel. The Johansens marketing team do listen to what you, our guests, tell them and also to what we as hoteliers suggest would improve the service given by the Guides.

We are very proud to have received this Award for Excellence 1993 and know that we, along with all the other entries in this Guide, will be striving to achieve the Johansens hallmark of "diversity and excellence for the discerning traveller".

Trevor Forecast

INTRODUCTION

By Jonathan Thompson, Director of Historic House Hotels Limited and Hartwell House in the Vale of Aylesbury, Winner of the Johansens 1993 Most Excellent Value for Money Award and Runner-up for the Luxury Hotel Award.

Historic House Hotels have for many years appeared in the Johansens Guides and our continued support emphasises the value we place on this publication. I appreciate the Most Excellent Value for Money Award which was presented to Hartwell House this year, and I am flattered to have been asked to write this introduction.

Hartwell House is the third Historic House Hotel following in the distinguished footsteps of Bodysgallen Hall in North Wales and Middlethorpe Hall in York. Historic House Hotels is a company dedicated to the rescue and restoration of architecturally interesting and historically valuable houses in order to turn them into first class hotels. Our houses are all at least three hundred years old and in our choice of decoration and furniture we have complemented the style and character of each one.

At Hartwell House we have more than just a beautiful building to offer our guests. There is a very pleasant sense of history, for the house was occupied for five years from 1809 by King Louis XVIII of France in exile in England from Napoleon. According to historians Louis enjoyed his time at Hartwell where he became popular with the local people. He spoke good English and took great pleasure in strolling in the garden to watch the progress of his roses and Camellias. Guests who visit Hartwell House can see his portrait, and that of his wife Marie Josephine, hanging above the staircase. His huge bedroom is known as the King's Room and he received visitors in the library, where he ultimately signed his Accession to the Throne which enabled him to return to France.

The parkland and gardens at Hartwell which were landscaped by a pupil of 'Capability' Brown have also been restored. There are many things to enjoy including a lake and no less than fifteen 18th century statues and follies. Hanging in the bar at Hartwell House are copies of paintings by Spanish artist Balthazar Nebot showing the original formal gardens which existed before the landscaping took place.

In addition to the pleasures of the house and our restaurant which has received a Michelin star for the third year in succession, there is the Hartwell Spa. Situated close to the house this contains a spacious swimming pool and whirlpool spa bath, steam room, saunas and gymnasium. In the Spa Buttery which overlooks the pool we have introduced a light menu as an alternative to our restaurant at lunch time. A woodland walk from the Spa leads to a walled garden which contains two all weather tennis courts and a pavilion.

I like to think that a stay at Hartwell provides a sense of occasion and we try to ensure that our visitors feel like guests in a private house - one to which we hope they want to return. Our aim is to provide the very best in terms of comfort and hospitality, and we are confident that our guests do indeed feel that this represents most excellent value for money for high quality for which Johansens rewarded us in 1993.

Jonathan Thompson

A VI-SPRING BED COULD CHANGE YOUR LIFE FOR GOOD

£50 VOUCHER

See page 479

ON AVERAGE, WE SPEND AROUND 25 years of our lives sleeping. It's something we know very little about, but it's also something few would deny the absolute importance of. Without a doubt, the best way to ensure good sleep is to sleep on a good bed. And you couldn't find a better bed to sleep on than a VI-SPRING.

Every VI-SPRING bed is hand-made by skilled craftsmen using only the very finest natural materials. Every one employs the system of individually pocketed springs which VI-SPRING originated in 1901. A system which has stood the test of time and remains unsurpassed to the present day in providing the best

ESTABLISHED 1901

possible all round posture support.

Recognising that different people have different sleeping requirements, there are 13 hand-made beds in the VI-SPRING range, offering a wide range of spring tensions, comfort and support levels. So no matter what your size, weight or shape, there's bound to be one that's ideal for you.

So if you'd like to improve your life overnight, replace your bed with a VI-SPRING. Visit your specialist VI-SPRING stockist who'll advise which one is exactly right for you. And you can rest knowing the change will do you good.

VI-SPRING

The Original Pocketed Spring Beds

INTRODUCTION

By Rick and Jill Stein of The Seafood Restaurant, Padstow, Cornwall, Winner of the Johansens 1993 Restaurant Award.

Were delighted to be named Johansens Restaurant of the Year for 1993 and even more pleased when we met the runners up at the Awards Lunch at The Dorchester and realised how strong the competition had been. Johansens Guide has been a very important source of business both for out restaurant and for the ten bedrooms above it and to be honoured with this award has been extremely valuable to us.

The Seafood Restaurant is on the quayside in the small fishing port of Padstow on the North Cornish coast. We specialise in fish and shellfish landed from boats, as the Good Food Guide once said, "a whelk's throw from the kitchen"!

We started the restaurant 18 years ago with not a lot of experience in cooking, running restaurants or hotels. We were lucky in that not a lot was expected by guests in any of those departments in the mid seventies when small hotels run like Fawlty Towers were quite the norm in the West Country. Over those eighteen years we have been able to develop at a natural pace so that our standards of food, service and accommodation are now well established. We certainly wouldn't want to start in today's more sophisticated catering world with the basic sort of knowledge of the business that we had when we first opened, but experience is the best of all teachers.

We would like to thank all those people who dined in our restaurant or stayed in our hotel who afterwards told Johansens how much they had enjoyed it. We look forward to seeing them all again and their friends and all other Johansens guests.

Rick and Jill Stein.

POTTER & MOORE · *Gilchrist & Soames*
LONDON

Potter & Moore and Gilchrist & Soames,
both traditional manufacturers of luxury toiletries, offer to the
select and discerning hotelier a wide variety of
high quality bath products.

The perfect touch to the perfect stay.

POTTER & MOORE. GILCHRIST & SOAMES. TELEPHONE: 0733 281000. FAX: 0733 281028

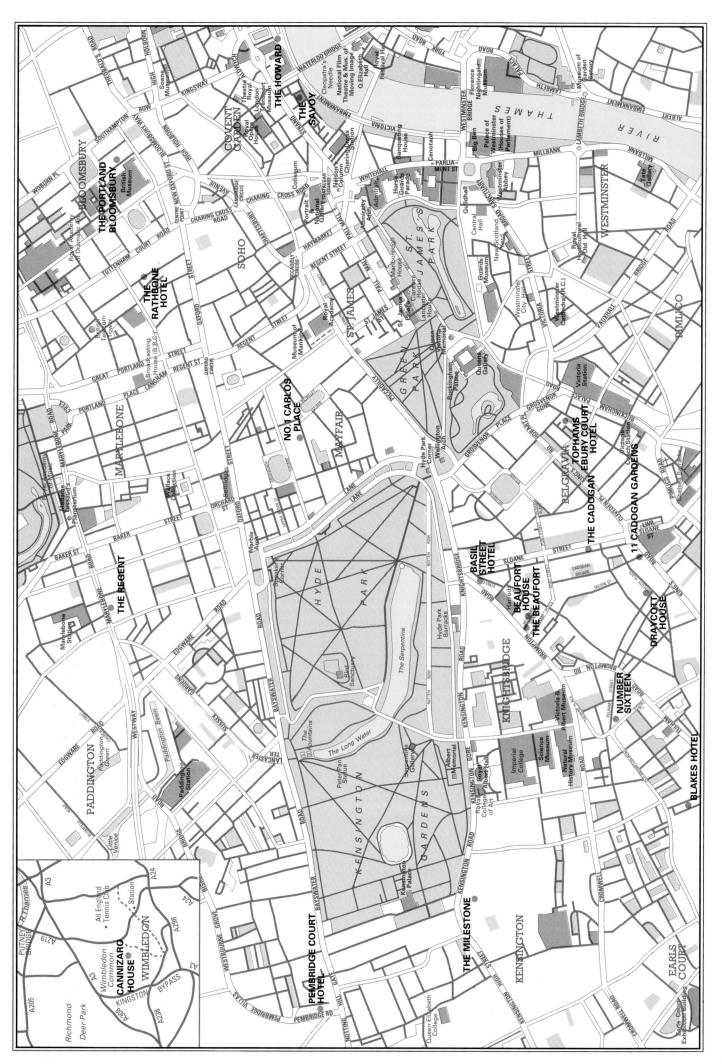

Johansens Recommended Hotels in

London

BASIL STREET HOTEL

BASIL STREET, LONDON SW3 1AH
TEL: 071-581 3311 FAX: 071-581 3693
FROM THE USA CALL TOLL FREE: UTELL 1-800 448 8355

The Basil feels more like an English home than an hotel. Privately owned by the same family for three generations, this Edwardian hotel is situated in a quiet corner of Knightsbridge, on the threshold of London's most exclusive residential area and best shopping facilities. Harrods, Harvey Nichols and other exclusive shops are only minutes away. The hotel offers modern comforts in an elegant traditional atmosphere. The spacious public rooms are furnished with antiques, paintings, mirrors and *objets d'art*. The lounge, bar and dining room are situated on the first floor, reached by the striking staircase that dominates the front hall. Bedrooms, all individually furnished, vary in size, style and décor. The hotel has a carvery/coffee shop and wine bar for lighter meals, alternatively dine by candlelight in the hotel restaurant. The Parrot Club, a lounge for the exclusive use of ladies, is a haven of rest in delightful surroundings. The Basil offers all the services of a modern, cosmopolitan hotel, yet ensures personal service. There is a discount scheme for regular guests. Close to museums and theatres. Near a multi-storey car park, multiple bus routes and Knightsbridge Underground station. Price guide: Single £110.50; double/twin £156.50; family room £215.50. Weekend rates are available.

THE BEAUFORT

33 BEAUFORT GARDENS, KNIGHTSBRIDGE, LONDON SW3 1PP
TEL: 071-584 5252 FAX: 071-589 2834 TELEX: 929200
FROM THE USA CALL TOLL FREE: 1-800 548 7764

Cited by Courvoisiers as 'one of the best hotels in the world', The Beaufort, owned by TV producer Diana Wallis, offers stylish hospitality to both the seasoned traveller and the first-time visitor to London. Situated in a quiet, tree-lined square only 100 yards from Harrods, The Beaufort is secluded yet convenient for shopping, business and sightseeing. The feel is one of a country house and guests are given a front-door key on arrival to come and go as they please. Although there is no restaurant, tremendous attention is given to guests' requirements. The price of the room includes food and drinks from the 24-hour bar, membership of a nearby health club and a superb breakfast, served on fine Wedgwood bone china. Each of the 28 air-conditioned bedrooms is stocked with sherry, Swiss chocolates, fruit and shortbread and furnished with the finest chintzes and wallpapers. On display throughout the hotel is an exceptional collection of over 400 original English floral watercolours. There is no service charge or tipping. Closed 22 December to 1 January. **Directions:** From the Harrods' exit of Knightsbridge Underground station, take the third turning on the left. Price guide: Single £110–£250; double/twin £150–£250.

BEAUFORT HOUSE APARTMENTS

45 BEAUFORT GARDENS, KNIGHTSBRIDGE, LONDON SW3 1PN
TEL: 071-584 2600 FAX: 071-584 6532
FROM USA CALL TOLL FREE: 1-800-323-5463

Situated in Beaufort Gardens, a quiet tree-lined Regency cul-de-sac in the heart of Knightsbridge, Beaufort House is an exclusive establishment comprising 22 self-contained and fully serviced luxury apartments. All of the benefits of a first-class hotel are combined with the privacy, discretion and comfort of home. The accommodation ranges in size from an intimate one-bedroomed apartment to a spacious, four-bedroomed apartment. Each bedroom has been individually decorated in a stylish fashion and each has its own en suite marble bathroom. Many of the bedrooms have views over Beaufort Gardens while several have west-facing balconies which are particularly attractive for long-stay guests. Fitted kitchens complete with modern appliances are an integral feature of each apartment. To ensure a perfect evening at home in London, cordon bleu caterers and waiting staff can be arranged when entertaining guests. A porter is on call 24 hours a day, in addition to a regular maid service. Expert management staff can arrange babysitting, taxis, tickets for shows and restaurant reservations. Conference facilities and executive support services are provided with confidentiality assured at all times. Complimentary membership to a private health club is offered to all guests for the duration of their stay. **Directions:** Beaufort Gardens leads off Brompton Road. Price guide: From £109 per night. Minimum 2 night stay.

BLAKES HOTEL

33 ROLAND GARDENS, LONDON SW7 3PF
TEL: 071-370 6701 FAX: 071-373 0442 TELEX: 8813500
FROM THE USA CALL TOLL FREE: 1-800 926 3173

Anouska Hempel, the celebrated London hotelier and fashion designer, created Blakes to offer style and elegance to the travelled connoisseur – and convenience and efficiency to the international business man or woman. *Architectural Digest* describes Blakes as 'bedrooms and suites, each a fantasy created with antiques, paintings, rare silks and velvets'. Blakes is just a 5-minute walk through the leafy streets of South Kensington to London's new centre of smart shops in Brompton Cross and a 5-minute taxi ride from Harrods. Its restaurant is one of the finest in London, open until midnight and providing 24-hour room service. If you are travelling on business, you can have a fax in your room, full secretarial facilities, courier service, CNN news and other satellite television stations. *Architectural Digest* calls Blakes 'Anouska Hempel's celebrated London refuge'. **Directions:** Roland Gardens is a turning off Old Brompton Road. South Kensington Underground station is 5 minutes' walk. Price guide: Single £130; double/twin £180–£295; suite £300–£575.

52 rms

THE CADOGAN

SLOANE STREET, LONDON SW1X 9SG
TEL: 071-235 7141 FAX: 071-245 0994 TELEX: 267893
FROM THE USA CALL TOLL FREE: Prima Hotels: 800 447 7462; Utell International 1800 44 UTELL; Supranational 1800 THE OMNI

The Cadogan is an imposing late-Victorian building in warm terracotta brick situated in a most desirable location in Sloane Street, Knightsbridge. It is well known for its association with Lillie Langtry, the 'Jersey Lily', actress and friend of King Edward VII, and her house in Pont Street now forms part of the hotel. Playright and wit Oscar Wilde was a regular guest at The Cadogan and his favourite Turret Room still bears his name. The Cadogan's elegant drawing room is popular for afternoon tea and the meals served in the restaurant combine imaginatively prepared food with value for money. The hotel has 70 comfortable bedrooms and suites all equipped to the highest standards. The Langtry Room on the ground floor, once the famous actress's drawing room, is a delightful setting for private parties, wedding receptions and small meetings. The hotel is an excellent base for shopping trips being close to Harrods and Harvey Nichols and Peter Jones. Business visitors will find its central position and easy access make it a most acceptable place to stay when visiting London. **Directions:** The hotel is halfway along Sloane Street at the junction with Pont Street. Price guide: Single £137.50–£157.50; double/twin £170–£190.

CANNIZARO HOUSE

WEST SIDE, WIMBLEDON COMMON, LONDON SW19 4UF
TEL: 081-879 1464 FAX: 081-879 7338 TELEX: 9413837

On your next visit to London, why not indulge yourself and experience the charm of an old English country house? An impressive feat of Georgian architecture, Cannizaro House is set on the edge of Wimbledon Common and its outlook over the park and gardens makes it a tranquil retreat from the hustle and bustle of central London, only a few miles away. Elegant furniture and rich fabrics create the luxurious style of the bedrooms, all individually designed with comfort in mind. Ornate plaster mouldings, oil paintings, huge floral displays and gilt-framed mirrors in the elegant bay-windowed drawing room are indicative of the finesse which is the hotel's hallmark. Run for several years under the management of Mr Ray Slade, the hotel extends the warmest of welcomes to its guests. With the kitchen in the hands of award-winning chef Nigel Couzens, the finest of classical and modern cuisine is offered, together with a most impressive, extensive wine list. Several intimate rooms are available for private dining – parties of up to 80 guests can be accommodated. **Directions:** Cannizaro House stands opposite Wimbledon Common. The nearest tube and British Rail station is Wimbledon. Price guide: Single £102–£118; double/twin £118–£210; suite £175–£320.

DRAYCOTT HOUSE APARTMENTS

10 DRAYCOTT AVENUE, CHELSEA, LONDON SW3 3AA
TEL: 071-584 4659 FAX: 071-225 3694

Draycott House stands in a quiet, tree-lined avenue in the heart of Chelsea. Housed in an attractive period building, the 13 apartments have been designed in individual styles to provide the ideal surroundings for a private or business visit, combining comfort, privacy and security with a convenient location. From spacious apartments with 3 bedrooms and 2 bathrooms to a superb penthouse with 2 bedrooms, most have their own balconies or terraces and overlook the private courtyard garden. Each apartment is full of home comforts. a private telephone line and television with video and fastext. Answerphones and fax machines can be installed on request. Complimentary provisions on arrival, milk and newspapers delivered daily. Resident housekeeper, daily maid service Monday to Friday. 24hr laundry/dry cleaning and laundry room. Garage parking included in the rental charge. Additional services arranged, such as cars, catering, travel and theatre arrangements, child minders and an introduction to an exclusive health club. The West End is within easy reach. Knightsbridge within walking distance. **Directions:** Draycott House is situated on the corner of Draycott Avenue and Draycott Place, close to Sloane Square. Price guide: From £715–£1,850 per week plus VAT.

THE HOWARD

TEMPLE PLACE, THE STRAND, LONDON WC2R 2PR
TEL: 071-836 3555 FAX: 071-379 4547 TELEX: 268047
FROM USA CALL TOLL FREE: BTH Hotels 1 800 221 1074

Situated where the City meets the West End, The Howard Hotel is ideal for business and leisure. With décor that echoes the grace of yesteryear, the hotel's interiors are charmingly furnished. Guests can enjoy first-class accommodation, service and cuisine. The air-conditioned bedrooms have French marquetry furniture, marbled bathrooms, satellite television, a fridge-bar and 24-hour room service. Many of them afford lovely views across the River Thames. The elegant Temple Bar is the ideal setting in which to relax with a cocktail apéritif before savouring the superb French cuisine in the famous Quai d'Or Restaurant, with its domed ceiling and Renaissance décor. A variety of suites and conference rooms can cater for up to 120 people. The rooms are equally suitable for dinner parties, luncheons, conferences and meetings. Full secretarial support services can be provided. The Howard's sister hotel, The Mirabeau in Monte Carlo, offers luxurious accommodation and is situated overlooking the sea. **Directions:** On the Embankment above the River Thames, 20 miles from Heathrow, about 1 mile from Charing Cross (underground and BR station). Price guide: Single £200; double/twin £226; suite £245–£465.

THE MILESTONE

1–2 KENSINGTON COURT, LONDON W8 5DL
TEL: 071-917 1000 FAX: 071-917 1010

The new and luxurious Milestone Hotel is situated opposite Kensington Palace. It enjoys uninterrupted views over Kensington Gardens and a remarkable vista of the royal parklands. A Victorian showpiece, this unique mansion has been meticulously restored to its original splendour while incorporating every modern facility. The 45 rooms and 12 suites are unusual in design, with antiques, elegant furnishings and private balconies. Guests may relax in the comfortable, panelled Park Lounge, which offers a 24-hour lounge service and menu. Cheneston's, the hotel's exceptional restaurant, has an elaborate carved ceiling, original fireplace, ornate windows, panelling –

and an oratory, which can be used for private dining. The exciting and innovative menu offers the latest in modern international cuisine. Stables Bar, fashioned after a traditional gentlemen's club, makes a convivial meeting place. The health and fitness centre offers guests the use of a solarium, spa bath, sauna and gymnasium. Some of London's finest shops and monuments are within walking distance. **Directions:** At the end of Kensington High Street, at the junction with Princes Gate. Price guide: Single £180–£195; double/twin £210–£260; suite £300–£500.

NO 1 CARLOS PLACE

NO 1 CARLOS PLACE, MAYFAIR, LONDON W1Y 5AE
TEL: 071-753 0744 FAX: 071-753 0731

In the very heart of Mayfair, in a perfect location for the capital's most fashionable streets, shops, theatres and restaurants, No 1 Carlos Place offers excellent serviced accommodation for visitors to London. Combining the independence and privacy of home with the luxury and high standards associated with the finest hotels, the 11 apartments are unusually spacious, ranging from one to four bedrooms, and are suitable for everyone from the solo executive to an entire family. No 1 Carlos Place has recently been refurbished to the highest standard by a team of talented interior designers, who have created an individual style for each apartment. Classically English in style with details taken from Europe and the East, the effect is elegant and relaxing. Each apartment features a beautifully furnished living area, dining room, bedrooms(s), luxury bathroom(s) and a fully fitted and equipped kitchen. The top-floor penthouse has its own roof garden. Services provided include: daily maid service, 24-hour porterage, TV and video, central heating and constant hot water, air conditioning. lift service to all floors, security systems and private safes, direct dial telephones. Other services provided on request. **Directions:** No 1 Carlos Place is situated between Park Lane and Berkeley Square. Price guide: £1,175–£2,900 per week.

NUMBER ELEVEN CADOGAN GARDENS

11 CADOGAN GARDENS, SLOANE SQUARE, KNIGHTSBRIDGE, LONDON SW3 2RJ
TEL: 071-730 3426 FAX: 071-730 5217

Number Eleven Cadogan Gardens was the first of the exclusive private town house hotels in London, and now, with the addition of Synergy, at Number One Cadogan Gardens – its new state-of-the-art health and beauty spa – it continues to take the lead. All hotel guests can enjoy free use of the spa facilities. Number Eleven remains traditional: no reception desk, a butler to meet you at the door, total privacy and security. It also offers the services you have a right to expect in the 1990s: round-the-clock room service offering excellent light meals and English breakfasts, a chauffeur-driven limousine for airport collection and sightseeing, and a private room which can accommodate 12 for a meeting and 30 for cock-tails. Another attraction is the Garden Suite, with its own private entrance, two large double bedrooms and a spacious drawing room overlooking the gardens. The hotel occupies four stately Victorian houses tucked away between Harrods and King's Road in a quiet, tree-lined square. Wood-panelled rooms, hung with oil paintings, are furnished with antiques and oriental rugs in a traditional, understated style. The fashionable shops and first-class restaurants of Knightsbridge and Belgravia are within easy walking distance. Theatre tickets can be arranged. **Directions:** Nearest tube is Sloane Square. Price guide: Single £89–£119; double/twin £132–£172; suite £220–£400.

THE NEW HEALTH AND BEAUTY SPA

Free to our hotel guests, Synergy at Number One Cadogan Gardens is the new health and beauty spa owned by Number Eleven. Once the elegant home of the American Club, Synergy now provides an atmosphere of quiet luxury, excellent facilities and the services of experts in the fields of beauty and complementary therapies. The Spa offers a fully equipped gym with a personal trainer and exercise studios, steam room, sauna, an aerobic pool, solarium and a café for light meals. Beauty treatments include massage, Thalgo facials, manicures, pedicures, electrolysis, lasertherapy, special anti-

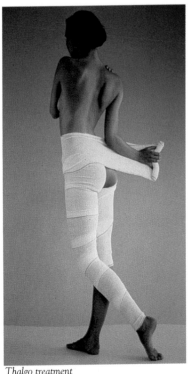

Thalgo treatment

pollution treatment and detoxifying body treatments. Complementary therapies include aromatherapy, shiatsu, homeopathy, reflexology, Hellerwork and physiotherapy. Yoga, tai chi, step aerobics exercise classes, Pilates and Callanetics are available. Here you can enjoy a health and beauty day for just £65 which includes full use of all club facilities, aerobics class, sunbed, facial or massage and lunch, or book in for a special Synergy stay of health, beauty and fitness from £130 per person, per day. Price guide: Free to hotel guests.

1 Cadogan Gardens, Sloane Square, Knightsbridge, London SW3 2RJ

NUMBER SIXTEEN

16 SUMNER PLACE, LONDON SW7 3EG
TEL: 071-589 5232 FAX: 071-584 8615 TELEX: 266638 SXTEEN

A passer-by may wonder what lies behind the immaculate pillared facade of Number Sixteen. Upon entering the hotel visitors will find themselves in an atmosphere of seclusion and comfort which has remained virtually unaltered in style since its early Victorian origins. The staff are friendly and attentive, regarding each visitor as a guest in a private home. The relaxed atmosphere of the lounge is the perfect place to pour a drink from the bar and meet friends or business associates. A fire blazing in the drawing room in cooler months creates an inviting warmth, while the conservatory opens on to a secluded walled garden, where drinks can be taken on summer evenings. Each spacious bedroom is decorated with a discreet combination of antiques and traditional furnishings. The rooms are fully appointed with every facility that the discerning traveller would expect. A light breakfast is served in the privacy of guests' rooms and a tea and coffee service is available throughout the day. Although there is no dining room at Number Sixteen, some of London's finest restaurants are just round the corner. The hotel is close to the West End, Knightsbridge, Chelsea and Hyde Park. **Directions:** Sumner Place is off Old Brompton Roadn near Onslow Square. South Kensington Underground Station is 2 minutes' walk away. Price guide: Single £60–£95; double/twin £130–£155.

PEMBRIDGE COURT HOTEL

34 PEMBRIDGE GARDENS, LONDON W2 4DX
TEL: 071-229 9977 FAX: 071-727 4982

Pembridge Court Hotel is a Victorian town house which has been restored to its former glory while providing all the modern facilities demanded by today's discerning traveller. Privately owned, the hotel is located very close to Portobello Road Antiques Market in quiet tree-lined gardens in the Royal borough of Kensington and Chelsea. Paul Capra has run this hotel for 22 years and along with his loyal, long-standing staff has created a genuinely welcoming ambience where guests are assured of the best in personal, friendly service. The 21 well-appointed rooms, the majority of which are de luxe, all have en suite

facilities. A fine collection of Victoriana, including antique costumes and prints, creates a period-style decorative theme. Caps Restaurant, with its informal atmosphere and attractive bar, is situated in the basement and offers a wide variety of reasonably priced bistro-style dishes. Summer or winter, Pembridge Court is ideally situated to take advantage of all that London can offer. **Directions:** Pembridge Gardens is a small turning off Notting Hill Gate/Bayswater Road, just 2 minutes from Portobello Road Antiques Market. Price guide: Single £80–£110; double/twin £100–£150.

THE PORTLAND BLOOMSBURY

7 MONTAGUE STREET, LONDON WC1B 5BP
TEL: 071-323 1717 FAX: 071-636 6498

Small can be beautiful, as this charming hotel in the fashionable district of Bloomsbury proves. Since opening in 1990, it has acquired an enviable reputation for its own brand of hospitality and elegance. Many features from the original Regency building are still in evidence: a marble-floored entrance leads into a lounge furnished with antiques, and a fine display of paintings decorates the walls. Beyond this room a beautiful little garden backing onto the British Museum provides a haven from the bustle of the city. All recently refurbished, the 27 en suite bedrooms combine the old and the new – Regency furnishings are cleverly matched with modern facilities, and, of course, 24-hour room service is provided. Owner Renzo Rapacioli has introduced a distinctly Italian influence, most notably in the style of the cooking: pastas, grilled meat and fish and sumptuous desserts are served in the hotel restaurant, open from breakfast to late evening. Close to Russell Square, the hotel is convenient for both the City and the West End. Covent Garden and the theatres are minutes away and staff are happy to help guests book tickets. Special weekend rates are offered. **Directions:** Russell Square tube station is on the Piccadilly Line with a direct link to Heathrow Airport. Price guide: Single £85; double/twin £120–£130.

THE RATHBONE HOTEL

RATHBONE STREET, LONDON W1P 1AJ
TEL: 071-636 2001 FAX: 071-636 3882

Situated in the heart of London's West End, in the area historically known as Fitzrovia, The Rathbone is a charming hotel with the feel of a stylish club, while offering the facilities and standard of service associated with a first-class hotel. Crystal chandeliers, comfy sofas, warm marble and rosewood panelling create an atmosphere of warmth and intimacy. The Peacock Restaurant has earned a formidable reputation, based on its outstanding cuisine and service. A selection from the finely balanced wine list is the perfect accompaniment to any meal. The elegant and spacious guest rooms and suites have Italian walnut furnishings and pastel fabrics and all have individual temperature control and air conditioning. En suite bathrooms are finished in pink marble and many are equipped with whirlpool baths. The hotel offers 24-hour room service and same-day laundry and dry cleaning. Two floors of the hotel are entirely non-smoking. Meetings can be accommodated in the impressive boardroom. Oxford Street is a 2-minute walk away; Soho, Theatreland, Covent Garden, Regent Street and Piccadilly are all close by. The City, London's financial centre, is a short journey away. **Directions:** The Rathbone is situated north of Oxford Street, close to Goodge Street underground station. Price guide: Single £110; double/twin £130; suite £185.

THE REGENT, LONDON

222 MARYLEBONE ROAD, LONDON NW1 6JQ
TEL: 071-631 8000 FAX: 071-631 8080

The Regent, London, part of the prestigious Regent International Hotels group, is a majestic, Victorian Grade II listed building located just opposite Marylebone Station, minutes from the capital's bustling West End. First opened in 1899, the Regent, London, has been sympathetically restored to offer today's guest a comfortable and relaxing haven from the pressures of the city, effortlessly blending the grandeur and finesse of a bygone era with the latest in visitors' requirements. Guests have complimentary access to the Regent Health Club, where facilities include an indoor swimming pool, whirlpool, sauna, steam room, 2 massage rooms and a fully equipped gymnasium. The extensive meeting and banqueting facilities – 9 lavishly decorated rooms in all – are fitted out with the latest technology. Guests are spoilt for choice on the dining front, too: there is the Dining Room, where Italian cuisine is served in casual elegance, the Cellars, for hot snacks and light meals, and the Winter Garden, open mid-morning for coffee and patisserie. Bedrooms are very spacious and exquisitely furnished with every facility from satellite TV to fax and computer ports. Sightseeing, shopping, Regent's Park, Hyde Park, the West End and theatres are all near at hand. Directions: undergrounds: Marylebone/Baker Street. Price guide: Double: £180–£255; suite: £280–£800.

THE SAVOY

THE STRAND, LONDON WC2R 0EU
TEL: 071-836 4343 FAX: 071-240 6040 TELEX: 24234

Built on the site of the medieval Palace of Savoy, the hotel was created in 1889 by Richard D'Oyly Carte, the legendary impresario, as a result of the success of his Gilbert and Sullivan operas. The Savoy has a very English tradition of service and individuality. Bedrooms are decorated and furnished in a variety of styles – traditional, art deco and contemporary – and all share a standard of unrivalled comfort. In the restaurant, with its stunning views of the Thames, classic dishes by the legendary chef Escoffier are recreated, while the Savoy Grill is the meeting place for leading lights in the arts, media and the City. The new Savoy Fitness Gallery boasts a roof-top swimming pool and state-of-the-art fitness facilities. Together with its sister hotels in The Savoy Group – The Berkeley in Knightsbridge and Claridge's in Mayfair – The Savoy offers a variety of short-break arrangements, some including dinner, others leaving one free to enjoy London at leisure – call 071-872 8080 for details. **Directions:** The Savoy is on the Strand, to the west of Lancaster Place and Waterloo Bridge, in the heart of London's theatre district. Price guide: Single £170; double/twin £195–£260, excluding VAT.

TOPHAMS EBURY COURT

28 EBURY STREET, BELGRAVIA, LONDON SW1W 0LU
TEL: 071-730 8147 FAX: 071-823 5966

Tophams Ebury Court evokes the charm of an English country house, yet is situated in the heart of Belgravia – one of London's most exclusive residential areas. Nick and Marianne Kingsford, the second generation of the same family to own and run the hotel for more than half a century, have made improvements and refurbishments without in any way denying the character of the original style. A variety of accommodation is offered, from compact single rooms to luxury four-poster bedrooms. The hotel garden room restaurant can be used for private lunch or dinner parties or meetings for up to 20 people. The hotel is named after its founders, Romer and Diana Topham, a family of artists whose paintings hang in the restaurant, where traditional English food is served for lunch and dinner. The location of Tophams Ebury Court makes it an ideal centre for sightseeing, shopping, visiting London's famous theatres and restaurants and walking in St James's and Hyde Parks. **Directions:** Three minutes' walk from Victoria Underground, bus and railway stations. Price guide: Single £55–£75; double/twin £80–£110.

For hotel location, see map on page 10

Johansens Recommended Hotels in

England

WENTWORTH HOTEL

WENTWORTH ROAD, ALDEBURGH, SUFFOLK IP15 5BD
TEL: 0728 452312/453253 FAX: 0728 454343

The Wentworth Hotel is ideally situated opposite the beach at Aldeburgh, on Suffolk's unspoilt coast. Aldeburgh has maritime traditions dating back to the 15th century which are still maintained today by the longshore fishermen who launch their boats from the beach. It has also become a centre for music lovers: every June the Aldeburgh International Festival of Music, founded by the late Benjamin Britten, is held at Snape Maltings. Privately owned by the Pritt family since 1920, the Wentworth has established a reputation for comfort and service, good food and wine, for which many guests return year after year. Relax in front of an open fire in one of the hotel lounges, or sample a pint of the famous local Adnam's ales in the bar, which also serves meals. Most of the 31 elegantly furnished bedrooms have en suite bathrooms and sea views. The restaurant offers an extensive menu for both lunch and dinner and there is a comprehensive wine list. The garden terrace is the perfect venue for a light lunch *alfresco*. Nearby, the Minsmere Bird Sanctuary will be of interest to nature enthusiasts, while for the keen golfer, two of Britain's most challenging courses are within easy reach of the hotel at Aldeburgh and Thorpeness. **Directions:** Aldeburgh is just 7 miles from the A12 between Ipswich and Lowestoft. Price guide: Single £55; double/twin £100.

THE ALDERLEY EDGE HOTEL

MACCLESFIELD ROAD, ALDERLEY EDGE, CHESHIRE SK9 7BJ
TEL: 0625 583033 FAX: 0625 586343

This privately owned award-winning hotel, dating from 1850, was refurbished from attic to cellar in 1989. It now has an attractive conservatory, 21 executive rooms and 11 de luxe rooms (each with a whirlpool bath), offering a choice of traditional decor or cottage-style accommodation. Attention is given to the highest standards of cooking; fresh produce, including fish deliveries twice daily, is provided by local suppliers. Specialities include light lunches featuring hot and cold seafood dishes, puddings served piping hot from the oven, and afternoon teas that include pastries baked in the hotel bakery which also produces a daily selection of unusual and delicious breads. The wonderfully mad wine list features over 1,000 wines and 200 champagnes. There are special wine tastings held monthly and also gourmet champagne dinners. In addition to the conference room, there is a suite of meeting and private dining rooms. Secretarial services and fax machines are available. The famous Edge walks are nearby, as are Tatton and Lyme Parks, Quarry Bank Mill and Dunham Massey. Manchester's thriving city centre is 15 miles away and the airport is a 20-minute drive. **Directions:** Follow M6 to M56 Stockport. Exit junction 6, take A538 to Wilmslow. Follow signs 1¾ miles through Alderley Edge, turn left at Volvo garage and hotel is 200 yards on the right. Price guide: Single £95–£103; double/twin £116–£150.

WHITE LODGE COUNTRY HOUSE HOTEL

SLOE LANE, ALFRISTON, EAST SUSSEX BN26 5UR
TEL: 0323 870265 FAX: 0323 870284

The White Lodge Country House Hotel lies majestically on a rise within 5 acres of glorious Sussex downland in the undisturbed Cuckmere Valley, with picturesque views of the ancient village of Alfriston. Exquisitely furnished with authentic period pieces and elegant drapery, White Lodge is a setting in which to enjoy the style and luxury of a former age, with every comfort and facility of the present day. There are three comfortable lounges, all light and airy, where guests can relax. The cocktail bar is the ideal place to sip an aperitif in congenial surroundings prior to dinner. Whether dining in the attractive Orchid Restaurant or the more intimate dining room, a high standard of service and cuisine is assured. Each bedroom offers every amenity the discriminating guest would expect, with decor to match the quiet elegance which is the hotel's hallmark. White Lodge is only 10 minutes' drive from Glyndebourne, while Brighton, Eastbourne and the port of Newhaven are all within easy reach. The hotel is a romantic setting for wedding celebrations, while for business purposes small conferences and seminars can be catered for. **Directions:** Alfriston is on the B2108 between the A27/A259. Access from the market cross via West Street. Price guide: Single £50; double/twin £75–£110.

BREAMISH COUNTRY HOUSE HOTEL

POWBURN, ALNWICK, NORTHUMBERLAND NE66 4LL
TEL: 066578 266/544 FAX: 066578 500

In the heart of Northumberland, close by the rambling Cheviot Hills, Breamish Country House Hotel is a fine Georgian-style building set in 5 acres of gardens and woodland, offering visitors a uniquely beautiful retreat from the pressures of the working week. The hotel was originally a 17th-century farmhouse converted in the 1800s into a hunting lodge. Now it is managed by Doreen and Alan Johnson, who have created an atmosphere of peace and hospitality for their many guests. There are 11 bedrooms, each sumptuously and individually furnished and all with private facilities. All are double-glazed with all modern conveniences. Pre-dinner drinks can be enjoyed in the comfortable drawing room, beside a log fire on winter evenings. In the restaurant, cordon bleu cooks prepare gourmet English cuisine with flair and imagination. To complement the food, the fine cellar offers many wines of distinction at competitive prices. Smoking is not permitted in the dining room. Activities available locally include riding, golf, course and game fishing. Northumberland is one of Britain's least spoilt regions, with mile upon mile of remote and lovely coastline. The area is also rich in history. **Directions:** Powburn is midway between Morpeth and Coldstream on the A697. Price guide (including dinner): Single: £65; double/twin: £108–£140.

LOVELADY SHIELD COUNTRY HOUSE HOTEL

NENTHEAD ROAD, ALSTON, CUMBRIA CA9 3LF
TEL: 0434 381203 FAX: 0434 381515

Two-and-a-half miles from Alston, England's highest market town, Lovelady Shield nestles in 3 acres of tranquil riverside gardens. Bright log fires in the library and drawing room enhance the hotel's welcoming atmosphere. Owners Kenneth and Margaret Lyons take great care to create a peaceful and tranquil haven where guests can relax. The five-course dinners created by chef Barrie Garton, rounded off by home-made puddings and a selection of English farmhouse cheeses has won the hotel AA 2 Red Stars and 2 Rosettes for food. Many guests first discover Lovelady Shield en route for Scotland. They then return to explore this beautiful and unspoiled part of England and experience the comforts of the hotel. Golf, fishing, shooting, pony-trekking and riding are available locally. The Pennine Way, Hadrian's Wall and the Lake District are within easy reach. Facilities for small conferences and boardroom meetings are available. Closed 3 January to mid-February. Special Christmas, New Year, winter and spring breaks are offered and special weekly terms. **Directions:** The hotel's driveway is by the junction of the B6294 and the A689, 2¼ miles east of Alston. Price guide (including dinner): Single £59–£74; double/twin £118–£142.

KIRKSTONE FOOT COUNTRY HOUSE HOTEL

KIRKSTONE PASS ROAD, AMBLESIDE, CUMBRIA LA22 9EH
TEL: 05394 32232

On your next visit to the Lake District, why not visit the Kirkstone Foot Country House Hotel? This charming 17th-century manor house stands in 2 acres of pretty, flower-filled gardens, overlooking Stock Ghyll which flows through the grounds. Such peace and tranquillity ensure that the tumults of the world will soon be forgotten. Inside, the atmosphere is warm and inviting: Kirkstone Foot's unique ambience has long been enjoyed by its oft-returning clientèle. Within the main house are 15 twin, double, family and single rooms, while a number of apartments and cottages in the grounds offer the privacy of self-contained accommodation. The hotel is managed by Andrew and Annabel Bedford, who continue to honour the English cultural tradition of good food and hospitality. A five-course dinner menu is changed daily and complemented by an extensive wine list. The staff reinforce the relaxing character of the hotel by combining attentive service with a friendly, informal manner – a sure recipe for success. With the magnificent scenery of the lakes and fells and golf, riding and water-sports facilities nearby, Kirkstone Foot has plenty to offer. Closed 3 January to early February. **Directions:** On Kirkstone Pass Road, off A591 at north end of Ambleside. Price guide (including dinner): Single £39.50–£68; double/twin £79–£116.

NANNY BROW HOTEL

CLAPPERSGATE, AMBLESIDE, CUMBRIA LA22 9NF
TEL: 05394 32036 FAX: 05394 32450

Designed and built in 1908 by a London architect for his own use, this beautiful country house remained a family home until 1952, when it was converted into an elegant hotel, now personally owned and run by Michael and Carol Fletcher. The hotel is set in 5 acres of peaceful gardens and woodlands and enjoys spectacular views across the Brathay Valley towards the Langdale Pikes. Guests can relax in the comfortable drawing room, elegant lounge-hall or Garden Room bar – there are log fires on chilly evenings. In the dining room, chef Richard Etherington prepares an imaginative 6-course dinner. The hotel has recently been awarded an AA Red Rosette for excellent cuisine. Much care has gone into creating the pretty chintzy bedrooms and four-poster suites, each one different. In the newer Garden Wing, luxury suites combine the traditional elegance of the original house with modern comfort. There is a spa bath and solarium and complementry use of the local private leisure centre. Facilities for management meetings and conferences are available. The hotel has fishing rights on the River Brathay, and the gardens lead directly onto Loughrigg Fell. Dogs are accepted by prior arrangement. Closed first 3 weeks of January. **Directions:** From Ambleside take A593 Coniston road for $1\frac{1}{2}$ miles; hotel is on right-hand side. Price guide (including dinner): Single £65; double/twin £110–£130; suite £150.

ROTHAY MANOR

ROTHAY BRIDGE, AMBLESIDE, CUMBRIA LA22 0EH
TEL: 05394 33605 FAX: 05394 33607

Situated half a mile from Lake Windermere, this Georgian listed building stands in 1 1/2 acres of grounds. The bedrooms include three beautifully furnished suites, two of which are in the lodge beside the manor and afford an unusual measure of space and privacy. One suite is equipped for five people and designed with particular attention to the comfort of guests with disabilities: it has a ramp leading to the garden and a spacious shower. Care and consideration are evident throughout. The menu is varied and meals are prepared with flair and imagination to high standards, complemented by an interesting wine list. For the actively inclined, residents have free use of the nearby Low Wood Leisure Club, with swimming pool, sauna, steam room, Jacuzzi, squash, sunbeds and a health and beauty salon. Permits are available for fishing, while locally guests can play golf, arrange to go riding, take a trip on a steam railway or visit Wordsworth's cottage. Small functions can be catered for with ease. Closed 2 January to 11 February. Represented in the USA by Josephine Barr: 800-323 5463. Each winter a full programme of special breaks with reduced rates is offered, as well as music, silver and antiques, bridge and cookery courses. **Directions:** 3/4 mile from Ambleside on the road to Coniston. Price guide: Single £69; double/twin £109–£122; suite £152.

ESSEBORNE MANOR

HURSTBOURNE TARRANT, ANDOVER, HAMPSHIRE SP11 0ER
TEL: 026 476 444 FAX: 026 476 473
As from May 1994 Tel: 0264 736 444 Fax: 0264 736 473

Esseborne Manor is small and unpretentious, yet stylish. The present house was built at the end of the 19th century and carries the name used to record details of the local village in the *Domesday Book*. It is set in a pleasing garden amid the rich farmland of the North Wessex Downs in a designated area of outstanding natural beauty. Michael and Frieda Yeo, who own and manage the house, have established the restful atmosphere of a private country home where guests can unwind and relax. There are just 12 comfortable bedrooms, each decorated and furnished to a high standard, with views of the gardens and surrounding countryside. During the winter, a log fire glows in the sitting room, where guests can enjoy an apéritif before dinner. The pretty dining room reflects the importance the owners place upon service and good food. Chef Andy Norman creates imaginative menus from carefully selected, fresh seasonal produce. In the grounds there is a herb garden, an all-weather tennis court, a croquet lawn and plenty of good walking beyond. Nearby Newbury racecourse has a busy programme of jumping and flat racing. Places to visit include Highclere Castle, Stonehenge, Salisbury, Winchester and Oxford. **Directions:** Midway between Newbury and Andover on the A343, $1\frac{1}{2}$ miles north of Hurstbourne Tarrant. Price guide: Single £84; double/twin £95–£125.

For hotel location, see maps on pages 458–464

TUFTON ARMS HOTEL

MARKET SQUARE, APPLEBY-IN-WESTMORLAND, CUMBRIA CA16 6XA
TEL: 07683 51593 FAX: 07683 52761

This distinguished Victorian coaching inn, owned and run by the Milsom family, has been refurbished to provide a high standard of comfort. The bedrooms evoke the style of the 19th century, when the Tufton Arms was one of the premier hotels in Victorian England. The kitchen is run under the auspices of David Milsom, who spoils guests for choice with a daily changing gourmet dinner menu complemented by a grill menu. Fresh produce from the fertile Vale of Eden is used and the restaurant is renowned for its fish dishes. Complementing the cuisine is an extensive wine list. There are conference and meeting rooms including the recently refurbished Hotlerfield Suite which can accommodate up to 120 people. Appleby, the historic county town of Westmorland, stands in splendid countryside and is ideal for touring the Lakes, Yorkshire Dales and Pennines. It is also a convenient stop-over en route to Scotland. Superb fishing for wild brown trout on a 24-mile stretch of the main River Eden, or for salmon on the lower reaches of the river, can be arranged. Shooting parties for grouse, duck and pheasant are a speciality. Appleby has an 18-hole moorland golf course. **Directions:** In centre of Appleby (bypassed by the A66), 38 miles west of Scotch Corner, 13 miles east of Penrith (M6 junction 40), 12 miles from M6 junction 38. Price guide: Single £50–£60; double/twin £70–£120; suite £130.

AMBERLEY CASTLE

AMBERLEY, NR ARUNDEL, WEST SUSSEX BN18 9ND
TEL: 0798 831992 FAX: 0798 831998

Amberley Castle is over 900 years old and is set between the rolling South Downs and the peaceful expanse of the Amberley Wildbrooks. Its towering battlements have breathtaking views while its massive, 14th-century curtain walls and mighty portcullis bear silent testimony to its fascinating history. Resident proprietors, Joy and Martin Cummings, have transformed this medieval fortress into a unique country castle hotel. They offer a warm, personal welcome and their hotel provides the ultimate in contemporary luxury, while retaining an atmosphere of timelessness. Guests can choose from four-poster, twin four-poster or brass double-bedded rooms. Each room is individually designed and has its own jacuzzi bath. The exquisite 12th-century Queen's Room Restaurant is the perfect setting for the highly creative cuisine of head chef Nigel Boschetti and his team. Amberley Castle is a natural first choice for romantic or cultural weekends, sporting breaks or confidential executive meetings. It is ideally situated for opera at Glyndebourne, theatre at Chichester and racing at Goodwood and Fontwell. It is easily accessible from London and the major air and channel ports. **Directions:** Amberley Castle is on the B2139, off the A29 between Fontwell and Bury. Price guide: Single £100; double/twin £130–£225.

AVISFORD PARK COUNTRY HOTEL

WALBERTON, ARUNDEL, WEST SUSSEX BN18 0LS
TEL: 0243 551215 FAX: 0243 552485/81

Avisford Park Hotel was created from what was an attractive but neglected Georgian manor house, set in 62 acres of delightful gardens and parkland. Although away from home, you will not be away from home comforts: each bedroom is attractively furnished and has views over the grounds. The bedrooms all have hairdryers, remote-control television, trouser press and hospitality tray. Executive rooms also have a personal safe and teletext television. Dinner is served in the Cedar Room Restaurant, where an imaginative menu prepared by chef Eamon Smith is offered. At lunchtime, a splendid buffet selection is provided. The terrace is the place to enjoy afternoon tea on sunny afternoons or an early-evening drink. Avisford Park is a popular venue for weddings, celebrations and corporate functions, which can be hosted in the Henty Room, Terrace Room or the Ballroom. After a session in the sauna or solarium, you can enjoy an invigorating swim in either the indoor or outdoor pool. There is a snooker room and, for the more energetic, squash and tennis courts. You can also improve your stroke-play on the 9-hole on-site golf course. Goodwood races, Arundel Castle and Chichester harbour are nearby. **Directions:** The hotel is set back from the A27 west of Arundel. Price guide: Single £70–£85; double/twin £106–£128; suite £128.

BAILIFFSCOURT

CLIMPING, WEST SUSSEX BN17 5RW
TEL: 0903 723511 FAX: 0903 723107

Gothic mullioned windows wink through the trees along the approach to Bailiffscourt. As you walk under the gnarled 15th-century beams you can sense the sombre dignity of the Middle Ages. Rooms interconnect through low doorways in a maze which completes a square around the courtyard. This 'perfectly preserved medieval house', architecturally and aesthetically correct in every detail, was built in the late 1930s at immense cost to satisfy a caprice of the late Lord Moyne. Constructed almost entirely from genuine bits of old buildings, this masterpiece is a splendid hotel with a warm and inviting atmosphere. Each bedroom is different and full of character –

some can only be described as vast – and nine have open log fires. The restaurant offers a varied menu and summer lunches can be taken alfresco in a fragrant rose-clad courtyard or the walled garden. Private dining rooms are available for weddings, conferences and meetings – companies can hire the hotel as their 'country house' for 2 or 3 days. Bailiffscourt is surrounded by tranquil parkland, with a golf practice area, outdoor pool and tennis courts. Climping Beach, 100 yards away, is ideal for wind-surfing. Nearby are Arundel with its Castle, Brighton, Chichester and Goodwood. **Directions:** Three miles south of Arundel, off the A259. Price guide: Single £65–£75; double/twin £95–£180.

PENNYHILL PARK HOTEL AND COUNTRY CLUB

LONDON ROAD, BAGSHOT, SURREY GU19 5ET
TEL: 0276 471774 FAX: 0276 473217

Bagshot has been a centre of hospitality since the early Stuart sovereigns, James I and Charles I, had a hunting lodge there. The Pennyhill Park Hotel continues this tradition. Built in 1849, this elegant mansion reflects its passage through Victorian and Edwardian times while providing every modern amenity. The bedrooms are outstanding: no two are identical, and infinite care has been invested in creating practical rooms with distinctive features. Impeccable service is to be expected, as staff are trained to formal, Edwardian standards. Cuisine is served in the dignified setting of the Latymer Restaurant, accompanied by a wine list that includes many rare vintages. During the day a light meal may be taken in the Orangery, which is part of the Pennyhill Country Club. Recreational facilities are available within the grounds, which span 120 acres and include landscaped gardens, parkland and a 3-acre lake. The Pennyhill Park is conveniently located only 27 miles from central London. **Directions:** From the M3, exit 3, take A322 towards Bracknell. Turn left before the lights into Bagshot village. Go through village; turn left onto the A30 London road. Go over lights, follow road for 3/4 mile, then turn right 50 yards past the Texaco garage. Price guide: Single £120; double/twin £138; suite £300.

THE ROYAL BERKSHIRE

LONDON ROAD, SUNNINGHILL, ASCOT, BERKSHIRE SL5 0PP
TEL: 0344 23322 FAX: 0344 27100/0344 874240

For over 100 years The Royal Berkshire was the home of the Churchill family. Now it is an elegant hotel, ideally located between Ascot racecourse and the Guards Polo Club. This Queen Anne mansion, built in 1705 by the Duke of Marlborough for his son, is set in 15 acres of gardens and woodlands. Guests have access to a wide range of leisure facilities including a putting green, indoor heated pool, squash court, whirlpool spa and sauna. The spacious interiors are smartly decorated in contemporary pastel shades, with the full-length windows bathing the rooms in light. Tea or drinks can be enjoyed in the drawing rooms or on the terrace with views across the lawns. The menu offers an eclectic choice of dishes to please connoisseurs of fine food. All meals are carefully prepared with meticulous attention to presentation. Some interesting vintages are included on the wine list. A series of well-equipped function rooms, combined with easy accessibility from Heathrow and central London, makes the Royal Berkshire a popular venue for business events. For golfers, Swinley, Sunningdale and Wentworth are all nearby. Royal Windsor and Eton are a short drive away. **Directions:** One mile from Ascot on the corner of A329 and B383. Nearest M25 exit is junction 13. Price guide: Single £105; double/twin £145; weekend rate £68 per person per night.

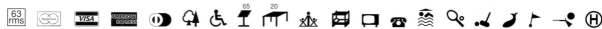

CALLOW HALL

MAPPLETON ROAD, ASHBOURNE, DERBYSHIRE DE6 2AA
TEL: 0335 343403 FAX: 0335 343624

The approach to Callow Hall is up a tree-lined drive through the 44-acre grounds. On arrival visitors can take in the splendid views from the hotel's elevated position, overlooking the valleys of Bentley Brook and the River Dove. The majestic building and Victorian gardens have been restored by resident proprietors, David and Dorothy Spencer, who represent the fifth generation of hoteliers in the Spencer family. Mineral water and home-made biscuits can be found in the spacious period bedrooms. Fresh local produce is selected daily for use in the kitchen, where the term 'home-made' comes into its own. Home-cured bacon, sausages, fresh bread, traditional English puddings and melt-in-the-mouth pastries are among the items prepared on the premises. Visiting anglers can enjoy a rare opportunity to fish for trout and grayling along a mile-long private stretch of the Bentley Brook, which is mentioned in Izaak Walton's *The Compleat Angler*. Callow Hall is ideally situated for touring the Peak District and Dovedale. Closed Christmas. **Directions:** Take the A515 through Ashbourne towards Buxton. At the Bowling Green Inn on the brow of a steep hill, turn left, then take the first right, signposted Mappleton, and the hotel is over the bridge on the right. Price guide: Single £65–£80; double/twin £90–£120.

HOLNE CHASE HOTEL

NR ASHBURTON, DEVON TQ13 7NS
TEL: 03643 471 FAX: 03643 453

A hunting estate in the 11th century, this ETB 4 Crowns Highly Commended hotel has been run in a professional yet friendly and informal fashion by the Bromage family for over 20 years. Most of the rooms at Holne Chase, including many of the individually furnished bedrooms, offer spectacular views over the Dart Valley. Deep sofas, easy chairs, log fires and books create a relaxing atmosphere, confirming the proprietors' aim to provide a sanctuary from the hustle and bustle of everyday life. A productive kitchen garden supplies the restaurant, where good quality, regional cooking can be enjoyed. Fly-fishermen can test the hotel's mile-long stretch of the River Dart, with its quarry of salmon and sea trout. Guided walks can be arranged from Holne Chase, which is a good base for exploring Dartmoor's open moorland and deep wooded valleys. It is also an area of archeological interest, having the largest concentration of Iron Age and prehistoric sites in Northern Europe. Hot-air ballooning, canoeing and riding can all be organised. Special breaks are available. **Directions:** Holne Chase is 3 miles north of Ashburton. To find the hotel, take the Ashburton turning off the A38, and follow the signs for Two Bridges. The hotel turning is on the right just after the road crosses the River Dart. Price guide: Single £60; double/twin £90.

RIVERSIDE COUNTRY HOUSE HOTEL

ASHFORD-IN-THE-WATER, NR BAKEWELL, DERBYSHIRE DE4 1QF
TEL: 0629 814275 FAX: 0629 812873

Ashford-in-the-Water lies in a limestone ravine of the River Wye in the Peak District National Park. Mentioned in the *Domesday Book*, it is a picture-postcard village of quaint, stone-built cottages. Near the village centre stands the Riverside Country House, an ivy-clad Georgian mansion, bounded by an acre of mature garden and river frontage. Oak panelling and inglenook fireplaces in the lounge create a sense of warmth – an ideal place to chat or curl up with a book. Using seasonally available game from the nearby Chatsworth estate and freshly caught fish, Master Chef Jerry Buckingham creates a series of exciting dishes. Dinner, complemented by fine wines, is served at antique tables set with gleaming silver, sparkling crystal and illuminated by candle-light. Prettily decorated bedrooms, with hand-made soft furnishings, all have private facilities. Ideally situated for visits to Chatsworth House, Haddon Hall and Hardwick Hall, the hotel is also convenient for access to the Derbyshire Dales, Lathkill and Dovedale. Bargain breaks offered for two to five-night stays. **Directions:** 1½ miles north of Bakewell on the A6 heading towards Buxton. Ashford-in-the-Water lies on the right-hand side of the river. The hotel is at the end of the village main street next to the Sheepwash Bridge. Price guide: Single £79; double/twin £85–£99.

TYTHERLEIGH COT HOTEL

CHARDSTOCK, AXMINSTER, DEVON EX13 7BN
TEL: 0460 21170 FAX: 0460 21291

Originally the village cider house, this 14th-century Grade II listed building has been skilfully converted into a spacious modern hotel, idyllically situated in the secluded village of Chardstock on the Devon/Dorset/Somerset borders. The hotel is owned and run by Frank and Pat Grudgings, who extend a warm welcome. The bedrooms, converted from former barns and outbuildings, are all individually designed, some with four-poster or half-tester beds, inglenook fireplaces and double Jacuzzis. The beautifully designed restaurant is housed in a Victorian-style conservatory, overlooking an ornamental lily pond with cascading fountain and wrought-iron bridge. Imaginative menus based on local ingredients are complemented by a carefully selected wine list. Special house parties are held at Christmas and New Year and bargain break weekends can be arranged. The hotel has an oudoor heated swimming pool, sauna, solarium and mini-gym. Riding, tennis, golf and clay pigeon shooting can be arranged locally. The hotel is ideally located for guests to explore the varied landscape of the South West and there are many historic houses and National Trust properties nearby. **Directions:** From Chard take A358 Axminster road; Chardstock signposted on right about 3 miles along. Price guide: Single £47–£55; double/twin £98–£123.

THE BELL INN

ASTON CLINTON, BUCKINGHAMSHIRE HP22 5HP
TEL: 0296 630252 FAX: 0296 631250

A former coaching house, The Bell Inn was reputedly once part of the Duke of Buckingham's estate, used by him as a stopover en route from his London house, Buckingham Palace, to his country seat at Stowe. Alterations to the building have been made over the years but the original façade remains very much as it was. Across the way, the stables and malthouse, once the Bell brewery, have been converted to provide additional hotel rooms. There are six rooms in the main house and 15 around the cobbled courtyard. All have en suite bathrooms. Some rooms have a four-poster bed and those in the Brewer's House have a sitting room overlooking a private garden. The hotel is run by Michael and Patsy Harris, who offer guests a warm welcome. In the restaurant, chef Jean-Claude McFarlane prepares excellent menus with flair and originality. There is a comprehensive wine list (some wines are sold in the hotel's wine shop). Private functions are catered for in the Pavilion or Writing Rooms. There is marvellous walking and riding in the nearby Chiltern Hills and a number of excellent golf courses in the vicinity. Woburn, Blenheim, Hatfield and Luton Zoo are all within easy reach. **Directions:** The Bell Inn is situated on the A41 between Tring and Aylesbury. Price guide: Single £92; double/twin £107; suite from £103.

HARTWELL HOUSE

OXFORD ROAD, NR AYLESBURY, BUCKINGHAMSHIRE HP17 8NL
TEL: 0296 747444 FAX: 0296 747450 TELEX: 837108 HART G

Standing in 90 acres of gardens and parkland landscaped by a pupil of 'Capability' Brown, Hartwell House has both Jacobean and Georgian facades. This beautiful house, brilliantly restored by Historic House Hotels, was the residence in exile of King Louis XVIII of France from 1809 to 1814. The large ground floor reception rooms, with oak panelling and decorated ceilings, have antique furniture and fine paintings which evoke the elegance of the 18th century. There are 47 individually designed bedrooms and suites, some in the house and some in Hartwell Court, the restored 18th-century stables. The dining room at Hartwell is the setting for memorable meals produced by head chef Aidan McCormack, winner of 1991, 1992 and 1993 Michelin stars. The Hartwell Spa adjacent to the hotel includes an indoor swimming pool, whirlpool spa bath, steam room, gymnasium, hairdressing and beauty salon. Situated in the Vale of Aylesbury, the hotel, which is a member of Relais et Chateaux, is only an hour from London and 20 miles from Oxford. Blenheim Palace and Woburn Abbey are nearby. Dogs are permitted only in the Hartwell Court bedrooms. **Directions:** On the A418 Oxford Road, 2 miles from Aylesbury. Price guide: Single £90–£116; double/twin £135–£213; suite from £215.

THE PRIORY HOTEL

HIGH STREET, WHITCHURCH, AYLESBURY, BUCKINGHAMSHIRE HP22 4JS
TEL: 0296 641239 FAX: 0296 641793

The Priory Hotel is a beautifully preserved, timber-framed house dating back to 1360. It is set in the picturesque conservation village of Whitchurch, 5 miles north of Aylesbury. With its exposed timbers, leaded windows and open fires, it retains all its traditional character and charm – a refreshing alternative to the all-too-familiar chain hotels of today. All 11 bedrooms are individually furnished and many of them have four-poster beds. At the heart of the hotel is La Boiserie Restaurant, where classical French cuisine is served in intimate surroundings. An imaginative à la carte fixed-price menu is offered, including a range of seasonal dishes. Start, for example, with a rich terrine of partridge, wild mushrooms and pistachios, then perhaps choose marinated saddle of venison in Cognac butter sauce and garnished with truffles. Specialities include fresh lobster and flambé dishes. The self-contained conference suite can be used for private lunches, dinners and receptions. Among the places to visit locally are Waddesdon Manor, Claydon House, Silverstone motor circuit and Oxford. Closed between Christmas and New Year's Eve; the restaurant also closes on Sunday evenings. **Directions:** Situated on the A413 4 miles north of Aylesbury. Price guide: Single £65–£80; double/twin £90–£110; suite £120.

HASSOP HALL

HASSOP, NR BAKEWELL, DERBYSHIRE DE45 1NS
TEL: 0629 640488 FAX: 0629 640577

The recorded history of Hassop Hall reaches back 900 years to the *Domesday Book*, to a time when the political scene in England was still dominated by the unceasing power struggle between the barons and the only real access to power was through possession of land. By 1643, when the Civil War was raging, the Hall was under the ownership of Rowland Eyre, who turned it into a Royalist garrison. It was the scene of several skirmishes before it was recaptured after the Parliamentary victory. Since purchasing Hassop Hall in 1975, Thomas Chapman has determinedly pursued the preservation of its outstanding heritage. Guests can enjoy the beautifully maintained gardens as well as the splendid countryside of the surrounding area. The bedrooms, some of which are particularly spacious, are well furnished and comfortable. A bridal suite is available for romantic occasions. A comprehensive dinner menu offers a wide and varied selection of dishes, with something to cater for all tastes. As well as the glories of the Peak District, places to visit include Chatsworth House, Haddon Hall and Buxton Opera House. Closed at Christmas. **Directions:** From M1 exit 29 (Chesterfield), take A619 to Baslow, then A623 to Calver; left at lights to B6001. Hassop Hall is 2 miles on right. Price guide: Single £65–£85; double/twin £75–£95; suite available – price on application. Inclusive rates available on request.

WROXTON HOUSE HOTEL

WROXTON ST MARY, NR BANBURY, OXFORDSHIRE OX15 6QB
TEL: 0295 730777 FAX: 0295 730800

Built of honeyed local stone, Wroxton House has undergone a sensitive restoration linking three village houses, dating from the 17th century, with a delightful clocktower wing and conservatory lounge. The relaxing character of the hotel is created by the carefully selected staff, who combine attentive service with friendliness and informality. The spacious and bright lounges contain thoughtfully chosen furnishings, comfortable armchairs and a profusion of flowers and plants. The 32 en suite bedrooms have been individually decorated and the original timbers preserved in many of the older rooms. The classic English styles complement the deeply polished woods of the furniture. Guests may dine by candlelight in the intimate restaurant, where a traditional Cotswold atmosphere is evoked by original beams, inglenooks, carved oak recesses, horse brasses and pewter. The expertly prepared menus display chef Gerväis Andrew's personal interpretation of classic British dishes which make imaginative use of the freshest local produce. Wroxton House Hotel is a popular choice with businessmen, as it offers good meeting facilities in a tranquil setting. Golf and riding can be arranged locally. **Directions:** Wroxton is 2 miles outside Banbury on the A422 Stratford-upon-Avon road. Price guide: Single £79; double/twin £89–£105.

HALMPSTONE MANOR

BISHOPS TAWTON, NR BARNSTAPLE, DEVON EX32 0EA
TEL: 0271 830321 FAX: 0271 830826

Set in 200 acres of rolling, north Devonshire countryside, Halmpstone Manor continues a 400-year tradition of hospitality. The name Halmpstone means 'holy boundary stone', from its original links with the ecclesiastical lands of Bishops Tawton. Proprietors Jane and Charles Stanbury have achieved a delightful combination of the formal and informal, to create a relaxing atmosphere of genuine warmth and quiet charm. Dinner is served in the distinctive early 16th-century wood-panelled dining room, where in winter an inviting log fire glows. Gourmet cuisine is prepared to the highest standards, with imaginative use of fresh local and exotic ingredients. Gleaming silver, sparkling glassware and beautiful china make for superbly presented meals. The tastefully co-ordinated bedrooms, luxuriously furnished with either four-poster or brass and coronet beds, all have sumptuous en suite facilities. Attentive and friendly service ensures that all guests' requirements are met. 2 AA Red Rosettes. Dogs are permitted in one of the bedrooms. Closed 10th December, re-opens 10th February. **Directions:** A361 to Barnstaple; A377 to Bishops Tawton. At end of village, turn left opposite BP filling station. Travel 2 miles further, turn right at Halmpstone Manor sign. Price guide: Single £65–£70; double/twin £80–£130.

AUDLEYS WOOD

ALTON ROAD, BASINGSTOKE, HAMPSHIRE RG25 2JT
TEL: 0256 817555 FAX: 0256 817500

Originally built as a Victorian country house for Sir George Bradshaw, publisher of railway timetables, Audleys Wood is set in 7 acres of gardens and lightly wooded parkland on the southern edge of Basingstoke, conveniently placed for the town centre and the M3. The restaurant, with its minstrels gallery, has been superbly restored. Here guests are offered a menu containing many creative, imaginative dishes, complemented by an extensive wine list which incorporates vintages of international repute. Each bedroom is individually decorated and provides every modern luxury. The public rooms are rich in magnificent carved oak features and fireplaces, providing a relaxing environment. The hotel is a perfect setting for senior-level management meetings; it has five conference rooms, one of which contains beautiful oak panelling from Tewkesbury Abbey. Private dinners can also be catered for. There is a golf driving net and putting green in the grounds and bicycles are available for guests who wish to explore the Hampshire countryside. Winchester, Silchester, Stratfield Saye – the Duke of Wellington's home – and the Watercress Steam Railway are just some of the places of interest to visit nearby. **Directions:** Audleys Wood lies off the A339 south of Basingstoke. Price guide: Single £90; double/twin £110. Special rates available at weekends.

TYLNEY HALL

ROTHERWICK, NR HOOK, HAMPSHIRE RG27 9AJ
TEL: 0256 764881 FAX: 0256 768141

Arriving at this hotel in the evening, with its floodlit exterior and forecourt fountain, you can imagine that you are arriving for a party in a private stately home. Grade II listed and set in 66 acres of stunning gardens and parkland tended by a team of six gardeners, Tylney Hall typifies the great houses of the past. Apéritifs are taken in the wood-panelled library bar; haute cuisine is served in the glass-domed Oak Room restaurant, complemented by conscientious service. The hotel was the 1990 winner of the AA Care and Courtesy Award and holds an AA Rosette for food and also AA 4 Red Stars. Extensive leisure facilities include indoor and outdoor heated swimming pools, multi-gym, sauna, tennis, croquet and snooker, while hot-air ballooning, archery, clay pigeon shooting, golf and riding can be arranged locally. Surrounding the hotel are wooded trails ideal for rambling or jogging. Functions for up to 100 are catered for in the Tylney Suite or Chestnut Suite, while more intimate gatherings are held in one of the other seven meeting rooms. The cathedral town of Winchester, Stratfield Saye House and Farnborough are all nearby. **Directions:** A33 to Basingstoke, left at end of dual carriageway. Take B3349 towards Hook, turn right to Rotherwick. Turn left to Newnham just after pond; hotel is 1 mile further on right. Price guide: Single £94–£135; double/twin £114–£160; suite £220.

CAVENDISH HOTEL

BASLOW, DERBYSHIRE DE45 1SP
TEL: 0246 582311 FAX: 0246 582312

Dating from the late-18th century, the original Peacock Hotel has been considerably upgraded and was re-opened as the Cavendish in 1975. Set on the Duke and Duchess of Devonshire's estate at Chatsworth, the hotel occupies a unique position and makes a marvellous base for visitors who wish to explore this part of Derbyshire. A warm welcome is assured from proprietor Eric Marsh who greets guests personally. All the well-equipped bedrooms overlook the estate and have en suite facilities. The hotel has a relaxed, homely feel which is enhanced by crackling log fires in cooler weather. The tasteful furnishings include antiques and fine art from the Devonshire Collection.

Meals are served throughout the day in the Garden Room Restaurant, where the informal atmosphere is in contrast to the other, more formal, dining room. Chef Nicholas Buckingham and his team have won many commendations for their creative cuisine. A footpath connects the hotel to the Chatsworth Estate where guests are welcome to stroll. Hardwick Hall, Haddon Hall, the Treak Cliff Cavern (the Blue John mine) and the Tramway Museum at Crich are all nearby. **Directions:** The hotel is on the A619 in Baslow, 9 miles west of Chesterfield; 15 miles from M1, junction 29. Price guide (excluding breakfast): Single £83; double/twin £99.

FISCHER'S

BASLOW HALL, CALVER ROAD, BASLOW, DERBYSHIRE DE45 1RR
TEL: 0246 583259

Situated on the edge of the magnificent Chatsworth Estate, Baslow Hall enjoys an enviable location surrounded by some of the country's finest stately homes and within easy reach of the Peak District's many cultural and historical attractions. Standing at the end of a winding Chestnut tree-lined driveway, this fine Derbyshire manor house was tastefully converted by Max and Susan Fischer into an award winning country house hotel in 1989. Since opening Fischer's have consistently maintained their position as one of the finest establishments in the Derbyshire/South Yorkshire regions. Whether you are staying in the area for private or business reasons, it is a welcome change to find a place that feels less like a hotel and more like a home combining comfort and character with an eating experience which is a delight to the palate. Max presides in the kitchen. He cooks with the seasons - finest English lamb in the spring and summer, Game in the autumn and winter. Herbs and salads are grown in the garden. Baslow Hall offers facilities for small conferences or private functions. Baslow is within 12 miles of the M1 motorway, Chesterfield and Sheffield. Fischer's is on the A623 in Baslow. A reduced room rate is available for guests staying for two or more consecutive nights. Price guide: Single £65–£80; double/twin £95–£120.

COMBE GROVE MANOR HOTEL & COUNTRY CLUB

BRASSKNOCKER HILL, MONKTON COMBE, BATH, AVON BA2 7HS
TEL: 0225 834644 FAX: 0225 834961

This is an exclusive 18th-century country house situated 2 miles from the beautiful city of Bath. Built on the hillside site of a Roman settlement, Combe Grove Manor is set in 82 acres of formal gardens and woodland, with magnificent views over the Limpley Stoke Valley. In addition to the Georgian Restaurant, where superb food is served, there is a private dining room, plus a wine bar and restaurant with a terrace garden. After dinner guests may relax with drinks in the elegant drawing room or library. The bedrooms are lavishly furnished, all with en suite facilities, two of them individually designed with Jacuzzi baths. Within the grounds are some of the finest leisure facilities in the South West,

including indoor and outdoor heated pools, a spa bath and steam room, four all-weather tennis courts, a 5-hole par 3 golf course and a two-tiered driving range. Visitors may use the Nautilus gym, aerobics studio, saunas and solaria or relax in the Clarins beauty room where a full range of treatments is offered. Separate from the manor house is the Garden Lodge which is ideal for conferences. ETB 5 Crowns Highly Commended. AA 4 Stars.
Directions: Set south-east of Bath on Brassknocker Hill, between Combe Down and Monkton Combe. Price guide: Single £98; double/twin £130; suite £235.

LUCKNAM PARK

COLERNE, NR BATH, WILTSHIRE SN14 8AZ
TEL: 0225 742777 FAX: 0225 743536

For over 250 years Lucknam Park has been a focus of fine society and aristocratic living, something guests will sense immediately upon their approach along the mile-long avenue lined with beech trees. Built in 1720, this magnificent country house hotel is situated just 6 miles from Bath on the southern edge of the Cotswolds. The delicate sense of historical context is reflected in fine art and antiques dating from the late Georgian and early Victorian periods. Michael Womersley's Michelin-starred cuisine can be savoured in the elegant restaurant, at tables set with exquisite porcelain, silver and glassware, accompanied with wines from an extensive cellar. Set within the walled gardens of the hotel is the Leisure Spa, comprising an indoor pool, sauna, solarium, steam room, whirlpool spa, gymnasium, beauty salon and snooker room. Numerous activities can be arranged on request, including hot-air ballooning, riding, golf and archery. Bowood House, Corsham Court and Castle Combe are among the many local places of interest. Represented in USA by Small Luxury Hotels of the World: telephone 800-544 7570 toll free. **Directions:** Fifteen minutes from M4, junctions 17 and 18. Price guide: Single £95; double/twin £140–£310.

THE QUEENSBERRY

RUSSEL STREET, BATH, AVON BA1 2QF
TEL: 0225 447928 FAX: 0225 446065

When the Marquis of Queensberry commissioned John Wood to build this house in Russel Street in 1772, little did he know that 200 years hence guests would still be being entertained in these elegant surroundings. An intimate town house hotel, The Queensberry is in a quiet residential street just a few minutes' walk from Wood's other splendours – the Royal Crescent, Circus and Assembly Rooms. Regency stucco ceilings, ornate cornices and panelling combined with enchanting interior decor complement the strong architectural style. However, the standards of hotel-keeping here are rather less traditional than the surroundings, with high-quality en suite bedrooms, room service and up-to-date office support for executives. The Olive Tree Restaurant is one of the leading restaurants in the Bath area. Having gained an admirable reputation at Homewood Park in the 1980s, proprietors Stephen and Penny Ross are thoroughly versed in offering hospitality. Represented in America by Josephine Barr. The hotel is closed for 2 weeks at Christmas. **Directions:** From junction 18 of M4, enter Bath along A4 London Road. Turn sharp right up Lansdown Road, left into Bennett Street, then right into Russel Street opposite the Assembly Rooms. Price guide: Single £89; double/twin £108.

THE PRIORY HOTEL

WESTON ROAD, BATH, AVON BA1 2XT
TEL: 0225 331922 FAX: 0225 448276

Lying in the seclusion of landscaped grounds, The Priory Hotel is in easy reach of some of Britain's finest architecture. Within walking distance of Bath city centre, this Gothic-style Bath stone building dates from 1835, when it formed part of a row of fashionable residences on the west side of the city. Visitors will sense the luxury as they enter the hotel: antique furniture, plush rugs and *objets d'art* add interest to the two spacious reception rooms and the elegant drawing room. Well-defined colour schemes lend an uplifting brightness throughout, particularly in the tastefully appointed bedrooms. French classical style is the primary inspiration for the cuisine, served in three interconnecting dining rooms which overlook the garden. An especially good selection of wines can be recommended to accompany meals. Private functions can be accommodated both in the Drawing Room and the Orangery, with garden access an added bonus. The Roman Baths, Theatre Royal, Museum of Costume and a host of bijou shops offer plenty for visitors to see. **Directions:** Leave M4 at junction 18 to Bath on A46. Enter city on A4 London road and follow signs for Bristol. Turn right into Park Lane which runs through Royal Victoria Park. Then turn left into Weston Road. The hotel is on the left. Price guide: Single £85; double/twin £150–£195.

STON EASTON PARK

STON EASTON, BATH, SOMERSET BA3 4DF
TEL: 0761 241631 FAX: 0761 241377

The internationally renowned hotel at Ston Easton Park is a Grade I Palladian mansion of notable distinction. A showpiece for some exceptional architectural and decorative features of its period, it dates from 1739 and has recently undergone extensive restoration, offering a unique opportunity to enjoy the opulent splendour of the 18th century. A high priority is given to the provision of friendly and unobtrusive service. The hotel has won innumerable awards for its décor, service and food. Jean Monro, an acknowledged expert on 18th century decoration, supervised the design and furnishing of the interiors, complementing the original features with choice antiques, paintings and *objets d'art*.

Fresh, quality produce, delivered from all parts of Britain, is combined with herbs and vegetables from the Victorian kitchen garden to create English and French dishes. To accompany the meal, a wide selection of rare wines and old vintages is stocked in the house cellars. The grounds, landscaped by Humphry Repton in 1793, consist of romantic gardens and parkland. The 17th-century Gardener's Cottage, close to the main hotel on the wooded banks of the River Norr, provides private suite accommodation. A Relais et Châteaux member. **Directions:** Eleven miles south of Bath on the A37 between Bath and Wells. Price guide: Single from £85; double/twin £135–£320.

POWDERMILLS HOTEL

POWDERMILL LANE, BATTLE, EAST SUSSEX TN33 0SP
TEL: 0424 775511 FAX: 0424 774540

Situated outside the historic Sussex town famous for the 1066 battle, Powdermills is an 18th century listed country house which has been skilfully converted into an elegant hotel. Nestling in 150 acres of parks and woodland, the beautiful and tranquil grounds feature a 7-acre specimen fishing lake, as well as three smaller lakes stocked with trout which guests may fish. Wild geese, swans, ducks, kingfishers and herons abound and a rare breed of Scottish sheep grazes nearby. Privately owned and run by Douglas and Julie Cowpland, the hotel has been carefully furnished with locally acquired antiques. On cooler days, log fires burn in the entrance hall, drawing room and library. The bedrooms – 2 with four-posters – are all individually furnished and decorated. The Orangery Restaurant has received many accolades and offers fine classical cooking. Guests may dine on the terrace in summer, looking out over the swimming pool and grounds. Light meals and snacks are available in the library. The location is ideal from which to explore the beautiful Sussex and Kent countryside and there are many villages and small towns in the area. **Directions:** From centre of Battle take the Hastings road south. After $^1/_4$ mile turn right into Powdermill Lane. After sharp bend, entrance is on right; cross bridge and lakes to reach hotel. Price guide: Single £40–£50; double/twin £70–£105.

THE MONTAGU ARMS HOTEL

BEAULIEU, NEW FOREST, HAMPSHIRE S042 7ZL
TEL: 0590 612324 FAX: 0590 612188

Situated at the head of the River Beaulieu in the heart of the New Forest, The Montagu Arms Hotel carries on a tradition of hospitality started 700 years ago. As well as being a good place for a holiday, the hotel is an ideal venue for small conferences. Each of the 24 bedrooms has been individually styled and many are furnished with four-poster beds. Choose from sumptuous suites, luxurious junior suites, superior and standard accommodation. All rooms are equipped with colour television, direct-dial telephones, radio and a trouser press. Dine in the oak-panelled restaurant overlooking the garden, where you can enjoy cuisine prepared by award-winning chef Simon Fennell. The menu is supported by an outstanding wine list. To help you relax, the hotel offers complimentary membership of an exclusive health club 6 miles away. Facilities there include a supervised gymnasium, large indoor ozone pool, Jacuzzi, steam room, sauna and beauty therapist. There is much to see and do around Beaulieu. Visit the National Motor Museum, Exbury Gardens or Bucklers Hard, or walk for miles through the beautiful New Forest. Special tariffs are available throughout the year. **Directions:** The village of Beaulieu is well signposted and the hotel commands an impressive position at the foot of the main street. Price guide: Single £67–£75; double/twin £95–£165.

WOODLANDS MANOR

GREEN LANE, CLAPHAM, BEDFORD, BEDFORDSHIRE MK41 6EP
TEL: 0234 363281 FAX: 0234 272390

Woodlands Manor is a secluded period manor house, set in acres of wooded grounds and gardens, only 2 miles from the centre of Bedford. The hotel is privately owned and a personal welcome is assured. In the public rooms, stylish yet unpretentious furnishings preserve the feel of a country house, with open fires in winter. The en suite bedrooms are beautifully decorated and have extensive personal facilities. All have views of the gardens and surrounding countryside. The elegantly proportioned restaurant, once the house's main reception room, provides an agreeable venue for dining. The menus balance English tradition with the French flair for fresh, light flavours, complemented by wines from well-stocked cellars. The private library is well suited to business meetings and intimate dinner parties. Woodlands Manor is conveniently located for touring: the historic centres of Ely, Cambridge and Oxford are within easy reach, and stately homes such as Woburn Abbey and Warwick Castle are not far away. The hotel is 2 miles from the county town of Bedford, with its riverside park and the Bunyan Museum. Other places of interest nearby include the RSPB at Sandy and the Shuttleworth Collection of aircraft at Biggleswade. **Directions:** Clapham village is 2 miles north of the centre of Bedford. Price guide: Single £TBA; double/twin £TBA.

THE MANOR HOUSE

NORTHLANDS, WALKINGTON, NORTH HUMBERSIDE HU17 8RT
TEL: 0482 881645 FAX: 0482 866501

Set in 3 acres of tree-lined grounds, overlooking horse paddocks and parkland, The Manor House occupies a tranquil position on the gentle, wooded flanks of the rolling Yorkshire Wolds. This late-19th-century retreat is perfect for those seeking relaxation. The bedrooms, with their open, attractive views, are individually furnished and decorated to the highest standard; guests will find themselves pampered with unexpected and useful personal comforts. Chef-patron Derek Baugh, formerly of The Dorchester Hotel, has evolved a distinctive, creative style of cuisine, and the connoisseur will find Lee Baugh's confections irresistible. Believing that the gourmet requires a sympathetic alliance between what he is eating and drinking, Derek has ensured that the wine list reflects his informed interest in European wines. On summer evenings, dinner may be taken in the conservatory, overlooking the south terrace and lawns. Horse-riding, clay pigeon shooting and golf can all be enjoyed locally, while there is racing at nearby Beverley, York and Doncaster. The Manor House won the 1990 RAC Small Hotel of the North Award. **Directions:** From Walkington on B1230 towards Beverley, turn left at traffic lights (following the brown hotel signs), then left and left again for the hotel. Price guide: Single £70–£80; double/twin £80–£110.

NEW HALL

WALMLEY ROAD, ROYAL SUTTON COLDFIELD, WEST MIDLANDS B76 8QX
TEL: 021-378 2442 FAX: 021-378 4637

Dating from the 12th century, this romantic hotel is reputedly the oldest fully moated manor house in England. To both the discriminating business and leisure visitor, the hotel is a feast for the eyes and palate, where a warm welcome and genuine hospitality awaits. Much acclaimed, New Hall proudly holds the coveted RAC Blue Ribbon Award and two AA Rosettes. Chef Glen Purcell creates imaginative dishes based upon the very best British ingredients and ideas. The cocktail bar and adjoining drawing room overlook the terrace from which a wood-clad bridge leads to the yew topiary, orchards, croquet lawn, putting green and trout-fishing pool, wooded arbours and sunlit glades.

Individually furnished bedrooms and suites offer every modern comfort and amenity for the executive and honeymoon couple alike. Surrounded by a rich cultural heritage, New Hall is convenient for Lichfield Cathedral, Warwick Castle, Stratford-upon-Avon and all that Birmingham has to offer is only 7 miles away. The Belfry Golf Centre is also nearby. Details of champagne breaks, opera, ballet, fishing, bridge and other weekends available on request. **Directions:** From exit 9 of M42, follow A4097 (ignoring signs to A38 Sutton Coldfield). At B4148 turn right. New Hall is 1 mile on left-hand side. Price guide: Single £93–£110; double/twin £105–£150; suite £175.

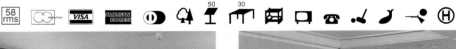

THE SWALLOW HOTEL

12 HAGLEY ROAD, FIVEWAYS, BIRMINGHAM B16 8SJ
TEL: 021-452 1144 FAX: 021-456 3442

The city's first five-star hotel offers comfort and service reminiscent of the truly grand hotels. Quiet corners, attentive service, sparkling chandeliers, polished marble and fine furnishings all combine to create an atmosphere of warm opulence. Acknowledgements of the standards of excellence have come quickly; the hotel has received the AA Courtesy and Care Award (one of only 17 hotels nationally), 4 AA Red Stars (one of 13 hotels), 3 AA Rosettes and a star for food in the Egon Ronay Guide and also awarded Caterer & Hotelkeeper 'Hotel of the Year' 1992. The 98 lavish bedrooms and suites offer all one would expect from a hotel of this calibre and with our award winning chef, Idris Caldora, dining is always memorable whether in the Sir Edward Elgar Restaurant, serving classical French cuisine, or Langtry's, where innovative English regional cooking is the speciality. In addition a self-contained suite of boardrooms and private dining rooms is available. Nowhere is luxury more apparent than in the Swallow Leisure Club, designed to an Ancient Egyptian theme and including a heated pool, steam room, fitness room and aerated pool. Hair and beauty care is offered in the salon. For business and pleasure The Swallow Hotel is the ideal venue. **Directions:** Five miles from M5 (junction 1) and $5\frac{1}{2}$ miles from M6 (junction 6) on A456 Hagley Road, just off Fiveways roundabout. Price guide: Single £97.50–£110; double/twin £120; suite £250.

DOWN HALL COUNTRY HOUSE HOTEL

HATFIELD HEATH, BISHOP'S STORTFORD, HERTFORDSHIRE CM22 7AS
TEL: 0279 731441 FAX: 0279 730416

Down Hall is an Italian-style mansion set in over 100 acres of woodland, park and landscaped gardens. The hotel is a splendid example of quality Victorian craftmanship, with many of the architectural details reproduced in the recently added West Wing. There is superb attention to detail throughout. The well-proportioned bedrooms have antique-style inlaid mahogany furniture and brass chandeliers. Italian granite is a feature of the luxurious en suite bathrooms. The hotel's public rooms offer comfort in the grand manner, with high ceilings, crystal chandeliers and paintings on the walls. There are two restaurants, offering English and International cuisine, with a wide selection of unusual dishes. For conferences, there are 26 meeting rooms, including 16 purpose-built syndicate rooms. Indoor and outdoor leisure facilities include a heated pool, whirlpool, sauna, croquet and putting lawns, giant chess, tennis courts and fitness trail. Down Hall is within access of London and Stansted Airport. For excursions, Cambridge, Constable country and the old timbered village of Thaxted are all within a few miles. **Directions:** Exit at junction 7 of M11. Follow the A414 towards Harlow. At the 4th roundabout follow the B183 to Hatfield Heath. Bear right towards Matching Green and the hotel is 1.3 miles on the right. Price guide: Single £80; double/twin £107.50.

MAINS HALL COUNTRY HOUSE HOTEL

MAINS LANE, SINGLETON, NR BLACKPOOL, LANCASHIRE FY6 7LE
TEL: 0253 885130 FAX: 0253 894132

Mains Hall is a Grade II listed house framed by trees and formal gardens, overlooking the River Wyre. Built in the 16th century by an order of monks, it later became a resting place for travellers. Its fascinating history continued under the ownership of the Fitzherbert family, when it was a sanctuary for Prince George, later George IV, who illicitly courted Maria Fitzherbert there. The Hall is reached via a long private drive and upon entering one senses an air of antiquity conveyed by the ancient oak panelling in the reception area. All 10 bedrooms have private or en suite facilities. Beautiful views can be appreciated from the dining room, where chef Simon Dobson's menus, including a new à la carte menu, cater for the most discerning palate. (Simon is a member of the prestigious Chefs' Culinary Circle.) The wine list comes with a useful commentary. The garden conservatory and 4-acre grounds make an ideal setting for private functions. Private river frontage allows for fishing and birdwatching. There are badminton lawns in the grounds, stabling for horses nearby and several golf courses in the vicinity. **Directions:** Leave the M55 at junction 3, following signs to Fleetwood on A585 for 5 miles (ignore signs to Singleton). The hall is 1/2 mile past the second set of traffic lights on the right-hand side. Price guide: Single: £50–£85; double/twin£65–£125.

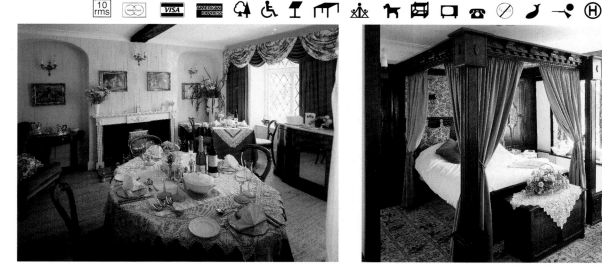

THE DEVONSHIRE ARMS COUNTRY HOUSE HOTEL

BOLTON ABBEY, SKIPTON, NORTH YORKSHIRE BD23 6AJ
TEL: 0756 710441 FAX: 0756 710564

The Duke and Duchess of Devonshire invite you to take a breath of fresh air at The Devonshire Arms Country House Hotel. Set in 12 acres in the heart of Wharfedale, this former coaching inn has been part of the Devonshire estate since 1753. It has been carefully restored and enlarged under the personal supervision of the Duchess of Devonshire to create a hotel which has charm, character and style. Rooms with stone-flagged floors and open fires are handsomely furnished with antiques and portraits from Chatsworth. All the bedrooms have been comfortably appointed with much attention to detail. An air of intimacy prevails in the Burlington restaurant where an inspirational menu combines the finest concepts of classical and modern cuisine while the wine list offers a diverse range of superior vintages. With five function rooms available, The Devonshire can accommodate all manner of private occasions with full professional and technical support. The Devonshire Club offers the best in leisure, health and beauty facilities. Special interest breaks reflect the traditions of a country house estate, such as splendid fly-fishing and clay pigeon shooting. The surrounding area has great appeal for those with an interest in history, geology or natural history. **Directions:** Off the A59 Skipton–Harrogate road at junction with the B6160. Price guide: Single £95–£100; double/twin £120–£140; suite £175.

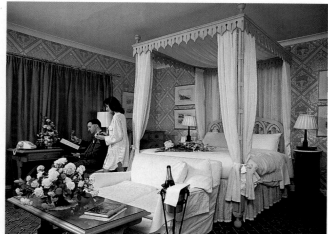

THE CARLTON HOTEL

EAST OVERCLIFF, BOURNEMOUTH, DORSET BH1 3DN
TEL: 0202 552011 FAX: 0202 299573

The Carlton Hotel is perfectly positioned upon Bournemouth's much-favoured East Cliff, with miles of golden sands below. For generations, public figures have enjoyed the care and charisma of The Carlton, which has provided hospitality to royalty, heads of state and ministers of the Crown. In recent years, leading designers have restyled the hotel to enhance the splendid turn-of-the-century features in accordance with modern taste. The interiors are a rich combination of classical furniture and contemporary decoration, creating an impression of space and opulence. The en suite bedrooms are furnished to the highest standards, while the exclusive suites are particularly luxurious. In the two-tier restaurant, decorated with blues, golds and shimmering crystal, guests are assured of international cuisine and fine wines. The versatile Meyrick Suite is suitable for banquets, wedding receptions, conferences or promotional events. For smaller functions, The Carlton offers its fully equipped executive suites. Relaxation or aerobic activity – either are options at the Carlton Health Club, with its comprehensive range of facilities. Luxury champagne breaks from £79 per person including 4-course dinner. **Directions:** The Carlton is on the corner of East Overcliff Drive and Meyrick Road, on the sea front. Price guide: Single £98; double/twin £150.

THE EDGEMOOR

HAYTOR ROAD, BOVEY TRACEY, SOUTH DEVON TQ13 9LE
TEL: 0626 832466 FAX: 0626 834760

Built in 1870, The Edgemoor Country House Hotel stands in a peaceful location in 2 acres of grounds on the eastern boundary of the Dartmoor National Park. Owned and managed by Rod and Pat Day, the hotel has recently undergone a programme of refurbishment and redecoration. There are 12 charming bedrooms, two of which are on the ground floor. All have en suite bathrooms and some have four-poster beds. The public rooms look over the hotel grounds and provide comfortable and sophisticated surroundings in which to enjoy your stay. In the restaurant, chef Edward Elliott prepares traditional English and French cuisine using local produce at all times. The wine list offers an interesting and varied selection. Bar meals are available at lunchtimes and in the evenings. Children are welcome and a special high-tea can be provided for them. With the hotel's close proximity to Dartmoor, walkers and naturalists are well catered for. Shooting and fishing can be arranged locally. Also worth a visit are Castle Drogo and the Becky Falls at Haytor. **Directions:** On leaving the M5, join the A38 in the direction of Plymouth. At Drumbridges roundabout, take A382 towards Bovey Tracey. At the second roundabout turn left and, after approximately $1/2$ mile, fork left at the sign for Haytor. Price guide: Single £44.75; double/twin £82.50.

WOOLLEY GRANGE

WOOLLEY GREEN, BRADFORD-ON-AVON, WILTSHIRE BA15 1TX
TEL: 0225 864705 FAX: 0225 864059

Woolley Grange is a 17th century Jacobean stone manor house set in 14 acres of formal gardens and paddocks. Standing on high ground, it affords southerly views of the White Horse at Westbury and beyond. Furnished with flair and an air of eccentricity, the interior décor and paintings echo the taste of owners, Nigel and Heather Chapman. Woolley Grange is gaining a reputation for outstanding cuisine and is highly rated in *The Good Food Guide*. Using local farm produce and organically grown fruit and vegetables from the Victorian kitchen gardens, chef Colin White has created a sophisticated style of country house food which aims to revive the focus on flavours. Children are particularly welcome; the owners have four of their own and they do not expect their young visitors to be 'seen but not heard'. In the Victorian coach house there is a huge games room and a well-equipped nursery with a full-time nanny available to look after guests' children 10am–6pm every day. A children's lunch and tea is provided daily. Nearby attractions include medieval Bradford-on-Avon, Bath, Longleat and Stonehenge. Riding can be arranged. **Directions:** From Bath on A363, fork left at Frankleigh House after town sign. From Chippenham, A4 to Bath, fork left on B3109; turn left after town sign. Price guide: Single £80; double/twin £92–£165.

FARLAM HALL HOTEL

BRAMPTON, CUMBRIA CA8 2NG
TEL: 06977 46234 FAX: 06977 46683

Farlam Hall was opened in 1975 by the Quinion and Stevenson families who over the years have managed to achieve and maintain consistently high standards of food, service and comfort. These standards have been recognised and rewarded by all the major guides and membership of Relais et Châteaux. This old border house, dating in parts from the 17th century, is set in mature gardens which can be seen from the elegant lounges and dining room, creating a relaxing and pleasing environment. The fine silver and crystal in the dining room ornament the quality of the English country house cooking produced by Barry Quinion and his team of chefs. There are 13 individually decorated bedrooms varying in size and shape, some having Jacuzzi baths, one an antique four-poster bed, and there are two ground floor bedrooms. This area offers many different attractions: miles of unspoiled countryside for walking, eight golf courses within 30 minutes of the hotel, Hadrian's Wall, Lanercost Priory and Carlisle with its castle, cathedral and museum. The Lake District, Scottish Borders and Yorkshire Dales each make an ideal day's touring. Winter and spring breaks are offered. Closed Christmas. **Directions:** Farlam Hall is 2½ miles east of Brampton on the A689, not in Farlam village. Price guide (including dinner): Single £95–£100; double/twin £170–£200.

MONKEY ISLAND HOTEL

BRAY-ON-THAMES, MAIDENHEAD, BERKSHIRE SL6 2EE
TEL: 0628 23400 FAX: 0628 784732

The name Monkey Island derives from the medieval Monk's Eyot. Circa 1723 the island was purchased by Charles Spencer, the third Duke of Marlborough, who built the fishing lodge now known as the Pavilion, and the fishing temple, both of which are Grade I listed buildings. The Pavilion's Terrace Bar, overlooking acres of riverside lawn, is an ideal spot for a relaxing cocktail, and the Pavilion Restaurant, perched on the island's narrowest tip with fine views upstream, boasts fine English cuisine, an award-winning cellar and friendly service. The River Room is suitable for weddings or other large functions, while the Regency-style boardroom is perfect for smaller parties. It is even possible to arrange exclusive use of the whole island for a truly memorable occasion. The Temple houses not only the comfortable bedrooms and suites but also the Wedgwood Room, with its splendid ceiling in high-relief plaster, and the octagonal Temple Room below. Monkey Island is 1 mile downstream from Maidenhead, within easy reach of Royal Windsor, Eton, Henley and London. Closed from 26 December to mid-January. Weekend breaks from £65 p.p. **Directions:** Take A308 from Maidenhead towards Windsor; turn left following signposts to Bray. On entering Bray, go right down Old Mill Lane, which goes over the M4; hotel is on left. Price guide: Single £70–£85; double/twin £90–£150.

TOPPS HOTEL

17 REGENCY SQUARE, BRIGHTON, EAST SUSSEX BN1 2FG
TEL: 0273 729334 FAX: 0273 203679

Quietly situated in Regency Square at the heart of Brighton, the Topps Hotel and Restaurant is only 2 minutes' walk from the sea and the Metropole Conference Centre, with the Lanes and Royal Pavilion nearby. This charming hotel offers an attractive alternative to the more anonymous large establishments in the vicinity and is under the personal supervision of resident proprietors, Paul and Pauline Collins. With its friendly welcome and efficient service, the Topps Hotel is certainly deserving of its name. The bedrooms are all elegantly appointed and every need of the discerning visitor has been anticipated. In the basement is the comfortable restaurant, where the emphasis is on freshness and simplicity. English and French influences are combined to create good but unpretentious cuisine. Brighton is often described as 'London-by-the-sea' – its urbane atmosphere and wide range of shops, clubs and theatres make it a popular town for visitors. Glyndebourne, Arundel, Chichester and Lewes are within easy reach and London is only 1 hour away by train. **Directions:** Regency Square is off King's Road (A259), opposite the West Pier. Price guide: Single £45–£84; double/twin £79–£99.

CHELWOOD HOUSE

CHELWOOD, NR BRISTOL, AVON BS18 4NH
TEL: 0761 490730 FAX: 0761 490730

Only minutes from Chew Valley Lake, Chelwood House enjoys an enviable location between Bristol, Bath and Wells – all cities of exceptional historic and cultural interest. A former dower house dating from 1681, the hotel's upper rooms enable visitors to take in far-reaching views over the meadows and rolling Mendip Hills. An impressive staircase leads to the guest rooms; three have four-poster beds of different national styles – French, Victorian and Chinese. Antique furniture, ornaments and paintings from the personal collection of owners Rudi and Jill Birk furnish the two lounges. Rudi Birk's Bavarian origins have a key influence on the cuisine – in addition to an English à la carte menu, a selection of traditional Bavarian dishes can be prepared. In 1990 the hotel's 'Restaurant in a Garden' opened, a conservatory dining room with plants, fountain and hand-painted murals, creating a lush setting for dinner. The hosts take credit for inspiring a convivial family atmosphere at this professionally run hotel, which represents good value for money. **Directions:** On the A37, 8 miles south of Bristol, between Pensford and Clutton. From Bath keep on the A368 through Chelwood village. Turn left at Chelwood Bridge traffic lights. Price guide: Single £49–£59.50; double/twin £69–£94. Special two day breaks available.

DANESWOOD HOUSE HOTEL

CUCK HILL, SHIPHAM, NR WINSCOMBE, SOMERSET BS25 1RD
TEL: 093 484 3145 FAX: 093 484 3824

A small country house hotel, Daneswood House stands in a leafy valley in the heart of the Mendip Hills – on a clear day, the views stretch as far as Wales. It was built by the Edwardians as a homeopathic health hydro and under the enthusiastic ownership of David and Elise Hodges it has been transformed into a charming hotel. Each bedroom is well furnished and individually decorated with striking fabrics. The honeymoon suite, with its king-sized bed, frescoed ceiling and antiques, is particularly comfortable. First-class cooking places equal emphasis on presentation and taste. Each dish is carefully prepared in a style that combines traditional English and French cooking with a nouvelle influence. During the summer, guests can dine alfresco and enjoy barbecued dishes such as Indonesian duck and baked sea bass with fennel and armagnac. There is a carefully selected wine list and a wide choice of liqueurs. The private conference lounge makes a quiet setting for meetings, while private functions can be catered for with ease. Awarded 2 AA Rosettes. Cheddar Gorge is 2 miles away, and Wells, Glastonbury, Bristol and Bath are nearby. Guide dogs only accommodated. **Directions:** Shipham is signposted from A38 Bristol–Bridgwater road. Go through village towards Cheddar; hotel drive is on left leaving village. Price guide: Single £57.50–£67.50; double/twin £69.50–£79.50; suite £112.

THORNBURY CASTLE

THORNBURY, NR BRISTOL, AVON BS12 1HH
TEL: 0454 281182 FAX: 0454 416188

Built in 1511 by Edward Stafford, 3rd Duke of Buckingham, Thornbury Castle was later owned by Henry VIII, who stayed here in 1535 with Anne Boleyn. Today it stands in 15 acres of regal splendour with its vineyard, high walls and the oldest Tudor garden in England. Rich furnishings are displayed against the handsome interior features, including ornate oriel windows, panelled walls and large, open fireplaces. The 18 carefully restored bedchambers retain many period details. In recent years, under the ownership of The Baron and Baroness of Portlethen, Thornbury Castle has received many accolades for its luxurious accommodation and excellent cuisine, including the 1992 *Johansens Most Excellent Value for Money Award*. Thornbury is an ideal base from which to explore Bath, Wales and the Cotswolds. Personally guided tours are available to introduce guests to the little-known, as well as the famous, places which are unique to the area. In addition, clay pigeon shooting, archery and golf may be enjoyed locally. Closed for 2 days in January. **Directions:** The castle is next to the parish church at the lower end of Castle Street. Price guide: Single £75–£85; double/twin £95–£200.

BUCKLAND MANOR

BUCKLAND, NR BROADWAY, GLOUCESTERSHIRE WR12 7LY
TEL: 0386 852626 FAX: 0386 853557

Set in an idyllic Cotswold valley, this fine gabled mansion house – parts of which date back to the 13th century – was tastefully converted in 1982 into an award-winning country house hotel. Guests can unwind far from the everyday hurly-burly and enjoy being cosseted in this friendly house. The bedrooms are of the highest standard, exquisitely furnished, with luxury bathrooms fed from the Manor's own spring water. Downstairs, the lounge and reception rooms feature impressive fireplaces, burnished oak panelling, antiques and plentiful displays of fresh flowers. Buckland Manor's resident manager is Nigel Power, previously of The Savoy and Hôtel du Rhône, Geneva. The head chef, Martyn

Pearn, trained at the Connaught Hotel in London and was previously head chef of the Michelin-starred La Reserve in Bordeaux. Given sufficient notice he will be happy to cook to order, and whatever the dish, only the best provisions are selected to meet the hotel's exacting standards. There are good recreational facilities at Buckland Manor in addition to the putting green and extensive gardens. Nearby attractions include the Vale of Evesham, Cheltenham and Stratford-upon-Avon. Closed for 3½ weeks from mid-January. **Directions:** Off the B4632 (formerly the A46). Price guide: Single £135–£260; double/twin £145–£270.

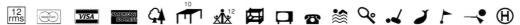

DORMY HOUSE

WILLERSEY HILL, BROADWAY, WORCESTERSHIRE WR12 7LF
TEL: 0386 852711 FAX: 0386 858636 TELEX: 338275 DORMY G

This former 17th-century farmhouse has been beautifully converted to a delightful hotel which retains much of its original character. With its oak beams, stone-flagged floors and honey-coloured local stone walls it imparts warmth and tranquillity. Dormy House provides a wealth of comforts for the most discerning guest. Each bedroom is individually decorated – some are furnished with four-poster beds – and suites are available. The restaurant is expertly managed by Saverio Buchicchio. Head Chef John Sanderson prepares a superb array of dishes, placing emphasis on considerations of both taste and healthy living. An extensive wine list including many half bottles, complements the cuisine. The versatile Dormy Suite is an ideal venue for conferences, meetings or private functions – professionally arranged to individual requirements. The hotel is surrounded on three sides by Broadway Golf Club, while the locality is an idyll for walkers. Stratford-upon-Avon, Cheltenham Spa, Hidcote Manor Garden and Sudeley Castle are all within easy reach. USA representative: Josephine Barr, 0101 708 251 4110. Closed 4 days at Christmas. **Directions:** Hotel is ½ mile off A44 between Moreton-in-Marsh and Broadway. Taking the turning signposted Saintbury, the hotel is first on left past picnic area. Price guide: Single £58–£80; double/twin £115–£135.

THE LYGON ARMS

BROADWAY, WORCESTERSHIRE WR12 7DU
TEL: 0386 852255 FAX: 0386 858611

The Lygon Arms, a magnificent Tudor building with numerous historical associations, stands in Broadway, acclaimed by some as 'the prettiest village in England', in the heart of the Cotswolds. Over the years much restoration has been carried out, emphasising the outstanding period features, such as original 17th century oak panelling and an ancient hidden stairway. The bedrooms are individually and tastefully furnished and offer guests every modern luxury combined with the elegance of an earlier age. The Great Hall, complete with a 17th century minstrels' gallery, and the smaller private dining rooms provide a fine setting for a well-chosen and imaginative menu. Conference facilities with all the latest communication equipment are available for up to 80 participants. Guests can enjoy a superb range of leisure amenities including all-weather tennis, indoor pool, gymnasium, billiards room, beauty salon, steam room, solarium and sauna. Golf can be arranged nearby. The many Cotswold villages; Stratford-upon-Avon, Oxford and Cheltenham are nearby, while Broadway itself is a paradise for the antique collector. **Directions:** Set on the right-hand side of Broadway High Street on the A44 in the direction of London to Worcester. Price guide: Single from £93; double/twin from £138 including Continental breakfast, excluding VAT at 17.5%

CAREYS MANOR HOTEL

BROCKENHURST, NEW FOREST, HAMPSHIRE SO42 7RH
TEL: 0590 23551 FAX: 0590 22799

Careys Manor, an elegant country house, dates from 1888 and is built on the site of a royal hunting lodge used by Charles II. Situated in 5 acres of landscaped grounds and surrounded by glorious New Forest countryside, the hotel is proud of the personal welcome and care it extends to its visitors. The comfortably furnished bedrooms are appointed to the highest standards. In the Garden Wing, there is a choice of luxury bedrooms, some opening directly onto the lawns and others with a balcony overlooking the pretty gardens. The restaurant offers fine English and French cuisine, prepared and presented to gourmet standards. A prestigious sports complex comprises a large indoor swimming pool with Jacuzzi, sauna, solarium and a Turkish steam room. In addition, guests can work out in the professionally supervised gymnasium, where there is also a room for massage, sports injury and beauty treatments. Wind-surfing, riding and sailing can all be enjoyed locally, while Stonehenge, Beaulieu, Broadlands, Salisbury and Winchester are a short distance away. Business interests can be catered for – there are comprehensive self-contained conference facilities. **Directions:** From M27 junction 1, follow A337 to Lymington. Careys Manor is on the left after 30 mph sign at Brockenhurst. Price guide: Single £69–£79; double/twin £89–£149.

NEW PARK MANOR

LYNDHURST ROAD, BROCKENHURST, NEW FOREST, HAMPSHIRE SO42 7QH
TEL: 0590 23467 FAX: 0590 22268

Hospitality is a centuries-old tradition at this former Royal hunting lodge, a restored manor house which dates back to the 17th century. Many of the original features have been incorporated into the decor – massive beams, ornate plasterwork and open fireplaces. The bedrooms, all equipped with modern facilities, are stylishly decorated with bright fabrics and co-ordinating colour schemes; the ground floor rooms also have verandahs leading onto the garden. Overlooking the park is the candle-lit restaurant, where visitors can choose from a menu that combines good English food with French style. Secluded in the New Forest, many types of outdoor pursuit can be undertaken from the hotel. New Park Manor has its own stables from which to ride out into the forest, and guests are welcome to bring their own horses. Polo is played every Saturday during the season and activities such as sailing and golf can be arranged. Business people are well provided for with two self-contained conference rooms, equipped with up-to-date audio-visual equipment, photocopying and secretarial services. Nearby: Beaulieu, Broadlands and gardens at Furzey, Spinners and Exbury. **Directions:** New Park Manor is 1/2 mile off the A337 between Lyndhurst and Brockenhurst. Price guide: Single £68; double/twin £114–£136.

RHINEFIELD HOUSE HOTEL

RHINEFIELD ROAD, BROCKENHURST, HAMPSHIRE SO42 7QB
TEL: 0590 22922 FAX: 0590 22800

Known locally as the 'jewel in the forest', at first sight the sheer grandeur of Rhinefield House surpasses all expectaitions. A hint of Italian Renaissance sweeps across ornamental gardens, with canals reflecting the mellow stonework. Lovingly restored to their original 1890s design, over 5,000 yew trees form the maze and formal parterres where a grass ampitheatre has beed carved out of the western slopes for summer evening concerts. The interiors are equally impressive, the journey through the rooms is a voyage of discovery. Authentically created in the style of a Moorish Palace, the Alhambra Room has Islamic inscriptions, onyx pillars and mosaic flooring. Fine cuisine is served in the elegant Armada Restaurant – so called after its splendid carving depicting the Spanish Armada. An airy sun-lit conservatory and attractive bedrooms appointed in accordance with the style of the house all add up to Rhinefield's appeal. The Grand Hall is an exact replica of Westminster Hall – an ideal setting for balls, society weddings and stylish banquets. A wide range of conference rooms and equipment is available for business events. Guests may unwind in the Atlantis Leisure Club with its plunge pool, solarium, sauna and gymnasium. Directions: A35 from Lyndhurst, or along Rhinefield Road from Brockenhurst. Price guide: Double/twin £95; single £75.

GRAFTON MANOR COUNTRY HOUSE HOTEL

GRAFTON LANE, BROMSGROVE, WORCESTERSHIRE B61 7HA
TEL: 0527 579007 FAX: 0527 575221

Closely associated with many of the leading events in English history, Grafton Manor's illustrious past can be traced back to Norman times. Commissioned in 1567, the present manor is set in several acres of gardens leading to a lake. Modern comfort and style are combined with the atmosphere of an earlier age. Pot-pourri from the hotel's 19th-century rose gardens scents the rooms and over 100 herbs are grown in a unique, chessboard-pattern garden. All the herbs are in regular use in the restaurant kitchen, where Simon Morris aims to 'produce only the best' for guests. Preserves made from estate produce are on sale. Meals are served in the 18th-century dining room, the focal point of Grafton Manor. Damask-

rose petal and mulberry sorbets are indicative of the inspired culinary style. Indian cuisine is Simon's award winning hobby and Asian dishes often complement the traditional English cooking. The fully equipped bedrooms have been meticulously restored and furnished, some with open fires on cooler evenings. Grafton Manor is ideally placed for Birmingham, the NEC and the International Conference Centre. It is an equally good base from which to explore the Worcestershire countryside. **Directions:** From M5 junction 5 proceed via A38 towards Bromsgrove. Bear left at first roundabout; Grafton Lane is first left after 1/2 mile. Price guide: Single £85; double/twin £95; suite £125.

THE OLD SWAN

MINSTER LOVELL, OXFORDSHIRE OX8 5RN
TEL: 0993 774441 FAX: 0993 702002

The Old Swan stands in Minster Lovell, a small Oxfordshire village nestling in the valley of the River Windrush, on the edge of the Cotswolds. This traditional inn, which stands in over 50 acres of grounds, dates back over 600 years. The original rustic character has been restored and combined with modern amenities and faultless service to provide tranquillity and privacy in a historic setting. The furnishings and decoration are of a high standard throughout, with many well-chosen antiques in all the rooms. All bedrooms are appointed for comfort and relaxation: each has an en suite bathroom and shower, mini bar, hairdryer and trouser press. Twenty-four-hour room service is available.

Patrons drive for miles to enjoy the outstanding food served in the Old Swan Restaurant. The à la carte menu offers a good choice of dishes, compiled from only the freshest ingredients, some of which are grown in the kitchen garden. The fully restored Mill House has been designed to offer state-of-the-art conference facilities and discreet business accommodation. Minster Lovell is ideal for tours of the Cotswolds, while Oxford is only 15 miles away. **Directions:** From A40 Oxford–Burford road, take B4047. Village is to the north. Follow signs for the Mill Conference Centre. Price guide: Single £60; double/twin £90.

THE PLOUGH

BOURTON ROAD, CLANFIELD, OXFORDSHIRE OX8 2RB
TEL: 036781 222 FAX: 036781 596

The Plough at Clanfield is an idyllic hideaway for the romantic at heart. Set in a sleepy Oxfordshire village on the edge of the Cotswolds, The Plough dates from 1560 and is a fine example of well-preserved Elizabethan architecture. When Hatton Hotels refurbished the hotel several years ago, great care was taken to preserve the charm and character of the interiors. Because there are only 6 bedrooms, guests can enjoy an intimate atmosphere and attentive, personal service. All the bedrooms are beautifully appointed to the highest standard and all have en suite bathrooms, four with whirlpool baths. At the heart of the hotel is the award-winning Tapestry Room Restaurant, regarded as one of the finest in the area. The cuisine is superbly prepared and impeccably served, with an interesting selection of wines. Two additional dining rooms are available for private entertaining. The hotel is an ideal base from which to explore the Cotswolds or the Thames Valley. There are many historic houses and gardens in the area, as well as racing at Newbury and Cheltenham. **Directions:** From Oxford, take the A420 for about 15 miles, then turn right to Faringdon. Go straight through the village on the main road. Clanfield is about 4 miles further on. Price guide: Single £60; double/twin £80–£95.

In association with MasterCard

THE BROOKHOUSE

ROLLESTON-ON-DOVE, NR BURTON UPON TRENT, STAFFORDSHIRE DE13 9AA
TEL: 0283 814188 FAX: 0283 813644

Originally built as a farmhouse in 1694, this attractive, ivy-clad William and Mary house stands in a tranquil position beside a gently flowing brook and lush gardens. Grade II listed, the building was converted into a hotel in 1976, and since then it has earned a good reputation for its friendly service and hospitality. Of particular interest are the pretty bedrooms, with four-poster, half-tester or Victorian brass beds. The bedding is trimmed with Nottingham lace. Downstairs, the décor and antique furniture are in keeping with the cosy cottage style. In the restaurant, soft wall-lighting and candles create an intimate atmosphere, while polished wooden tables are set with silver and crystal. The food is of a consistently high quality. An extensive menu presents a wide choice to suit all tastes. Small private functions can be catered for: fax, photo-copying and secretarial services can be arranged for business meetings. Serious hikers and ramblers alike will find plenty of good walking in the nearby Derbyshire Dales and Peak District. Notable local attractions include the Shugborough Estate, Calke Abbey, Haddon and Kedleston Halls. **Directions:** Rolleston is just outside Burton upon Trent between the A50 to Stoke-on-Trent and the A38 to Derby. Price guide: Single £65–£75; double/twin £85–£95.

THE ANGEL HOTEL

BURY ST EDMUNDS, SUFFOLK IP33 1LT
TEL: 0284 753926 FAX: 0284 750092

Immortalised by Charles Dickens as the hostelry where Mr Pickwick enjoyed an excellent roast dinner, The Angel Hotel prides itself that it continues to offer a first-class service to travellers, as indeed it has done since it first became an inn in 1452. It has several historical associations: during the Civil War Suffolk was the backbone of the parliamentary cause, the Committee for Suffolk meeting frequently at The Angel. Visitors to the hotel have the immediate impression of a hotel that is loved and nurtured by its owners. In the public rooms, guests will appreciate the carefully chosen ornaments and pictures, fresh flowers and log fires. Bedrooms are individually furnished and decorated and all have en suite bathrooms. Extra touches, such as hairdryers and trouser-presses, add to the comfort and warm welcome. The elegant dining room, overlooking the ancient abbey, serves classic English cuisine, including succulent roasts. There is a downstairs restaurant providing lighter meals in the modern style. The Angel is within an hour of east coast ferry ports and 30 minutes from Stansted Airport. Nearby there is racing at Newmarket and several golf courses within easy reach. Bury St Edmunds is an excellent centre for touring East Anglia. **Directions:** The hotel is situated in the centre of the town. Price guide: Single £69–£79; double/twin £99–£115; suite £125.

RAVENWOOD HALL

ROUGHAM, BURY ST EDMUNDS, SUFFOLK IP30 9JA
TEL: 0359 70345 FAX: 0359 70788

Dating from 1530 when Henry VIII was on the throne of England, this fine Tudor building with its elaborate oak carving is now an excellent country house hotel. While the period decor and furnishings reflect its history, the bedrooms are very comfortable and have private bathrooms. Fresh local produce forms the basis of the classic, modern English cooking which guests can enjoy in the impressive restaurant; it has a beamed ceiling and a massive fireplace. Facilities at the hotel include an outdoor heated swimming pool, an all-weather tennis court and croquet lawn. Golfers are well catered for: there are two courses nearby. Fishing and riding are also available and resident director, Craig Jarvis, takes pride in organising a splendid day's game shooting for guests. With the support of his efficient staff, he does all he can to ensure the guest' wellbeing. Set amid landscaped lawns and mature woodland, Ravenwood Hall is convenient for horse-racing at Newmarket, and for visiting the historic, university city of Cambridge. The hotel also has original banqueting facilities for up to 200 people. Price guide: Single £59–£77; double/twin £87–£97. Directions; situated 2 miles east of Bury St Edmunds off the A45.

HOWFIELD MANOR

CHARTHAM HATCH, NR CANTERBURY, KENT CT4 7HQ
TEL: 0227 738294 FAX: 0227 731535

At Howfield Manor great care has been taken to preserve a long tradition of hospitality dating back to 1181, while discreetly providing modern comforts. Originally part of the Priory of St Gregory, this historic country house is set in 5 acres of secluded grounds with a formal English rose garden. The hotel has an authentic priest hole and, in the Priory Bar, striking *trompe l'oeil* murals. Illuminated under the floor of the Old Well Restaurant is the ferned ancient well, which was the main source of water for the monks who lived here 800 years ago. Guests can choose from an extensive range of menus to cater for every occasion – from an intimate à la carte meal for two to a gourmet dinner party in the self-contained conference and banqueting suite. The well-furnished bedrooms have been thoughtfully equipped. Located only 2 miles from the cathedral city of Canterbury, Howfield Manor makes an ideal base for touring this area and as a stopping-off point to and from the continent. Special weekend breaks are also available. **Directions:** From A2 London–Dover road, follow signs for Chartham Hatch after the Gate Service Station, then follow straight on for 2¼ miles. Hotel is on left at junction with A28. Price guide: Single £62.50; double/twin £79.50–£90.

THE MANOR HOUSE

CASTLE COMBE, CHIPPENHAM, WILTSHIRE SN14 7HR
TEL: 0249 782206 FAX: 0249 782159 TELEX: 449931 MANOR G

Exclusive·HOTELS·UK·

The Manor House at Castle Combe enjoys a setting of idyllic tranquillity: 26 acres of gardens and parkland, a gently flowing trout stream, and the romance of a terraced Italian garden. All the rooms have been lovingly restored in sympathy with their historical significance, and many interesting features have been revealed such as stone fireplaces and a grain-drying kiln dating from the 14th century. The bedrooms are individually furnished to a luxurious standard, in keeping with the history of the house. A friendly relaxed atmosphere, excellent service, food and guest care are combined in this charming country house. Castle Combe 18-hole championship golf course adjoins the hotel grounds. A stroll through the village of Castle Combe, unchanged for almost 200 years and believed by many to be 'England's prettiest village', is itself a magical experience. **Directions:** Fifteen minutes' drive from junctions 17 and 18 of the M4, or 20 minutes from the M5/M4 intersection. Twelve miles from Bath (2 hours from central London). Approached directly from A420 and B4039. Price guide: Single £95; double/twin £115; suite £250.

BROCKENCOTE HALL

CHADDESLEY CORBETT, NR KIDDERMINSTER, WORCESTERSHIRE DY10 4PY
TEL: 0562 777876 FAX: 0562 777872

The Brockencote estate consists of 70 acres of landscaped grounds surrounding a magnificent hall. There are a gatehouse, half-timbered dovecote, lake, some fine European and North American trees and an elegant conservatory. The estate dates back 300 years and the style of the building reflects the changes which have taken place in fashion and taste over the years. At present, the interior combines classical architectural features with contemporary creature comforts. As in most country houses, each of the bedrooms is different: all have their own character, complemented by tasteful furnishings and decor. The friendly staff provide a splendid service under the supervision of owners Alison and Joseph Petitjean. Head chef, Eric Bouchet specialises in traditional French cuisine with occasional regional and seasonal specialities. Brockencote Hall is an ideal setting for those seeking peace and quiet in an unspoiled corner of the English countryside. Located a few miles south of Birmingham, it is convenient for business people and sightseers alike – it makes a fine base for touring historic Worcestershire. **Directions:** Exit 4 from M5 or exit 1 from M42. Brockencote Hall is beside the A448 at Chaddesley Corbett between Bromsgrove and Kidderminster. Price guide: Single £75; double/twin £90–£115.

EASTON COURT HOTEL

EASTON CROSS, CHAGFORD, DEVON TQ13 8JL
TEL: 0647 433469

Easton Court is a 15th-century, Grade II listed, thatched Tudor house with many historic connections, particularly literary ones. Both Evelyn Waugh – who wrote *Brideshead Revisited* here – and Patrick Leigh Fermor found inspiration in this tranquil setting amid the glorious Devon countryside. The sensitive restoration of the hotel has removed none of its old-world charm and period features such as exposed granite walls, oak beams and a great inglenook fireplace, complete with bread oven, have been retained. For those of a literary bent, there is a superb library housing a fascinating collection of old tomes. The tastefully furnished bedrooms have lots of interesting nooks and crannies and offer wonderful rural and moorland views. The menus in the attractive restaurant vary with the seasons and special diets can be catered for by prior arrangement. Dartmoor's mystery and grandeur lie 'on the doorstep' of the hotel, offering an endless variety of breathtaking walks, while Exmoor, Lynton and the rugged North Devon coast are a short journey away. Castle Drogo, Fernworthy Reservoir and Exeter are among the many other local places of interest. Closed January. **Directions:** From Exeter, take the A30. At the first roundabout take the A382 signposted Moretonhampstead. Price guide: Single £45–£55; double/twin £70–£80. Seasonal short breaks available.

GIDLEIGH PARK

CHAGFORD, DEVON TQ13 8HH
TEL: 0647 432367/432225 FAX: 0647 432574

Gidleigh Park enjoys an outstanding reputation among connoisseurs for its comfort and gastronomy. It has collected a clutch of top culinary awards for its imaginative cuisine (The Times Hotel Restaurant of the Year 1989, Egon Ronay Hotel of the Year 1990), and the Gidleigh Park wine list is one of the best in Britain. Master chef Shaun Hill was one of the first British members of L'Académie Culinaire de France. Service throughout the hotel is faultless. The en suite bedrooms – two of them in a converted chapel – are luxuriously furnished with antiques. The public rooms are elegantly appointed, and during the cooler months a fire burns merrily in the lounge's impressive fireplace.

Set amid 40 secluded acres in the Teign Valley, Gidleigh Park is 1½ miles from the nearest road. Two croquet lawns, an all-weather tennis court and a splendid water garden can be found in the grounds. Guests can swim in the river or explore Dartmoor on foot or horse-back. There are 14 miles of trout, sea trout and salmon fishing, as well as golf facilities nearby. Gidleigh Park is a Relais et Châteaux member. **Directions:** Approach from Chagford: go along Mill Street from Chagford Square. Fork right after 150 yards, cross into Holy Street at factory crossroads and follow lane for 1½ miles. Price guide (including dinner): Single £190–£300; double/twin £270–£360.

CHEDINGTON COURT

CHEDINGTON, NR BEAMINSTER, DORSET DT8 3HY
TEL: 0935 891265 FAX: 0935 891442

Situated in the Dorset Hills near the borders of Somerset and Devon, Chedington Court stands 700 feet above sea level and commands magnificent views over the surrounding countryside. This striking Jacobean-style mansion is set in 10 acres of grounds which contain ancient trees, a variety of shrubs, sweeping lawns, terraces and an ornamental water garden. Proprietors Philip and Hilary Chapman aim to provide a high standard of comfort, delicious food and a good selection of fine wines in beautiful surroundings. All ten bedrooms are elegantly decorated and have en suite bathrooms. The equally fine public rooms include a conservatory full of unusual plants. Taking pride of place among the leisure facilities is the 3,400-yard, par 74, 9-hole golf course, which attracts players of all handicaps. There is also a billiard room, croquet lawn and putting green. In this part of the world there are numerous small, unspoiled villages and charming towns to explore. Lulworth Cove, Lyme Regis, Dorchester, Weymouth and the splendid coastlines of Dorset and South Devon can be easily reached by car. **Directions:** Just off the A356, 4½ miles south-east of Crewkerne at Winyard's Gap. Price guide: Single £49–£71; double/twin £78–£120.

PONTLANDS PARK COUNTRY HOTEL & RESTAURANT

WEST HANNINGFIELD ROAD, GREAT BADDOW, NR CHELMSFORD, ESSEX CM2 8HR
TEL: 0245 476444 FAX: 0245 478393

Pontlands Park is a fine Victorian mansion, originally built for the Thomasin-Foster family in 1879. It became a hotel in 1981. The Victorian theme is still much in evidence, tempered with the best of contemporary interior styling. Immaculate public rooms – the conservatory-style Garden Room, the residents' lounge with its deep sofas and the relaxed ambience of the Victorian bar – are designed with guests' comfort in mind. Beautifully furnished bedrooms have co-ordinated fabrics and well-defined colour schemes. Diners are offered a selection of imaginative menus, with fine wines and attentive service. On Friday and Saturday evenings there is a menu of speciality Italian dishes. Within the grounds, Trimmers Leisure Centre has indoor and outdoor swimming pools, Jacuzzis, saunas and a solarium. The beauty salon offers many figure-toning, hairstyling and beauty treatments. Meetings and private dinners for from 2 to 36 guests can be accommodated, and functions for up to 200 guests can be held in the marquee. Closed 26 December to 4 January (but open for New Year's Eve). **Directions:** From A12 Chelmsford bypass take Great Baddow intersection (A130). Take first slip-road off A130 to Sandon/Great Baddow; bear left for Great Baddow, then first left for West Hanningfield Road. Price guide: Single £82.50; double/twin £121.

THE GREENWAY

SHURDINGTON, CHELTENHAM, GLOUCESTERSHIRE GL51 5UG
TEL: 0242 862352 FAX: 0242 862780

Set amid gentle parkland with the rolling Cotswold hills beyond, The Greenway is an Elizabethan country house with a style that is uniquely its own – very individual and very special. Renowned for the warmth of its welcome, its friendly atmosphere and its immaculate personal service, The Greenway is the ideal place for total relaxation. The public rooms with their antique furniture and fresh flowers are elegant and spacious yet comfortable, with roaring log fires in winter and access to the formal gardens in summer. The 19 bedrooms all have private bathrooms and are individually decorated with co-ordinated colour schemes. Eleven of the rooms are located in the main house and the larger rooms are in the converted Georgian coach house immediately next door to the main building. The conservatory dining room overlooks the sunken garden and lily pond, providing the perfect backdrop to superb cuisine of international appeal complemented by an outstanding selection of wines. Situated in one of Britain's most charming areas, The Greenway is well placed for visiting the spa town of Cheltenham, the Cotswold villages and Shakespeare country. **Directions:** On the outskirts of Cheltenham off the A46 Cheltenham–Stroud road, $2^1/_2$ miles from the city centre. Price guide: Single £85; double/twin £120–£175.

ON THE PARK

EVESHAM ROAD, CHELTENHAM, GLOUCESTERSHIRE GL52 2AH
TEL: 0242 518898 FAX: 0242 511526

On The Park is an exclusive town house hotel situated in the elegant spa town of Cheltenham. It enjoys a favourable aspect overlooking the beautiful Pittville Park. A classic example of a Regency villa, the atmosphere inside is one of warmth and sophistication, akin to that of a smart country house. The 12 intimate and restful bedrooms are individually styled and furnished with antiques, offering everything that one would expect to find in a small, luxury hotel. Each room has a private bathroom en suite, colour satellite television, direct-dial telephone, hairdryer and refreshments. A board meeting room for 16 people is available. Guests can enjoy some of the best modern British cooking on offer today in the epicurean restaurant, where fresh produce is meticulously prepared with imagination and flair to produce well-balanced menus. The wine list has been carefully selected to offer something for all tastes. Cheltenham, with its Regency architecture, attractive promenade and exclusive shops, has plenty to offer visitors and is set in the heart of the Cotswolds. Cheltenham racecourse has a busy National Hunt programme. For details of terms during Gold Cup week, apply well in advance. Dogs accommodated by prior arrangement. **Directions:** Opposite Pittville Park, 5 minutes' walk from town centre. Price guide: Single £74.50; double/twin £94; junior suites £109.

THE BIRCHES HOTEL

CARDEN PARK, CHESTER, CHESHIRE CH3 9DQ
TEL: 0829 731000 FAX: 0829 250539

Set in over 1200 acres of magnificent Cheshire countryside, Carden Park is one of Europe's leading Hotel, Golf, Sporting and Leisure resorts. Within the resort is The Birches Hotel which offers an outstanding level of comfort and service rarely found elsewhere today. All 83 suites – complete with satellite TV and CD hi-fi system are exquisitely designed and decorated to a five star standard around Mediterranean-style garden courtyards. The only variation is in the choice of accommodation – from the luxurious suites of the hotel itself to the the traditional Country Cottages, respectfully restored to combine the atmosphere of the past with modern comfort. Within the estate there is a fine selection of restaurants from Le Croquet providing international cuisine overlooking "The Great Lawn" to the Par 3 Brasserie with views over the Carden Academy, Europe's finest golf tuition centre. Every business and private function can be accommodated at The Birches and afterwards guests may enjoy the many sporting facilities that the hotel can provide: clay pigeon and game shooting, riding, tennis, croquet, fishing, archery and a 9 and 18 hole championship golf course. **Directions:** 8 miles south of Chester on A534, 1 ¹/₂ miles from A41 Broxton roundabout towards Wrexham. Price guide: Single £85; double/twin: £120; suite £150–£250.

BROXTON HALL COUNTRY HOUSE HOTEL

WHITCHURCH ROAD, BROXTON, CHESTER CH3 9JS
TEL: 0829 782321 FAX: 0829 782330

Built in 1671 by a local landowner, Broxton Hall is a black-and-white half-timbered building set in 5 acres of grounds and extensive gardens amid rolling Cheshire countryside. The medieval city of Chester is 8 miles away. The hotel provides every modern comfort while retaining the ambience of a bygone age. The reception area reflects the character of the entire hotel, with its magnificent Jacobean fireplace, plush furnishings, oak panelled walls and carved mahogany staircase. On cool evenings log fires are lit. The well-appointed bedrooms are furnished with antiques and have en suite bathrooms as well as every modern comfort. Overlooking the gardens, the restaurant receives constant praise from regular diners. French and English cuisine is served, using local game in season and freshly caught fish. There is an extensive wine list. Breakfast may be taken in the sunny conservatory overlooking the lawned gardens. The hotel is an ideal venue for business meetings and conferences. Broxton Hall is the perfect base from which to visit the North Wales coast and Snowdonia. There are a number of excellent golf courses nearby, and racecourses at Chester and Bangor-on-Dee. **Directions:** Broxton Hall is on the A41 Whitchurch-Chester road, 8 miles between Whitchurch and Chester. Price guide: Single £55–£60; double/twin £65–£85.

THE CHESTER GROSVENOR

EASTGATE STREET, CHESTER CH1 1LT
TEL: 0244 324024 FAX: 0244 313246

The Chester Grosvenor, occupying part of a estate that has been in his family for over 900 years, is owned by the Duke of Westminster. Recently awarded the Egon Ronay Cellnet Guide Hotel of the Year 1993. Epitomising the grandeur of the hotel is the splendid stairwell, above which shimmers the stunning 'Grosvenor chandelier'. Italian furniture, French silks and skilled British craftsmanship feature in the sumptuously fitted bedrooms, with 24-hour room service provided. Visitors can expect to enjoy highly regarded cuisine, whether in the opulent surroundings of the Arkle restaurant, or in the more relaxed, Parisian-style brasserie. An outstanding wine list names over 900 bins. The purpose-built function rooms can accommodate everything from board meetings to conferences of up to 250 delegates (theatre style). The leisure suite offers multi-gym, sauna and solarium; swimming can be arranged as well as outdoor pursuits such as riding, hot-air ballooning, falconry and clay pigeon shooting on a nearby country estate. **Directions:** In the centre of Chester on Eastgate Street. Car parking via Newgate Street NCP. Price guide: Single £125–£150; double/twin £196–£230; suites £270–£400

CRABWALL MANOR

PARKGATE ROAD, MOLLINGTON, CHESTER, CHESHIRE CH1 6NE
TEL: 0244 851666 FAX: 0244 851400 TELEX: 61220 CRAWAL G

Crabwall Manor can be traced back to Saxon England, prior to the Norman Conquest. The present Grade II listed manor at the heart of the hotel is believed to have originated from a Tudor farmhouse, with successive occupants enlarging the building over the ages. Set in 11 acres of wooded parkland on the outer reaches of Chester, the hotel has achieved a fine reputation under the ownership of Carl Lewis. A relaxed ambience is enhanced by staff who combine attentive service with friendliness and care. Bathrobes and sherry are among the many extras to be found in the bedrooms and luxury suites. Brightly printed drapes and pastel shades lend a freshness to the decor of the spacious lounge and reception areas, while a log fire crackling away in the inglenook fireplace adds warmth. Chef Michael Truelove, formerly of The Box Tree Restaurant in Ilkley, introduces a classic French influence to traditional English dishes. Manchester and Liverpool Airports are 30 minutes away by road. Chester, the Wirral and North Wales are all easily accessible. **Directions:** Go to end of M56, ignoring signs to Chester. Follow signs to Queensferry and North Wales, taking the A5117 to the next roundabout. Left onto the A540, towards Chester for 2 miles. Crabwall Manor is on the right. Price guide: Single £95; double/twin £135; suite £165. Weekend rates available.

ExCLUSIVE ·HOTELS· UK

NUNSMERE HALL

TARPORLEY ROAD, SANDIWAY, CHESHIRE CW8 2ES
TEL: 0606 889100 FAX: 0606 889055

Set in peaceful Cheshire countryside and surrounded on three sides by a lake, Nunsmere Hall epitomises the elegant country manor where superior standards of hospitality still exist. Wood panelling, antique furniture, exclusive fabrics, Chinese lamps and magnificent chandeliers evoke an air of luxury. The 32 bedrooms, with spectacular views of the lake and gardens, are beautifully appointed with king-size beds, comfortable breakfast seating and marbled bathrooms containing soft bathrobes and toiletries. The Brocklebank, Delamere and Oakmere business suites are air-conditioned, soundproofed and offers excellent facilities for boardroom meetings, private dining and seminars. The Garden Restaurant has a reputation for fine food and uses only fresh seasonal produce. County Restaurant of the Year in the 1993 Good Food Guide. A snooker room is provided, while there are several golf courses and Oulton Park Racing Curcuit nearby and the Cheshire Polo Club is next door. Archery and golf practice nets are available in the grounds. Although secluded, Nunsmere is convenient for major towns and routes. AA and RAC 4 Star, ETB 5 Crowns Highly Commended. **Directions:** Leave M6 at junction 18 northbound or 19 southbound, take A556 to Chester (approximately 12 miles). At second set of traffic lights turn left onto A49. Hotel is 1 mile on left. Price guide: Single £95; double/twin £120–£150; suite £185–£225.

ROWTON HALL HOTEL

WHITCHURCH ROAD, ROWTON, CHESTER CH3 6AD
TEL: 0244 335262 FAX: 0244 335464

Standing in 8 acres of gardens and pastureland on the outskirts of the city of Chester, Rowton Hall enjoys far-reaching views across the Cheshire Plains to the Welsh hills. Built as a private residence in 1779, the hall is renowned for the informal country-house atmosphere which welcomes all its guests. It retains many original features, including a Robert Adam fireplace and superb carved staircase. The conservatory-style Hamilton Lounge, overlooking the garden, is the perfect place to enjoy morning coffee, afternoon tea or cocktails, while the Cavalier Bar is ideal for a lunchtime snack. The bedrooms are furnished with chintzy fabrics and all have en suite bathrooms. In the Langdale Restaurant, which has earned a first-class reputation, chef Roger Price's à la carte and table d'hôte menus can be sampled in elegant and restful surroundings. Fresh vegetables and herbs are supplied by the hall's kitchen garden. Hotel guests have complimentary use of Hamiltons Leisure Club – facilities include a swimming pool, multi-gym, sauna and solarium. There are 5 conference/meeting rooms accommodating up to 200. The hotel offers special weekend rates. **Directions:** From the centre of Chester, take the A41 towards Whitchurch. After 3 miles, turn right to Rowton village. The hotel is in the centre of the village. Price guide: Single £67–£82; double/twin £88–£95; suite £125.

THE MILLSTREAM HOTEL

BOSHAM, NR CHICHESTER, WEST SUSSEX PO18 8HL
TEL: 0243 573234 FAX: 0243 573459

A village rich in heritage, Bosham is depicted in the Bayeux Tapestry and is associated with King Canute, whose daughter is buried in the local Saxon church. Moreover, sailors from the world over navigate their way to Bosham, which is a yachtsman's idyll on the banks of Chichester Harbour. The Millstream consists of a restored 18th-century malthouse and adjoining cottages linked to the Grange, a small English manor house. Cane and pine bedroom furnishings are complemented by chintz fabrics and pastel décor. Period furniture, a grand piano and bowls of freshly cut flowers feature in the drawing room. A stream meanders past the front of the delightful gardens, where traditional herbs are grown for use by the *chef de cuisine*. Whatever the season, care is taken to ensure that the composition and presentation of the dishes reflects high standards. An extensive buffet selection is offered in the summer months and includes specialities like lobster, crab and salmon. During the winter, good-value 'Hibernation Breaks' are available. **Directions:** From A259, 4 miles west of Chichester, take Walton Lane to Bosham; the hotel is situated on the right. Price guide: Single £59–£69; double/twin £89–£109.

STANTON MANOR

STANTON SAINT QUINTIN, NR CHIPPENHAM, WILTSHIRE SN14 6DQ
TEL: 0666 837552 FAX: 0666 837022

Set just off the beaten track in 5 acres of leafy gardens, there has been a home at Stanton Manor for over 900 years. The original house was listed in the *Domesday Book* and was later owned by Lord Burghley, Elizabeth I's chief minister. The Elizabethan dovecote in the garden bears witness to that period, although the present building dates largely from the 19th century. The bedrooms are furnished in a homely, country style and several offer views over Wiltshire farmland. Choices from the à la carte menu might include a starter of king prawns and mussels provençale or chicken liver parfait followed, for a main course, by saddle of spring lamb in a brandy, tomato and tarragon sauce. A variety of light meals is available in either the lounge or the bar. Proprietors Elizabeth and Philip Bullock are usually at hand to ensure that a friendly, personal service is extended to all their visitors. The Roman city of Cirencester, Chippenham, and a wealth of pretty villages all invite exploration. **Directions:** Leave the M4 at junction 17 and join the A429 towards Cirencester. After ¹/₂ mile, turn left to Stanton Saint Quintin; Stanton Manor is on the left in the village. Price guide: Single £68; double/twin £82.

CHARINGWORTH MANOR

NR CHIPPING CAMPDEN, GLOUCESTERSHIRE GL55 6NS
TEL: 038678 555 FAX: 038678 353

The ancient manor of Charingworth lies amid the gently rolling Cotswold countryside, just a few miles from the historic towns of Chipping Campden and Broadway. The 14th-century manor house overlooks its own 50-acre grounds and offers peace, tranquillity and breathtaking views. Inside, Charingworth is an historic patchwork of intimate public rooms with log fires burning during the colder months. There are 24 individually designed bedrooms, all furnished with antiques and fine fabrics. Outstanding cuisine is regarded as being of great importance and guests at Charingworth are assured of imaginative dishes. Great emphasis is placed on using only the finest produce and the AA has awarded the cuisine two Rosettes. There is an all-weather tennis court within the grounds, while inside, a beautiful swimming pool, sauna, steam room, solarium and billiards room are available, allowing guests to relax and unwind. Hidcote Manor Gardens, Batsford Arboretum, Stratford-upon-Avon, Oxford and Cheltenham are all within easy reach. Short-break rates are available on request. **Directions:** Charingworth Manor is on the B4035 between Chipping Campden and Shipston-on-Stour. Price guide: Single £85; double/twin £110–£175.

THE COTSWOLD HOUSE

HIGH STREET, CHIPPING CAMPDEN, GLOUCESTERSHIRE GL55 6AN
TEL: 0386 840330 FAX: 0386 840310

The Cotswold House takes pride of place on Chipping Campden's historic High Street, described by Trevelyn as 'the most beautiful street left in this island'. The beauty and harmony of this unique setting are reflected within the hotel, where antiques, choice fabrics, works of art and vast bowls of freshly cut flowers complement the elegant Regency architecture, creating a warm and welcoming atmosphere where friendly, efficient service is the hallmark. There are 15 very comfortable bedrooms, ranging from the whimsical Aunt Lizzie's Room to a wonderfully 'over the top' Four-Poster Room. In the Restaurant, eating from one of Raymond Boreham's menus is always a pleasure. Seasonal variety and fresh, local produce combine to give a new meaning to the words 'English cooking'. An extensive wine list, a delightful garden vista and soothing piano-playing add to the experience. A private dining room is available for small parties, weddings and conferences. The Cotswold House is perfectly located for visiting the many famous houses and gardens nearby and is just a short drive from Stratford-upon-Avon, Warwick, Oxford and Cheltenham Spa. Special short-stay breaks are available all year, except at Christmas when the hotel is closed. **Directions:** Chipping Campden lies 2 miles east of the A44 on the B4081. Price guide: Single £65–£80; double/twin £95–£130; four poster £145.

THE WHITE HART HOTEL

MARKET END, COGGESHALL, ESSEX CO6 1NH
TEL: 0376 561654 FAX: 0376 561789

A historic, family-run hotel, The White Hart is situated in the Essex town of Coggeshall, where it has played an integral part for many years. In 1489 The White Hart became the town's meeting place when the adjoining Guildhall was destroyed by fire. Now part of the original Guildhall, dating from 1420, forms the residents' lounge, and features magnificent roof timbers hewn from sweet chestnut. Sympathetically restored throughout, the hotel has been comfortably appointed with much attention to detail. All the en suite bedrooms have been decorated with bright fabrics to reflect the hotel's colourful character. Heavily timbered and spacious, the restaurant enjoys a good reputation locally. The table d'hôte and à la carte menus feature a choice of Italian dishes with a particular emphasis on seafood and shellfish. Pasta is freshly made on the premises, and aromatic sauces and tender cuts of meat figure prominently on the menu. The restaurant now has AA 2 Crowns. Coggeshall is noted for its abundance of antiques shops. It is also convenient for Colchester and Chelmsford and the ferry ports of Felixstowe and Harwich. **Directions:** Coggeshall is just off the A120 between Colchester and Braintree. From the A12 follow signs through Kelvedon, then take B1024. Price guide: Single £61.50; double/twin £82–£130.

COULSWORTHY HOUSE HOTEL

COMBE MARTIN, NORTH DEVON EX34 0PD
TEL: 0271 882463

Coulsworthy House Hotel stands in 6 acres of grounds in a quiet, rural setting on the western boundary of Exmoor National Park, in a region that, for its size, has as much beauty and variety of coastline and countryside as anywhere in Britain. The house originates in the main from 1750, although parts of the farmhouse date back over 600 years. An unusual hotel, it is family-owned and run by the Anthonys and the Osmonds, who offer an informal, friendly, house-party atmosphere. Alison Osmond's country-style cooking is of an uncompromisingly high standard and, by using the finest local ingredients, she creates dishes that are delicious, varied and generous. A variety of drinks is offered at the bar, including real ale, local cider and 24 single malt whiskies. The bedrooms are decorated in keeping with the period character of the house. Golf, clay pigeon shooting and fishing (river, lake and sea) are all available in the vicinity, and several riding stables offer the chance to explore Exmoor on horse-back. There are many country houses and gardens to visit. Closed mid-December to mid-February. **Directions:** From A39 at Blackmoor Gate take Combe Martin road; hotel is signposted after 2 miles. Price guide (including dinner): Single £55–£120; double/twin £110–£160.

MORTONS HOUSE HOTEL

CORFE CASTLE, DORSET BH20 5EE
TEL: 0929 480988 FAX: 0929 480820

Mortons House dates back to 1590. The original manor house was built in the shape of an E to honour Queen Elizabeth I and is linked by underground tunnels to nearby Corfe Castle. The hotel is idyllically situated in the midst of the historical village of Corfe Castle, which is flanked by the Purbeck Hills. Leading from the entrance hall, with its original stone fireplace, is the magnificent oak-panelled drawing room, lined with exotic friezes carved by Indonesian sailors. A chief priority of proprietors Mr and Mrs Langford is creating good British cooking of a consistently high standard. Prepared with flair and imagination by chef Pierre Mathiot are such dishes as collops of venison with wild mushrooms, walnuts and a port wine sauce, and paupiettes of sea trout filled with spinach and smoked salmon. In the summer, guests can enjoy their morning coffee, lunch and Dorset cream teas in the attractive, walled gardens. Nearby is the famed Dorset coast, with its sandy bays and cliff walks taking in landmarks such as Durdle Door and Lulworth Cove. Also worth a visit are the homes of Thomas Hardy and Lawrence of Arabia, Kingston Lacy Estate and Compton Acres, one of the finest Japanese gardens in Britain. **Directions:** Mortons House Hotel is situated in East Street, the main road through Corfe Castle. Price guide: Single £55; double/twin £80–£96.

NAILCOTE HALL

NAILCOTE LANE, BERKSWELL, NR COVENTRY, WARWICKSHIRE CV7 7DE
TEL: 0203 466174 FAX: 0203 470720

Nailcote Hall is a charming Elizabethan country house hotel set in 15 acres of gardens and surrounded by Warwickshire countryside. Built in 1640, the house was used by Cromwell during the Civil War and damaged by troops prior to the assault on Kenilworth Castle. Ideally located in the heart of England, Nailcote Hall is within 15 minutes' drive of the castle towns of Kenilworth and Warwick, Coventry Cathedral, Birmingham International Airport/Station and the NEC. Situated at the centre of the Midlands motorway network, Birmingham city centre, the ICC and Stratford-upon-Avon are less than 30 minutes away. Leisure facilities include indoor swimming pool, gymnasium, solarium and sauna. Outside are all-weather tennis courts, petanque, croquet, a 3-hole golf course and putting green. The hotel is associated with Stoneleigh Deer Park Golf Club. In the intimate Tudor surroundings of the Oak Room restaurant, the chef will delight you with superb cuisine, while the cellar boasts an extensive choice of international wines. Forty en suite bedrooms offer luxury accommodation, and elegant facilities are available for conferences, private dining and corporate hospitality. **Directions:** Situated 6 miles south of Birmingham International Airport/ NEC on the B4101 Balsall Common–Coventry road. Price guide: Single £95–£120; double/twin £115–£165.

CRATHORNE HALL HOTEL

CRATHORNE, NR YARM, CLEVELAND TS15 0AR
TEL: 0642 700398 FAX: 0642 700814

Part of the Virgin group, Richard Branson's Crathorne Hall was the last great stately home built in the Edwardian era. Now a splendid country house hotel, it is set in 15 acres of woodland overlooking the River Leven and the Cleveland Hills. True to their original fashion, the interiors have elegant antique furnishings complementing the grand architectural style. There is no traffic to wake up to here: just the dawn chorus, all the comforts of a luxury hotel and, if desired, a champagne breakfast in bed. From a simple main course to a gastronomic dinner, the food is of the highest quality, complemented by a comprehensive wine list. Whether catering for conferences, product launches, wedding receptions or a quiet weekend for two, professional, courteous service is guaranteed. In the grounds guests can play croquet, follow the jogging track or try clay pigeon shooting with a tutor on a layout designed to entertain the beginner and test the expert. Hot-air ballooning, fishing, archery and tennis can be arranged. The Yorkshire Dales, Durham and York are nearby. **Directions:** From A19 Thirsk–Teesside road, turn to Yarm and Crathorne. Follow signs to Crathorne village; hotel is on left. Teesside Airport and Darlington rail station are both 7 miles; a courtesy collection service is available. Price guide: Single £90; double/twin £105–£160.

CRICKLADE HOTEL AND COUNTRY CLUB

COMMON HILL, CRICKLADE, WILTSHIRE SN6 6HA
TEL: 0793 750751 FAX: 0793 751767

Built at the turn of the last century by a wealthy German émigré, this interesting house has been skillfully restored. Set in extensive, secluded grounds in the heart of rural Wiltshire, the hotel offers a diverse range of attractions – from quiet tranquillity to the most modern sporting facilities. The leisure complex includes a 9-hole golf course (plus on-site golf professional to offer tuition), *en tout cas* tennis, indoor swimming pool, a gymnasium, hot spa bath, solarium and full-size snooker tables. Each smartly furnished bedroom is fully equipped with teletext TV, hairdryer and trouser press. From the conservatory lounge, fine views can be enjoyed over the Marlborough Downs. The restaurant offers a varied and interesting menu to suit all tastes, with the emphasis on fresh local produce and careful presentation. With the new extension, large functions can be catered for and the Cricklade is particularly recommended for conferences. Up to 150 delegates can be accommodated in the self-contained suite of exhibition rooms. Live entertainment and dinner dances are regular events, and barbecues are held in the warmer months. The hotel is well placed for visits to the Cotswolds, Cirencester, Bath and Gloucester. **Directions:** From M4 junctions 15/16, M5 junction 11; situated on the B4040 Cricklade–Malmesbury road. Price guide: Single £76–£80; double/twin £90–£95.

OCKENDEN MANOR

OCKENDEN LANE, CUCKFIELD, WEST SUSSEX RH17 5LD
TEL: 0444 416111 FAX: 0444 415549

Set in 9 acres of gardens in the centre of the Tudor village of Cuckfield, this hotel is an ideal base from which to discover Sussex and Kent, the Garden of England. First recorded in 1520, Ockenden Manor has become a hotel of great charm and character. The bedrooms all have their own individual identity: climb your private staircase to Thomas or Elizabeth, look out across the lovely Sussex countryside from Victoria's bay window or choose Charles, with its handsome four-poster bed. The restaurant, with its beautifully painted ceiling, is a dignified setting in which to enjoy acclaimed cuisine. 'Modern English' is how the chef describes his culinary style, offering an à la carte menu with a daily table d'hôte choice to include fresh seasonal produce and herbs from the hotel garden. An outstanding, extensive wine list offers, for example, a splendid choice of first-growth clarets. Spacious and elegantly furnished, the Ockenden Suite welcomes private lunch and dinner parties. A beautiful conservatory is attached to the Ockenden Suite, this opens to the lawns, where marquees can be set up for summer celebrations. The gardens of Nymans, Wakehurst Place and Leonardslee are nearby, as is the opera at Glyndebourne. **Directions:** In the centre of Cuckfield on the A272. Less than 3 miles east of the A23. Price guide: Single £68–90; double/twin £90; exec double/twin from £130.

HALL GARTH GOLF & COUNTRY CLUB HOTEL

COATHAM MUNDEVILLE, NR DARLINGTON, COUNTY DURHAM DL1 3LU
TEL: 0325 300400 FAX: 0325 310083

From the style of its architecture and décor to the warmth of its hospitality, Hall Garth is English through and through. The older parts of the hotel date back to 1540, although there are many Georgian and Victorian features. The hotel boasts it's own 9-hole par 74 golf course built to championship standards and USGA specifications and will be playable in April 1994 making this one of the most popular holiday and business locations in the north east. Lovingly furnished with interesting antiques, Hall Garth has 40 comfortable bedrooms, five with four-poster beds. The style of Hugo's restaurant combines local seasonal produce to create an interesting and imaginative menu which changes weekly, complemented by an extensive wine list. Home-made bar meals and real ales are offered in the Stables Bar, a few yards from the main house. Leisure facilities include a grass tennis court, indoor heated pool, Jacuzzi, sauna, steam room, solarium and gymnasium with all the latest cardio-vascular equipment. The Brafferton Suite is the ideal venue for conferences, banquets, weddings and other social occasions. Durham, Darlington's railway museum and the North Yorkshire Moors are among the local attractions. **Directions:** Turn off A1(M) north of Darlington onto the A167 (signposted to Darlington); hotel is ¹/₂ mile on left. Price guide: Single £70–£80; double/twin £90–£100.

HEADLAM HALL

HEADLAM, NR GAINFORD, DARLINGTON, COUNTY DURHAM DL2 3HA
TEL: 0325 730238 FAX: 0325 730790

This magnificent Jacobean mansion is set in 3 acres of formal gardens in the quiet countryside of rural Teesdale. Originally built in the 17th century, the hall was home for 150 years to the Brocket family and more recently to Lord Gainford. Since 1979 Headlam Hall has been owned and personally run by the Robinson family. The grounds include a small private trout water enclosed by ancient yew and beech hedges. The hotel has a tennis court, croquet lawn, a fine swimming pool, sauna and snooker room. All the bedrooms are individually furnished, and the restaurant provides the best of traditional English cuisine. The main hall features a magnificent carved oak fireplace and open staircase, while the Georgian drawing room opens onto a stepped terrace, overlooking the lawns. There are 4 separate conference and meeting rooms including the Edwardian Suite holding up to 200 people. A free night's accommodation and champagne breakfast are provided for newly-weds holding their reception here. Fishing and golf can be enjoyed nearby and Barnard Castle and Durham are only a short drive away. Closed Christmas Day. Dogs by prior arrangement. **Directions:** Headlam is 2 miles north of Gainford off the A67 Darlington–Barnard Castle road. Price guide: Single £55–£70; double/twin £70–£85; suite £85.

BRANDSHATCH PLACE HOTEL

FAWKHAM VALLEY ROAD, FAWKHAM, KENT DA3 8NQ
TEL: 0474 872239 FAX: 0474 879652

Set amidst 12 acres of private parkland and gardens, Brandshatch Place is a distinguished Georgian residence built for the Duke of Norfolk in 1806. Approached along an impressive tree-lined drive, it offers a peaceful getaway from London, only 20 miles to the north. The hotel has been carefully renovated and now offers every modern amenity, from banqueting and conference rooms to a fully equipped leisure complex. All 29 bedrooms are pleasantly decorated and fully appointed, and the attentive room service takes care of requests for early-morning tea to three-course meals. Downstairs, in the relaxing surroundings of the restaurant, the dinner menu might, any evening, include casserole of seafish or sirloin of beef slowly braised in claret with bay leaves and delicate spices. After your meal enjoy a relaxing drink in our library bar. You are always welcome to use Fredericks, our sports and leisure complex with its indoor pool, squash courts, badminton and tennis courts, plus sauna, steam room and solarium and full size snooker tables. Business and private functions are easily accommodated in the 7 conference and syndicate rooms, complete with audio-visual facilities. **Directions:** From M25 junction 3 follow A20 south, then signs to Fawkham Green, hotel is on the left about $1/2$ mile before Fawkham village. Price guide: Single: £75; double/twin £90.

MAISON TALBOOTH

STRATFORD ROAD, DEDHAM, COLCHESTER, ESSEX CO7 6HN
TEL: 0206 322367 FAX: 0206 322752

In the north-east corner of Essex, where the River Stour borders with Suffolk, is the Vale of Dedham, an idyllic riverside setting immortalised in the early 19th century in the paintings of John Constable. One summer's day many years later, in 1952, the young Gerald Milsom enjoyed a 'cuppa' in the Talbooth tea room and soon afterwards took the helm at what would develop into Le Talbooth Restaurant. Business was soon booming and the restaurant built itself a reputation as one of the best in the country. By 1969 Gerald had branched out, and Maison Talbooth was created in a nearby Edwardian rectory, to become, as it still is, a vanguard of England's premier country house hotels. Indeed, in

1982 Gerald Milsom became the founder member of the Pride of Britain group. With its atmosphere of tranquil opulence, Maison Talbooth has ten spacious guest suites which all have an air of quiet luxury. Every comfort has been provided, and for an extra touch of romance, some of the plush bathrooms have large round baths with gold taps. Although a full breakfast is served, the hotel doesn't have a restaurant as it is just a pleasant 1/2-mile stroll to Le Talbooth Restaurant, where first-class cuisine is served. **Directions:** Dedham is about a mile from the A12 between Colchester and Ipswich. Price guide: Single £82.50–£107.50; double/twin £102.50–£137.50; suite £137.50. Telephone for details of special weekend breaks.

MAKENEY HALL COUNTRY HOUSE HOTEL

MAKENEY, MILFORD, DERBYSHIRE DE56 0RU
TEL: 0332 842999 FAX: 0332 842777

Set in a tranquil location on the River Derwent, Makeney Hall is surrounded by over 6 acres of beautifully landscaped gardens just 10 minutes' drive from Derby. Founded by the Stutt family with cotton-spinning wealth, this quiet, spacious hotel, with its mid-Victorian features, offers guests a warm, distinctive welcome. The carefully chosen décor imparts an air of bygone comfort. Bedrooms in the main house are spacious and individually appointed and many overlook the gardens. A splendid covered courtyard gives access to a further eighteen new rooms. Guests may dine in Lavinia's restaurant, where expert cooking and fresh local produce create cuisine of the highest standard. The fare is British in flavour and a selection of fine wines is available. Makeney Hall's Conference and Banqueting suites can accommodate wedding receptions and business meetings of up to 130 visitors. Places of interest locally include the Derwent Valley – an area of outstanding natural beauty – the Peak District, the stately homes of Chatsworth and Haddon Hall, and Alton Towers. **Directions:** From M1 (exits 25 or 28) head for Derby and A38 northbound. Follow A6 (signposted Matlock). Makeney is signposted at Milford, 6 miles NW of Derby. Price guide: Double-twin: from £62.50; suite: from £100.

SUMMER LODGE

SUMMER LANE, EVERSHOT, DORSET DT2 0JR
TEL: 0935 83424 FAX: 0935 83005

A charming Georgian building, idyllically located in Hardy country, the Summer Lodge was formerly the dower house of the Earls of Ilchester. Now it is a luxurious hotel where owners Nigel and Margaret Corbett offer their visitors a genuinely friendly welcome, encouraging them to relax as if in their own home. The bedrooms have views over the 4-acre sheltered gardens or overlook the village rooftops across the meadowland. In the dining room, with its French windows that open on to the garden, the cuisine is highly regarded. Fresh local produce is combined with the culinary expertise of chef Edward Denny to create a distinctive brand of English cooking. The unspoiled Dorset countryside, and coastline 12 miles south, make for limitless exploration, and bring to life the setting of *Tess of the d'Urbevilles* and the other Hardy novels. Many National Trust properties and gardens in the locality are open to the public. There are stables, golf courses and trout lakes nearby. Summer Lodge has recently earned the distinction of becoming a member of Relais et Châteaux. **Directions:** The turning to Evershot leaves the A37 halfway between Dorchester and Yeovil. Once in the village turn left into Summer Lane and the hotel entrance is 150 yards on the right. Price guide: Single £100; double/twin £125–£225.

THE WHITE HART HOTEL

HIGH STREET, DORCHESTER-ON-THAMES, OXFORDSHIRE OX10 7HN
TEL: 0865 340074 FAX: 0865 341082

This comfortable small hotel was years ago a coaching inn on the main road. Now it lies peacefully in the midst of a rural community with its ancient abbey, its quaint shops and its winding streets around it. The picturesque old village of Dorchester has been by-passed. The White Hart still bears the emblem of King Richard II but today the hotel is modern and luxurious. The suites and bedrooms have been imaginatively designed to maximise the appeal of their interesting features and cottage-style charm, while all offer superb private facilities. The Friary Restaurant, with its warm and congenial atmosphere, is the setting for fine cuisine accompanied by a good choice of wines from around the world, while simpler fare is served in the Abbey Room Restaurant. The White Hart Hotel is ideally located to accommodate small senior level conferences and business meetings, being only 45 minutes from Heathrow and 8 miles from Oxford. There is much to see in the area, including Blenheim Palace, Henley-on-Thames, the City and University of Oxford and the village of Dorchester itself. **Directions:** The White Hart is easily spotted in the High Street in Dorchester-on-Thames. Price guide: Single £66.50; double/twin £87.

LUMLEY CASTLE HOTEL

CHESTER-LE-STREET, COUNTY DURHAM DH3 4NX
TEL: 091 389 1111 FAX: 091 389 1881/091 387 1437

The origins of this magnificently preserved castle go back to the 9th century, although the main building dates from the 14th century. Sympathetic refurbishment over the ages has transformed it into an international hotel offering an exciting blend of ancient history and modern luxury. The bedrooms are uniquely furnished, from the genuine Queen Anne four-poster in the King James' Suite to the rustic charm and old beams of the courtyard rooms. Subdued lighting, hidden corridors and secret passages enhance the delightful atmosphere of the hotel. Well-chosen wines and delicious cooking tempt the palate in the candle-lit restaurant, where medieval pillars support a multi-domed ceiling. The popular weekly Elizabethan Banquets are now in their 24th year. They are held in the Baron's Hall, where guests enjoy a five-course feast while tuneful troubadours entertain them from the minstrels gallery. Medieval Memories and Murder Mystery weekends are also held. For conferences and functions, a full-time professional is available to discuss individual needs. Closed Christmas Day, Boxing Day and New Year's Day. **Directions:** From A1(M) take A693/A167 to Chester-le-Street and Durham. At the second roundabout take first left to Lumley Castle. Price guide: Single £60–£102; double/twin £98–£135; suite £160.

GRINKLE PARK HOTEL

EASINGTON, SALTBURN-BY-THE-SEA, CLEVELAND TS13 4UB
TEL: 0287 640515 FAX: 0287 641278

Grinkle Park Hotel is a refurbished 19th-century mansion, surrounded by 35 acres of parkland and gardens containing many varieties of azalea and rhododendron. The hotel's lake is home to local wildfowl and peacocks strut about the grounds. Guests can enjoy tea taken in the Camellia Room, play croquet, tennis, billiards or snooker, or simply relax in the majestic entrance hall lounge. For the more energetic, there is a jogging trail. The individually designed bedrooms are named after local places, flora and birds, and every luxury the discerning guest would expect is provided. Dinner is by candle-light; table d'hôte and à la carte menus present a wide choice of dishes with the emphasis on presentation and quality. The hotel's location between unspoiled coastline and the North York Moors National Park ensures the availability of outdoor activities, such as climbing, freshwater and sea fishing, swimming, golf and moorland walks. **Directions:** Grinkle Park Hotel is situated 9 miles from Guisborough, signed left, off the main A171 Guisborough–Whitby road. Price guide: Single £65; double/twin £80–£90.

THE EVESHAM HOTEL

COOPERS LANE, OFF WATERSIDE, EVESHAM, WORCESTERSHIRE WR11 6DA
TEL: 0386 765566 FAX: 0386 765443

National awards for 'friendly eccentricity' suggest that a stay at The Evesham Hotel will be memorable. Indeed, the emphasis here is on unconventional hotel-keeping, informality and fun! Originally a Tudor farmhouse, the hotel was extended and converted into a Georgian mansion house in 1810. Privately owned and managed by the Jenkinson family since the mid-1970s, guests can be assured of prompt, friendly service and a relaxed atmosphere. Each of the 40 en suite bedrooms is furnished complete with a teddy bear and a toy duck for the bath. The restaurant offers delicious cuisine from a very imaginative and versatile menu, accompanied by a list of unusual wines. John Jenkinson claims that the eclectic wine list 'enjoys great notoriety' and that the hotel can offer a wide selection of drinks. The indoor swimming pool has a seaside theme, and guests have access to squash and tennis at a nearby sports club. The peace of the 2¹/₂-acre garden belies the hotel's proximity to the town – a 5-minute walk away. In the gardens are six 300 year-old mulberry trees and a magnificent Cedar of Lebanon, planted in 1809. The hotel is a good base from which to explore the Cotswolds, Stratford-upon-Avon and the Severn Valley. Closed Christmas. **Directions:** Coopers Lane lies just off Waterside (the River Avon). Price guide: Single £60–£68; double/twin £88–£98.

DUNSFORD MILLS COUNTRY HOUSE HOTEL

DUNSFORD, NR EXETER, DEVON EX6 7EF
TEL: 0647 52011 FAX: 0647 52988

Situated on the edge of the River Teign in the beautiful Teign Valley, and inside the Dartmoor National Park, Dunsford Mills is ideally placed for exploring one of England's last wildernesses and visiting the historic city of Exeter. The fully restored mill, set in 10 acres of grounds, has 10 spacious en suite bedrooms, all furnished to a high standard. Overlooking the river, the lounge bar, with its large, open fireplace and oak beams, is a comfortable room for relaxation. The restaurant occupies the original working area of the flour mill. Here, the water flows under the building through the original, 15-foot working waterwheel, now enclosed in a glass-and-oak-beam case. Since the hotel opened the restaurant has been concentrating on a high standard of quality cuisine and imagination for presentation which has now built up a good reputation to constant returning guests, along with a carefully selected wine list. Proprietors Steuart and Susan Veitch are very active in the running of this beautifully kept hotel and assure all their guests of a memorable stay. Riding and golf nearby. Children aged up to 2, and over 12 welcome. **Directions:** Situated west of Exeter on the B3212, 5 miles from East Moretonhampstead. Price guide: Single £41.50–£47.50; double/twin £63–£90.

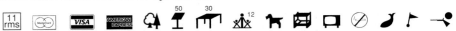

ST OLAVES COURT HOTEL

MARY ARCHES STREET, EXETER, DEVON EX4 3AZ
TEL: 0392 217736 FAX: 0392 413054

St Olaves Court Hotel stands in a private walled garden just 400 yards from Exeter Cathedral. When owners Raymond and Ute Wyatt arrived in 1991, the hotel already had a good reputation; however, they optimistically undertook the pursuit of excellence. With their experience of running a leading Speyside hotel, they had a clear idea of the high standards of hospitality to be achieved. A major coup was the recruitment of head chef Lee Jones, a dedicated perfectionist with an almost obsessional passion for cooking. In the new kitchens he prepares innovative *cuisine moderne*, focusing on taste, flavour and presentation. St Olaves is fast earning a reputation as one of the leading restaur-ants in the South West. Meals are served in the candle-lit Golsworthy Restaurant, where the very reasonably priced food has already been awarded 2 AA Rosettes. Each of the 15 Georgian-style bedrooms has been well appointed. A decanter of sherry can be found in each room and the executive rooms have Jacuzzi baths. A fast-growing city, Exeter's attractions include its Cathedral, museums and Northcott Theatre. Closed 25 December to 3 January. **Directions:** Follow signs to city centre, then signs to Mary Arches P (parking); hotel entrance is opposite. Price guide: Single £60–£80; double/twin £70–£95.

FALMOUTH (Mawnan Smith)

In association
with MasterCard **MasterCard**

MEUDON HOTEL

MAWNAN SMITH, NR FALMOUTH, CORNWALL TR11 5HT
TEL: 0326 250541 FAX: 0326 250543

Set against a delightfully romantic backdrop of densely wooded countryside between the Fal and Helford Rivers, Meudon Hotel is a unique, superior retreat: a luxury, family-run establishment which has its origins in two humble 17th century coastguard's cottages. The French name comes from a nearby farmhouse built by Napoleonic prisoners of war and called after their homonymous home village. Set in nearly 9 acres of fertile gardens – laid out by landscape gardener 'Capability' Brown, and now coaxed annually into early bloom by the mild Cornish climate – Meudon Hall is safely surrounded by 200 acres of beautiful National Trust land and the sea. All bedrooms enjoy spectacular views over sub-tropical gardens. Modern appliances are standard. Bedrooms are all en suite, and furnishings include Parker Knoll, ViSpring and Austinsuite. Many a guest is enticed by the cuisine to return: in the restaurant (or the gardens during nice weather), fresh seafood and kitchen garden produce is served with wines from a judiciously compiled list. There are opportunities locally for fishing, sailing and walking. Golf is free. **Directions:** From Truro take A39 for 7 miles, then A394 for 1 mile. Over Helston road, follow signs to Mawnan. Turn left at the Red Lion, Meudon is 1 mile on. Price guide (including dinner): Single £65-£85; double/twin £120–£150; suite £160–£200.

134

NANSIDWELL COUNTRY HOUSE

MAWNAN, NR FALMOUTH, CORNWALL TR11 5HU
TEL: 0326 250340 FAX: 0326 250440

Lying at the head of a wooded farmland valley, Nansidwell Country House is bounded by several acres of grounds between National Trust coastland and the Helford River. Bearing witness to the mild climate, the 5 acres of sub-tropical gardens are ablaze with colour throughout the seasons, from January when the Camellias appear, through to autumn when the banana trees bear fruit. The philosophy of proprietors Jamie and Felicity Robertson is that their guests should experience the atmosphere of an amiable, well-run country house. That so many guests return each year is a credit to the hotel. The bedrooms are prettily furnished and offer every comfort. Chef Anthony Allcott places an emphasis on fresh, local produce, particularly seafood such as lobster, mussels and oysters, served in generous portions and accompanied by an interesting wine list. For the sports enthusiast, there are no fewer than five 18-hole golf courses within a short drive, as well as both sea fishing and reservoir trout fishing. Wind-surfing, sailing, riding and bowls can all be enjoyed in the vicinity and, of course, there is unlimited scope for enjoying the area's natural beauty. Closed 27 December to 1 February. **Directions:** From A39, take A394 Helston road. After 1 mile follow sign for Mabe/Mawnan Smith. Price guide (including dinner): Single £95–£105; double/twin £140–£190.

TRELAWNE HOTEL

MAWNAN SMITH, NR FALMOUTH, CORNWALL TR11 5HS
TEL: 0326 250226 FAX: 0326 250909

A very friendly welcome awaits guests, who will be enchanted by the beautiful location of Trelawne Hotel, on the coast between the Rivers Fal and Helford. Large picture windows in the public rooms, including the attractively decorated, spacious lounge, ensure that guests take full advantage of the panoramic views of the ever-changing coastline. The bedrooms are charming, many with views of the ocean. The soft colours of the décor, the discreet lighting and attention to detail provide a restful atmosphere, in harmony with the Wedgwood, fresh flowers and sparkling crystal in the restaurant. The menu changes daily and offers a variety of inspired dishes, including local seafood, game and fresh vegetables. Recreational facilities include a putting green and a games room, with snooker, table-tennis and darts. The Royal Duchy of Cornwall is an area of outstanding beauty, with many National Trust and English Heritage properties to visit and a range of leisure pursuits to enjoy. Trelawne Hotel offers its own golf package at no less than ten fine courses. 'Slip Away Anyday' spring, autumn and winter breaks. Closed January. A Hospitality Hotel of Cornwall. AA Rosette. **Directions:** From A39 take A394 Helston road. After 1 mile follow sign for Mabe/Mawnan Smith. Price guide: Single £67–£73; double/twin £120–£132. Including dinner.

FLITWICK MANOR

CHURCH ROAD, FLITWICK, BEDFORDSHIRE MK45 1AE
TEL: 0525 712242 FAX: 0525 712242

Flitwick Manor is a classical English house of the late-17th and early-18th centuries, approached along a magnificent avenue of towering lime trees. It is set in 50 acres of quiet rolling gardens, with a castellated, walled kitchen garden, hot house, a listed 18th-century folly in grotto form, an ornamental pond and a 12th-century ironstone church, all ringed by woodland. There is also an all-weather tennis court, two croquet lawns and a putting green. The bedrooms all have views of the park; the restaurant has an excellent reputation and is acclaimed by all the major food guides. The finest dishes are prepared with skill and dedication from local venison, fish and home-grown herbs. The vaulted cellars hold a comprehensive selection of the finest wines. Mahogany furniture and family portraits add to the sybaritic atmosphere. The library doubles as a private dining room and is used for small meetings. Flitwick lies in an enviable position 40 miles from central London, equidistant from Oxford and Cambridge, with Woburn to the west. Motor racing, golf and water-sports are available nearby. Fishing, shooting and horse-riding can be arranged. **Directions:** Flitwick is on the A5120 just north of the M1 junction 12. Price guide: Single £78; double/twin £98–£190; suite £155.

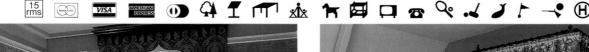

ALEXANDER HOUSE

TURNER'S HILL, WEST SUSSEX RH10 4QD
TEL: 0342 714914 FAX: 0342 717328

Alexander House is a magnificent mansion set in 135 acres of parkland, comprising manicured lawns, landscaped gardens and a secluded, gently sloping valley which forms the head of the River Medway. One of England's most luxurious hotels, it provides a dignified atmosphere where each person is regarded as an individual guest in an English country house. The interiors are spacious and splendidly decorated to emphasise the many original features and impressive works of art. Guests are offered a choice of suites or bedrooms, all lavishly furnished with particularly good bathrooms. The head chef has created a gourmet menu emphasising both classic English dishes and French cuisine. The wine cellars are stocked with a fine selection of French wines, vintage ports, brandies and armagnacs, and rare liqueurs. In recent years, Alexander House has collected many accolades, including – for 5 consecutive years – the RAC Blue Ribbon for outstanding quality. Music recitals, garden parties (for up to 250) and luncheons with guest speakers are among the events held here. Good conference facilities are available. A chauffeur-driven Daimler limousine can take guests to Gatwick Airport within minutes. **Directions:** Alexander House is situated on the B2110, 1 mile east of Turner's Hill crossroads, towards East Grinstead. Price guide: Single £115–£160; double/twin £165; suite £210–£260.

ASHDOWN PARK HOTEL

WYCH CROSS, FOREST ROW, ASHDOWN FOREST, EAST SUSSEX RH18 5JR
TEL: 0342 824988 FAX: 0342 826206

Ashdown Park is a grand, rambling 19th century mansion overlooking almost 200 acres of landscaped gardens, parkland, forests and, beyond, the rolling South Downs. Built in 1867, the hotel is situated within easy reach of Gatwick Airport, London and the South Coast, and provides the perfect backdrop for every occasion, from a weekend getaway to a honeymoon or business convention. The hotel is subtly furnished throughout to satisfy the needs of escapees from urban stress. The 44 bedrooms have been individually designed and luxuriously appointed – several with elegant four-poster beds, all with up-to-date amenities. Downstairs, past sprouting potted ferns, archways and high balustrades, is the handsome restaurant, where the painstakingly compiled menu and wine list are complemented by discreetly attentive service in soigné surroundings. Guests seeking relaxation retire to the indoor swimming pool and sauna, or amble through the gardens and nearby woodland paths; the more energetic indulge in squash, pitch-and-putt, bowling and/or croquet. There are also facilities close by for riding, clay-pigeon shooting, archery and fishing. **Directions:** East of A22 at Wych Cross on road signposted to Hartfield. Price guide: Single from £90; double/twin from £110; suite from £145.

LANGSHOTT MANOR

LANGSHOTT, HORLEY, SURREY RH6 9LN
TEL: 0293 786680 FAX: 0293 783905

This beautifully restored Grade II listed Elizabethan manor house is tucked away down a quiet country lane, set in 3 acres of tranquil gardens and ponds. For guests' recreation there is a croquet lawn and all around walks can be enjoyed through woodland and countryside. The sense of peace and seclusion belies Langshott Manor's proximity to Gatwick Airport, only 8 minutes' drive away. This delightful country house hotel was acquired by its present owners, Patricia and Geoffrey Noble, in 1986. Under their personal management, guests are offered the warmest welcome and old-fashioned hospitality. Their loving restoration of the manor is reflected in the convivial atmosphere and character of this charming old house, with its seven finely furnished bedrooms. Guests can relax in the four oak-panelled reception rooms, which all have log fires. Delicious traditional English cuisine is served in either the dining room or in the privacy of the Gallery. Small business or social functions can be accommodated and the hotel has full business communications. Free car parking (2 weeks) and luxury courtesy car to Gatwick airport are available. **Directions:** From A23 in Horley take Ladbroke Road (Chequers Hotel roundabout) to Langshott. The manor is 3/4 mile on the right. Price guide: Single £78–£93; double/twin £90–£149.

NUTFIELD PRIORY

NUTFIELD, REDHILL, SURREY RH1 4EN
TEL: 0737 822066 FAX: 0737 823321

Built in 1872 by the millionaire MP, Joshua Fielden, Nutfield Priory is an extravagant folly embellished with towers, elaborate carvings, intricate stonework, cloisters and stained glass, all of which have been superbly restored to create an unusual country-house hotel. Set high on Nutfield Ridge, the priory has far-reaching views over the Surrey and Sussex countryside, while being within easy reach of London. The elegant lounges and library have ornately carved ceilings and antique furnishings. Unusually spacious bedrooms – some with beams – enjoy views over the surrounding countryside. Fresh fruit is a thoughtful extra. The cloistered restaurant provides a unique environment in which to enjoy the high standard of cuisine, complemented by an extensive wine list. Conferences and private functions can be accommodated in the splendid setting of one of the hotel's 10 conference rooms. Fredericks sports and leisure club, adjacent to the hotel, provides all the facilities for exercise and relaxation that one could wish for, including a swimming pool, sauna, spa, solarium, gym, steam room and snooker room. **Directions:** Nutfield is on the A25 between Redhill and Godstone and can be reached easily from junctions 6 and 8 of the M25. From Godstone, the priory is on the left just after the village. Price guide: Single £90–£100; double/twin £110–£170; suite £205.

Exclusive
·HOTELS·
UK

SOUTH LODGE HOTEL

LOWER BEEDING, NR HORSHAM, WEST SUSSEX RH13 6PS
TEL: 0403 891711 FAX: 0403 891766

From its elevated position in the heart of West Sussex, South Lodge has commanding views over the rolling South Downs. The house was originally built as a family home by Frederick Ducane Godman, an eminent 19th-century botanist and explorer, and the hotel's 90-acre grounds are evidence of his abiding passion – many of the shrubs and trees were planted by him. There is also a fine Victorian rock garden. The hotel prides itself on the warm welcome extended to guests, ensuring a memorable stay. Wood panelling and open fires in the reception rooms create an atmosphere of comfortable elegance and the luxuriously appointed bedrooms offer every modern amenity. From the south-facing dining room there are views over the rolling Sussex countryside, from where comes much of what features on the menu, perfectly complemented by a comprehensive yet carefully chosen wine list. Private and business functions can be catered for in one of the private rooms. South Lodge offers a wide variety of sporting and leisure facilities, including croquet, tennis and clay pigeon shooting, golf, fishing and riding. Nearby attractions include Glyndebourne and Chartwell, Leonardslee gardens and racing at Goodwood, Plumpton and Brighton. **Directions:** South Lodge is situated on the A 281 at Lower Beeding, south of Horsham. Price guide: Single £90–£110; double/twin £110–£175; suite £205–£255.

STOCK HILL COUNTRY HOUSE HOTEL

GILLINGHAM, DORSET SP8 5NR
TEL: 0747 823626 FAX: 0747 825628

Offering the type of comfort and hospitality in an English country house that once was enjoyed by only the lucky few, Stock Hill is a fine late-Victorian edifice set in Thomas Hardy's Wessex near the south coast. Owners Peter and Nita Hauser have painstakingly restored the building and its grounds to their present aspect. At Stock Hill, visitors will encounter accommodation, food and service of an exceptionally high standard. Public and private rooms are characterised by a judicious choice of furnishings, designer materials and antique pieces. All 9 bedrooms are well appointed, clean and comfortable. Peter takes responsibility for the cuisine at Stock Hill. An Austrian, he places great emphasis on his puddings – the house meringue Suchard and roasted hazelnut and vanilla parfait Schmankerl are particularly addictive – although every item on the extensive menu is delicious. The kitchen garden supplies much of the produce and local fish is a feature of the menu. Stock Hill won the Egon Ronay Hosts of the Year Award for 1993, alongside many other accolades from leading guides. Tennis and croquet may be enjoyed in the the grounds, and fishing can be arranged. **Directions:** From the M3 take the A303, then turn south to the B3081 to Gillingham. Price guide: (including dinner): Single £85–£95; double/twin £160–£210.

THE WIND IN THE WILLOWS

DERBYSHIRE LEVEL, GLOSSOP, DERBYSHIRE SK13 9PT
TEL: 0457 868001 FAX: 0457 853354

At this charming small hotel, guests will discover a convivial combination of friendliness and professionalism. The hotel has benefited from the continuity provided by proprietors Anne and Peter Marsh, a mother-and-son team who have been running The Wind in the Willows for the past 12 years – and each year has seen a careful upgrading of the interior. Set in the marvellous scenery of the Peak District National Park and the Pennine Hills, the totally relaxed atmosphere of this early Victorian house is further protected by 5 acres of land and gardens on three sides and the Park and golf course on the other. In recognition of its high standards, the hotel was voted the 1991 RAC Best Small Hotel in the North of England. Home-cooked food at its best is served in a private dining room which occasionally admits non-residents. The pretty bedrooms have some interesting individual features and all have private shower/bathrooms; the Erika Louise room has an attractive Victorian bathroom. Riding, pot-holing and gliding can be arranged locally. **Directions:** One mile east of Glossop on the A57, 400 yards down the road opposite the Royal Oak. Price guide: Single £55–£75; double/twin £65–£95.

HATTON COURT HOTEL

UPTON HILL, UPTON ST LEONARDS, GLOUCESTERSHIRE GL4 8DE
TEL: 0452 617412 FAX: 0452 612945

Hatton Court is a picturesque, ivy-clad manor house perched on an escarpment 600 feet above sea level, with superb views over the wonderful scenery of the Severn Valley and Malvern Hills. The hotel, set in 37 acres of beautifully maintained gardens and green pastures, has been lovingly refurbished. Its bedrooms, while offering visitors every modern comfort and providing considerate extras, retain the charm and atmosphere of a bygone age. The award-winning restaurant features the best of traditional English and classic cuisine created from fresh, local produce; the menus vary with the seasons but are always complemented by an extensive and well-chosen wine list. The sports enthusiast can enjoy fishing, golf, squash, pony-trekking and clay pigeon shooting nearby. The hotel now has the added benefit of a small health and relaxation suite which includes a sauna, solarium, Jacuzzi and exercise bike. Places to visit include the elegant spa towns of Bath and Cheltenham, the Wildfowl and Wetlands Trust at Slimbridge, Prinknash Abbey, Berkeley Castle and Stratford-upon-Avon. Special breaks are available – details can be supplied on request. **Directions:** Hatton Court is located 3 miles south of Gloucester on the B4073 Gloucester–Painswick road, off the A46. Price guide: Single £75–£85; double/twin £90–£99.

MICHAELS NOOK

GRASMERE, CUMBRIA LA22 9RP
TEL: 05394 35496 FAX: 05394 35765

Built in 1859 and named after the eponymous shepherd of Wordsworth's poem, Michaels Nook has long been established as one of Britain's leading country house hotels. Opened as a hotel in 1969 by Reg and Elizabeth Gifford, it overlooks Grasmere Valley and is surrounded by gardens and trees. Reg is a respected antiques dealer, and the hotel's interior reflects his appreciation of English furniture, rugs, prints and porcelain. There are two suites, and twelve individually designed bedrooms, all with en suite bathrooms. In the acclaimed restaurant, polished tables are set with fine crystal and china. The best ingredients are used to create dishes memorable for their delicate flavours and artistic presentation. The panelled Oak Room, with its stone fireplace and gilt furnishings, can be booked for private parties and executive meetings. Leisure facilities at the nearby Wordsworth Hotel are available to guests, as is free golf at Keswick Golf Club, Monday–Friday. Michaels Nook is, first and foremost, a home where comfort is the watchword. **Directions:** Approaching Grasmere on the A591 from the south, ignore signs for Grasmere Village and continue to The Swan Hotel on the right. There turn sharp right and follow the lane uphill for 400 yds to Michaels Nook. Price guide (including dinner): Single £110; double/twin £170–£265; suite £290–£360.

WHITE MOSS HOUSE

RYDAL WATER, GRASMERE, CUMBRIA LA22 9SE
TEL: 05394 35295

Set in a fragrant garden of roses and lavender, White Moss House was once owned by Wordsworth, who often rested in the porch here between his wanderings. Built in 1730, it overlooks beautiful Rydal Water, onto which guests may take the hotel's rowing boat. Many famous and interesting walks through fells and lakeland start from the front door. Guests have free use of the local leisure club and swimming pool. It has been described by a German gourmet magazine as 'probably the smallest, most splendid hotel in the world'. Proprietors Peter and Susan Dixon have created an intimate family atmosphere with a marvellous degree of comfort and attention to detail. The five bedrooms in the main house and the two in the Brockstone Cottage Suite are individually furnished, and all have lake views. Chef Peter Dixon has won international acclaim for his culinary skills. The restaurant is deservedly famous for food prepared with imagination and style – 'the best English food in Britain', said *The Times* – and offers an extensive wine list of over 300 bins. Closed early December to early March. **Directions:** White Moss House is off the A591 between Rydal Water and Grasmere, on the right as you drive north to Grasmere. Price guide (including dinner): Single £80–£85; double/twin £130–£175.

THE WORDSWORTH HOTEL

GRASMERE, NR AMBLESIDE, CUMBRIA LA22 9SW
TEL: 05394 35592 FAX: 05394 35765

In the very heart of the English Lakeland, The Wordsworth Hotel combines AA 4 Star sophistication with the magnificence of the surrounding fells. Set in its own grounds in the village of Grasmere, the hotel provides first-class, year-round facilities for both business and leisure travellers. It has a reputaion for the high quality of its food, accommodation and hospitality. Comfortable bedrooms have well-equipped bathrooms, and there are two suites with whirlpool baths. 24-hour room service is available for drinks and light refreshments. Peaceful lounges overlook landscaped gardens, and the heated indoor pool opens on to a sun-trap terrace. There is a jacuzzi, mini-gym, sauna and solarium. As well as a Cocktail Bar, the hotel has its own pub, "The Dove and Olive Branch", which has accolades from The Good Pub Guide. In "The Prelude Restaurant" menus offer a good choice of dishes, prepared with skill and imagination from the freshest produce. The Wordsworth Hotel is a perfect venue for conferences, incentive weekends and corporate entertaining. Three function rooms are available with highly professional back-up. Lakeland's principal places of interest are all within easy reach. **Directions:** The hotel is located next to the village church. Price guide: Single £58.50; double/twin £105–£142; suite £195.

THE ANGEL POSTING HOUSE AND LIVERY

91 THE HIGH STREET, GUILDFORD, SURREY GU1 3DP
TEL: 0483 64555 FAX: 0483 33770

The Angel, a delightful historic coaching inn, has stood in Guildford High Street since the 16th century. This timber-framed building has welcomed many famous visitors, including Jane Austen and Charles Dickens. Today, with easy access to Gatwick, Heathrow, the M4, M3 and M25, the Angel is ideally placed for both business and pleasure. The galleried lounge with its oak-beamed Jacobean fireplace and 17th-century parliament clock is a welcome retreat from the bustle of the nearby shops. The panelled Oak Room restaurant serves a wide choice of superb English and Continental cuisine together with fine wines and impeccable service. The Crypt, with its vaulted ceiling and intimate atmosphere also offers some of the finest gourmet dining in Surrey, and the charming bedrooms and suites, decorated with soft furnishings and fabrics, are all unique. Excellent communications, presentation facilities and 24-hour service make this a good choice for business meetings. Private dinners, buffets, dances and wedding receptions can also be catered for. **Directions:** From M3 junction 3 take the A322; or from M25 junction 10 take the A3. The Angel is in the centre of Guildford, within the pedestrian priority area – guests should enquire about vehicle access when booking. Price guide (room only): Single £105–140; double/twin £105–£140; suite £160.

WEST LODGE PARK

COCKFOSTERS ROAD, HADLEY WOOD, BARNET, HERTFORDSHIRE EN4 0PY
TEL: 081-440 8311 FAX: 081-449 3698

West Lodge Park is a country house hotel standing in 34 acres of Green Belt parkland and gardens, including a lake and arboretum, yet only 12 miles from the centre of London. Run by the Beale family for more than 45 years, the hotel was originally a gentleman's country seat, rebuilt in 1838 on the site of an earlier keeper's lodge. Entering the hotel, one feels as if one is stepping into a private house. In the public rooms, antiques, original paintings and period furnishings create a civilised and restful atmosphere and log fires burn in winter. All the bedrooms, which enjoy country views, have private bathroom, remote control TV with Teletext, radio and telephone. The restaurant has views over the gardens during the day and a warm, intimate atmosphere in the evenings. Residents enjoy free membership and a free taxi to the luxurious nearby David Lloyd leisure centre, with a 25 metre indoor pool, indoor tennis, gym etc. Hatfield House and St Albans' Abbey are 15 minutes' drive away. AA and RAC 4 stars; 2 RAC merit symbols. Also in the *Which? Hotel Guide*. **Directions:** The hotel is situated on A111 one mile north of Cockfosters Underground Station and one mile south of Junction 24 on M25. By underground, take Piccadilly line to Oakwood, then taxi to hotel (2 miles). Price guide: Single £53–£99; double/twin £69.50–£140; suite £140.

HOLDSWORTH HOUSE

HOLDSWORTH ROAD, HOLMFIELD, HALIFAX, WEST YORKSHIRE HX2 9TG
TEL: 0422 240024 FAX: 0422 245174

Holdsworth House is a haven of quality and charm standing 3 miles north of Halifax in the heart of Yorkshire's West Riding. Built in 1633, it was acquired by the Pearson family over 30 years ago. With care, skill and professionalism they have created a hotel and restaurant of considerable repute. The interior of the house, with its polished panelling and open fireplaces, has been carefully preserved and embellished with fine antique furniture and ornaments. The comfortable lounge opens onto a pretty courtyard and overlooks the herb garden and gazebo. The restaurant comprises three beautifully furnished rooms, enabling private dinners to be catered for with ease. Exciting modern English and continental cuisine is meticulously prepared and presented, complemented by a thoughtfully compiled wine list. Each bedroom has its own style – from the four split-level suites to the two single rooms designed for wheelchair access. This is the perfect base from which to explore the Pennines, the Yorkshire Dales and Haworth – the home of the Brontë family. 1993 Which County Hotel of the Year. Closed Christmas. **Directions:** From M1 junction 42 take M62 westbound to junction 26. Follow A58 to Halifax (ignore signs to town centre). At Burdock Way roundabout take A629 to Keighley; after 1 1/2 miles go right into Shay Lane; hotel is 1 mile, on right. Price guide: Single £60–£74; double/twin £86–£90; suite £100.

THE BOAR'S HEAD HOTEL

RIPLEY, HARROGATE, NORTH YORKSHIRE HG3 3AY
TEL: 0423 771888 FAX: 0423 771509

Overlooking the village stocks and cobbled market square of Ripley, one of Britain's most beautiful and historic estate villages, The Boar's Head is a 4 Star hotel of genuine charm, comfort and quality. Each of the 25 en suite bedrooms has been individually decorated and furnished; most of the beds are king-sized. Fine portraits, paintings and prints from nearby Ripley Castle grace the walls. The restaurant menu is outstanding, created under the auspices of leading chef David Box (formerly of The Savoy and Claridges) and complemented by a wide selection of reasonably priced, good quality wines. Good bar meals, along with Theakstons traditional ale served straight from the wood, have also generated popular appeal. Guests can enjoy a game of tennis or try fly-fishing on the 20-acre lake. Or they can stroll through the delightful walled gardens and grounds of Ripley Castle, home of the National Hyacinth Collection and an admirable array of tropical plants. Many lovely walks through glorious countryside lead from the village. Ripley is only 10 minutes from Harrogate and 40 minutes from York, so there is plenty to see and do. **Directions:** Ripley is just off the A61, between Harrogate and Ripon. The hotel is situated on the market square in the centre of the village. Price guide: Single £80; double/twin £98; suite £115.

GRANTS HOTEL

SWAN ROAD, HARROGATE, NORTH YORKSHIRE HG1 2SS
TEL: 0423 560666 FAX: 0423 502550

Towards the end of the last century, Harrogate became fashionable among the affluent Victorian gentry, who came to 'take the waters' of the famous spa. Today's visitors have one advantage over their Victorian counterparts – they can enjoy the hospitality of Grants Hotel, the creation of Pam and Peter Grant. The friendly welcome, coupled with high standards of service, ensures a pleasurable stay. All the bedrooms are attractively decorated and have en suite bathrooms. Downstairs, guests can relax in the comfortable lounge or take refreshments out to the terrace gardens. Drinks and light meals are available at all times from the cocktail bar, whereas dinner is a more formal occasion in the air-conditioned Chimney Pots restaurant. Cooking is in the modern English style, with old favourites adapted to accommodate more contemporary tastes – a blend which meets with the approval of local gourmets. Located less than 5 minutes' walk from Harrogate's Conference and Exhibition Centre, Grants offers its own luxury suite of meeting and syndicate rooms, the Herriot Suite. The Royal Pump Room Museum and the Royal Baths Assembly Rooms are nearby. **Directions:** Swan Road is in the centre of Harrogate, off the A61 to Ripon. Price guide: Single £87.50–£93.50; double/twin £102.50–£137.

HOB GREEN HOTEL AND RESTAURANT

MARKINGTON, HARROGATE, NORTH YORKSHIRE HG3 3PJ
TEL: 0423 770031 FAX: 0423 771589

Hob Green is a small country house hotel set in 870 acres of farm and woodland. The gardens, which include a croquet lawn, have won awards regularly in the Harrogate District Best Kept Garden Competition. The hall and drawing room are furnished with a combination of antique and contemporary furniture, while crackling fires in the winter months create a warm and welcoming atmosphere. Overlooking manicured lawns, with views towards the ha-ha, fields and woodland, is the restaurant, where guests can enjoy interesting and varied cooking, incorporating fresh vegetables from the garden. The comfortably appointed bedrooms also have fine views. Markington is the perfect setting for equestrian enthusiasts, as the Yorkshire Riding Centre, run by two former Olympic dressage team members, is located in the village and offers some of the best riding facilities in Europe. Golf, fishing, cricket and horse-racing are all within easy reach of the hotel. Fountains Abbey, Markenfield Hall, Ripley Castle and the cathedral cities of York and Ripon are also nearby. **Directions:** Follow the A61 Harrogate–Ripon road for about 4 miles, then turn left to Markington at Wormald Green. Go through the village of Markington and the hotel is 1 mile on the left. Price guide: Single £65–£75; double/twin £80–£98; suite £115.

EXCLUSIVE ·HOTELS· UK

NIDD HALL

NIDD, HARROGATE, NORTH YORKSHIRE HG3 3BN
TEL: 0423 771598 FAX: 0423 770931

A long, curling, tree-flanked driveway leads to this imposing country mansion. Set in 45 acres of beautiful parkland and gardens, Nidd Hall is the epitome of the English country manor, combining a rare blend of historical elegance and modern amenities with the very highest standards of comfort, service and cuisine. All the bedrooms have been tastefully designed and luxuriously appointed and the elegant restaurant, renowned for its superb menu, offers an extensive wine list and wonderful views across the terrace. Conference facilities at Nidd Hall have been carefully designed to meet most corporate needs, from a board meeting in the Oak Room to a product launch in the Courtyard Suite. Leisure Club facilities include squash, tennis, sauna, plunge pool and gymnasium. Clay pigeon shooting and boating on the lake can be arranged. Nidd Hall is easily accessible by air, road and rail and also provides an executive helipad in the grounds. Herriot country is close by, as are the historic cities of Harrogate and York. Directions: A61 Harrogate to Ripon. At Ripley roundabout turn right on to the B6165 towards Knaresborough. The hotel is 1 mile further on the left. Price guide: Single £90–£115; double/twin £135–£150; suite £195–£230.

LYTHE HILL HOTEL

PETWORTH ROAD, HASLEMERE, SURREY GU27 3BQ
TEL: 0428 651251 FAX: 0428 644131

Cradled by the Surrey foothills in a tranquil, wealden setting is the enchanting Lythe Hill Hotel. It is an unusual cluster of ancient buildings – parts of which date from the 14th century. While most of the beautifully appointed accommodation is in the more modern main hotel, there are five charming bedrooms in the Tudor House. In keeping with this style, it is no surprise to find that there is a choice of two restaurants. In the main hotel restaurant, the cooking is in the English tradition whereas superb French cuisine is served in the Auberge de France, the oak-panelled dining room which overlooks the lake and parkland. An exceptional wine list offers over 200 wines from more than a dozen countries. Its situation, easily accessible from London, Gatwick and Heathrow, together with good facilities make the Lythe Hill Hotel suitable for both business meetings and private dinners. National Trust hillside adjoining the hotel grounds provides delightful walking and views over the surrounding countryside. The area is steeped in history, with the country houses of Petworth, Clandon and Uppark to visit as well as racing at Goodwood and polo at Cowdray Park. Brighton and the south coast are only a few miles away. **Directions:** Lythe Hill lies about $1^1/_2$ miles from the centre of Haslemere, east on the B2131. Price guide: Single £74; double/twin £95–£100; suite £110–£160.

BEL ALP HOUSE

HAYTOR, NR BOVEY TRACEY, SOUTH DEVON TQ13 9XX
TEL: 0364 661217 FAX: 0364 661292

Peace and tranquillity are guaranteed at the Bel Alp House, with its spectacular outlook from the edge of Dartmoor across a rolling patchwork of fields and woodland to the sea, 20 miles away. Built as an Edwardian country mansion and owned in the 1920s by millionairess Dame Violet Wills, Bel Alp has been lovingly restored by proprietors Roger and Sarah Curnock, whose personal attention ensures their guests' enjoyment and comfort in the atmosphere of a private home. Sarah takes charge of the cooking and the five-course menu is changed daily. She uses only the best local produce and her meals are complemented by Roger's well-chosen and comprehensive wine list. Of the nine en suite bedrooms, two still have their original Edwardian basins and baths mounted on marble plinths, and all have views over the gardens. An abundance of house plants, open log fires and restful colours complement the family antiques and pictures to create the perfect environment in which to relax. AA Rosette. Bel Alp is ideally situated for exploring Devon and parts of Cornwall: Plymouth, famed for Drake and the Pilgrim Fathers, Exeter with its Norman cathedral, and National Trust properties Castle Drogo and Cotehele Manor House are all within an hour's drive. **Directions:** Bel Alp is off the B3387 Haytor road, 2½ miles from Bovey Tracey. Price guide: Single £72–£84; double/twin £126–£144.

THE CARLTON HOTEL

ALBERT STREET, HEBDEN BRIDGE, WEST YORKSHIRE HX7 8ES
TEL: 0422 844400 FAX: 0422 843117

The Carlton is an unusual town house hotel, centrally situated on the first and second floors of the old Co-operative Society building, dating from 1867. Following a full refurbishment of this Victorian emporium, The Carlton Hotel was able to continue serving the local community, while also attracting a much wider, international clientele. A lift takes visitors from the entrance hall up to the elegant reception area where a friendly welcome waits. The 18 en suite bedrooms are individually appointed with attractive furnishings, satellite TV and hospitality bars. In the elegant restaurant an international and imaginative menu is served, suitable for business lunches or a relaxing evening meal.

Conference parties and banquets can be accommodated in the Hard Castle Suite. Set at the head of the Calder Valley, Hebden Bridge is a thriving mill town, with many quaint antiques and craft shops. Guests who are staying on a special 2-night break can play golf free of charge at Mount Skip Golf Course. A boat trip on the Rochdale Canal is a leisurely way to spend an afternoon. Enquire for details about weekend and midweek breaks. **Directions:** Entering Hebden Bridge on the A646, turn down Hope Street, a one-way street nearly opposite the marina, which runs into Albert Street. The hotel is on the left. Price guide: Single £55–£64; double/twin £64–£74.

THE FEVERSHAM ARMS HOTEL

HELMSLEY, NORTH YORKSHIRE YO6 5AG
TEL: 0439 70766 FAX: 0439 70346
As from January 1994 Tel: 0439 770766 Fax: 0439 770346

This historic coaching inn, rebuilt in 1855 of mellow Yorkshire stone by the Earl of Feversham, has been owned and managed by the Aragues family since 1967. Set in over an acre of walled garden, The Feversham Arms has been updated to a high standard to offer every modern convenience, while special care has been taken to preserve the character and charm of the older parts of the hostelry. The bedrooms are individually furnished and some have special features such as four-poster beds and de luxe bathrooms. Open fires blaze in the winter months. The attractive candle-lit Goya Restaurant serves English, French and Spanish cooking and, by relying on fresh local produce, offers seasonal variety. There is a delicious fish and seafood menu. To accompany dinner, a good wine list includes a wide selection of Spanish wines and clarets. Situated in the North York Moors National Park and close to many golf courses, this comfortable and welcoming hotel is ideal for sporting pursuits as well as for touring the moors, dales, coast and the medieval city of York. Dogs by arrangement. **Directions:** From the A1 take the A64, then take the York north bypass (A1237) and then the B1363. Alternatively, from the A1 take the A168 signposted to Thirsk, then the A170. Price guide: Single £55–£65; double/twin £70–£80. Bonanza breaks available all year.

THE PHEASANT

HAROME, HELMSLEY, NORTH YORKSHIRE YO6 5JG
TEL: 0439 71241/70416
As from January 1994 Tel: 0439 771241/770416

The Pheasant Hotel is rich in oak beams and open log fires, and offers additional accommodation, set apart from the main building, in a charming, 16th century thatched cottage. The Binks family, who built the hotel and now own and manage it, have created a relaxed, friendly atmosphere which is part of the warm Yorkshire welcome all guests receive. The bedrooms and suites are brightly decorated in an attractive, cottage style and all are complete with en suite facilities. Traditional English cooking is the speciality of the restaurant, many of the dishes prepared using fresh fruit and vegetables grown in the hotel gardens. During the summer, guests may chat or relax on the terrace overlooking the pond. The recent opening of a new indoor heated swimming pool is an added attraction. Sporting activities available locally include swimming, riding, golf and fishing. York is just a short drive away, as are a host of historic landmarks including Byland and Rievaulx Abbeys and Castle Howard of *Brideshead Revisited* fame. Also nearby is the magnificent North York Moors National Park. Dogs by arrangement. Closed Christmas, January and February. **Directions:** From Helmsley, take the A170 towards Scarborough; after 1/4 mile turn right for Harome. Hotel is near the church in the village. Price guide (including dinner): Single £50–£56; double/twin £104–£112.

STOCKS

ALDBURY, NR TRING, HERTFORDSHIRE HP23 5RX
TEL: 044285 341 FAX: 044285 253

Stocks House was first mentioned in 1176, since when it has had an illustrious history, including a period as a training school for Playboy 'Bunny' girls! Under its present ownership, extensive development has seen the addition of conference and leisure facilities, including an 18-hole (6,904 yards) golf course. Amenities include riding and livery stables, four all-weather tennis courts, a gymnasium and the country's largest heated indoor Jacuzzi. Balloon flights, blindfold driving, laser shooting and archery can also be arranged, with corporate hospitality packages a speciality. Each of the very distinctive bedrooms is individually appointed and all offer views over the grounds to the Chilterns beyond. Fine plasterwork, tapestries, crisp linen and porcelain set the tone of the elegant Tapestry Restaurant. Stocks makes an ideal setting for small board meetings and senior-level conferences. Comfortable meeting rooms provide a peaceful working environment, while behind the scenes a professional staff attend to all aspects of the occasion. **Directions:** From M1 exit 8, take A41 towards Aylesbury; hotel is 3 miles beyond Berkhamsted. Price guide: Single £70; double/twin £80–£90; suite £120.

WHITE FRIARS HOTEL

BOREHAM STREET, HERSTMONCEUX, EAST SUSSEX BN27 4SE
TEL: 0323 832355 FAX: 0323 833882

A warm welcome awaits visitors to the White Friars Hotel, which enjoys peaceful views over surrounding farmland and the rolling Sussex Weald. A Grade II listed building dating from 1721, this quintessentially English country house is characterised by comfortable rooms with oak beams, fresh flowers and deep sofas. Since his arrival here in 1991, owner Philip White has raised standards. Guests are assured of good, attentive service befitting a hotel of this calibre. All the bedrooms are well appointed, some with four-poster beds for a touch of romance. Several rooms are situated within a converted stable block. With its classic moulded ceilings and panelled walls, the Ashburnham Restaurant is an elegant setting for dinner. Carefully chosen menus include seasonal choices, fresh vegetables and scrumptious puddings. The cellar restaurant is a less formal setting for a meal. Up to 32 delegates can be accommodated in the intimate meeting room. Among the many nearby attractions, guests can visit Herstmonceux Castle, Rudyard Kipling's home 'Batemans', Bodiam Castle, Battle Abbey, Michelham Priory and Pevensey Castle. **Directions:** On the A271 east of Herstmonceux village. Price guide: Single £45–£60; double/twin £55–£75.

NUTHURST GRANGE

HOCKLEY HEATH, WARWICKSHIRE B94 5NL
TEL: 0564 783972 FAX: 0564 783919

The most memorable feature of this friendly country house hotel is its outstanding restaurant. Chef-patron David Randolph and his team have won many accolades for their imaginative menus, described as 'English, cooked in the light French style'. Diners can enjoy their superb cuisine in the three adjoining rooms which comprise the restaurant and form the heart of Nuthurst Grange. The rest of the house is no less charming – the spacious bedrooms have a country house atmosphere and are appointed with extra luxuries such as an exhilarating air-spa bath, a trouser press, hairdryer and a safe for valuables. For special occasions there is a room furnished with a four-poster bed and a marble bathroom. There are fine views across the 7½ acres of landscaped gardens. Executive meetings can be accommodated at Nuthurst Grange – within a 12-mile radius of the hotel lie Central Birmingham, the NEC, Stratford-upon-Avon, Coventry and Birmingham International Airport. Sporting activities available nearby include golf, canal boating and tennis. **Directions:** From M42 exit 4 take A3400 signposted Hockley Heath (2 miles, south). Entrance to Nuthurst Grange Lane is ¼ mile south of village. Also, M40 (exit 16 – southbound only), take first left, entrance 300 yards. Price guide: Single £89; double/twin £99–£119; suite £135.

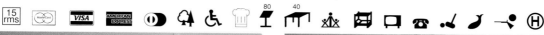

THE WORSLEY ARMS HOTEL

HOVINGHAM, YORK, NORTH YORKSHIRE YO6 4LA
TEL: 0653 628234 FAX: 0653 628130

The Worsley Arms is an attractive stone-built Victorian coaching inn in the heart of Hovingham, a pleasant and unspoiled Yorkshire village with a history stretching back to Roman times. The hotel, which overlooks the village green and is set amid delightful gardens, was built in 1841 by the baronet Sir William Worsley. It is still owned and run by the Worsley family whose home, Hovingham Hall, is nearby. Elegant, traditional furnishings and open fires create a welcoming and restful atmosphere. The spacious sitting rooms are an ideal place to relax over morning coffee or afternoon tea, or to meet friends and chat in the comfortable bar. The restaurant, with its 18th-century paintings and displays of fresh flowers, offers creatively prepared dishes, including game from the estate, cooked and presented with flair. The en suite bedrooms range in size and are all prettily decorated and well appointed, with 24-hour room service available. There is plenty to do nearby, including tennis, squash, jogging and scenic walks along nature trails. Also, guests can explore the majestic beauty of the Dales and spectacular Yorkshire coastline or discover the many historic abbeys, battlefields, stately homes and castles nearby. **Directions:** Hovingham is on the B1257, 8 miles from Malton and Helmsley. Price guide: Single £62–£72; double/twin £84–£90.

BAGDEN HALL HOTEL & GOLF COURSE

WAKEFIELD ROAD, SCISSETT, NR HUDDERSFIELD, WEST YORKSHIRE HD8 9LE
TEL: 0484 865330 FAX: 0484 861001

Bagden Hall is set in 40 acres of parkland, yet less than 10 minutes from the M1. It was built in the mid-19th century by local mill owner George Norton as a home for his family, whose portraits still hang in the foyer. Lovingly restored by current owners the Braithwaite family, Bagden has been transformed into an elegant hotel. The grounds comprise of magnificent lawns, superb landscaped gardens with a lake and an 18th century boathouse. Inside, the hotel has recently undergone a major programme of renovation and now has all the facilities one would expect of a modern hotel while retaining its original character. Each of the 17 bedrooms – one with four-poster – has en suite facilities. The oak-panelled lounge bar and adjoining conservatory have views over the lawns to the lake, making this an ideal setting for relaxing with a drink before moving on to the Glendale Restaurant. Here, traditional and modern English food with classical French influences is served amid tasteful surroundings. There is a fine wine list to complement the food. For golfers, there is a 9-hole par 3/4 golf course on site. **Directions:** From south, leave M1 at junction 38, taking A637 towards Huddersfield. Take A636 to Scissett. From north, leave M1 at junction 39, taking A636 to Scissett. Hotel is $^1/_2$ mile through village on left. Price guide: Single £60; double/twin £80–£100.

THE OLD BRIDGE HOTEL

1 HIGH STREET, HUNTINGDON, CAMBRIDGESHIRE PE18 6TQ
TEL: 0480 52681 FAX: 0480 411017

The Old Bridge is a handsome, 18th-century edifice standing on the banks of the River Ouse close to the centre of Huntingdon, a thriving market town and the birthplace of Oliver Cromwell. The hotel has been decorated in keeping with its original character. In the panelled dining room and main lounge, sumptuous fabrics, quality prints and beautiful furnishings impart a sense of elegance. Each of the 26 guest rooms is unique in its style and decor – all have been luxuriously appointed with every attention to detail, and with a full complement of facilities. The restaurant exemplifies British cooking at its best – traditional dishes are interpreted with imagination and flair and the menu is balanced by an exceptional wine list. The Terrace, painted with a series of delightful murals by Julia Rushbury, offers a simpler style in a more informal setting, with an extensive cold buffet at lunchtime. Private parties or business lunches can be accommodated in the Cromwell Room and a fully integrated business centre is available for executive meetings. Guests can enjoy boating trips from the private jetty or visit nearby Cambridge, Ely and Newmarket. **Directions:** Huntingdon is on the A604 driving north or A1 driving south. The hotel is set off the inner ring road in the town. Price guide: Single £69.50–£92; double/twin £95–£120.

ROMBALDS HOTEL

WEST VIEW, WELLS ROAD, ILKLEY, WEST YORKSHIRE LS29 9JG
TEL: 0943 603201 FAX: 0943 816586

This 160-year-old Georgian hotel, set on the edge of Ilkley Moor, is run under the personal supervision of Ian and Jill Guthrie, now in their 13th year of ownership. The restaurant is a special feature and serves excellent, freshly prepared dishes, using seasonally available produce from local suppliers. Sundays at the hotel are renowned: guests are treated to an 'Edwardian Breakfast' and, in the evening, a superb roast dinner. The list of 140 wines includes something for every taste. Facilities for conferences and private functions are available in the coach house, which in 1989 was awarded the White Rose Award for Excellence and Innovation by the Yorkshire and Humberside Tourist Board. Two service flats are available for monthly letting. Ilkley is the gateway to the Yorkshire Dales National Park and close to the area made famous by the Brontës. Historical attractions nearby include Bolton, Fountains and Rievaulx Abbeys, Castle Howard and Harewood House. **Directions:** Ilkley is on the A65 Leeds–Skipton road. At traffic lights on the A65 in the town centre, turn into Brook Street, cross The Grove to enter Wells Road. The hotel is 600 yards up Wells Road on the left-hand side. There is a car park to the rear of the hotel. Price guide: Single £60–£85; double/twin £90–£108; suite £120–£150.

HINTLESHAM HALL

HINTLESHAM, IPSWICH, SUFFOLK IP8 3NS
TEL: 0473 652268 FAX: 0473 652463

An epitome of grandeur, Hintlesham Hall is a house of evolving styles: its splendid Georgian facade belies its 16th-century origins, to which the red-brick Tudor rear of the hall is a testament. The Stuart period also left its mark, in the form of a magnificent carved-oak staircase leading to the north wing of the hall. The combination of styles works extremely well, with the lofty proportions of the Georgian reception rooms contrasting with the timbered Tudor rooms. The decor throughout is superb – all rooms are individually appointed in a discriminating fashion. Iced mineral water, toiletries and towelling robes are to be found in each of the comfortable bedrooms. The herb garden supplies many of the flavours for the well-balanced menu which will appeal to the gourmet and the health-conscious alike, complemented by a 300-bin wine list. Bounded by 175 acres of rolling countryside, leisure facilities include the hall's own 18-hole championship golf course, saunas, steam room, spa bath, tennis, croquet and snooker. Guests can also explore Suffolk's 16th-century wool merchants' villages, its pretty coast, 'Constable country' and Newmarket. **Directions:** Hintlesham Hall is 4 miles west of Ipswich on the A1071 Sudbury road. Price guide: Single £88; double/twin £97–£160; suite £178.

PEACOCK VANE

BONCHURCH VILLAGE ROAD, BONCHURCH, ISLE OF WIGHT PO38 1RJ
TEL: 0983 852019 FAX: 0983 854796

Sheltered by St Boniface Down and surrounded by landscaped gardens, the Peacock Vane is a fine Victorian house situated in the charming fishing hamlet of Bonchurch on the south coast of the Isle of Wight. The hotel has been completely refurbished and carefully restored to assure guests of every comfort and generous hospitality. The furnishings have been chosen to reflect the Victorian era, when poets and authors walked the hallways and ate and drank in opulent splendour. The décor throughout is elegant, rich and elaborate, with flamboyant use of gold set against deep red fabric. The en suite bedrooms are sumptuously appointed with an abundance of period paintings and antique furnishings, as well as a host of modern conveniences. An early-evening drink can be enjoyed in the drawing room, with its grand piano, flowing drapes and twinkling chandelier, before proceeding to the Ivory Room Restaurant, where the menus offer delicious English and French cuisine. The Directors' dining room is ideal for private dinners, cocktail parties or business meetings. The Peacock Vane is a short drive from the island's many attractions, including Osborne House, Carisbrooke Castle, Cowes and the splendid coastline. **Directions:** Bonchurch is on the A3055 Shanklin–Ventnor road. Hotel is in the village centre by the pond. Price guide: Single £50; double/twin £65–£85.

ST MARTIN'S HOTEL

THE ISLAND OF ST MARTIN'S, ISLES OF SCILLY TR25 0QW
TEL: 0720 22092 FAX: 0720 22298

This stunning location and beautiful hotel are for those seeking to get away for total relaxation. The Isles of Scilly, unknown to many, are a small group of islands 28 miles South West of Lands End. The third largest, St Martin's, renowned for its white sand beaches, is home to the St Martin's Hotel. Twenty four attractively designed rooms and suites with colours and fabrics to evoke a restful atmosphere, provide luxury amidst some of the most spectacular scenery in Britain. Cuisine of the highest quality featuring, naturally, all manner of local fish and seafood is served in the first floor restaurant with its wonderful sea and island views. Other facilities include comfortable lounges, bar and indoor heated pool. Boats leave the hotel daily to visit other islands, including Tresco with its famous botanical gardens. Fishing, sailing and diving are popular, or try snorkelling amongst Atlantic grey seals for an unforgettable experience. The islands are a safe haven for children to enjoy their very own 'Treasure Island' and St Martin's is also a unique setting for corporate and incentive meetings. **Directions:** By air from Heathrow (via Newquay), Exeter and Penzance or by sea from Penzance. The hotel will assist with all travel arrangements. Price guide (including dinner): Single £90–£114; double/twin £130–£200; suite £160–£260.

MEADOW HOUSE

SEA LANE, KILVE, SOMERSET TA5 1EG
TEL: 0278 741546 FAX: 0278 741663

With its origins dating from around 1600, Meadow House was enlarged in Georgian times to become a rectory. Standing in 8 acres of grounds, the hotel is entirely surrounded by countryside with rolling meadows and woodland and has views encompassing the nearby Quantocks, Bristol Channel and Welsh coast. A stream feeds the hotel pond as it wends its way to the sea only a few minutes' walk away. Unspoiled Kilve Beach is renowned for its rock formations, fossils and spectacular cliff views. The spacious bedrooms are comfortably furnished and guests will find mineral water, fresh flowers and biscuits when they arrive. French windows open on to a large, south-facing terrace overlooking the garden, which is a profusion of colour during the summer. Antiques, curios and books abound in the drawing room and study, while blazing log fires create a cosy atmosphere. Guests may dine in the main restaurant or in the adjoining conservatory. The frequently changing menu pays particular attention to English recipes, using fruit and vegetables from the kitchen garden whenever possible. The wine list is exceptional. Dogs can be accommodated in some rooms. **Directions:** Leave M5 at junction 23. Join A39 at Bridgwater. Turn right at Kilve into Sea Lane; hotel is ½ mile on left. Price guide: Single £55; double/twin £80.

MILL HOUSE HOTEL

KINGHAM, OXFORDSHIRE OX7 6UH
TEL: 0608 658188 FAX: 0608 658492

With unsparing attention to detail, owners John and Valerie Barnett have lavished great care on this delightful former mill to make it one of the more attractive hotels in the Cotswolds. It is set in 7 acres of gardens bordered by a trout stream. The bedrooms are all elegantly appointed and most offer superb views of the rolling countryside. There is a comfortable lounge with deep armchairs and sofas, open log fires and a beamed ceiling. The restaurant provides cooking of the highest standards; the menus are changed daily to take advantage of the very best of fresh, seasonal produce. The interiors are enhanced by beautiful flower arrangements and fragrant pot-pourri, which scents the rooms and hallways. With the whole of the historic Cotswolds on the doorstep, Mill House makes the ideal base from which to explore the multitude of quaint villages in this region, as well as Blenheim Palace and Stratford-upon-Avon. AA and RAC 3 Stars; holder of both AA and RAC Restaurant Awards. **Directions:** From the A40/M40 westbound, heading towards Cheltenham, turn right at the roundabout towards Burford, through Chipping Norton. Price guide: Single £45–£60; double/twin £70–£100.

CONGHAM HALL

GRIMSTON, KING'S LYNN, NORFOLK PE32 1AH
TEL: 0485 600250 FAX: 0485 601191

Dating from the mid-18th century, this stately manor house is set in 40 acres of paddocks, orchards and gardens, including its own cricket pitch. The conversion from country house to luxury hotel in 1982 was executed with care to enhance the elegance of the classic interiors. Proprietors Christine and Trevor Forecast have, however, retained the atmosphere of a family home. Christine's particular forté is flower arranging, and her displays enliven the decor throughout, while the delicate fragrance of home-made pot-pourri perfumes the air. Winners of the Johansens Hotel Award for Excellence 1993. Antique furniture and attractive fabrics complement the Georgian style of the bedrooms. In the Orangery restaurant, guests can relish modern English cooking. The origin of many of the flavours is explained by the herb garden, with over 100 varieties for the chef's use. Even the most discerning palate will be delighted by the choice of wines. Congham Hall is an ideal base for touring the countryside of West Norfolk, as well as Sandringham, Fakenham races and the coastal nature reserves. A video of the hotel and vicinity is available, for which a £10 returnable deposit is required. **Directions:** Grimston is on the B1153 which runs between the A47 King's Lynn–Norwich road and the A148. Price guide: Single £72; double/twin £97; suite £170.

BUCKLAND-TOUT-SAINTS

GOVETON, KINGSBRIDGE, DEVON TQ7 2DS
TEL: 0548 853055 FAX: 0548 856261

Situated in rural South Devon, Buckland-Tout-Saints was built in 1690, when William, Prince of Orange, and Mary were on the throne of England. The hotel re-opened in April 1992 under the ownership of experienced hoteliers John and Tove Taylor, with their son George. They are continuing the tradition of country house entertaining, promoting the feeling of being a privileged guest in a private house. On the first floor, four de luxe rooms and two suites are decorated in harmony with the period setting. Six smaller rooms on the second floor have Provence-style shuttered windows and lovely views. In the pine-panelled Queen Anne Restaurant, simple, crisp linen, china and glassware provide elegant surroundings for dinner. 2 AA Rosettes, Pride of Britain. Chef Alastair Carter prepares imaginative English and French dishes which are presented in the modern English style. An extensive range of wines provides something to enhance each meal. Kingsbridge, 2 miles away, is a bustling market town, while Dartmouth is further round the coast. The wilds of Dartmoor, Dartington Glassworks, numerous quaint fishing ports and several National Trust properties are nearby. Children and dogs by prior arrangement. **Directions:** Signposted from the A381 between Totnes and Kingsbridge. Price guide: (including dinner) Single £75; double/twin £150–£170; suite £190.

RAMPSBECK COUNTRY HOUSE HOTEL

WATERMILLOCK, LAKE ULLSWATER, NR PENRITH, CUMBRIA CA11 0LP
TEL: 07684 86442 FAX: 07684 86442

A beautifully situated hotel, Rampsbeck Country House stands in 18 acres of landscaped gardens and meadows leading to the shores of Lake Ullswater. Built in 1714, it first became a hotel in 1947, before the present owners acquired it in 1983. Thomas and Marion Gibb, with the help of Marion's mother, Marguerite MacDowall, completely refurbished Rampsbeck with the aim of maintaining its character and adding only to its comfort. Most of the well-appointed bedrooms have lake and garden views. Three have a private balcony and the suite has a small patio. In the elegant drawing room, a log fire burns and French windows lead to the garden. Guests and non-residents are welcome to dine in the intimate candle-lit restaurant. Imaginative menus offer a choice of delicious dishes, carefully prepared by head chef Andrew McGeorge and his team. A good bar lunch menu offers light snacks as well as hot food. Guests can stroll through the gardens, play croquet or fish from the lake shore. Lake steamer trips, riding, golf, sailing, wind-surfing and fell-walking are available nearby. Closed from the first week in January to mid-February. Dogs by arrangement only. **Directions:** Leave M6 at junction 40, take A592 to Ullswater. At T-junction at lake turn right; hotel is 1½ miles on left. Price guide: Single £48–£70; double/twin £75–£120; suite £140.

THE ARUNDELL ARMS

LIFTON, DEVON PL16 0AA
TEL: 0566 784666 FAX: 0566 784494

A 250-year-old former coaching inn near Dartmoor, The Arundell Arms is one of England's best-known sporting hotels. Americans travel 3,000 miles to fish the hotel's 20 miles of private waters on the River Tamar for salmon, trout and sea trout. The Arundell has a two professional fishing instructors and runs a wide range of fly-fishing courses throughout the year. Also renowned as a shooting lodge, the driven snipe shoots have an international following. The hotel takes great pride in the cuisine prepared by French-trained chef Philip Burgess who has been given the honour of being elected Master Chef of Great Britain and was formerly with L'Écu de France in London. With its slate floors, crackling fires, paintings and antiques, The Arundell Arms epitomises old-world charm. It is a splendid base for visits to the historic houses and gardens, the moors and quaint fishing villages of Devon and Cornwall. Only 45 minutes' drive from Exeter and Plymouth, it is also ideal for the business executive as it can be reached by fast roads from all directions: an elegant and spacious conference suite is available. **Directions:** Lifton is approximately 1/4 mile off the A30 and 2 miles east of Launceston and the Cornish border. Price guide: Single £54–£60; double/twin £88–£94.

HOPE END HOTEL

HOPE END, LEDBURY, HEREFORDSHIRE HR8 1JQ
TEL: 0531 633613 FAX: 0531 636366

Hope End is a most romantic small hotel, set in 40 acres of restored 18th-century listed parkland. This very individual Georgian hotel provides total peace and an opportunity to enjoy an idle holiday amid rural surroundings. Formerly the childhood home of poet Elizabeth Barrett Browning, the building has been refurbished to offer discreet comfort. Nine en suite bedrooms are furnished with antiques and paintings, while the absence of TV ensures complete tranquillity. An extraordinary range of organic fruit, vegetables and herbs is grown in the walled kitchen garden. Free-range eggs, milk, yoghurt, local beef, lamb, fish and game in season are used in the kitchen. Fresh home-made bread is always available, along with a wide selection of farmhouse cheeses and the hotel's own spring water. Chef-patronne Patricia Hegarty prepares delicious dishes in the English country style, to a high standard that has earned both national acclaim and 3 AA Rosettes. The wine list includes over 150 labels, with some rare vintages. Hope End is an ideal touring base as the Welsh Marches, Cotswolds and Malvern Hills are nearby. Closed from mid-December to mid-February. **Directions:** Two miles north of Ledbury, just beyond Wellington Heath. Price guide: Single £87; double/twin £99.

42 THE CALLS

42 THE CALLS, LEEDS, WEST YORKSHIRE LS2 7EW
TEL: 0532 440099 FAX: 0532 344100

This remarkable hotel is simply unique. Converted from an old riverside corn mill, it is run as a very personal and luxurious hotel by Jonathan Wix and his general manager John Knaggs, in a peaceful location in the centre of Leeds. Shops, offices and theatres are within a few minutes' walk. The bedrooms have been individually decorated and furnished, taking full advantage of the many original features from small grain shutes to massive beams, girders and old machinery. Each room has three telephones, ten-channel TV (including French and German stations), a fresh filter coffee machine, complimentry toffees and cordials, luxury toiletries, trouser press and hair dryer. Stereo CD players are fitted in all the bedrooms and a library of disks is available to guests. Every comfort has been provided with full-size desks, handmade beds and armchairs, a liberal scattering of eastern rugs and beautiful bathrooms. Valet car parking and 24-hour room service are offered. Next door to the hotel is the very stylish Brasserie 44 where guests will always be offered a table and their meals can be charged to their hotel account. **Directions:** M1 junction 46, follow signs to Harrogate, turn right by Tetley's Brewery. Go over Crown Point Bridge, then immediately left down a narrow cobbled street; No 42 is 200 yards on the left. Price guide: Single £95–£125; double/twin £100–£130; suite £135–£195.

HALEY'S HOTEL & RESTAURANT

SHIRE OAK ROAD, HEADINGLEY, LEEDS, WEST YORKSHIRE LS6 2DE
TEL: 0532 784446 FAX: 0532 753342

Haley's Hotel is a Victorian house located on a tree-lined lane in a quiet suburb of the city and within walking distance of the Yorkshire Cricket Club's home ground at Headingley. Skilfully fashioned into a town house hotel, Haley's combines style with comfort and convenience. All the bedrooms are individually furnished, while the public rooms are graced with antiques. In Haley's Restaurant, with its two AA Rosettes, chef, Chris Baxter and his team prepare a daily choice of fixed price and à la carte menus. The Bramley Room and Library provide excellent venues for private meetings, lunch or dinner parties. Despite the richness of the furnishings and decor, it is the staff who set Haley's apart.

Each member of the team is dedicated to making a visit to the hotel a truly memorable experience, working to promote an atmosphere reminiscent of the Victorian age. It is with great pride that Haley's has won the *North Eastern Loo of the Year Award* for the third consecutive year and was also the AA Best New Hotel in the North of England 1991/92. **Directions:** Shire Oak Road is off the main A660 Otley road which forms the primary route from the city centre to Otley, Ilkley and Leeds/Bradford Airport. Price guide: Single £95; double/twin £112; suite £165.

        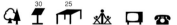

MONK FRYSTON HALL

MONK FRYSTON, LEEDS, NORTH YORKSHIRE LS25 5DU
TEL: 0977 682369 FAX: 0977 683544

This mellow old manor house, with origins dating back to the time of William the Conqueror, is of great architectural interest. The mullioned and transomed windows, and the family coat of arms above the doorway, are reminiscent of Monk Fryston's fascinating past. In 1954 the hall was acquired by the Duke of Rutland, who has since created an elegant hotel for the 20th century, while successfully preserving the strong sense of heritage and tradition. The bedrooms, ranging from cosy, to airy and spacious, all have private en suite bathrooms and are appointed to a high standard. A comprehensive menu offers a wide choice of traditional English dishes with something to suit all tastes.

From the hall, the terrace leads to landscaped Italian gardens which overlook an ornamental lake and are a delight to see at any time of year. Wedding receptions and dinner-dances are catered for in the oak-panelled Haddon Room with its splendid carved fireplace. The Rutland Room makes a good conference venue. Monk Fryston Hall is an ideal choice for business people, tourists or those seeking a relaxing break. York is 16 miles, Leeds 14 miles and Harrogate 18 miles away. **Directions:** Three miles off A1, on the A63 towards Selby in the centre of Monk Fryston. Price guide: Single £65–£85; double/twin £92–£110.

QUORN COUNTRY HOTEL

66 LEICESTER ROAD, QUORN, LEICESTERSHIRE LE12 8BB
TEL: 0509 415050 FAX: 0509 415557

Located in the heart of rural Leicestershire, Quorn Country Hotel has easy access to major road, rail and air links, making it an ideal base for visiting the East Midlands. Far from the hurly-burly of city life, the Quorn stands in 4 acres of landscaped gardens which dip down to the River Soar. A friendly welcome awaits guests. A magnificent reception hall, with a Minster fireplace, panelled walls, mahogany staircase, oil paintings and well-chosen antiques, reflect the high standards of style and comfort. The bedrooms have been equipped with attention to every detail. Particular emphasis is given to the enjoyment of food, with the Orangery and the Shires Restaurant offering two culinary styles and atmospheres. Classically inspired decor, hand-painted murals and a delightful trompe l'œil painting create the composed ambience of the Orangery, which contrasts with the cosy intimacy of the Shires, with its alcoves and low-beamed ceilings. Interesting menus featuring top quality local produce offer a variety of choice, and the traditional Sunday lunch is a speciality. AA 4 Stars; RAC Merit awards for excellence in cuisine, hospitality and comfort. **Directions:** Situated in the bypassed centre of Quorn (Quorndon) village, 5 miles from the M1 (junction 23), between Leicester and Loughborough. Price guide: Single £80; double/twin £110; suite £125.

TIME OUT HOTEL

15 ENDERBY ROAD, BLABY, LEICESTER LE8 3GD
TEL: 0533 787898 FAX: 0533 787898

This early Victorian doctor's house, converted into a modern comfortable hotel, provides an ideal venue for the business traveller or for those seeking peace and tranquillity. The croquet lawn, lily pond and regular summer barbecues entice guests into the garden, while the bar and lounge are havens for a convivial drink or quiet read. The en suite bedrooms are light and airy, delightfully furnished and extremely cosy. There is a wonderful choice of seasonal, fresh produce on the menu with an extensive, yet reasonably priced wine list to complement your meal. The surroundings and decor make the function rooms ideal for receptions, meetings and conferences. The hotel is well equipped with leisure facilities including a heated indoor swimming pool, sauna, solarium, gymnasium and Jacuzzi. There is also a warm, cosily furnished brasserie offering a selection of hot and cold dishes. There is much to see in the surrounding area such as Belvoir Castle, Charnwood Forest and Leicester Cathedral. Sporting interests catered for include football, cricket, first-class rugby, horse-racing and motor-racing. Special weekend leisure breaks are available. Closed 26 to 30 December and 1 January. **Directions:** Ideally situated 4 miles from Leicester, 2 miles from the M1 (junction 21) on the B582. Price guide: Single £45–£55; double/twin £75.

HOAR CROSS HALL HEALTH SPA RESORT

HOAR CROSS, NR YOXALL, STAFFORDSHIRE DE13 8QS
TEL: 0283 75671 FAX: 0283 75652

Hoar Cross Hall is a health spa resort in a stately home. Rated one of the top three health spas in Britain. This Grade II listed building, situated in acres of formal gardens and woodland, has all the charm of a luxury country residence, combined with the most innovative and comprehensive health spa facilities on offer. Seventy luxury en suite bedrooms are furnished with either half-tester, crown-tester or four-poster beds. The opulent public areas retain most original features including panelling, mouldings and fireplaces. Dining is an experience combining healthy eating with à la carte choices. Fully equipped meeting facilities for up to 30 delegates offers the ideal venue for 'Healthy Executive'

conferences. Specialising in hydrotherapy, over thirty beauty & fitness therapists are on hand to relieve life's stresses. Outdoor activities range from hard-court tennis and 9-hole golf improvement to croquet and bicycles. Price includes accommodation, breakfast, lunch, dinner, unlimited use of all indoor and outdoor facilities in addition to a number of inclusive treatments. (For your complete relaxation minimum guest age is 16 years). Corporate half-board rates available – details on request. **Directions:** From Lichfield turn off A51 onto A515 towards Ashbourne. Go through Yoxall and turn left to Hoar Cross. Price guide (fully inclusive, see above): Single £98; double/twin £196.

SWINFEN HALL

SWINFEN, NR LICHFIELD, STAFFORDSHIRE WS14 9RS
TEL: 0543 481494 FAX: 0543 480341

Swinfen Hall is a luxurious country house hotel built in the mid-18th century under the supervision of local architect Benjamin Wyatt. The money lavished on this dream residence is evident today in Swinfen Hall's sweeping balustraded Minstrels' Gallery and superb stucco ceilings crafted by Italian artisans. Elsewhere, fine architectural touches include the splendid carved-wood lobby ceiling, plus magnificent panelling, tiled fireplaces and tiny details. Owned by Helen and Victor Wiser, Swinfen is expertly managed by Simon Hastie, who ensures a quality of service and hospitality befitting such a setting. In the restaurant and private dining room, guests can select from fresh fish, beef and local game

(the breakfast menu is famed for its choice and value). A sun-filled banqueting hall with oak-panelled walls and magnificent Grinling Gibbons carvings is available for receptions and dinner dances. Bedrooms, decorated in pastel shades, are light, airy and comfortable, with period furnishings and modern conveniences including hospitality trays and hairdryers. Birmingham, and the International Airport are only 20 minutes away, and places to visit include Tamworth Castle and Lichfield Cathedral. **Directions:** Exit M42 at junctions A5. Lichfield is signposted off A5. Price guide: Single £65–£85; double/twin £85–£95; suite £105–£125.

ROWLEY MANOR

LITTLE WEIGHTON, NR HULL, NORTH HUMBERSIDE HU20 3XR
TEL: 0482 848248 FAX: 0482 849900

This ivy-clad Georgian manor stands in 34 acres of lawns, rosebeds and parkland. Formerly a rectory, it was acquired in 1928 by a shipping magnate who installed panelling by Grinling Gibbons in the study and an unusual water temple in the garden. A giant outdoor chess board further adds to guests' enjoyment of the grounds. Attractive interiors have been decorated in a style that befits the dignified form of the rooms – period furniture, gilt-framed mirrors and oil paintings. The bedrooms all have views of the grounds and offer comfortable accommodation. An interesting menu is presented in the elegant dining room, including a good choice of seafood 'fresh from the quayside'. A permanent deluxe marquee attached to the Green Room can cater for up to 180 people. Personally managed by owners Mario and Christine Ando, Rowley Manor is ideally located for visitors to the Hull and Beverley areas, yet its rural setting in the Yorkshire Wolds offers plenty of scope for exploration. **Directions:** Located between Hull and Beverley. Leave M62/A63 at the South Cave signpost. Take the A1034 to South Cave, turn right at the clock tower and follow the signs to Rowley. Price guide: Single £50–£60; double/twin £65–£85.

LOWER SLAUGHTER MANOR

LOWER SLAUGHTER, NR BOURTON-ON-THE-WATER, GLOUCESTERSHIRE GL54 2HP
TEL: 0451 820456 FAX: 0451 822150

A delightful old Manor House, crafted from Cotswold stone by a local mason in 1658, is now the home of Audrey and Peter Marks, previously of Rookery Hall. Situated on the edge of one of the Cotswolds' prettiest villages, the Manor is an ideal retreat where one can relax in pleasant surroundings. The picturesque walled garden is a superb setting for the centuries-old dovecote, one of the finest in England. Elegant public rooms have fine paintings, antiques and log fires blazing in the winter. Exceptionally spacious bedrooms offer all modern comforts while retaining their charm. Chef Julian Ehlers serves modern and traditional country-house cooking, using fresh produce from local suppliers and herbs from the garden. The cellar provides a wide selection of fine wines from Burgundy, Bordeaux and the New World. A warm welcome, courteous service and general ambience remind guests of country house entertaining of an intimate scale in days gone by. There is an indoor heated swimming pool, sauna, all-weather tennis court, and croquet lawn. The position, setting and location of the Manor makes it an ideal base for touring the beautiful Cotswold countryside, villages and market towns. A self-contained conference suite offers complete privacy. **Directions:** From the A419, follow the sign to The Slaughters; the Manor is on right when entering the village. Price guide: Single £120–£185; double/twin £170–£250.

WASHBOURNE COURT HOTEL

LOWER SLAUGHTER, GLOUCESTERSHIRE GL54 2HS
TEL: 0451 822143 FAX: 0451 821045

Situated in the centre of the village of Lower Slaughter, in the heart of the Cotswolds, Washbourne Court Hotel is a magnificent 17th century building. Owned and managed by the Pender family and assisted by a professional team, the hotel prides itself on offering quality accommodation and friendly, personal service. Much of the original character and charm of the place has been retained, with traditional beamed ceilings, flagstone floors and mullioned windows. During the summer months, guests can enjoy a drink on the riverside terrace or, in winter, indoors in front of an old-fashioned log fire. Modern English cuisine is served to a high standard in the Riverside Restaurant, where guests dine by candlelight. The menus make full use of local produce and there is a fine wine list. The restaurant has recently been awarded an AA Rosette. There are several bedrooms in the main building; alternatively, choose one of the Barn rooms, incorporating the original beams, or one of the cottage-style suites. The surrounding area is renowned for its beauty and there are many gentle walks. The Fosse Way, one of the famous Roman roads, is $1/_2$ a mile away. **Directions:** Washbourne Court is $1/_2$ a mile from the A429 Fosse Way between Stow-on-the-Wold and Cirencester. Price guide: Single £65–£75; double/twin £88; suite £125.

THE FEATHERS

BULL RING, LUDLOW, SHROPSHIRE SY8 1AA
TEL: 0584 875261 FAX: 0584 876030

Ludlow has been described as the most beautiful and historic small town in England and the hotel's situation makes it ideal for exploring 'Housman' country and enjoying the glorious scenery of the Teme, Severn and Wye Valleys and the Welsh Marches. Described in the *New York Times* by historian Jan Morris as 'the most handsome inn in the world', this lovely Jacobean building is now a hotel with a fine reputation for food and comfort. The interiors are richly decorated with elaborate carvings, ornamented plaster ceilings, original panelling, coats of arms and antiques. What was formerly the kitchen is now the setting for the Housman Restaurant, while the Prince Charles Banqueting Room is designed in the style of a baronial hall. During the summer, the Courtyard Restaurant is especially attractive for alfresco dining. All 40 bedrooms have en suite facilities, colour television, direct-dial telephone, radio, tea-/coffee-/chocolate-making facilities and a mini-bar. Guests can choose to stay in one of eight four-poster bedrooms. There is a lift to the upper floors. The Feathers has good conference facilities for corporate events and there is a billiard room for guests' enjoyment. **Directions:** Ludlow is on the A49 north of Hereford (access from the M5 via Worcester, Droitwich or Kidderminster). Price guide: Single £75; double/twin £104; suite £124.

PASSFORD HOUSE HOTEL

MOUNT PLEASANT LANE, LYMINGTON, HAMPSHIRE SO41 8LS
TEL: 0590 682398 FAX: 0590 683494

Passford House Hotel, the former home of Lord Arthur Cecil, is situated on the edge of the New Forest in 9 acres of grounds and beautifully maintained gardens. The hotel boasts a superb leisure centre, featuring a spa pool, solarium, gym and indoor and outdoor swimming pools. The bedrooms, one of which has a four-poster bed, provide every modern comfort and convenience. In addition, two suites are available: one of these is situated across the old stable yard and comprises two en suite bedrooms, lounge and kitchen. The elegant restaurant offers an imaginative and tempting menu complemented by fine wines. Two miles away, the old Georgian town of Lymington has a good shopping centre, thriving Saturday market, two impressive marinas and superior yachting facilities. Just a short drive away are Beaulieu, the cathedral cities of Winchester and Salisbury and ferry ports to the Isle of Wight and France. The New Forest district has five golf courses and, for those interested in riding, there are many stabling and trekking centres. Milford-on-Sea is the nearest beach, 4 miles away. **Directions:** At Lymington leave the A337 at the Tollhouse Inn, then take the first turning right; the hotel is on the right-hand side. Price guide: Single £72; double/twin £101–£140.

PARKHILL HOTEL

BEAULIEU ROAD, LYNDHURST, NEW FOREST, HAMPSHIRE SO43 7FZ
TEL: 0703 282944 FAX: 0703 283268

Reached by way of a winding drive through glorious parkland from the scenic route between Lyndhurst and Beaulieu, Parkhill, situated in an elevated position with superb views across open forest and heathland, is perfect for a restful break or holiday and makes the ideal venue for special business meetings and small conferences offering a charming New Forest remoteness coupled with an excellence of standards and service. Dining at Parkhill is very much an integral part of your overall pleasure. The restaurant offers a most tranquil setting with fine views across the lawns, where deer can frequently be seen grazing. The cuisine is a delicious blend of modern and classical English cooking, where local fresh produce is used to create appetising menus, balanced by a carefully chosen and well-stocked cellar. Parkhill is also an ideal base for touring not only the delightful surrounding areas, but also the many places of interest which are all within easy driving distance, including Exbury Gardens, home to one of the world's finest collections of rhododendrons and azaleas, Broadlands, the home of Lord Mountbatten, the *Mary Rose* in Portsmouth Dockyard, and the graceful cathedral cities of Salisbury and Winchester. **Directions:** From Lyndhurst take the B3056 to Beaulieu; Parkhill is about 1 mile from Lyndhurst on your right. Price guide: Single from £45–£64; double from £90–£128.

THE LYNTON COTTAGE HOTEL

NORTH WALK, LYNTON, NORTH DEVON EX35 6ED
TEL: 0598 52342 FAX: 0598 52597

Once the residence of a knight of the realm, The Lynton Cottage Hotel gives a breathtaking view of the Lyn Valley and Lynmouth Bay – a spectacular sight to greet visitors approaching along the winding drive. Dating back to the 17th century, the hotel combines period charm with modern comforts. The 18 en suite bedrooms & suites, including a recent addition on the ground floor, are individually decorated with taste and style and equipped to reflect the perfectionist approach of enthusiastic proprietors John and Masie Jones. Under the auspices of chef Leon Balanche, innovative cuisine is prepared with flair, finesse and an influence of French culinary style. AA Rosette Awarded.

Gastronomic house parties have proved popular on regular weekends throughout the year, offering guests an opportunity to enjoy the finest gourmet cooking accompanied by wines carefully selected for the occasion. Other special breaks available include mystery whodunnit and champagne weekends. Riding, clay pigeon shooting, golf and salmon fishing are all available locally and the hotel is an ideal base from which to discover the rugged beauty of Exmoor and the Valley of Rocks. Closed January. **Directions:** From M5 take A39 to Porlock then on to Lynton, where the hotel is on the North Walk. Price guide (including dinner): Single £57–£75; double/twin £110–£140.

THE BRIDGE HOTEL

PRESTBURY, CHESHIRE SK10 4DQ
TEL: 0625 829326 FAX: 0625 827557

The Bridge Hotel is situated in the centre of the village of Prestbury, one of the prettiest villages in the North West of England. Originally dating from 1626, The Bridge today combines the old world charm of an ancient and historic building with the comfort and facilities of a modern hotel, yet within easy reach of Manchester Airport and major motorways. The public rooms have retained much of the inn's original character, with oak panelling and beams in the bar and reception area. The bedrooms, many of which overlook the River Bollin, are decorated to the highest standard, with 6 rooms in the old building and a further 17 in a recently added wing. In the attractive galleried dining room, table d'hôte and à la carte menus offer traditional English cuisine. There is an extensive selection of wines to accompany your meal. Conference and banqueting facilities are available. Places to visit nearby include the Peak District National Park, Chatsworth, Tatton Park and Liverpool's Albert Dock. While enjoying a quiet location, the hotel is convenient for Manchester, just 30 minutes away, Liverpool, and the medieval city of Chester, which is under 40 minutes' drive. **Directions:** In the centre of the village next to the church. Prestbury is on the A538 from Wilmslow to Macclesfield. Price guide: Single £77; double/twin £84-£94.

CLIVEDEN

TAPLOW, BERKSHIRE SL6 0JF
TEL: 0628 668561 FAX: 0628 661837 TELEX: 846562

Cliveden, Britain's only 5-star hotel that is also a stately home, is set in 376 acres of National Trust private gardens and parkland, overlooking the Thames. As the former home of Frederick, Prince of Wales, three Dukes and the Astor family, Cliveden has been at the centre of Britain's social and political life for over 300 years. It is exquisitely furnished in a classically English style, with a multitude of oil paintings, antiques and *objets d'art* set against elaborate carved panelling, chiselled colonnades and ornate plasterwork. The spacious guest rooms and suites are appointed to the most luxurious standards, with every comfort assured. One of the greatest pleasures of eating at Cliveden is in the choice of dining rooms and the scope of the menus. The French Dining Room, with its original Madame de Pompadour rococo decoration, is the finest 18th-century *boiserie* outside France. Alternatively, relish the Michelin-starred cuisine of chef Ron Maxfield. The Pavilion offers a full range of health and fitness facilities and beauty therapies. Guests can ride Cliveden's horses over the estate or enjoy a leisurely cruise on an Edwardian launch. Comprehensively equipped, The Churchill Boardroom provides self-contained business meeting facilities. **Directions:** Situated on B476, 2 miles north of Taplow. Price guide: Single £205; double/twin £240; suite £515.

FREDRICK'S HOTEL & RESTAURANT

SHOPPENHANGERS ROAD, MAIDENHEAD, BERKSHIRE SL6 2PZ
TEL: 0628 35934 FAX: 0628 771054

'Putting people first' is the guiding philosophy behind the running of this sumptuously equipped hotel and, indeed, is indicative of the uncompromising service guests can expect to receive. Set in 2 acres of grounds, Fredrick's overlooks the fairways and greens of Maidenhead Golf Club beyond. The immaculate reception rooms are distinctively styled to create something out of the ordinary. Minute attention to detail is evident in the 37 bedrooms, all immaculate with gleaming, marble-tiled bathrooms, while the suites have their own patio garden or balcony. A quiet drink can be enjoyed in the light, airy Wintergarden lounge before entering the air-conditioned restaurant. Amid the elegant décor of crystal chandeliers and crisp white linen, fine gourmet cuisine is served which has received recognition from leading guides for many years. Particularly suited to conferences, four private function rooms with full secretarial facilities are available. Helicopter landing can be arranged. Easily accessible from Windsor, Henley, Ascot, Heathrow and London. Closed 24-30 December. **Directions:** Leave M4 at exit 8/9, take A404(M) and leave at first turning signed Cox Green/White Waltham. Turn into Shoppenhangers Road; Fredrick's is on the right. Price guide: Single £130–£140; double/twin £165–£175; suite £240.

CHILSTON PARK COUNTRY HOUSE

SANDWAY, LENHAM, NR MAIDSTONE, KENT ME17 2BE
TEL: 0622 859803 FAX: 0622 858588 TELEX: 966154 CHILPK G

This magnificent Grade I listed mansion, one of England's most richly decorated hotels, was built in the 13th century and remodelled in the 18th century. Now sensitively refurbished, the hotel's ambience is enhanced by the lighting at dusk each day of over 200 candles. The marble hall and drawing room offer guests an opportunity to relax and to admire the outstanding collection of antiques. Owners Martin and Judith Miller, who are renowned antiques experts (their annual *Miller's Guide to Antiques* is a best-seller), have made the entire hotel a treasure trove for their many interesting *objets d'art*. The opulently furnished bedrooms are fitted to a high standard and many have four-poster beds. Good, fresh English cooking is offered in each of Chilston's five dining rooms, where outstanding menus are supported by a excellent wine list. In keeping with the traditions of a country house, a wide variety of sporting activities is available, such as good rough shooting, fishing in the natural spring lake and punting. **Directions:** Take junction 8 off the M20, then A20 to Lenham Station. Turn left into Boughton Road. Go over the crossroads and M20; Chilston Park is on the left. Price guide: Single £70–£145; double/twin £90–£190.

CRUDWELL COURT HOTEL

CRUDWELL, NR MALMESBURY, WILTSHIRE SN16 9EP
TEL: 0666 577194 FAX: 0666 577853

Crudwell Court is a 17th-century rectory, set in 3 acres of Cotswold walled gardens. The pretty, well-established grounds have lily ponds and a garden gate leading through to the neighbouring Saxon church of All Saints. Completely refurbished in recent years, the old rectory has been decorated with bright, cheery colours. Sunshine yellow in the sitting room, warm apricot in the drawing room and shades of buttercream and blue in the bedrooms lend a fresh feel to this hotel. Visitors enter through a flagstoned hall to discover rooms with comfortable seating and plenty of books to read. In the panelled dining room guests will find a weekly changing menu, which is best described as modern Anglo-French. Cooked to order, the meals are a feast for the eye as well as the palate. The restaurant has recently been extended into a new conservatory, which may also be used for private functions. Nearby are the market towns of Tetbury, Malmesbury and Cirencester, the picturesque villages of Castle Combe and Lacock and numerous stately homes. **Directions:** Crudwell Court is on the A429. Travelling towards Cirencester, when you reach the village of Crudwell turn right (signposted Oaksey) opposite the Plough pub, and the hotel is on the left. Price guide: Single £50; double/twin £90.

WHATLEY MANOR

EASTON GREY, MALMESBURY, WILTSHIRE SN16 0RB
TEL: 0666 822888 FAX: 0666 826120

This Grade II listed manor, set around a central courtyard, stands in 12 acres of grounds running down to a peaceful stretch of the River Avon. Originally built in the 17th century, Whatley Manor was refurbished by a wealthy sportsman in the 1920s and many of the present buildings date from that period. While the hotel's interior is furnished to a high standard, an emphasis has always been placed on maintaining a relaxed, informal atmosphere, enhanced by pine and oak panelling, log fires and the effect of warm colours in the lounge and drawing room. Similarly, the dining room combines elegance with intimacy and overlooks the gardens. Snooker and table-tennis facilities are provided in the original saddle rooms and there is also a sauna, solarium and Jacuzzi. Guests can fish in the River Avon within the hotel grounds. With the Cotswolds, the cities of Bath, Bristol and Cheltenham and many places of historic interest nearby, Whatley Manor is the perfect place for long weekend breaks, for which the special terms ensure good value. 2 night weekend breaks from £109. **Directions:** The hotel is on the B4040 between Easton Grey and Malmesbury. Price guide: Single £85–£96; double/twin £112–£136.

THE COTTAGE IN THE WOOD

HOLYWELL ROAD, MALVERN WELLS, WORCESTERSHIRE WR14 4LG
TEL: 0684 573487 FAX: 0684 560662

The Malvern Hills – the home and inspiration for England's most celebrated composer, Sir Edward Elgar – are the setting for The Cottage in the Wood. The hotel occupies 7 acres of thickly wooded grounds, perched high on the hillside. With its breathtaking views across the Severn Valley plain, it won acclaim from the *Daily Mail* for 'the best view in England'. Formerly attached to the Blackmore Park seat of Sir Thomas Hornyold, it now comprises three buildings: the Georgian Dower House, Beech Cottage and Coach House. The cottage-style furnishings of all the bedrooms are simple and cosy and the Coach House bedrooms have sun-trap balconies and patios. An essentially English menu is complemented by a wine cellar with labels from Europe, Australia, America and Chile. To counter any gastronomic indulgence, guests can take an exhilarating trek straight from the hotel grounds to the breezy summits of the Malverns. The Victorian spa town of Great Malvern is nearby, as is the Three Counties Showground and the cathedral cities of Worcester, Gloucester and Hereford. The hotel is personally run by John and Sue Pattin and family. **Directions:** Three miles south of Great Malvern on A449, turn into Holywell Road opposite Jet petrol station. Hotel is 250 yards on right. Price guide: Single £67; double/twin £93–£130.

ETROP GRANGE

THORLEY LANE, MANCHESTER AIRPORT, MANCHESTER M22 5NR
TEL: 061-499 0500 FAX: 061-499 0790

Since Etrop Grange was built in 1780, the world around it has changed completely. When William Moss, dressed in powder wig and stockings, stood and admired his fine gardens then, did he ever imagine how dramatic those changes would be? More than 200 years on, Etrop Grange has not only survived but has been lovingly restored to its former glory. Owners John and Susan Roebuck have transformed this elegant residence into an establishment with a reputation for superb cuisine, exquisite accommodation and a friendly atmosphere. The original coach house has been restored to create additional bedrooms and suites along with excellent conference facilities. As well as the obvious advantage of its proximity to Manchester Airport, Etrop Grange is ideally located in many other ways, being easily reached from anywhere in the UK. There is a chauffer driven Jaguar to take guests to and from the airport. Long term car parking available with reduced accommodation rates for holiday travellers from Autumn 1993. **Directions:** Leave M56 at junction 5 towards Manchester Airport. At roundabout take the first exit and follow signs for Etrop Grange. Price guide: Single £63–£113; double/twin £72–£121; suite from £107.

THE IVY HOUSE HOTEL

HIGH STREET, MARLBOROUGH, WILTSHIRE SN8 1HJ
TEL: 0672 515333 FAX: 0672 515338

The Ivy House Hotel is an 18th-century Grade II listed building, overlooking Marlborough High Street. Built in 1707 for the Earl of Aylesbury, it has been refurbished to display the many architectural features of the changing eras. Beyond the reception area, guests may relax in the Churchill Lounge, with its antique furniture. Facing the sun terrace, at the rear of the building, is the elegant Palladian-style Garden Restaurant. The cooking is to a high standard, reflecting both traditional and progressive styles. The purpose-built Beeches Conference and Banqueting Suite provides a venue for business meetings, while the Marlborough Suite is suitable for private dinner parties. The Ivy House is professionally run by owners David Ball and Josephine Scott, who offer guests a comfortable stay which is extremely good value for money. The ancient archaeological sites of Silbury Hill, Stonehenge and Avebury are easily accessible by car, as are the Marlborough Downs and the Savernake Forest. Close by are the stately homes of Bowood House, Littlecote, Corsham Court and Blenheim Palace. **Directions:** The hotel is in Marlborough High Street, just off the A4 from Bath. Price guide: Single £59; double/twin £71.

DANESFIELD HOUSE

MEDMENHAM, MARLOW, BUCKINGHAMSHIRE SL7 3ES
TEL: 0628 891010 FAX: 0628 890408

Danesfield House is situated between Henley and Marlow in 65 acres of outstanding grounds and formal gardens, overlooking the River Thames, with panoramic views across the Chiltern Hills. Only 30 miles from London, this stunning Victorian Gothic edifice is centrally located for the events of the English Season. Fully refurbished, the hotel opened in 1991, perfectly suited for its role as a luxury hotel offering the highest levels of service and hospitality 24 hours a day. Notable among the impressive interiors are the grand drawing room with its magnificently carved timber ceiling, the spacious banqueting hall inspired by Versailles and the 89 superbly appointed bedrooms and suites.

The two elegant and stylish restaurants – Oak Room and Loggia – present an exciting diversity of culinary choice. For corporate events and meetings a full range of state-of-the-art business facilities is available. In addition to the three conference rooms, the grand banqueting hall is a fine venue for large functions. Shooting, riding, polo, gliding and hot-air ballooning can be arranged, as can temporary membership of local golf clubs. Nearby are many pretty villages, including Pangbourne, Goring and Hambleden. **Directions:** Between M4 and M40 on A4155 between Marlow and Henley-on-Thames. Price guide: Single £125; double/twin £150; suite £230.

RIBER HALL

MATLOCK, DERBYSHIRE DE4 5JU
TEL: 0629 582795 FAX: 0629 580475

A listed historical building, starred in its class, Riber Hall dates from the 1400s, although much of the manor house is Elizabethan. Having survived through the ages, Riber Hall underwent extensive restoration in 1970 to lead to its present status as a prestigious hotel. The original features are very much in evidence, with exposed beams and large fireplaces creating a fitting backdrop to the antique furniture and period decor. Quietly located around an attractive courtyard, the bedrooms provide many extras and most have whirlpool spa baths. Acknowledged as a restaurant of distinction, Riber Hall offers a comprehensive wine list, game when in season and a wide choice of delicious dishes in an intimate atmosphere, enhanced by fine Wedgwood bone china and cut glass. Conferences, wedding receptions and small dinner parties can be privately catered for. The tranquillity of the setting can be appreciated in the walled garden and orchard, while energetic types can pit their skills against the tennis-trainer ball machine on the all-weather court. The Peak National Park beyond beckons explorers, while Chatsworth House, Haddon Hall, Hardwick Hall and Calke Abbey are nearby. **Directions:** Twenty minutes from junction 28 of M1, off A615 at Tansley; 1 mile further to Riber. Price guide: Single £78; double/twin £92.

FIFEHEAD MANOR

MIDDLE WALLOP, STOCKBRIDGE, HAMPSHIRE SO20 8EG
TEL: 0264 781565 FAX: 0264 781400

Middle Wallop, along with its sister villages of Nether Wallop and Over Wallop, is to the first-time visitor an idyll of rural England – quaint thatched cottages, a charming Saxon church and the Wallop Brook winding sleepily through. An integral part of the village history is Fifehead Manor, whose foundations reputedly date from the 11th century, when it was attached to the estates of the Saxon Earl Godwin. The first American president, George Washington, was a direct descendant of a 15th-century Lord of the Manor of Wallop Fifehead. Nowadays, as a comfortable hotel, the sense of history is reflected in the beamed rooms, leaded windows and the timelessly courteous hospitality. Among the attractive bedrooms are some which have been adapted for guests with disabilities. Evidence of a minstrels' gallery can be seen in the dining room, which was probably the main hall during medieval times. An inventive team of chefs use their culinary skills to produce a delicious menu with a hint of Gallic inspiration. Nearby are Stonehenge, Wilton House and Salisbury and Winchester Cathedrals. Riding can be arranged. **Directions:** Fifehead Manor is at the west end of the village on the A343. Price guide: Single £50–£60; double/twin £75–£95.

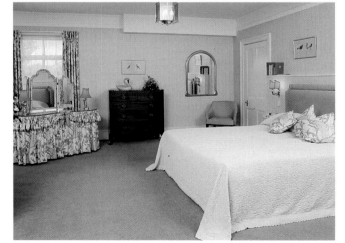

PERITON PARK HOTEL

MIDDLECOMBE, NR MINEHEAD, SOMERSET TA24 8SW
TEL: 0643 706885 FAX: 0643 706885 REF PP

Bordering on the northern fringe of the Exmoor National Park, the elevated position of this handsome country house affords the visitor magnificent views of the West Somerset hills, with flashes of the Bristol Channel beyond. Through the dawn mists the early riser may be rewarded by the spectacle of a herd of red deer grazing on the moorland below the hotel. Set in 4 acres of woodland, this residence, built in 1875, is now owned by Richard and Angela Hunt whose aim is to run a select hotel in the style of a country gentleman's home. In this they have succeeded – the decor and furnishings in the well-proportioned rooms have been enlivened with warm autumn colours to create a restful impression. The wood-panelled restaurant, with its double aspect views over the grounds, has been completely renovated. Imaginative use of Somerset and West Country produce has earned Periton Park a reputation for gastronomic excellence. The combination of heathered moorland, sheltered coombes and rugged coastline makes the hotel an ideal base for walking and field sports, while riding is available from the stables adjacent to the hotel. **Directions:** Periton Park is situated off the A39 on the left just after Minehead, in the direction of Lynmouth and Porlock. Price guide: Single £60; double/twin £88.

THE ANGEL HOTEL

NORTH STREET, MIDHURST, WEST SUSSEX GU29 9DN
TEL: 0730 812421 FAX: 0730 815928

The Angel Hotel, a 16th century coaching inn, set in formal Elizabethan gardens in the historic market town of Midhurst, offers a warm welcome, comfortable accommodation and fine food. The buildings have been sympathetically restored to provide hospitality in a splendid English setting. New owners Nicholas Davies and Peter Crawford-Rolt bring with them a wealth of experience, the former from the world of business, the latter from previously owning Beechfield House in Beanacre. Two restaurants offer a choice of dining. In the informal brasserie, the emphasis is on fresh seafoods and there is a daily changing menu of hearty roasts, casseroles and pies. An extensive menu in the Cowdray Room includes a wide choice of char-grilled meats and fish, accompanied by an imaginative wine list. Company presentations, seminars and exhibitions can all be held here, as can weddings: a marquee can be erected on the lawn for larger parties. The 17 individually furnished bedrooms, some with four-posters, all have en suite bathrooms and offer every comfort. The Angel is well placed to enjoy polo at Cowdray Park, racing at Goodwood and visits to Petworth House and Arundel Castle. **Directions:** From the A272, the hotel is on the left as the town centre is approached from the east. Price guide: Single from £55; double/twin from £70; suite £130.

THE SPREAD EAGLE HOTEL

SOUTH STREET, MIDHURST, WEST SUSSEX GU29 9NH
TEL: 0730 816911 FAX: 0730 815668 TELEX: 86853 SPREAG G

Dating from 1430, when guests were welcomed to the tavern here, The Spread Eagle is one of England's oldest hotels. Throughout the centuries, including its time as a famous coaching inn, the influences of successive eras have been preserved both in the architecture and decorative features of the hotel. Heavy polished timbers, Tudor bread ovens and a series of Flemish stained-glass windows are among the many noteworthy features. Innovative cooking forms the basis of the meals, served in the dining room, with its huge, coppered inglenook fireplace and dark oak beams hung with traditional Sussex Christmas puddings. Colourful, co-ordinated fabrics and antique furnishings make for attractive bedrooms, all fully appointed. The 17th-century Jacobean Hall is an ideal venue for meetings – or perhaps a medieval banquet complete with minstrels! A secluded courtyard garden is flanked, in the summer, by climbing roses and clematis. The stately homes at Petworth, Uppark and Goodwood are all within a short drive, with Chichester Cathedral, the Downland Museum and Fishbourne Roman Palace among the many local attractions. Cowdray Park Polo Club is only 1 mile away. **Directions:** Midhurst is on the A286 between Chichester and Milford. Price guide: Single £59–£85; double/twin £78–£140; suite £140.

MOORE PLACE HOTEL

THE SQUARE, ASPLEY GUISE, MILTON KEYNES, BEDFORDSHIRE MK17 8DW
TEL: 0908 282000 FAX: 0908 281888

This elegant Georgian mansion was built by Francis Moore in the tranquil Bedfordshire village of Aspley Guise in 1786. The original house, which is set on the village square, has been sympathetically extended to create extra rooms. The additional wing has been built around an attractive courtyard with a rock garden, lily pool and waterfall. The pretty Victorian-style conservatory restaurant, with its floral tented ceiling and festooned drapes, serves food that rates among the best in the area. Vegetarian options can always be found on the menus, which offer dishes prepared in the modern English style and balanced with a selection of fine wines. The 54 bedrooms are well appointed with many amenities, including a trouser press and hairdryer. Banquets, conferences and dinner parties can be accommodated in three private function rooms: all are decorated in traditional style yet are equipped with the latest audio-visual facilities. The hotel is close to Woburn Abbey, Dunstable Downs, Whipsnade Zoo and the city of Milton Keynes. Its central location and accessibility to the motorway network make Moore Place Hotel an attractive choice, whether travelling on business or for pleasure. **Directions:** Only 2 minutes' drive from the M1 junction 13. Price guide: Single £49.50; double/twin £65–£150.

THE BEACON COUNTRY HOUSE

BEACON ROAD, MINEHEAD, SOMERSET TA24 5SD
TEL: 0643 703476 FAX: 0643 402668

This elegant Edwardian building is surrounded by 20 acres of grounds visited by red deer and home to badgers and peacocks. From the hotel's woods there is direct access to Exmoor and to a winding coastal path. Although extensively refurbished, the building has maintained the characyer of a fine country house. All the public rooms are tastefully furnished to create a comfortable and relaxing atmosphere, and a superb, domed, glass conservatory affords views of the gardens and sea beyond. Co-owner and master chef, Pennie Fulcher-Smith, compiles an imaginative menu which places emphasis on fresh local produce, and, although a wide variety of dishes is offered, Pennie is happy to cater for all tastes. There is also an extensive wine list. The individually styled bedrooms are as elegantly furnished as the rest of the hotel and provide every modern facility. There is a livery adjacent to the hotel and riding or shooting breaks are available by arrangement. The Beacon Country house is an ideal base for those touring the West Country and Exmoor. **Directions:** Leave the M5 at junction 25 to Minehead on the A358. Continue along Townsend Road; right at T-junction, second left at Blenheim Road, first left into Marlett Road. Straight over into Burgundy Road; round hairpin bend, hotel is at end of Beacon Road on the right. Price guide: Double/twin £70–£80; single £55

For hotel location, see maps on pages 458–464

THE KINGS ARMS INN HOTEL & RESTAURANT

MONTACUTE, SOMERSET TA16 6UU
TEL: 0935 822513 FAX: 0935 826549

This Elizabethan coaching inn, situated in one of Somerset's unspoiled villages, is built, like many of the local houses, of Ham stone, which has mellowed beautifully over the centuries to produce the warm, honeyed hues seen today. Inside, the distinctive character and features have been preserved – the natural stone walls in the lounge, mullioned windows and uneven floors all add to the relaxed charm of this friendly hotel. The décor lends a refreshing and cheery feel to the interiors, with soft, pastel shades and pretty floral fabrics. The quietly situated bedrooms are well furnished and offer many comforts. In the elegant Abbey Room a good menu offers a range of classical English dishes in addition to some more unusual choices such as hot scallops and mussels tossed in seaweed. Extensive lunch and supper menus are also available in the Pickwick Bar, which has the convivial atmosphere of an English country inn. Nearby is Montacute House, one of the most notable stately homes in the area and a showpiece of Tudor architecture. Brympton d'Evercy, Sherborne Castle, Yeovilton Air Museum and Cricket St Thomas Wildlife Park are all in the vicinity – and the south coast is only 30 minutes' drive away. **Directions:** The Kings Arms is 3^1/$_2$ miles from Yeovil on the A3088. Price guide: Single £46–£59; double/twin £64–£79.

THE MANOR HOUSE HOTEL

MORETON-IN-MARSH, GLOUCESTERSHIRE GL56 0LJ
TEL: 0608 50501 FAX: 0608 51481

This former 16th-century manor house and coaching inn is set in beautiful gardens in the Cotswold village of Moreton-in-Marsh. The Manor House Hotel has been tastefully extended and restored, yet retains many of its historic features, among them a priest's hole and secret passages. The 39 well-appointed bedrooms have been individually decorated and furnished. The restaurant offers traditional English cooking using only the freshest ingredients, accompanied by an expertly selected wine list. For the guest seeking relaxation, leisure facilities include an indoor heated swimming pool, spa bath and sauna. Sports enthusiasts will also find that tennis, golf, horse-riding and squash can be arranged locally. The spacious conference facilities are set apart from the rest of the hotel. Modern business facilities, combined with the peaceful location, make this an excellent venue for executive meetings. It is also an ideal base for touring, with many attractions nearby, including Stratford-upon-Avon, Warwick and the fashionable centres of Cheltenham, Oxford and Bath. **Directions:** The Manor House Hotel is located on the A429 Fosse Way near the junction of the A44 and A429 north of Stow-on-the-Wold. Price guide: Single £77; double/twin £115–£130.

ROOKERY HALL

WORLESTON, NANTWICH, NR CHESTER, CHESHIRE CW5 6DQ
TEL: 0270 610016 FAX: 0270 626027

Built in 1816, Rookery Hall is a Grade II listed building overlooking the verdant Cheshire Plain. Later in the 19th century, Baron Von Schroder, a Bavarian merchant banker, introduced the dramatic restyling that can be seen today. He created a new façade for the back of the house and added a schloss-like tower to remind him of his homeland. Sweeping lawns, an immense kitchen garden, lily pond, fountain and riverside meadows are encompassed within the 200-acre grounds. The reception rooms, with polished panelling and ornate plasterwork, are richly decorated with antiques and sumptuous fabrics. Traditional English fayre with European influences is the hallmark of the menu. Meat and fish dishes are lightly cooked to preserve their natural flavours and vegetables are prepared *al dente*. An outstanding list of 200 wines is offered. Recreational facilities which can be arranged on the premises include hot-air ballooning. Good conference facilities are provided within the converted stables. **Directions:** From M6 junction 16 take the A500 to Nantwich, then the B5074 to Worleston. Price guide: Single £95–£145; double/twin £115–£170; suite £215–£240.

THE PENTIRE ROCKS HOTEL

NEW POLZEATH, NR ROCK, NORTH CORNWALL PL27 6US
TEL: 0208 862213 FAX: 0208 862259

Set amid the spectacular scenery of the North Cornwall coast, the Pentire Rocks Hotel is a small, friendly hotel owned and managed by Clive and Christine Mason. It retains the personal touch that only family ownership can bring and provides the perfect base from which to explore this picturesque area of the West Country. The conservatory lounge is the ideal place to relax and there is an open fire on chilly evenings. There is also a smaller TV lounge. The bar area is a comfortable meeting place for an apéritif. All 15 bedrooms have en suite facilities and offer a level of comfort that more than justifies the hotel's AA 2-star status. AA Rosette for cuisine. Guests may choose from the à la carte or table d'hôte menus. The wine list would satisfy the most discerning palate. Service is attentive and friendly. There is a superb outdoor heated swimming pool. The North Cornwall coastal footpath runs just outside the hotel, while for the less energetic there are many magnificent houses and gardens to visit nearby. Surfers are well catered for at Polzeath, one of the safest and cleanest beaches in the West Country. **Directions:** From Launceston bypass, follow North Cornwall sign to Camelford and Wadebridge. Then head towards Port Isaac and follow signs to New Polzeath. Price guide: Single £38–£48; double/twin £76–£96. Special golf/breaks are available on request.

DONNINGTON VALLEY HOTEL & GOLF COURSE

OLD OXFORD ROAD, DONNINGTON, NEWBURY, BERKSHIRE RG16 9AG
TEL: 0635 551199 FAX: 0635 551123

Uncompromising quality is the hallmark of this hotel and its 18-hole golf course that opened in 1991. The grandeur of the Edwardian era has been captured by the striking decor of the hotel's reception area with its splendid wood-panelled ceilings and impressive overhanging gallery. Each individually designed bedroom has been thoughtfully equipped to guarantee comfort and peace of mind. In addition to the standard guest rooms Donnington Valley offers a number of non-smoking rooms, family rooms, superior executive rooms and luxury suites. With its crackling log fire and elegant surroundings, the Piano Bar is an ideal place to meet friends or, alternatively, enjoy the relaxed ambience of the Golf Bar. Guests may dine in either the Gallery Restaurant or the more formal à la carte restaurant – both offer fine international cuisine complemented by an extensive choice of wines and liqueurs. The golf course is the perfect place to spend a relaxing weekend working on your handicap or to mix business with pleasure. Special corporate golfing packages are offered and tournaments can be arranged. Purpose-built conference suites offer the flexibility to meet the demands of today's executive meeting. **Directions:** Easily accessible from M4 junction 13. From Newbury take B4494 Oxford road north. Price guide: Single £89; double/twin £96.

FOLEY LODGE HOTEL

STOCKCROSS, NEWBURY, BERKSHIRE RG16 8JU
TEL: 0635 528770 FAX: 0635 528398

Set in the heart of beautiful Berkshire, this former Victorian hunting lodge has been developed into a luxury country house hotel. The individually designed and furnished bedrooms overlook trees, garden and open countryside, while the elegant lounge and cocktail bar are perfect venues for an apéritif, or for a chance to relax and enjoy the atmosphere of the house. The attractive Victorian décor in the à la carte restaurant reflects the superb quality of the hotel's fine French and traditional English cuisine. Head Chef, Ian Webb, uses the best ingredients to prepare his inventive dishes; the menus are changed daily. The octagonal pagoda leisure complex is in the style of a grand Victorian conservatory. Lush greenery, a mezzanine restaurant and a snooker table surround the circular pool. Comprehensive facilities are available to ensure that conference and business meetings run smoothly. Themed activity breaks include racing weekends with visits to Newbury races and Lambourn stables, hot-air ballooning, or a 'Country Impressions' weekend of fishing and shooting. Among the nearby attractions are Oxford and Highclere Castle. **Directions:** Foley Lodge is in the village of Stockcross on the B4000, 1½ miles west of Newbury and close to the M4, A4 and A34. Price guide: Single £90; double/twin £110; suite from £140 (Room only).

HOLLINGTON HOUSE HOTEL

WOOLTON HILL, NR NEWBURY, BERKSHIRE RG15 9XR
TEL: 0635 255100 FAX: 0635 255075

Hollington House Hotel, England's newest luxury country house hotel, opened in July 1992. The Elizabethan-style house, built in 1904, is set in 14 acres of mature woodland gardens, adjacent to 250 acres of private parkland. Prior to returning to the UK after an absence of 32 years, John and Penny Guy created and owned Burnham Beeches Hotel, near Melbourne, which became Australia's first Relais et Châteaux hotel. No expense has been spared in their endeavours to achieve similar standards of excellence here. The 20 individually designed bedrooms are furnished with antiques and paintings and have sumptuous bathrooms. Elegant reception rooms, an oak-panelled, galleried hall and private boardroom are among the many splendid features of the house. Their chef serves a modern style of cooking with flair and innovation, based on traditional English and French cuisine. Outside, there is a solar-heated swimming pool, tennis court and croquet lawn, and the surrounding countryside offers opportunities for walking, shooting, hunting and horse-racing. Conference, wedding and weekend packages available. **Directions:** From A343 Newbury– Andover road, follow signs for Hollington Herb Garden. Price guide: Single from £80; deluxe double/twin from £110; junior suite from £165.

LAKESIDE HOTEL ON LAKE WINDERMERE

LAKESIDE, NEWBY BRIDGE, CUMBRIA LA12 8AT
TEL: 05395 31207 FAX: 05395 31699 TELEX: 65149

Lakeside Hotel has a unique location by the water's edge on the banks of Lake Windermere, with gardens running down to the lake shore. This peaceful setting offers beautiful views of the lake and surrounding mountains. A former coaching inn, the hotel has been fully refurbished to provide all the comforts and amenities expected by today's traveller. The traditional character has been retained, with original panelling and beams creating a comfortable atmosphere. Most of the en suite bedrooms overlook the lake, while the ground floor de luxe rooms have French windows and a patio that leads to the gardens and water's edge and there are two suites with Jacuzzis. Guests may dine in either of two restaurants, where extensive menus offer a wide selection of dishes, including Cumbrian specialities and a good choice for vegetarians. A fully equipped conference centre provides flexible accommodation that can be tailored to specific requirements. A varied range of leisure activities can be incorporated into the business programme. No visit is complete without a trip on the lake, by speedboat, motor launch or pleasure steamer, directly from the hotel's private moorings. Closed 2–9 January. **Directions:** From M6 junction 36 join A590 to Newby Bridge, turn right over bridge towards Hawkshead; hotel is 1 mile on right. Price guide: Single £70–£95; double/twin £110–£150; suite £150–£180.

LINDEN HALL HOTEL AND HEALTH SPA

LONGHORSLEY, MORPETH, NORTHUMBERLAND NE65 8XF
TEL: 0670 516611 FAX: 0670 788544

Ivy-clad, hidden away among 450 acres of fine park and woodland in mid-Northumberland, Linden Hall is a superb Georgian country house within easy reach of Newcastle-upon-Tyne. An impressive mile-long drive sweeps up to its main door where, upon entering, the visitor will discover a relaxed, dignified atmosphere enhanced by gracious marble hearths, antiques and period pieces. Refugees from urban stress will be delighted to find every fitness and relaxation requirement catered for at the health and beauty spa: beauty therapy treatments, fitness and steam room, swimming pool, sun terrace and solarium are all available on the premises. The 52 bedrooms are individually and elegantly furnished. Some rooms have four-poster beds; each has its own private bathroom, supplied with thoughtful extras. The Linden Pub serves informal drinks and the Dobson Restaurant, with panoramic views of the Northumberland coastline, serves delicious food, imaginatively prepared. Wedding receptions, banquets, dinner parties and business conferences can be held in comfort in any one of Linden Hall's conference and banqueting suites. **Directions:** From Newcastle take A1 north for 15 miles, then A697 toward Coldstream and Wooler. The hotel is 1 mile north of Longhorsley. Price guide: Single £85-£99.50; double/twin £115-£175; suite: £190-£210.

HOTEL BRISTOL

NARROWCLIFF, NEWQUAY, CORNWALL TR7 2PQ
TEL: 0637 875181 FAX: 0637 879347

The Hotel Bristol has been personally run since 1927 by four generations of the Young family, overlooking the superb golden sands of Tolcarne Beach and the rolling surf of the Atlantic Ocean. The hotel has been lovingly restored, combining the grand proportions of the 1930s with an array of modern comforts. The bedrooms, most with sea views, are spacious and well furnished, and five new suites have been added to provide an extra sense of luxury. An extensive seasonal menu is offered in the restaurant, with fresh local fish and seafood dishes being particular favourites, followed by delicious puddings smothered in Cornish cream. A conference hall provides for large meetings and parties. There is an indoor swimming pool, table-tennis and a full-sized billiard table; a sauna, solarium, beauty salon and hairdressing service are also available. Golf, bowling, riding, sailing and fishing can all be arranged locally. The spacious ballroom is the venue for regular live entertainment. The hotel is also an ideal base for exploring the rugged and unspoiled beauty of the Cornish coastline. Newquay offers a range of attractions, including the zoo and Trenance Leisure Park. **Directions:** The hotel is on the Tolcarne cliffs at the entrance to Newquay. Price guide: Single £45–£55; double/twin £75–£90.

PASSAGE HOUSE HOTEL

KINGSTEIGNTON, NEWTON ABBOT, DEVON TQ12 3QH
TEL: 0626 55515 FAX: 0626 63336

Overlooking the Teign Estuary, the Passage House Hotel has been designed to take advantage of the clear and panoramic views. Drawing inspiration from the natural beauty of the surrounding landscapes, the interior colour schemes are soft, muted shades of grey, blue and pink. The bedrooms provide every comfort, while the Penthouse rooms have a private terrace. The relaxing theme is continued in the reception rooms, with natural pale wood and mirrors enhancing the sense of space and light. Five-course table d'hôte and à la carte menus offer imaginatively prepared Devon recipes, using the freshest local fare, including Teign salmon, oysters and game. Throughout the hotel the service is extremely friendly and efficient. For active guests, there is a fully equipped leisure club, comprising indoor pool, hydro-spa, steam room, sauna, solarium and gymnasium. Sailing, water-skiing and golf are available locally. Racing fans should note that the hotel is located adjacent to Newton Abbot racecourse. The Devon heartland is rich in historical monuments, and the rugged scenery of Dartmoor is only minutes from the hotel. Special rate breaks available. **Directions:** Turn off A380 onto A381, follow signs to racecourse. Turn left at mini-roundabout; hotel is first left. Price guide: Single £59; double/twin £75.

REDWORTH HALL HOTEL & COUNTRY CLUB

REDWORTH, NR NEWTON AYCLIFFE, COUNTY DURHAM DL5 6NL
TEL: 0388 772442 FAX: 0388 775112

Redworth Hall is a 17th-century, tastefully converted manor house situated in 25 acres of parkland and woods, which contain many varieties of mature and rare trees. There are 100 en suite bedrooms, some of which are suitable for guests with disabilities and/or incorporate loop systems for the hard of hearing. The furnishings throughout range from antique to fine reproduction. The hotel's health club includes a heated indoor swimming pool, which has a hoist for guests with disabilities, a spa bath, sunbeds, steam bath, two squash courts, a sauna, snooker tables, a fully equipped gymnasium and all-weather tennis courts. There is an indoor play area and an outdoor adventure playground for children. Conference and day meetings can be held in the Surtees Suite (capacity 300), the Baronial Hall (150) and eight syndicate rooms (20 each). In the Baronial Hall, 'The Land of the Prince Bishops' medieval banquets are held throughout the year. Parking for up to 200 cars. Guests may savour innovative cuisine in the elegant Crozier Blue Room Restaurant, or alternatively dine in the airy Conservatory Restaurant, featuring a traditional carvery and contemporary à la carte menu. **Directions:** From A1(M) take A68 to Corbridge for 2 miles. At roundabout take A6072; hotel is 2 miles on left. Price guide: Single £93–£103; double/twin £115–£130; suite £150.

NORFOLK MEAD HOTEL

COLTISHALL, NORWICH, NORFOLK NR12 7DN
TEL: 0603 737531 FAX: 0603 737521

On the edge of the Norfolk Broads, standing in 12 acres of delightful gardens which dip gently down to a long frontage with the River Bure, is the Norfolk Mead Hotel. A Georgian manor house dating back to 1740, the hotel has undergone sensitive restoration to ensure that, while the original character has been preserved, all modern comforts have been provided. The style is refreshingly simple: a light, airy feel to the rooms has been achieved with chintz fabrics and pastel shades. The dining room, which overlooks the garden, offers a wide variety of dishes, beautifully presented and very reasonably priced. The 2-acre

fishing lake is well stocked with coarse fish, and rowing dinghies are available for 'messing about on the river'. For guests bringing their own boats, there is a slipway and off-river mooring which they may use. There are sailing and riding facilities nearby. Coltishall itself has a number of specialist antiques shops, while Anne Boleyn's home at Blickling Hall is well worth a visit. The unspoiled north Norfolk coastline and the cathedral city of Norwich are a short drive away. Closed at Christmas. **Directions:** Coltishall lies on the B1150 between Norwich and North Walsham. Price guide: Single £55; double/twin £75–£95.

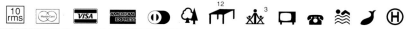

PARK FARM HOTEL & LEISURE

HETHERSETT, NORWICH, NORFOLK NR9 3DL
TEL: 0603 810264 FAX: 0603 812104

Park Farm Hotel occupies a tranquil and secluded location in beautifully landscaped grounds 5 miles south of Norwich. Luxuriously decorated bedrooms are equipped with every convenience. For those wishing to pamper themselves, executive rooms provide additional comforts, including four-poster beds and Jacuzzi baths. A superb leisure complex to suit all ages has been carefully incorporated alongside the original Georgian house. It includes a heated swimming pool, sauna, steam room, solarium, spa-bath, gymnasium and aerobics studio. There is a hard tennis court as well as croquet and putting on the front lawns. Up to 60 diners can be accommodated in the comfortable Georgian restaurant, renowned for its high standard of cuisine and service, with a wide selection of menus complemented by a fine choice of wines. The owners' close involvement in the day-to-day management of Park Farm ensures its continuing popularity. Five conference rooms, catering from 10 to 120 people, are ideal for functions. Weddings and conferences a speciality. The Norfolk Broads, coast and Norwich with its market, Castle Museum and cathedral are nearby. **Directions:** By road, just off A11 on B1172, 8 miles from Norwich Airport, 6 miles from Norwich rail station and 5 miles from Norwich bus station. There is a light aircraft landing strip and helipad in the grounds. Price guide: Single £70–£100; double/twin £80–£120; suite £130.

PETERSFIELD HOUSE HOTEL

LOWER STREET, HORNING, NR NORWICH, NORFOLK NR12 8PF
TEL: 0692 630741 FAX: 0692 630745

Petersfield House Hotel is set slightly back from the banks of one of the most attractive reaches of the River Bure. Surrounded by 2 acres of landscaped gardens, it occupies a choice position at the heart of Broadland. The charming location and private moorings are discreetly secluded, away from the crowds. However, Broadland has plenty of things to do: sailing can be enjoyed throughout the area and there are open regattas in the summer. Horning is midway between the medieval city of Norwich and the sweeping Norfolk coast. At the hotel, a regular Saturday night dinner-dance attracts many guests and non-residents. Varied fixed price and extensive à la carte menus are offered in the restaurant, where a comprehensive list of over 60 wines offers the ideal accompaniment to dinner. The bedrooms, many recently refurbished, are bright, comfortable and with en suite bathrooms. Most rooms overlook the well-tended gardens which feature a delightful lily pond, fountain and flintstone moon gate that links the gardens to a small woodland glade. The Petersfield is family-owned and managed, and guests can be assured of personal attention at all times. **Directions:** From Norwich ring road, take A1151 to Wroxham. At Hoveton take the A1062 to Horning; hotel is in centre of the village. Price guide: Single £60; double £75.

SPROWSTON MANOR HOTEL

WROXHAM ROAD, NORWICH, NORFOLK NR7 8RP
TEL: 0603 410871 FAX: 0603 423911

This imposing country house, built originally in 1559 and then largely rebuilt in the 19th century, stands at the end of an oak-lined driveway in 10 acres of parkland, just 3 miles from Norwich. The bedrooms, all en suite and some with four-posters, have views over the hotel's parkland setting and are spacious and comfortable. The hotel has two restaurants: in The Orangery, lavishly draped Gothic arched windows provide the perfect setting in which to enjoy the finest table d'hôte cuisine. The more traditional Manor Restaurant has been restored to classic splendour with mahogany columns, oil paintings and crystal chandeliers. The à la carte menu offers a good choice of dishes.

The large indoor swimming pool and leisure club, with spa bath, pool bar, fitness studio, steam rooms and sauna, are open to hotel residents free of charge. Solarium and beauty salon charged as taken. With its well-equipped conference rooms, the hotel is an excellent venue for social and business functions. Adjoining the hotel is the 18-hole Sprowston Park Golf Club, with floodlit driving range. The city of Norwich, Sandringham, the Norfolk Broads and the Norfolk coast are all within easy reach. **Directions:** From Norwich, take the Wroxham Road (A1151) and follow signs to Sprowston Park. Price guide: Single £75–£95; double/twin £75–£95 per person.

LANGAR HALL

LANGAR, NOTTINGHAMSHIRE NG13 9HG
TEL: 0949 60559 FAX: 0949 61045

Set in the Vale of Belvoir, Langar Hall is the family home of Imogen Skirving. Built in 1830, it combines the standards of good hotel-keeping with the hospitality and style of country house living. Having received a warm welcome, guests can enjoy the atmosphere of a private home that is much loved and cared for. The 12 en suite bedrooms are individually designed and comfortably appointed. The public rooms feature fine antique furnishings and most rooms afford beautiful views of the garden, park and moat. As well as a collection of paintings from the 19th and 20th centuries on display in the pillared dining room, exhibitions by contemporary artists are regularly held here.

Imogen and her chef collaborate to produce an excellent, varied menu of modern British food. For the perfect start to the weekend it is worth booking early for a special Friday night break which combines a leisurely dinner with an entertaining in-house theatre performance. Murder weekends and evenings are also popular. It is an ideal venue for small boardroom meetings. Dogs can be accommodated by arrangement. **Directions:** Langar is accessible via Bingham on the A52, or Cropwell Bishop from the A46 (both signposted). The house adjoins the church and is hidden behind it. Price guide: Single £60–£80; double/twin £85–£115.

HAMBLETON HALL

HAMBLETON, OAKHAM, RUTLAND, LEICESTERSHIRE LE15 8TH
TEL: 0572 756991 FAX: 0572 724721

Hambleton Hall enjoys a spectacular location overlooking Rutland Water and is surrounded by gardens and woodland. Since 1979, when proprietors Tim and Stefa Hart converted this comfortable Victorian hall into a country house hotel and restaurant, Hambleton Hall has become highly regarded by all the major guide books. An enthusiastic and professional staff ensure that the service is impeccable, yet friendly. Avoiding the catalogue approach to furnishing, the interiors are classically appointed, with a stylish collection of furniture, pictures and odds and ends that create an elegant and relaxing ambience. Displays of fresh flowers are always in evidence – an artistic combination of foliage from the hedgerows and blooms from Nine Elms market. In the summer, the menu is particularly strong in fresh fish and shellfish, accompanied by the best vegetables, herbs and salads of the season; in winter, a variety of game is featured, notably fallow venison, partridge, wild duck and woodcock. Supporting the cuisine is an award-winning wine list. Burghley House and Belton are nearby, as are the antiques shops of Oakham, Uppingham and Stamford. Hambleton Hall is a Relais et Châteaux member. **Directions:** In the village of Hambleton, signposted from the A606, 1 mile east of Oakham. Price guide: Single £95; double/twin £95–£250.

For hotel location, see maps on pages 458–464

LE MANOIR AUX QUAT' SAISONS

GREAT MILTON, OXFORD, OXFORDSHIRE OX44 7PD
TEL: 0844 278881 FAX: 0844 278847

Le Manoir, set in 27 acres of gardens and woodlands, is one of Britain's outstanding hotels. The manor's history can be traced back over 750 years and it has welcomed many famous visitors, including Oliver Cromwell. The restaurant, widely acknowledged as Britain's finest, overlooks the landscaped gardens. It has established a reputation for culinary excellence, with a varied menu offering seasonal specialities. The cuisine is largely the creation of internationally renowned chef-patron Raymond Blanc, whose dishes are close to perfection. The wine list, in keeping with the food, is extensive and imaginative. Bedrooms are beautifully appointed and the overall impression is of spaciousness and comfort, matched by faultless service. Indeed, a stay at Le Manoir is an unforgettable experience. Oxford, Woodstock and Blenheim are just a short drive away and there are several sporting facilities available in the vicinity. Le Manoir is a Relais et Châteaux member and won the Johansens Luxury Hotel Award for Excellence 1992. **Directions:** From London, travel on M40 and turn off at junction 7 (A329 to Wallingford). From Birmingham and the North, leave M40 at junction 8 and follow signs to Wallingford (A329). After about 1½ miles, take second turning on right, signposted Great Milton Manor. Price guide: Single £165; double/twin £165.

For hotel location, see maps on pages 458–464

STUDLEY PRIORY

HORTON-CUM-STUDLEY, OXFORD, OXFORDSHIRE OX33 1AZ
TEL: 0865 351203 FAX: 0865 351613

Studley Priory, its exterior little altered since Elizabethan days, is conveniently located only 7 miles from both the main London–Oxford road and the dreaming spires of Oxford. There is a sense of timeless seclusion in the setting of 13 acres of wooded grounds with their fine views of the Cotswolds, the Chilterns and the Vale of Aylesbury. The bedrooms range from single rooms to the Elizabeth Suite, which has a half-tester bed dating from around 1700. Cots are available for young children. The restaurant, offering the best of English and French cuisine, provides a seasonally changing menu created from fresh local produce and complemented by an extensive and well-balanced wine list. Good conference facilities are available and wedding parties and banquets can be accommodated. Studley Priory is ideally placed for visits to Blenheim Palace, the Manors of Waddesdon and Milton, Broughton Castle, the Great Western Museum of Railways and also horse-racing at Ascot, Newbury and Cheltenham. Clay pigeon shooting and many other activities can be arranged at the hotel and there are riding facilities nearby. **Directions:** Leave M40 at junction 8. The hotel is situated at the top of the hill in the village of Horton-cum-Studley. Price guide: Single £88; double/twin £98–£150; suite £210.

WESTON MANOR

WESTON-ON-THE-GREEN, OXFORDSHIRE OX6 8QL
TEL: 0869 50621 FAX: 0869 50901

Weston Manor has been the showpiece of the lovely village of Weston-on-the-Green, 6 miles from Oxford, since the 11th century. The ancestral home of the Earls of Abingdon and Berkshire, it was once the home of Henry VIII. The manor house, set in 13 acres of beautiful gardens and grounds, has been sympathetically restored to retain its fine architectural features and historic charm. Facilities include an outdoor heated swimming pool during the summer months and a well-kept croquet lawn. The en suite bedrooms offer guests every modern convenience. The Baronial Hall, with its magnificent vaulted ceiling and original, 15th-century linenfold oak panelling, is the setting for the best of traditional and modern English cooking. The conference facilities offer business clients professional support and expertise amid peaceful surroundings. Weston Manor is ideally placed for visits to Blenheim Palace, Woodstock, Broughton Castle, Waddesdon Manor, Claydon House and the University of Oxford. Weston Manor is part of the Hidden Hotels group. The hotel is 35 minutes' drive from the M25, 45 minutes from Birmingham and the NEC, and 2 hours' drive from Manchester. **Directions:** B430 2 miles from M40 junction 9, just off the new section of the A34. Price guide: Single £75; double/twin £95–£120.

THE SEAFOOD RESTAURANT

RIVERSIDE, PADSTOW, CORNWALL PL28 8BY
TEL: 0841 532485 FAX: 0841 533344

Owners Rick and Jill Stein describe this as 'a restaurant with some quite luxurious rooms above', and over the past 17 years they have built up an international reputation for the most innovative fish and shellfish cuisine. The restaurant stands on the estuary bank in the enchanting North Cornish fishing port of Padstow, along a stretch of coastline noted for its outstanding natural beauty. Opposite the restaurant is the quay where the lobster boats and trawlers unload their haul, so the fish comes straight from the sea into the kitchen and so to the table, with the unmistakable flavour and fine texture that only freshly caught fish can have. The menu is simple and unfussy, the décor bright and the atmosphere lively and informal, to complement the holiday mood. The bedrooms are comfortably furnished in the same style and most of them command fine views over the harbour; several of the bathrooms are richly panelled with mahogany. A full English or Continental breakfast is served in the restaurant – residents can watch the boats while they eat. Nearby are sandy beaches where water-sports – particularly surfing – can be enjoyed, clifftop walks and golf courses. Closed from just before Christmas to end of January. **Directions:** Opposite the quay in Padstow. Free car parking opposite. Price guide: Single £34–£85; double/twin £65–£105.

THE PAINSWICK HOTEL

KEMPS LANE, PAINSWICK, GLOUCESTERSHIRE GL6 6YB
TEL: 0452 812160 FAX: 0452 814059 TELEX: 43605

Crouched between the rolling Cotswold valleys is the village of Painswick, where medieval cottages lie hugger mugger with fine Georgian merchants' houses. Standing at the hub of this architectural gem is the Painswick Hotel, built in 1790 in Palladian style and formerly the home of wealthy village rectors. The hotel's 20 bedrooms have fine fabrics, soft furnishings, antiques and *objets d'art* which, combined with the luxury toiletries, baskets of fresh fruit, books and magazines provided, create the feeling of staying in a comfortable private house. A team of young chefs takes great pride in creating delicious, tempting cuisine. Much use is made of locally reared Cotswold meat, wild Severn salmon, game, Vale of Evesham vegetables and fresh shellfish from a seawater tank. Quiet meals, weddings, family occasions or extravagant dinners can be enjoyed in the private dining rooms, as can board meetings or senior management conferences. An interesting feature of the garden is the unusual grotto, designed by a past vicar to amplify his voice in practice for preaching sermons! Rich in heritage, the Cotswolds are also a happy hunting ground for antiques buyers. Dogs by arrangement. **Directions:** Painswick is on the A46 between Stroud and Cheltenham. The hotel is behind the church. Price guide: Single £65–£95; double/twin £95–£130.

TEMPLE SOWERBY HOUSE HOTEL

TEMPLE SOWERBY, PENRITH, CUMBRIA CA10 1RZ
TEL: 07683 61578 FAX: 07683 61958

Temple Sowerby House overlooks Cross Fell, the highest peak in the Pennines, noted for its spectacular ridge walk. This old Cumbrian farmhouse, formerly the principal residence of the village, is set in 2 acres of gardens and guests are assured of peace and tranquillity. Proprietors Peter and Anne McNamara offer a warm, hospitable and friendly family service upon which the hotel prides itself. There are two dining rooms – the panelled room with its cosy atmosphere and the Rose Room which overlooks the garden. Delicious, home-cooked dishes might include a starter of asparagus cheese tart with lemon cream, followed by venison steak in kumquat and orange liqueur, rounded off with a pudding of apricot and mango profiteroles in caramel sauce. Individually furnished bedrooms all have private bathrooms. Four of the rooms are situated in the Coach House, just yards from the main house, overlooking the cobbled yard and garden. During the winter, apéritifs are taken by the fireside, while in the summer, guests can sip drinks on the terrace and enjoy views across the fells. Lakes Ullswater and Derwentwater, the Borders, Scottish lowlands, Hadrian's Wall and Yorkshire Dales are within easy reach by car. **Directions:** Temple Sowerby lies on the A66, 5 miles from exit 40 of the M6, between Penrith and Appleby. Price guide: Single £45; double/twin £60–£66.

THE HAYCOCK

WANSFORD-IN-ENGLAND, PETERBOROUGH, CAMBRIDGESHIRE PE8 6JA
TEL: 0780 782223 FAX: 0780 783031 TELEX: 32710 HAYCOK G

The Haycock has been described as a hotel of great charm and character, where nothing is too much trouble for the staff. Overlooking the historic bridge that spans the River Nene, the hotel maintains much of its personality while providing a full range of contemporary comforts. An award-winning restoration programme has created an additional 28 bedrooms. All are colourful, individually designed and furnished to a high standard. A purpose-built ballroom is a popular venue for a wide range of events, from May Balls, wedding receptions, Christmas parties and casino nights to the East Anglian Wine Festival. The Business Centre has also made its mark; it is well equipped with all facilities and offers the flexibility to cater for meetings, car launches, product seminars and national conferences. Amid this activity the Tapestry and Orchard Rooms, bar and terrace all provide traditional hospitality combined with great charm – as does the restaurant, with its wine list attracting particular attention. The Haycock offers such a diverse range of amenities – including a new country pursuits programme – that every need can be accommodated. **Directions:** Clearly signposted on A1 a few miles south of Stamford, on A1/A47 intersection west of Peterborough. Price guide: Single £68–£85; double/twin £85–£98; suite £130.

ALSTON HALL

ALSTON, HOLBETON, NR PLYMOUTH, DEVON PL8 1HN
TEL: 075530 555 FAX: 075530 494

Alston Hall is an impressive Edwardian manor house set in over 4 acres of lightly wooded parkland with expansive views across the soft rolling hills to the sea beyond. Located in one of the most beautiful, unspoiled regions of South Devon, midway between Plymouth and Kingsbridge near to the village of Holbeton in the South Hams, Alston Hall provides peace and tranquillity – the perfect place in which to relax and unwind. The oak-panelled Great Hall, with its balustraded minstrels gallery and stained-glass windows, acts as an elegant drawing room in which to relax with a drink or after-dinner coffee. The Peony Room Restaurant draws inspiration from traditional English and French culinary styles. The menu, which caters for all tastes, makes good use of fresh seafood and local farm produce. Alston Hall invites guests to enjoy the good life. In addition to the 20 delightful bedrooms, spacious public rooms and conference facilities, guests can use the Leisure Club during their stay. Facilities include both indoor and outdoor swimming pools, sauna, solarium, croquet and two all-weather tennis courts. AA Red Rosette. **Directions:** From A379, follow signs to Holbeton/Alston. Continue for about 4 miles to Battisborough Cross. Take first right signed Alston Hall. Price guide: Single £70; double/twin £85–£95.

THE DUKE OF CORNWALL HOTEL

MILLBAY ROAD, PLYMOUTH, DEVON PL1 3LG
TEL: 0752 266256 FAX: 0752 600062

Regarded by John Betjeman as the finest example of Victorian architecture in Plymouth, The Duke of Cornwall Hotel is a listed building which has welcomed guests for more than 125 years. The interior has been sympathetically restored in keeping with the era in which it was built. The 69 en suite bedrooms, some with four-posters, offer every modern comfort, with colour TV, radio, tea and coffee making facilities, trouser press and hairdryer. The elegantly refurbished public rooms are beautifully proportioned. In the Devonshire Restaurant, imaginative dishes are cooked to order using only fresh produce. An extensive wine list featuring wines from around the world accompanies the menus. The hotel is an ideal conference venue, catering for up to 300 delegates. Directly opposite is the Pavilions Conference, Exhibition and Entertainments Centre with its leisure complex. Plymouth has a variety of attractions, all within easy reach of the hotel. The city stands at the mouth of the River Tamar, with magnificent scenery all around, while the rugged beauty of Dartmoor is within a short drive. There are several historic houses nearby, as well as golf, sailing and other water-sports. **Directions:** On arrival in Plymouth, follow signs for the Continental Ferry Port or for the Plymouth Pavilions. Price guide: Single £64.50; double/twin £74.50–£85; suite £115.

MOORLAND LINKS HOTEL AND RESTAURANT

YELVERTON, NR PLYMOUTH, DEVON PL20 6DA
TEL: 0822 852245 FAX: 0822 855004

Surrounded by 9 acres of well-kept grounds in a superlative setting, the Moorland Links Hotel is a dignified country retreat with spectacular views of remote and romantic moorland scenery. Over the past 10 years, since its takeover by Forestdale Hotels, the residence has been internally updated and extended with luxurious effect: stylishly decorated throughout with plush furniture, pastel walls and interesting prints, the Moorland guarantees a pleasurable and stress-free stay for business visitors and holidaymakers alike. All 30 en suite bedrooms have been individually designed and decorated with comfort in mind; little extras in each include trouser press, remote-control TV and hairdryers. After apéritifs in the lounge, guests may proceed to the restaurant overlooking the lawns, to sample first-class cooking prepared by chef Stephen Holmes, who can summon up everything from Japanese prawn dumplings to spicy vegetable tortillas, plus traditional dishes. Private and business functions are held in the various engagement rooms and marquee. The wildly beautiful Dartmoor National Park is a magnet for walkers; Plymouth, Buckland Abbey and golf are closeby. **Directions:** A38 Exeter-Plymouth; A386 towards Tavistock for about 5 miles on to open moorland. Hotel signposted 1 mile on. Price guide: Single £59.95–£65; double/twin £75.90–£85.90; suite £105–£120.

THE MANSION HOUSE

THAMES STREET, POOLE, DORSET BH15 1JN
TEL: 0202 685666   FAX: 0202 665709

A sophisticated Georgian town residence, The Mansion House Hotel is set in a prime location just off Poole's busy quayside, on a quiet cul-de-sac adjacent to St James's Church – offering its visitors a calm retreat from the hubbub. Restored by its owners, The Mansion House provides every modern luxury. From the entrance hall a splendid staircase sweeps up to an elegant hallway featuring statuesque marble pillars. Pretty bedrooms demonstrate the personal touch; all are distinctively styled and named after a famous Georgian or Victorian character. A drink and a crudité in the Canadian Redwood Cocktail Bar – a popular haunt of local business people – is the ideal prelude to a fine meal. Good, English gourmet cooking is served in the panelled Dining Club restaurant. Lunches and lighter meals are also offered downstairs in the less formal Members' Bar, where stone walls and stripped oak furniture create a rustic atmosphere. Two conference rooms provide good private meeting facilities. For the sports enthusiast, all manner of water activities are available, while local places of interest include the Isle of Purbeck and Corfe Castle. **Directions:** Thames Street runs between The Quay and West Street by Poole Bridge. Price guide: Single £75–£85; double/twin £95–£115.

THE LUGGER HOTEL

PORTLOE, NR TRURO, CORNWALL TR2 5RD
TEL: 0872 501322 FAX: 0872 501691

Welcome westward – that is the warm invitation from the Powell family at The Lugger Hotel, which affords comfort and fabulous views seaward. Built in the 17th century, and originally a smugglers' inn, it is situated at the very water's edge of a picturesque Cornish cove on the beautiful Roseland Peninsula. In the panelled restaurant the menu features English and Continental dishes accompanied by a wide choice of wines. Fresh, local seafood is a speciality, with crab and lobster particular favourites, followed by a choice of home-made puddings or a deliciously indulgent Cornish ice-cream parfait topped with clotted cream. Each of the charming, cottage-style bedrooms has en suite facilities and additional features in the hotel include a solarium and sauna. The Roseland Peninsula has a hectic calendar of local events throughout the year, such as sheepdog trials, horse shows and carnivals, and during April and May, the Cornish Garden Festival presents an opportunity to enjoy a spectacular variety of parks and gardens. Both freshwater and deep-sea fishing can be arranged – even shark fishing! ETB 4 Crowns Commended. Closed mid Nov to early February. **Directions:** A390 from Plymouth, B3287 from St Austell to Tregony, and A3078 to Portloe. Price guide (including dinner): Single £60–£65; double/twin £120–£136.

THE GIBBON BRIDGE

NR CHIPPING, FOREST OF BOWLAND, LANCASHIRE PR3 2TQ
TEL: 0995 61456 FAX: 0995 61277

You will be 'Forever the Richer' having stayed at The Gibbon Bridge, set in award winning grounds abounding with trees, wildlife and a tarn. Now in their 10th year, Janet Simpson and her enthusiastic, attentive team provide a welcome retreat well placed for exploring Lancashire's heritage in the Forest of Bowland; yet only 20 minutes from the M6 and London/Glasgow railway at Preston. The 8 bedrooms and 22 suites include four-poster, half-tester, and Gothic brass beds, Jacuzzi baths and the Staple Oak Suite's private garden. The restaurant is renowned for its traditional and imaginative dishes using fresh herbs and vegetables from the kitchen garden and complemented by the extensive wine list. Elegant, unintrusive conference facilities incorporate up-to-date audio-visual and communication equipment. Leisure facilities feature a health & beauty salon, steam room, and an all-weather tennis court. Numerous sporting activities can be arranged. **Directions:** M6 exit 32, A6 to Broughton, B5269 to Longridge, follow signs to Chipping. Turn right at 'T' junction in village – hotel one mile. Price guide: Single £60; double/twin £75; suite £95–£180.

CHEQUERS HOTEL

CHURCH PLACE, PULBOROUGH, WEST SUSSEX RH20 1AD
TEL: 0798 872486 FAX: 0798 872715

A warm welcome awaits visitors to this historic hotel built during the reign of Queen Anne. Situated on a sandstone ridge, Chequers has enviable views across the beautiful Arun Valley to the South Downs beyond. Mindful of the needs of today's traveller, owners John and Ann Searancke have ensured that modern amenities have been carefully blended with old-world charm and comforts. The hotel has recently enjoyed a programme of refurbishment further to enhance its facilities. All 11 bedrooms have private facilities, 10 of which are en suite. There are 4 bedrooms on the ground floor and 3 family rooms. Public rooms are comfortably furnished, with a log fire in the lounge on winter evenings. In warmer weather, guests may linger over an apéritif on the patio or in the secluded garden, before dining in the restaurant, where the traditional English menu changes daily. The hotel and the adjacent meadow, is set in the heart of the local conservation area which passes the old Roman Stane Street. It is conveniently placed for the Roman city of Chichester, Arundel Castle and the Sussex coast. Packed lunches can be provided. ETB 4 Crowns Highly Commended; 2 RAC Merit Awards. **Directions:** At the top of the hill, at the northern end of the village, the hotel is opposite the church. Price guide: Single £44.50–£49.50; double/twin £69–£79.

THE RICHMOND GATE HOTEL AND RESTAURANT

RICHMOND HILL, RICHMOND-UPON-THAMES, SURREY TW10 6RP
TEL: 081-940 0061 FAX: 081-332 0354

The Richmond Gate, with its walled Victorian garden and delightful period style conservatory, is set at the top of Richmond Hill overlooking the Royal Richmond Park and the Thames. Originally four 18th century houses, the transition from private homes to hotel occurred some 50 years ago. At its heart is Morshead House, built in 1831. This was previously owned by Miss Morshead, a popular society figure renowned for her dinner parties – initiating the tradition of fine dining and hospitality. The bedrooms are furnished in period style that offers comfort and convenience. The newly refurbished Gates Restaurant is certainly the centrepiece of the hotel. Chef, Michel Deville, has created a superb traditional British menu supported by a fine wine list – including a selection of vintages from the hotel's own prizewinning vineyard in Kent. A variety of function rooms, with experienced staff, ensure the success of weddings, meeting and private events. Local attractions include Hampton Court Palace, Syon Park House and Gardens, Kew Gardens and Chiswick House as well as the Royal Park and the River Thames. Weekend breaks, featuring entry to one of the attractions, are available from just £96 for two nights half board, £136 for three nights. **Directions:** Almost facing the Star & Garter Home at the top of Richmond Hill. Price guide: Single £65–£90; double/twin £80–£115.

THE CHASE HOTEL

GLOUCESTER ROAD, ROSS-ON-WYE, HEREFORDSHIRE HR9 5LH
TEL: 0989 763161 FAX: 0989 768330

The Chase Hotel, just a few minutes' walk from the centre of Ross-on-Wye, is a handsome Regency mansion standing in pleasant grounds. Careful restoration of the interiors has recaptured the elegance and craftsmanship of the past. After an apéritif in the Chase Bar, guests are ushered into the dining room where the tall windows and voluminous drapes make a striking impression. Chef Ken Tait favours a modern British approach to cooking, with a distinct Continental influence. He uses fine local produce, such as Herefordshire beef, game and fresh vegetables in combination, to create dishes that give an unexpected subtlety to traditional ingredients. When the bedrooms were renovated, great care was taken to preserve their original Georgian character: the effect was then softened with comfortable furniture and appealing fabrics. Unobtrusive, up-to-the-minute amenities have been provided in each room and en suite bathroom. The function suites can accommodate a host of events. The surrounding area offers an infinite variety of places to visit, including Hereford Cathedral, Symonds Yat, Monmouth and the Forest of Dean. **Directions:** From M50 exit 4 turn left at roundabout signposted Gloucester and right at first roundabout signposted 'Town Centre'. Hotel is ½ mile on left-hand side. Price guide: From £60–£100

PENGETHLEY MANOR

NR ROSS-ON-WYE, HEREFORDSHIRE HR9 6LL
TEL: 0989 87211 FAX: 0989 87238

Lord Chandos, a favourite of Mary Tudor, appears to have acquired Pengethley Estate around 1544, and it was here that he built the original Tudor house. Although much of the building was ravaged by fire in the 19th century, some parts survived – notably the oak panelling in the entrance hall – and it was rebuilt as a Georgian manor house in 1820. The en suite bedrooms reflect the traditional character of a former country squire's home. Drawing on the best produce that rural Herefordshire can offer, the menu includes Wye salmon, prime Hereford beef and tender Welsh lamb. Fresh herbs, grapes for future wine production and soft fruit are all grown within the manor boundaries. A complete vegetarian menu is also available. Throughout their stay at Pengethley, guests will find the service always attentive, but never intrusive. Chandos House is a purpose-built conference suite which can cater for business and social events. For leisure, there is a snooker room, a well-stocked trout lake, a 9-hole golf improvement course and an outdoor heated pool. Riding and hot-air ballooning can be arranged. The Wye Valley and Welsh border are not very far away and the Malvern Hills are nearby. **Directions:** Four miles from Ross-on-Wye, 10 miles from Hereford on the A49. Price guide: Single £70–£115; double/twin £100–£160.

PETERSTOW COUNTRY HOUSE

PETERSTOW, ROSS-ON-WYE, HEREFORDSHIRE HR9 6LB
TEL: 0989 62826 FAX: 0989 67264

In 1987, Jeanne and Mike Denne fell in love with a dilapidated rectory by the side of the church of St Peter and surrounded by 28 acres of woodland and pasture. With careful determination, they set about restoring the house into a delightful family home. By late 1989 they opened Peterstow Country House to share its beauty with guests from all over the world. Upon entering the spacious hall, with its flagstone floor and grand winding staircase, the relaxed atmosphere is immediately apparent. The nine bedrooms are Georgian or Victorian in style, ranging from half-tester suites to double- and twin-bedded rooms. Peterstow's centrepiece is its restaurant, where modern English cooking and French cuisine are served, accompanied by a list of choice European and New World wines. New flavour combinations are always being developed, using seasonal vegetables, fruit and organic produce. Specialist weekends are arranged throughout the year: for example, activity weekends, paint finishing courses, golf or clay pigeon shooting during the day will be followed by cocktails and a gourmet dinner in the evening. Accolades include an AA Rosette and ETB 4 Crowns Highly Commended. Good walking country, the Welsh Marches and the Wye Valley are nearby. **Directions:** On the A49, 3 miles north of Ross-on-Wye. Price guide: Single £38.50–£69; double/twin £60–£90.

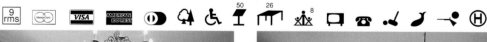

SYKESIDE COUNTRY HOUSE HOTEL

RAWTENSTALL ROAD END, HASLINGDEN, ROSSENDALE, LANCASHIRE BB4 6QE
TEL: 0706 831163 FAX: 0706 830090

Sykeside, the former home of Lancashire composer Alan Rawsthorne, is a Grade II listed mansion built in 1883, set in almost 3 acres of beautiful gardens. The building has been sensitively refurbished and retains many fine features, such as the magnificent leaded stained-glass entrance porch, yet offers its guests every modern comfort. A Victorian-style conservatory provides a relaxing morning coffee, afternoon tea or pre-dinner area. All the bedrooms have been furnished to a high standard. The executive en suite rooms offer an extra touch of luxury with Jacuzzi or sauna baths, while one of the bedrooms has been specially designed and equipped with the disabled guest in mind. The lounge, with extensive views over the front lawns, has a marble and brass fireplace with an open fire. Delicious English cooking, relying on fresh local produce, combined with a well-chosen wine list, is served in the relaxing atmosphere of the restaurant. Guide dogs only are accommodated. **Directions:** From south take M66 from M62. Go to end of M66, onto A56 link. Take first exit, A680 right at roundabout. Go right at lights, then left into hotel drive. From north, M65, take A56 link and A681 exit. Price guide: Single £57–£90; double/twin £72–£100.

EAST LODGE COUNTRY HOUSE HOTEL

ROWSLEY, MATLOCK, DERBYSHIRE DE4 2EF
TEL: 0629 734474 FAX: 0629 733949

East Lodge Country House Hotel was originally built as the East Lodge to Haddon Hall. Expanded to its present size in Victorian times, it was sold as a private home by the Duke of Rutland in the 1920s. It is now the home and business of John and Angela Beecroft, who offer a warm welcome to their visitors. Interior decor is in the country house style and each room has its own distinctive colour scheme. The lounge, dining room, licensed bar and spacious hall are comfortably appointed with furnishings of pine, mahogany and solid oak. The four-course menus are changed daily 'to avoid boring the residents', says John. In the 10 acres of attractive gardens, the wide variety of trees and shrubs offers an ever-changing display of foliage. East Lodge is only 4 miles from Matlock, with its spa baths, and 3 miles from Bakewell, home of the famous Bakewell Pudding. The hotel is ideally suited for touring all parts of Derbyshire, particularly Dovedale and the spectacular scenery of the Peak District, which is a must for walkers. A short drive away are Chatsworth House, the tramway museum at Crich, and Buxton with its theatre and Roman baths. ETB 4 Crowns Highly Commended. **Directions:** By the junction of the A6 and Beeley Road. Price guide: Single £50–£55; double/twin £75–£90.

BROOMHILL LODGE

RYE FOREIGN, RYE, EAST SUSSEX TN31 7UN
TEL: 0797 280421 FAX: 0797 280402

Imposing and ivy-bedecked, Broomhill is a dramatic mock-Jacobean construction towering above 3 green acres and dating back to the 1820s, when it was commissioned by a prominent local banker. Giving pleasing views over rolling East Sussex terrain, the hotel has been renovated with care by its new owners to offer a standard of accommodation as impressive as the architecture. Relaxed, informal, yet unerringly professional, the management and staff have quickly established an elegant, comfortable and warm place to stay. All 12 rooms are equipped with en suite bath or shower rooms and all modern conveniences. Four-poster bedrooms are available. A splendid new conservatory -style restaurant serves innovative cuisine expertly prepared. A fixed-price menu offers a wide choice (3-course lunch £14.50, dinner £18.50) and a typical menu might include calamares, then venison with cranberries followed by chocolate torte. Special tariffs apply for bookings of two or more nights. The hotel has a full-size snooker table and a sauna. Sports available locally include windsurfing, sailing, angling, clay-pigeon shooting and golf on the famous links nearby. Hastings, Winchelsea, Romney Marsh and Battle Abbey are all nearby and worth visiting. **Directions:** 1½ miles north of Rye on A268. Price guide: Single £42; double/twin £84.

BARNSDALE LODGE

THE AVENUE, RUTLAND WATER, NR OAKHAM, RUTLAND, LEICESTERSHIRE LE15 8AH
TEL: 0572 724678 FAX: 0572 724961

Situated in the heart of the ancient county of Rutland, amid unspoiled countryside, Barnsdale Lodge overlooks the rippling expanse of Rutland Water. Guests are invited to enjoy the hospitality offered by hosts The Hon. Thomas Noel and Robert Reid (who is also host at his sister hotel, Normanton Park). Although the hotel is set within a restored 17th-century farmhouse, the atmosphere and style are distinctively Edwardian. This theme pervades throughout, from the courteous service to the furnishings – including chaises-longues and plump, upholstered chairs. The 17 en suite bedrooms evoke a mood of relaxing comfort. Traditional English cooking and fine wines are served in the Edwardian-style dining rooms. A silver trolley of prime roast beef is always available. Elevenses, buttery lunches, afternoon teas and suppers may be enjoyed in the bar, drawing rooms or courtyard. There are three conference rooms and facilities for wedding receptions and parties. A baby-listening service and safe play area are provided for children. Belvoir and Rockingham Castles and Burghley House are nearby. Rutland Water offers a wide range of water sports, as well as being of interest to nature lovers including a Butterfly Farm. **Directions:** Barnsdale Lodge is situated on the A606 Oakham–Stamford road. Price guide: Single £49.50; double/twin £69.50; suite £79.50.

NORMANTON PARK HOTEL

NORMANTON PARK, RUTLAND WATER SOUTH SHORE, RUTLAND, LEICESTERSHIRE LE15 8RP
TEL: 0780 720315 FAX: 0780 721086

Situated alongside the famous 'submerged' church overlooking England's largest man-made reservoir, Normanton Park Hotel, sister hotel to Barnsdale Lodge, has been meticulously restored from its origins as the coach house to Normanton Park Hall. The Grade II listed hotel is set in 4 acres of grounds, which were landscaped in the 18th century and have one of the country's oldest Cedar of Lebanon trees. Many of the public rooms and bedrooms overlook the lake, which provides a wide range of leisure pursuits including fly and coarse fishing, boat hire, windsurfing, kite-flying, cycling, walking and birdwatching. The Sailing Bar offers a warm welcome, and a good variety of meals, snacks and drinks is served throughout the day. Designed on an orangery theme, the delightful restaurant offers a gourmet's choice of both à la carte and reasonably priced Sunday lunch table d'hôte menus. The reception hall, decorated with ancient bellows and a blazing log fire in cooler months, makes a relaxing lounge area for guests, diners and conference delegates alike. Many stately homes and National Trust properties are nearby and the A1 is easily accessible. Ample parking available. **Directions:** From the A1, take A606 at Stamford towards Oakham; turn along the south shore road towards Edith Weston. Price guide: Single £49.50; double/twin £69.50; suite/lake view £79.50.

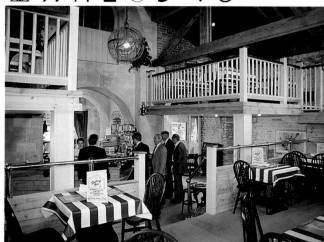

ST MICHAEL'S MANOR HOTEL

FISHPOOL STREET, ST ALBANS, HERTFORDSHIRE AL3 4RY
TEL: 0727 864444 FAX: 0727 848909

The medieval foundations of this imposing manor house still form part of its cellars. Originally constructed in 1512, the fascinating history of St Michael's Manor is reflected in the diversity of architectural features – from its William and Mary structure to the recent Victorian-style conservatory – which blend together surprisingly well. Part of the early Tudor building, the Oak Lounge, makes a good reception area for private functions, with its fine Elizabethan plastered ceiling displaying *fleur de lys* and stylised floral bosses. Chintz fabrics and pastel colours create a relaxing impression that complements the amiable welcome which has earned the hotel an RAC Merit Award for Hospitality. In the elegant, chandeliered restaurant an extensive menu offers international cooking with something to suit all tastes. The Bar Lounge leads to 5 acres of award-winning gardens, where the resident collection of wildfowl can be seen paddling about in the ornamental lake. The heart of Roman Verulamium is a 5-minute walk away, with its Roman Theatre and Hypocaust, museums, cathedral and antiques shops. Dogs accommodated by arrangement. **Directions:** Fishpool Street runs from the Abbey at the junction of the A5183 and A1081. The hotel is a few minutes walk from the town centre. Price guide from: Single £70; double/twin £80.

SOPWELL HOUSE HOTEL & COUNTRY CLUB

**COTTONMILL LANE, SOPWELL, ST ALBANS, HERTFORDSHIRE AL1 2HQ
TEL: 0727 864477 FAX: 0727 844741 TELEX: 927828 SOPWEL**

The opening of a country club and health spa has firmly established Sopwell House among the area's leading hotels. An elegant Georgian manor, it offers a high degree of comfort and service while retaining a country house ambience. Peacefully set in 12 acres, surrounded by unspoiled countryside, Sopwell House is 30 minutes from London and 22 miles from Heathrow – ideal for executives or for a leisure break. The individually furnished bedrooms are all well equipped and many have four-poster beds. Overlooking the gardens, the distinctive Magnolia conservatory restaurant boasting 2 AA Rosettes provides modern cuisine from an imaginative seasonal menu. State-of-the-art health and leisure facilities include an ozone-purified swimming pool, fitness centre and a full range of specialist beauty treatments. Bejerano's Brasserie serves light, healthy dishes, including vegetarian options. A purpose-built conference centre, incorporating an impressive ballroom, offers excellent provision for banquets, dances and corporate events. Woburn Abbey, Hatfield House and St Albans' Roman sites are nearby. The hotel is convenient for the M1, M10, M25 and local railway station (Thameslink is 20 minutes to King's Cross). Dogs by arrangement. Special breaks are available. **Directions:** Take A1081 from A414 Hatfield–St Albans road. Price guide: Single £68; double/twin £85.

THE GARRACK HOTEL

BURTHALLAN LANE, ST IVES, CORNWALL TR26 3AA
TEL: 0736 796199 FAX: 0736 798955

This intimate, family-run hotel, secluded and full of character, is set in 2 acres of gardens with views over Porthmeor Beach and beyond to St Ives Bay. Most of the bedrooms in the original house are in keeping with the style of the building. The additional rooms are modern in design and have wonderful sea views. All rooms have private bathrooms and baby-listening facilities. Superior rooms have either four-poster beds or whirlpool baths. A new ground-floor room has been fitted for guests with disabilities. Visitors return year after year to enjoy informal yet professional service, with the emphasis on good food and hospitality. The restaurant, overlooking the bay, specialises in seafood especially fresh lobsters. Over 70 labels from ten different regions are offered on the wine list. Relaxation is assured here – there are log fires, an indoor swim/spa pool, sauna, solarium and cardiovascular gym. Ample car parking is available. Porthmeor Beach, just below the hotel, is renowned for surfing. Riding, golf, bowls and sea-fishing can be enjoyed locally. St Ives, with its harbour, is famous for its association with English artists work now hanging in the St Ives Tate Gallery. Dogs by prior arrangement. **Directions:** A30–A3074–B3311–B3306. Go ¹/₂ mile, turn left at mini-roundabout, hotel is 300 yards further on. Price guide: Single £39.50–£55.50; double/twin £79–£111.

THE WELL HOUSE

ST KEYNE, LISKEARD, CORNWALL PL14 4RN
TEL: 0579 342001

The West Country is one corner of England where hospitality and friendliness are at their most spontaneous, and nowhere more so than at The Well House, just beyond the River Tamar. New arrivals are entranced by their first view of this lovely Victorian country manor. Its façade wrapped in rambling wisteria and jasmine trailers is just one of a continuous series of delights including top-quality service, modern luxury and impeccable standards of comfort and cooking. The hotel is professionally managed by proprietor Nick Wainford, whose attention to every smallest detail has earned his hotel numerous awards (among them the AA 2 Red Stars and 1989 Catey Newcomer of the Year). From the tastefully appointed bedrooms there are fine rural views, and each private bathroom offers luxurious bath linen, soaps and gels by Roger & Gallet. Continental breakfast is served in bed – or a traditional English breakfast may be taken in the dining room. Chef David Woolfall selects fresh, seasonal produce to create his superbly balanced and presented cuisine. Tennis, swimming and croquet are on offer, and the Cornish coastline offers matchless scenery and walking territory. **Directions:** Leave A38 at Liskeard, take A390 to town centre, bearing left on approach; pass Market Cross, take B3254 to St Keyne Well and hotel. Price guide: Single £60; double/twin £67.50–£105.

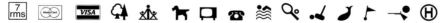

THE NARE HOTEL

CARNE BEACH, VERYAN-IN-ROSELAND, TRURO TR2 5PF
TEL: 0872 501279 FAX: 0872 501856

The Nare Hotel overlooks the fine sandy beach of Gerrans Bay, facing south, and is sheltered by The Nare and St Mawes headlands. In recent years extensive refurbishments have ensured comfort and elegance without detracting from the country house charm of this friendly hotel. All the bedrooms are within 100 yards of the sea, many with patios or balconies to take advantage of the outlook. While dining in the restaurant, with its colour scheme of soft yellow and green, guests can enjoy the sea views from three sides of the room. Local seafoods such as lobster, and delicious home-made puddings, served with Cornish cream, are specialities, complemented by an interesting range of wines.

Surrounded by sub-tropical gardens and National Trust land, the peaceful seclusion of The Nare is ideal for lazing or for exploring the coastline and villages of the glorious Roseland Peninsula. Facilities include concessionary golf, hotel boat and water sports. Guests arriving by train can be met by prior arrangement at Truro. Closed 6 January to mid-February. Helicopters can land on the premises. **Directions:** Follow road to St Mawes; 3 miles after Tregony Bridge turn left for Veryan. The hotel is 1 mile from Veryan. Price guide: Single £43–£103; double/twin £86–£176.

BOLT HEAD HOTEL

SOUTH SANDS, SALCOMBE, SOUTH DEVON TQ8 8LL
TEL: 0548 843751 FAX: 0548 843060

Bolt Head Hotel occupies a spectacular position overlooking Salcombe Estuary, where the mild climate ensures a lengthy holiday season. New improvements have ensured that guests can enjoy a fine range of modern comforts during their stay. The bedrooms are, furnished to a high standard, all with good en suite bathrooms, and there are family suites available complete with a baby-listening service. The light and sunny lounge is ideal for relaxation, or guests may sit on the adjoining sun terrace with sweeping views of the sea. In the air-conditioned restaurant special care is taken to cater for all tastes. Both English and French cuisine is prepared, with freshly caught fish, lobster and crab delivered daily, as well as wholesome farm produce and local cheeses. Palm trees surround the heated outdoor swimming pool on the sunny terrace. There is a good golf course within a few miles of the hotel. Riding, sailing and wind-surfing can be arranged. Sea fishing trips can be organised and private moorings are available. The hotel is directly adjacent to miles of magnificent National Trust cliff land at Bolt Head. Dogs by arrangement. Closed mid-November to mid-March. **Directions:** Please contact the hotel for directions. Price guide (including dinner): Single from £64; double/twin from £128; superior rooms available.

THE MARINE HOTEL

CLIFF ROAD, SALCOMBE, DEVON TQ8 8JH
TEL: 0548 844444 FAX: 0548 843109

The Marine Hotel occupies an enviable position right on the water's edge, with fine views across one of Devon's most beautiful estuaries. Salcombe is a charming little sailing resort with a mild climate and picturesque location, close to four golden beaches and many peaceful coves. Countless visitors have enjoyed the special atmosphere of The Marine Hotel during its distinguished 100-year history. Most of the hotel's 50 en suite bedrooms have a balcony overlooking the sea. The food served in the restaurant is superb, where the emphasis is naturally upon freshly caught fish and seafood. In addition to the spacious lounge, there is also a library, where guests are welcome to browse through the books.

Waves, the hotel's indoor relaxation and leisure complex, offers recreational facilities for the whole family, including a well-equipped fitness room, Jacuzzi, sauna, solarium and hair and beauty salon. Snacks and drinks are served in the poolside brasserie and also from the bar. As well as providing private moorings, the hotel can arrange sailing tuition, the hire of sailing boats, deep-sea fishing, water-skiing and wind-surfing. **Directions:** Leave A38 at Totnes, then follow A381 to Kingsbridge and thereafter to Salcombe as signposted. Price guide: Single £77–£87; double/twin £140–£160 including dinner.

SOAR MILL COVE HOTEL

SOAR MILL COVE, SOUTH DEVON TQ7 3DS
TEL: 0548 561566 FAX: 0548 561223

Soar Mill Cove Hotel is owned and loved by the Makepeace family who, with their dedicated staff, provide a special blend of friendly yet professional service. The hotel's spectacular setting is a flower-filled combe, facing its own sheltered sandy bay and entirely surrounded by hundreds of acres of dramatic National Trust coastland. While it is perhaps one of the last truly unspoiled corners of South Devon, Soar Mill Cove is only 15 miles from the motorway system (A38). All the bedrooms are at ground level, each with a private patio opening onto the gardens. Private guests will not find any conferences here. In winter, crackling log fires and efficient double glazing keep the cold weather at bay. Both the indoor and outdoor pools are spring-water fed, the former being maintained all year at a constant 88°F. Imaginative and innovative cuisine reflects the very best of the west of England; fresh crabs and lobster caught in the bay are a speciality. Soar Mill Cove is situated midway between Plymouth and Torquay and close to the old ports of Salcombe and Dartmouth. Dogs by prior arrangement. Closed 1 November to 12 February. **Directions:** A384 to Totnes, then A381 to Soar Mill Cove. Price guide: Single £40–£68; double/twin £80–£120.

HACKNESS GRANGE

NORTH YORK MOORS NATIONAL PARK, SCARBOROUGH YO13 0JW
TEL: 0723 882345 FAX: 0723 882391

Set in 11 acres of splendid parkland, Hackness Grange cuts a stylish architectural dash at the edge of the River Derwent. Built in 1849 and recently renovated, this 26 bedroom country house has been equipped with all the facilities the modern visitor requires, from the newly furnished bedrooms to the indoor swimming pool. As a result, the house and converted stable block offer luxury accommodation richly redolent of a former age. Outside, parking is available for 50 cars in the private car park. Upstairs, the management have ensured that the individually styled and centrally heated bedrooms contain every convenience, from en suite bathroom and mini-bar to child-listening and tea/coffee-making facilities. Attention to guests' needs continues downstairs, where in the restaurant a five-course luncheon menu prepared by chef Sheila Cowlson and eaten overlooking the lake is exceptional value at £10 (as is the dinner menu at £17.50). Before or after dining, guests can enjoy a drink in the large, comfortable adjacent bar. Activities on the premises include swimming, pitch & putt and tennis; there is also trout fishing on the Derwent. **Directions:** Take A64 York-Scarborough road until left turn to Seamer on to B1261, and through to East Ayton. Take 1st right to Hackness village and hotel is 4 mins on right. Price guide: Single £60; double/twin £90–£110; suite £110.

WREA HEAD COUNTRY HOTEL

SCALBY, NR SCARBOROUGH, NORTH YORKSHIRE YO13 0PB
TEL: 0723 378211 FAX: 0723 371780

Wrea Head Country Hotel is a Victorian country house built in 1881 and situated in 14 acres of wooded and landscaped grounds on the edge of the North York Moors National Park, yet only 3 miles from Scarborough. Scenic drives can take in the quaint coastal villages of Robin Hood's Bay, Runswick and Straithes, as well as historic Whitby. A little further afield are Castle Howard and the city of York with its famous Minster and city walls both steeped in history. The house is furnished with many antiques and paintings, and the interesting panelled main hall and inglenook fireplace, with blazing log fires in the winter, add a

cheerful welcome. All the bedrooms are individually decorated to the highest standard, most having delightful views of the garden. The elegant Russell Flint Restaurant serves the best traditional English fare using fresh local produce and only the finest ingredients, complemented by an interesting wine list. The hotel is open all year and offers weekend breaks throughout. **Directions:** Follow the A171 north from Scarborough, past the Scalby Village sign until hotel is signposted. Follow the road over the ford and then turn first left up the drive to the hotel. Price guide: Single from £49.50; double/twin from £89.

CHARNWOOD HOTEL

10 SHARROW LANE, SHEFFIELD, SOUTH YORKSHIRE S11 8AA
TEL: 0742 589411 FAX: 0742 555107

Charnwood Hotel is a listed Georgian mansion dating from 1780. Originally owned by John Henfrey, a Sheffield Master Cutler, it was later acquired by William Wilson of the Sharrow Snuff Mill. Restored in 1985, this elegant 'country house in town' is opulently furnished, with colourful flower arrangements set against attractive décor. The bedrooms are decorated in a country style, with the Woodford suite designed specifically to meet the requirements of a family. Two dining rooms are available for experiencing the gourmet skills of chef Stephen Hall. Dignified and formal, Henfrey's Restaurant offers cuisine to match the surroundings, while traditional French fare is the order of the day at Brasserie Leo. A library has been added recently and facilities are available to cater for large functions. While approximately a mile from Sheffield city centre, with its concert hall, theatre and hectic night-life, Charnwood Hotel is also convenient for the Peak District National Park. The spa town of Buxton and the historic Abbeydale Industrial Hamlet are nearby. **Directions:** Sharrow Lane is near the junction of London Road and Abbeydale Road, 1¹/₂ miles from city centre. Junction 33 from the M1. Price guide: Single £65–£75; double/twin £80–£90.

WHITLEY HALL HOTEL

ELLIOTT LANE, GRENOSIDE, SHEFFIELD, SOUTH YORKSHIRE S30 3NR
TEL: 0742 454444 FAX: 0742 455414

Carved into the keystone above one of the doors is the date 1584, denoting the start of Whitley Hall's lengthy country house tradition. In the bar is a priest hole, which may explain the local belief that a tunnel links the house with the nearby 11th-century church. In the 18th century, the house was a prestigious boarding school, with Gothic pointed arches and ornamentation added later by the Victorians. Attractively refurbished, Whitley Hall is now a fine hotel with all the amenities required by today's visitors. Stone walls and oak panelling combine with richly carpeted floors and handsome decoration. A sweeping split staircase leads to the spacious bedrooms, all of which have en suite bathrooms. Varied yet unpretentious cooking is served in generous portions and complemented by a wide choice from the wine cellar, including many clarets and ports. Peacocks strut around the 30-acre grounds, which encompass rolling lawns, mature woodland and two ornamental lakes. Banquets and private functions can be held in the conference suite. **Directions:** Leave M1 at junction 35, following signs for Chapeltown (A629), go down hill and turn left into Nether Lane. Go right at traffic lights, then left opposite Arundel pub, into Whitley Lane. At fork turn right into Elliott Lane; hotel is on left. Price guide: Single £58–£70; double/twin £74–£90.

CHARLTON HOUSE HOTEL

CHARLTON ROAD, SHEPTON MALLET, SOMERSET BA4 4PR
TEL: 0749 342008 FAX: 0749 346362

Charlton House Hotel, listed as being of architectural and historical interest, has been converted from a 17th-century manor house. The hotel stands in 6 acres of lawns, woods and gardens – including a trout lake. The grounds run alongside the River Sheppey and make a tranquil setting for waterside walks. Each bedroom varies in style, some decorated in pretty pastel shades, others quaint and beamed. In the coach house annexe, there is a spacious suite and a family room. Use of first-class ingredients is the key to good cooking, with an imaginative range of dishes offering something to suit every taste. Dusky pink decor is offset by crisp, white table linen, fresh flowers, silver and soft candlelight. The chandelier-hung conservatory extends the area of the restaurant, allowing guests to enjoy the gardens while dining in comfort. Leisure facilities include a tennis court and Swedish-style indoor swimming pool, and golf can be played at Mendip, 2 miles away. Wedding receptions, functions and conferences can be catered for. Special Bank Holiday breaks are available. Charlton House is a good base for exploring the Mendips, Wells, Cheddar Gorge, Glastonbury, Longleat, Bath and Bristol. **Directions:** The hotel is $1/2$ mile from the centre of Shepton Mallet on the A361 to Frome. Price guide: Single £75–£95; double/twin £95–£125.

ALBRIGHT HUSSEY HOTEL AND RESTAURANT

ELLESMERE ROAD, SHREWBURY, SHROPSHIRE SY4 3AF
TEL: 0939 290523/71 FAX: 0939 291143

A 16th century moated manor house, this Grade II listed building stands in 4 acres of grounds and landscaped gardens, fronted by a moat with Australian black swans and a variety of ducks. The house has been fully restored and refurbished by the present owners, Vera and Franco Subbiani, and their son Paul. Although only recently converted to a hotel, Albright Hussey has quickly gained a reputation for the high standard of accommodation. This is supported by the excellence of the cuisine and the restaurant is open for lunch and dinner every day. Exposed beams and leaded windows are features of the cosy public rooms. Antique furnishings enhance the atmosphere of luxury – one of the spacious bedrooms has a four-poster spa bath as well as a four-poster bed. All have en suite bathrooms. The hotel provides comfort and luxury under the personal supervision of the owners and has recently been awarded 2 AA Rosettes as well as the 3 RAC Merit Award for restaurant, comfort and hospitality. Local landmarks include the former Roman city of Viroconium and Ironbridge Gorge, birthplace of the Industrial Revolution. **Directions**: The hotel is $2^1/_2$ miles from Shrewsbury town centre on the A528 Ellesmere road. Price guide: Single £65–£80; double/twin £85–£100. Midweek & weekend breaks from £45 per person per night sharing a room.

HOTEL RIVIERA

THE ESPLANADE, SIDMOUTH, DEVON EX10 8AY
TEL: 0395 515201 FAX: 0395 577775 TELEX: 42551

The Hotel Riviera is splendidly positioned at the centre of Sidmouth's esplanade, overlooking Lyme Bay. With its mild climate and the beach just on the doorstep, the setting echoes the south of France and is the choice for the discerning visitor in search of relaxation. Handsome 18th- and 19th-century architecture abounds in Sidmouth, and behind the hotel's fine Regency facade lies an alluring blend of old-fashioned service and present-day comforts. Glorious sea views can be enjoyed from the recently redesigned and refurbished en suite bedrooms, all of which are fully appointed and have many thoughtful extras like hairdryers, fresh flowers and complimentary toiletries. Traditional Devonshire cream teas are served in the lounge or outside on the patio. In the elegant bay-view dining room, guests are offered a fine choice of dishes from the extensive menus, with local seafood and fish being a particular speciality. Arrangements can be made for guests to play golf, while bowls, croquet, tennis, putting, sailing and fishing are available nearby. Explore the many delightful villages of East Devon's rolling countryside and coastline, or just enjoy pottering around Sidmouth, with its enduring architectural charm. **Directions:** The hotel is situated at the centre of the esplanade. Price guide (including dinner): Single £58–£78; double/twin £106–£146; suite £138–£158.

THE GREAT HOUSE AT SONNING

SONNING-ON-THAMES, BERKSHIRE RG4 0UT
TEL: 0734 692277 FAX: 0734 441296

The original White Hart Hotel – the heart of the 4 acre Great House Estate – enjoys a splendid riverside setting. On this site a 13th century ale house stood beside the ferry crossing into Oxfordshire. The gardens lead towards the river, and there are private moorings for guests who visit by boat. The accommodation is distributed between the original hotel, the 16th century palace yard buildings, the 17th century Coach House and a 19th century house in the grounds, formerly the house of the playwright Sir Terence Rattigan. All of the rooms are comfortably appointed, several of them with four-poster beds, all with en suite facilities. The Moorings Restaurant overlooks an attractive terrace, with lawns and gardens leading towards the Thames. Table d'hôte and à la carte menus offer a good choice at both lunch and dinner. Barbecues are regularly held in the summer. Small meetings, receptions and private dinner parties can be held in the Sonning Suite, while for larger occasions there are five function rooms. **Directions:** Sonning is signposted off the A4, 4 miles east of Reading. The Great House is on the right-hand side just before the bridge. Price guide: Single £TBA; double/twin £TBA.

WHITECHAPEL MANOR

NR SOUTH MOLTON, NORTH DEVON EX36 3EG
TEL: 0769 573377 FAX: 0769 573797

A listed Grade I building, Whitechapel Manor is a quintessentially English country house set in terraced, walled gardens of lawn roses and clipped yew hedges, surrounded by meadow and woodland. The entrance hall has a perfect Jacobean carved oak screen; elsewhere, William and Mary plasterwork and panelling, complete with painted overmantles, have been preserved. Guests can relax in the Great Hall with an afternoon tea of home-made Devon honey cake or freshly baked scones with raspberry jam and clotted cream. The cuisine is modern French which has won wide international acclaim. Local game and seafood are served in season, as well as fresh local vegetables and Devon farmhouse cheeses. The large bedrooms which overlook the garden and the smaller, cosy rooms which look over woodland are thoughtfully appointed for comfort. A superb country breakfast, including herb sausages and home-made chutneys, gets the day off to a good start. Exmoor's leafy combes, wild moorland and dramatic coastline are nearby. **Directions:** From Bristol leave M5 at junction 27. Follow signs to Barnstaple and South Molton. After 30 minutes, at roundabout signposting South Molton, turn right to Whitechapel. Price guide: Single £65; double/twin from £98. Special breaks available all year round.

THE SWAN HOTEL

MARKET PLACE, SOUTHWOLD, SUFFOLK IP18 6EG
TEL: 0502 722186 FAX: 0502 724800

Rebuilt in 1659, following the disastrous fire which destroyed most of the town, The Swan was remodelled in the 1820s, with further additions in 1938. The hotel provides all modern services while retaining its classical dignity and elegance. Many of the antique-furnished bedrooms in the main hotel offer a glimpse of the sea, while the garden rooms – decorated in a more contemporary style – are clustered around the old bowling green. The drawing room has the traditional character of an English country house and the reading room upstairs is perfect for quiet relaxation or as the venue for a private party. The daily menu offers dishes ranging from simple, traditional fare through the

English classics to the chef's personal specialities. An exciting selection of wines is offered. Almost an island, Southwold is bounded on three sides by creeks, marshes and the River Blyth – making it a paradise for birdwatchers and nature lovers. Barely changed for a century, the town, built around a series of greens, has a fine church, lighthouse and golf course. Music lovers flock to nearby Snape Maltings for the Aldeburgh Festival. Winner of Country Living Gold Award for the Best Hotel 1993/94. **Directions:** Southwold is off the A12 Ipswich–Lowestoft road. The Swan Hotel is in the town centre. Price guide: Single £42–£75; double/twin £86–£140; suite £150.

THE GEORGE OF STAMFORD

ST MARTINS, STAMFORD, LINCOLNSHIRE PE9 2LB
TEL: 0780 55171 FAX: 0780 57070

The George, a beautiful, 16th century coaching inn, retains the charm of its long history, as guests will sense on entering the reception hall with its oak travelling chests and famous oil portrait of Daniel Lambert. Over the years, The George has welcomed a diverse clientele, ranging from highwaymen to kings – Charles I and William III were both visitors. At the heart of the hotel is the lounge, its natural stone walls, deep easy chairs and softly lit alcoves imparting a cosy, relaxed atmosphere, while the blazing log fire is sometimes used to toast muffins for tea! The flair of Julia Vannocci's interior design is evident in all the expertly styled, fully appointed bedrooms. Exotic plants, orchids, orange trees and coconut palms feature in the Garden Lounge, where a choice of hot dishes and an extensive cold buffet are offered. Guests may also dine alfresco in the courtyard garden. The more formal, oak-panelled restaurant serves imaginative but traditional English dishes and an award-winning list of wines. Superb facilities are incorporated in the Business Centre, converted from the former livery stables. Special weekend breaks available. **Directions:** Stamford is 1 mile from the A1 on the B1081. The George is in the town centre opposite the gallows sign. Car parking is behind the hotel. Price guide: Single from £60–£81; double/twin from £99–£108; suite £148–£154.

WHITEHALL

CHURCH END, BROXTED, ESSEX CM6 2BZ
TEL: 0279 850603 FAX: 0279 850385

Set on a hillside overlooking the delightful rolling countryside of north-west Essex is Whitehall, one of East Anglia's leading country hotels. While its origins can be traced back to 1151, the manor house is ostensibly Elizabethan in style, with recent additions tastefully incorporated. Traditional features such as beams, wide fireplaces and log fires blend well with the contemporary, fresh pastel shades and subtle-hued fabrics. A spectacular vaulted ceiling makes the dining room an impressive setting for dinner, with an à la carte or six-course set menu offering many delicious concoctions. For large private functions, the timbered Barn House is an ideal venue, where guests can enjoy the same high standards of cuisine found in the restaurant. Overlooked by the old village church is the attractive Elizabethan walled garden. Whitehall is only a short drive from London's newest international airport at Stansted and easily accessible from the M11 motorway, while Cambridge and Newmarket are only 30 minutes' drive away. **Directions:** Take junction 8 from the M11, follow Stansted Airport signs to new terminal building and then signs for Broxted. Price guide: Single £75–£95; double/twin £105–£155.

STAPLEFORD PARK

NR MELTON MOWBRAY, LEICESTERSHIRE LE14 2EF
TEL: 057284 522 FAX: 057284 651

Had Queen Victoria not forbidden Edward, Prince of Wales, to buy this grand stately home, it would now have been a country seat of the monarchy. However, her concern that he would be corrupted by the Leicestershire hunting set prevented the acquisition. Instead, Bob and Wendy Payton have turned it into a highly acclaimed hotel. The most important privately owned stately home to be converted into a hotel, it has won many awards for its relaxed, casual, yet sophisticated approach to hospitality. Set in woods and parkland, it is a splendid centre for country pursuits. Clay pigeon shooting, tennis, ballooning and fishing are all available on site, while equestrian sports, game shooting and golf can be organised locally. Leading contemporary designers have created 35 highly individual bedrooms and suites, each luxuriously appointed. Intricate carvings by Grinling Gibbons adorn the fine dining room, where diners may enjoy first-class modern cuisine. There are excellent facilities for large receptions and conferences. The area is rich in local heritage: places to visit include Chatsworth, Burghley House and Belvoir Castle. **Directions:** Stapleford is signposted from the B676 Melton Mowbray–Saxby road, and from the A606 Melton Mowbray– Oakham road. Price guide: Double/twin £125–£195; suite £200–£285.

LITTLE THAKEHAM

MERRYWOOD LANE, STORRINGTON, WEST SUSSEX RH20 3HE
TEL: 0903 744416 FAX: 0903 745022

One of the finest examples of a Lutyens Manor house, Little Thakeham is the home of Tim and Pauline Ratcliff who have carefully preserved the feeling of a family home. There are two suites and seven bedrooms all furnished in character with the house. The restaurant, also open to non-residents serves traditional English food based on local produce such as Southdown lamb and shellfish from the South Coast. The set menu changes daily and there is an excellent cellar. Outside the gardens were created in the style of Gertude Jekyll and recently have been the subject of restoration. There is a heated swimming pool and croquet lawn in the grounds. The famous country houses of Goodwood, Petworth and Arundel Castle are nearby, racing enthusiasts are well served with Goodwood, Fontwell and Plumpton Park. Antique collectors will not be disappointed, there are shops in Arundel, Petworth and Chichester. **Directions:** From Storrington, take B2139 to Thakeham. After about 1 mile turn right into Merrywood Lane. Hotel is 400 yards on left. Price guide: Single £95; double/twin £150; suite £200.

THE GRAPEVINE HOTEL

SHEEP STREET, STOW-ON-THE-WOLD, GLOUCESTERSHIRE GL54 1AU
TEL: 0451 830344 FAX: 0451 832278

Set in the pretty town of Stow-on-the-Wold, regarded by some as the jewel of the Cotswolds, The Grapevine Hotel has an atmosphere which makes visitors feel welcome and at ease immediately upon their arrival. The outstanding personal service provided by a loyal team of staff is perhaps the secret of the hotel's success – nothing is too much trouble for them. This, along with the exceptionally high standard of overall comfort and hospitality, earned The Grapevine the 1991 *Johansens Hotel Award for Excellence* – a well-deserved accolade. Beautifully furnished bedrooms, including six superb garden rooms across the courtyard, offer every facility. Visitors can linger over imaginative cuisine in the relaxed and informal atmosphere of the conservatory restaurant, with its unusual canopy of trailing vines. AA Rosette awarded for food. Whether travelling on business or for pleasure, The Grapevine is a hotel that guests will wish to return to again and again. The local landscape offers unlimited scope for exploration, whether to the numerous stone-cottaged villages tucked away in the Cotswolds or to the nearby towns of Cheltenham, Cirencester and Stratford-upon-Avon. Special bargain breaks are available. Closed over Christmas/New Year. Directions: Sheep Street is part of the A436 in the centre of Stow-on-the-Wold. Price guide: Single £66–£89; double/twin £92–£138.

For hotel location, see maps on pages 458–464

WYCK HILL HOUSE

WYCK HILL, STOW-ON-THE WOLD, GLOUCESTERSHIRE GL54 1HY
TEL: 0451 831936 FAX: 0451 832243

Wyck Hill House is a magnificent Cotswold mansion built in the early 1700s, reputedly on the site of an early Roman settlement. It is set in 100 acres of wooded and landscaped gardens, overlooking the beautiful Windrush Valley. The hotel has been tastefully restored and the bedrooms individually furnished to combine superb antiques with modern comforts. There is a suite with a large, antique four-poster bed, which is perfect for honeymoons and special occasions. The cedar-panelled library is an ideal room in which to read, if you wish, and to relax with morning coffee or afternoon tea. The award-winning restaurant provides the highest standards of modern British cuisine from the freshest seasonally available local produce. The menus are complemented by a superb wine list. Wyck Hill House hosts several special events, including opera, travel talks, cultural weekends and a variety of theme activities. The hotel is an ideal base from which to tour the university city of Oxford and the Georgian city of Bath. Cheltenham, Blenheim Palace and Stratford-upon-Avon are just a short drive away. Special price 2-night breaks are available. **Directions:** One-and-a-half miles south of Stow-on-the-Wold on the A424 Stow–Burford road. Price guide: Single £65; double/twin £95–£115; suite £170.

In association
with MasterCard
MasterCard

BILLESLEY MANOR

BILLESLEY, ALCESTER, NR STRATFORD-UPON-AVON, WARWICKSHIRE B49 6NF
TEL: 0789 400888 FAX: 0789 764145

Three miles from Stratford-upon-Avon, Billesley Manor is set in 11 acres of delightful grounds with a typically English topiary garden and ornamental pond. Ten centuries of history and tradition welcome guests to this magnificent house in the heart of Shakespeare country. Billesley Manor has been extensively refurbished in recent years, blending old and new to create a hotel that is impressive, spacious and comfortable. Guests may stay in a suite, an oak-panelled four-poster room or one of the well-appointed modern rooms – all have a large bathroom and a good range of facilities. The panelled Tudor and Stuart Restaurants have won awards for their fine food and service, including 3 AA Rosettes in 1993. Billesley Manor is particularly suitable for residential conferences and meetings, offering self-contained amenities and seclusion. In addition to the many on-site leisure activities, like the attractive sun patio, pool and mini-golf, weekend breaks can include hot-air ballooning, shooting and riding. The hotel is ideal for visiting the Royal Shakespeare Theatre, Warwick Castle and the Cotswolds. **Directions:** From M40 (exit 15) follow A46 towards Evesham and Alcester. Three miles beyond Stratford-upon-Avon turn right to Billesley. Price guide: Single £99; double/twin £135; suite £180.

ETTINGTON PARK HOTEL

ALDERMINSTER, STRATFORD-UPON-AVON, WARWICKSHIRE CV37 8BS
TEL: 0789 450123 FAX: 0789 450472

A Gothic mansion is nothing if not grand, and, positively exuding grandeur, Ettington Park rises majestically over 40 acres of Warwickshire parkland, surrounded by terraced gardens and carefully tended lawns, where guests can wander at will to admire the pastoral views. The interiors are breathtaking, their striking opulence enhanced by flowers, beautiful antiques and original paintings. Amid these elegant surroundings guests can relax totally, pampered with every luxury. On an appropriately grand scale, the 48 bedrooms and superb leisure complex, comprising an indoor heated swimming pool, spa bath, solarium and sauna, make this a perfect choice for the sybarite. The menu reflects the best of English and French cuisine, served with panache in the dining room, with its elegant 18th century rococo ceiling and 19th century carved family crests. The *bon viveur* will relish the fine wine list. Splendid conference facilities are available: the panelled Long Gallery and 14th century chapel are both unique venues. Riding is a speciality, while clay pigeon shooting, archery and fishing can also be arranged on the premises. **Directions:** From M40 junction 15 (Warwick) take A46 signposted Stratford, then left-hand turn onto A3400. Ettington is 5 miles south of Stratford-upon-Avon off the A3400. Price guide: Single £115; double/twin £145; suite £180.

SALFORD HALL HOTEL

ABBOT'S SALFORD, NR EVESHAM, WORCESTERSHIRE WR11 5UT
TEL: 0386 871300 FAX: 0386 871301

Between Shakespeare's Stratford-upon-Avon, the rolling Cotswolds and the Vale of Evesham is the Roman village of Abbot's Salford. Steeped in history, Salford Hall is a romantic Grade I listed manor house. It was built in the late 15th century as a retreat for the monks of Evesham Abbey and the imposing stone wing was added in the 17th century. Essentially unchanged, stained glass, a priest hole, exposed beams, oak panelling and original decorative murals are examples of the well-preserved features of the interior. The period charm is doubly appealing when combined with modern comforts, gracious furnishings, delicious food and an extensive selection of fine wines. Reflecting the past associations of the hall, the bedrooms are named after historical figures, and all are individually appointed with antique furniture and luxury fittings. Guests may relax in the Hawkesbury lounge, formerly a medieval kitchen, the conservatory lounge or on the sunny terrace within the walled flower garden. Facilities include snooker, a sauna and a solarium. Special weekends are arranged for hot-air ballooning, horse-racing, touring the Cotswolds, discovering Shakespeare and murder mysteries. Closed Christmas and New Year. **Directions:** Abbot's Salford is 8 miles west of Stratford-upon-Avon on A439 towards Vale of Evesham. Price guide: Single £TBA; double/twin £TBA.

WELCOMBE HOTEL AND GOLF COURSE

WARWICK ROAD, STRATFORD-UPON-AVON, WARWICKSHIRE CV37 0NR
TEL: 0789 295252 FAX: 0789 414666 TELEX: 31347

A splendid Jacobean-style mansion dating from 1869, the aptly named Welcombe Hotel stands in 157 acres of rolling parkland, much of which was owned by Shakespeare. One of the foremost hotels in the heart of England, it is also renowned for its fully equipped 18-hole golf course. The magnificent lounge, with its striking black marble fireplace, ornate floor-to-ceiling oak panelling, deep armchairs and bright flower arrangements, typifies the immaculate style of the hotel's interior. Exquisitely decorated, the restaurant is light, airy and spacious – an elegant setting overlooking the extensive formal gardens. The finest English and French cuisine is impeccably prepared, with particular emphasis on delicate sauces and presentation. A well-balanced wine list includes a wide selection of half bottles. Whether staying in one of the suites or bedrooms, guests will find the accommodation appointed to the highest standards. From small meetings to large-scale conferences, the Welcombe Hotel can offer amenities to ensure the event runs smoothly. The centre of Stratford-upon-Avon is only 1 mile away. Closed 28 December to 2 January. **Directions:** Five miles from exit 15 of M40, on A439. 1 mile from Stratford-upon-Avon. Price guide: Single £95; double/twin £135–£195; suite £350.

THE SWAN DIPLOMAT

STREATLEY-ON-THAMES, BERKSHIRE RG8 9HR
TEL: 0491 873737 FAX: 0491 872554

In a beautiful setting on the bank of the River Thames, this hotel offers visitors comfortable accommodation. All of the 46 bedrooms, many of which have balconies overlooking the river, are appointed to high standards with individual decor and furnishings. The elegant Riverside Restaurant, with its relaxing waterside views, serves fine food prepared by chef Christopher Cleveland, complemented by a good choice of wines. Moored alongside the restaurant is the Magdalen College Barge, which is a stylish venue for meetings and cocktail parties. Business guests are well catered for – the hotel has six attractive conference suites. Reflexions Leisure Club is superbly equipped for fitness programmes and beauty treatments, with facilities including a heated 'fit' pool; rowing boats and bicycles may be hired. Squash, riding and clay pigeon shooting can all be arranged. Special theme weekends are offered, such as bridge weekends and murder mystery breaks. Events in the locality include Henley Regatta, Ascot and Newbury races, while Windsor Castle, Blenheim Palace, Oxford and London's airports are easily accessible. **Directions:** The hotel lies just off the A329 in Streatley village. Price guide: Single £85–£99; double/twin £114–£125.

In association
with MasterCard **MasterCard**

PRIDE OF BRITAIN MEMBER

PLUMBER MANOR

STURMINSTER NEWTON, DORSET DT10 2AF
TEL: 0258 472507 FAX: 0258 473370

An imposing Jacobean building of local stone, occupying extensive gardens in the heart of Hardy's Dorset, Plumber Manor has been the home of the Prideaux-Brune family since the early 17th century. Leading off a charming gallery hung with family portraits are six very comfortable bedrooms. The conversion of a natural stone barn lying within the grounds, as well as the courtyard building, has added a further ten spacious bedrooms, some of which have window seats overlooking the garden and the Divelish stream. Three interconnecting dining rooms comprise the restaurant, where a good choice of imaginative, well-prepared dishes is presented, supported by a wide-ranging wine list. Chef

Brian Prideaux-Brune's culinary prowess has been recognised by all the major food guides. Lunches are served by arrangement. The Dorset landscape, with its picture-postcard villages such as Milton Abbas and Cerne Abbas, is close at hand, while the south coast villages of Lyme Regis and Lulworth are only 30 miles away. Riding can be arranged locally: however, if guests wish to bring their own horse to hack or hunt with local packs, the hotel provides free stabling on a do-it-yourself basis. Closed during February. **Directions:** Plumber Manor is 2 miles south west of Sturminster Newton on the Hazelbury Bryan road, off the A357. Price guide: Single £60–£75; double/twin £80–£120.

THE MILL HOTEL

WALNUT TREE LANE, SUDBURY, SUFFOLK CO10 6BD
TEL: 0787 375544 FAX: 0787 373027

Standing on the banks of the River Stour, overlooking the mill pond and water meadows, is The Mill Hotel. It is situated on the edge of the Suffolk market town of Sudbury, birthplace of the portrait artist Thomas Gainsborough whose house nearby is now a museum and art gallery. Extensive refurbishments have recently been completed and the hotel is ideally suited to serve both as a holiday and business centre. Much of the original character has been retained and defines the style of the reception rooms and the comfortable, en suite bedrooms. The Meadow Bar, with its two open log fires blazing in winter, is divided from the restaurant by the 102-year-old mill wheel – an attractive centrepiece which still works today. Dating back 300 years, the millhouse is the setting for the restaurant which offers a comprehensive choice of dishes. Two well-equipped meeting rooms can accommodate medium-sized conferences. The Mill Hotel has fishing rights to an adjacent stretch of the River Stour – renowned for its good coarse fishing. Suffolk's unspoiled medieval villages, old churches and coastline are easily accessible. Sudbury is central to the whole of East Anglia and Stansted Airport is within easy reach. A small fee is levied for accommodating dogs. **Directions:** Sudbury is on the A134 Colchester–Bury St Edmunds road. Price guide: Single £50–£55; double/twin £78–£98 Room only.

THE CASTLE at TAUNTON

CASTLE GREEN, TAUNTON, SOMERSET TA1 1NF
TEL: 0823 272671 FAX: 0823 336066

The Castle at Taunton is steeped in the drama and romance of English history. Once a Norman fortress, it has been welcoming travellers to the town since the 12th century. In 1685, the Duke of Monmouth's officers were heard "roystering at the Castle Inn" before their defeat by the forces of King James II at Sedgemoor. Shortly after, Judge Jeffreys held his Bloody Assize in the Great Hall of the Castle. Today the Castle lives at peace with its turbulent past but preserves the atmosphere of its ancient tradition. The Chapman family have been running the hotel for over 40 years and in that time it has acquired a worldwide reputation for the warmth of its hospitality. Laurels in Michelin, Egon Ronay and the AA also testify to the excellence of the Castle's kitchen and cellar. Located in the heart of England's beautiful West Country, the Castle is the ideal base for exploring a region rich in history. This is the land of King Arthur, King Alfred, Lorna Doone's Exmoor and the monastic foundations of Glastonbury and Wells. Roman and Regency Bath, Longleat House and the majestic gardens of Stourhead. All this and much more can be discovered within easy driving distance of Taunton. **Directions:** Exit M5 junction 25 and follow signs for town centre. Price guide: Single £65; double/twin £89.90–£99.90.

THE MOUNT SOMERSET

LOWER HENLADE, TAUNTON, SOMERSET TA3 5NB
TEL: 0823 442500 FAX: 0823 442900

Standing high on the slopes of the Blackdown Hills, this elegant Regency house, designed by an Italian architect, has seen little alteration over the years. All the main rooms retain their period features, the restoration work having been carried out in sympathy with the character of the building. Service is professional and the atmosphere relaxing. The spacious public rooms include the beautifully furnished Regency drawing room, where guests may take tea, coffee or an apéritif. Refreshments are also served on the West Terrace. There are 11 luxurious bedrooms, all with their own bathrooms and most with views over the Somerset countryside. The restaurant specialises in modern English cuisine, with the emphasis on fresh produce, home-grown where possible – preserves are home-made, bread and croissants baked daily on the premises, and the hotel has its own smokehouse. Outside there are acres of lovely grounds in which to stroll and relax. Golf, riding, horse racing and even hot-air ballooning are all available nearby. **Directions:** From junction 25 on M5 take A358 Ilminster road. Go through Henlade village, then turn right towards Stoke St Mary before dual carriageway. After 1/2 mile turn left at T-junction. Hotel is 150 yards on right. Price guide: Single £90-£110; double/twin £110-£200.

BUCKATREE HALL HOTEL

THE WREKIN, WELLINGTON, TELFORD, SHROPSHIRE TF6 5AL
TEL: 0952 641821 FAX: 0952 247540

Buckatree Hall Hotel, with its own lake and gardens, stands in woodland at the foot of Wrekin Hill in Telford, yet is only 1 mile from the M54. Many of the 62 bedrooms have balconies overlooking either the lake or the gardens, and some rooms have hi-tech waterbeds. All bedrooms are en suite with baths and aqua-lisa showers, garment presses, refreshment facilities, hairdryers, 5-channel satellite TV and direct-dial telephone. Additional features in the Lady Executive Rooms include ironing facilities, double locks and door spy-holes. The 2-storey Penthouse Suite has a whirlpool bath. The Terrace Restaurant, with its pink decorative theme, offers a wide choice of English and Continental dishes. The adjoining Fountain Room can be booked for private dinner parties. Enjoy a drink by the carved fireplace in the split-level Liszt Lounge or the Brahms Bar. The Champagne conference and banqueting suite is ideal for dinner dances or weddings. Foremost among the local attractions is the famous open-air museum at Ironbridge. As the birthplace of England's industrial revolution in the early 18th century, Ironbridge is a world heritage site. Weekend breaks from £96 p.p. for 2 nights dinner, bed and breakfast. **Directions:** Leave M54 at junction 7, turn left and first left again. Mid-week Price guide: Single £69–£72; double/twin £79–£82; suite £92–£125.

MADELEY COURT

TELFORD, SHROPSHIRE TF7 5DW
TEL: 0952 680068 FAX: 0952 684275

Madeley is a veritable gem of a residence. Its characteristic manor-house façade stands virtually unaltered since the 16th century when it was mainly built, while its interior has been recently expertly rejuvenated – with respect for its history – to provide accommodation suitable for all who stay there whether for pleasure or on business. Furnishings have been judiciously selected to enrich Madeley's period appeal: scatterings of fine fabrics, handsome antique pieces and elaborate fittings all accentuate the historic atmosphere, and ensure that every guest leaves with an indelible impression. Bedrooms, whether located in the old part of the Court or in the newer wing, are quiet and full of character; some offer whirlpool baths and views over the lake, all are en suite. At the heart of Madeley is the original 13th century hall, where the restaurant, awarded a coverted AA Rosette is now located, serving inventive food of the highest standard, with a wine list to match. The Brasserie offers a more informal setting. Business meetings and private functions are happily catered for in the three rooms available. Places of interest nearby include: Ironbridge Gorge, Shrewsbury, Powys Castle and Weston Park. Directions: 4 miles from junction 4 of M54; follow A442 then B4373. Signposted Dawley then Madeley. Price guide: Single £78; double/twin £98; suite £110.

CALCOT MANOR

NR TETBURY, GLOUCESTERSHIRE GL8 8YJ
TEL: 0666 890391 FAX: 0666 890394

This delightful old manor house, built of Cotswold stone, offers guests peace and tranquillity amidst acres of rolling countryside. Calcot Manor is situated in the southern Cotswolds close to the historic town of Tetbury. The building itself dates back to the 15th century and was a farmhouse until 1983. Its beautiful stone barns and stables include one of the oldest tithe barns in England, built in 1300 by the Cistercian monks from Kingswood Abbey. These buildings form a quadrangle and the sight of the stone glistening in the dawn or glowing in the dusk is quite a spectacle. Calcot achieves the rare combination of professional service and cheerful hospitality without any hint of over formality. The atmosphere is one of peaceful relaxation. All the cottage style rooms are beautifully appointed as are the public rooms. A recent addition is a charming cottage providing four family suites with the sitting areas convertable into children's bedrooms equipped with toys, baby listening system and a safe outdoor play area. At the heart of Calcot Manor is its star rated restaurant. Its superb cooking is one of the main reasons for Calcot Manor's enduring popularity and dinner is very much the focus of a memorable stay. **Directions:** From Tetbury, take the A4135 signposted Dursley; Calcot is on the right after 3½ miles. Price guide: Single £75–£100; double/twin £87–£125; family suites £125.

THE CLOSE HOTEL

LONG STREET, TETBURY, GLOUCESTERSHIRE GL8 8AQ
TEL: 0666 502272 FAX: 0666 504401

This distinguished hotel, built over 400 years ago by a successful wool merchant, has been refurbished to the highest standard. The hotel is renowned for its luxury accommodation, and the individually styled bedrooms are truly elegant. All have superb hand-painted decorated bathrooms. The cuisine, served in the charming Adam dining room, is delicious and imaginative and there is an exceptional choice of wines from an extensive cellar. The restaurant overlooks a walled garden, and you can enjoy a quiet drink on the terrace. The hotel now has a purpose-built suite for top-level management meetings and corporate entertainment for up to 24 people. Many first-class sporting facilities are within easy reach, including racing at Cheltenham, motor racing at Castle Combe, golf, riding and hot-air ballooning. The hotel is also an ideal base to explore the Cotswolds. **Directions:** The hotel is on the main street of Tetbury, called Long Street. Tetbury is on the A433, 20 minutes from Bath. Price guide: Single £85; double/twin £95.

THE SNOOTY FOX

MARKET PLACE, TETBURY, GLOUCESTERSHIRE GL8 8DD
TEL: 0666 502436 FAX: 0666 503479

This old coaching inn dating back to the 16th century is situated right in the heart of the quaint old market town of Tetbury. Built of mellow-hued stone, The Snooty Fox dominates the historic market place in the town centre. The hotel has been imaginatively refurbished by Hatton Hotels, who have carefully maintained its considerable period character. There are 12 individual and charming en suite bedrooms which are decorated to convey the warm and homely atmosphere of a bygone age. All are well appointed and comfortable. The public areas and restaurant are steeped in history and are full of antiques and fine oil paintings. The prints that decorate the walls depict the hotel's long association with the famous Beaufort Hunt. The Snooty Fox is still a favourite meeting place for the local community of this famous Royal town. Guests can choose either to dine in the elegant restaurant or to enjoy the splendid food from the bar menu. Facilities for executive meetings can be arranged and the hotel is the perfect destination for business and short breaks throughout the year. **Directions:** The Snooty Fox is situated in the centre of Tetbury facing the market square. Price guide: Single £60; double/twin £80–£95.

CORSE LAWN HOUSE HOTEL

CORSE LAWN, NR TEWKESBURY, GLOUCESTERSHIRE GL19 4LZ
TEL: 0452 780479/771 FAX: 0452 780840

Though only 6 miles from the M5 and M50, Corse Lawn is a completely unspoiled, typically English hamlet in a peaceful Gloucestershire backwater. The hotel, an elegant Queen Anne listed building set back from the village green, stands in 12 acres of gardens and grounds, and still displays the charm of its historic pedigree. Visitors can be assured of the highest standards of service and cooking: Baba Hine is famous for the dishes she produces, while Denis Hine, of the Hine Cognac family, is in charge of the wine cellar. The service here, now in the hands of son Giles, is faultlessly efficient, friendly and personal. As well as the renowned restaurant, there are three comfortable drawing rooms, a large lounge bar, a private dining-cum-conference room for up to 45 persons, and a similar, smaller room for up to 20. A tennis court, heated swimming pool and croquet lawn adjoin the hotel, and most sports and leisure activities can be arranged. Corse Lawn is ideal for exploring the Cotswolds, Malverns and Forest of Dean. **Directions:** Take A438 towards Ledbury for 4 miles, turn left onto the B4211 by Corse Lawn sign, go 1 mile and the hotel is on the right. Price guide: Single £70–£80; double/twin £90–£100.

PUCKRUP HALL

PUCKRUP, TEWKESBURY, GLOUCESTERSHIRE GL20 6EL
TEL: 0684 296200 FAX: 0684 850788

Lying between the Cotswolds and the Malvern Hills, set in 140 acres of parkland, Puckrup Hall Hotel and Golf Club is the country house hotel of the future. The original Regency manor house, built in the 19th century has been tastefully extended to combine the most up-to-date hotel and leisure facilities with a taste of England's past. A superb 18 hole golf course complements the extensive hotel amenities and leisure facilities, which include aerobics studio, swimming pool, spa bath, solarium, steam room and gymnasium all supported by a beauty treatment centre and créche. Each of the 84 luxury en suite bedrooms are furnished to the highest standard with all the facilities expected of a country house hotel. The 12 conference and private dining rooms can accommodate between 10 and 200 people for a meeting, presentation or dinner dance. An extensive range of cuisine is available from fine dining in the à la carte restaurant, a variable and exciting choice of menu in "Balharries Brasserie" or a light snack in the coffee lounge. A refreshing drink in the "Limes" bar makes a welcome finish to a game of golf or as somewhere to relax and enjoy a game of snooker. **Directions:** Puckrup Hall is 2 miles north of Tewkesbury on the A38, and only a few minutes from junction 8 of the M5, via junction 1 of the M50. Price guide: Single/double/twin £69.50–£95; suite £110–£125.

THE LIVERMEAD HOUSE

SEA FRONT, TORQUAY, DEVON TQ2 6QJ
TEL: 0803 294361 FAX: 0803 200758

Built in 1820, The Livermead House was one of many early Victorian villas which sprang up to form the new resort town of Torquay. Personally owned and run by the Rew family, the house has been enlarged and extensively modernised since then. The superb seafront location offers panoramic views over Torbay. There are 65 comfortable bedrooms: all have en suite bathrooms and superior rooms have sea views. The well-appointed lounges and public rooms conjure up the elegance and grandeur of a former era. In the elegant silver-service restaurant, traditional menus with a wide choice of dishes are complemented by a carefully compiled wine list. The hotel grounds are extensive and offer many facilities, including a swimming pool and tennis court. Squash and snooker are also available as well as a sauna, solarium and small gym. Business conferences and other functions such as wedding receptions and banquets are catered for. The Livermead House is within easy reach of many of the south-west's places of natural and historic interest, such as Dartmoor and the South Hams, and the cathedral city of Exeter. There are several National Trust properties in the area. **Directions:** From Exeter, take the A380 to Torquay, then follow the signs for the seafront. Price guide: Single £32–£58; double/twin £64–£116.

ORESTONE MANOR

ROCKHOUSE LANE, MAIDENCOMBE, TORQUAY, DEVON TQ1 4SX
TEL: 0803 328098 FAX: 0803 328336

Orestone Manor is an elegant Georgian building set in 2 acres of secluded gardens in an area of outstanding natural beauty overlooking Lyme Bay. Run by resident proprietors Mike and Gill Staples, the atmosphere is relaxed. The Manor has been substantially extended since it was built in the early-19th century. The main lounge has a unique pitch-pine ceiling and some bedrooms feature gables. Each en suite bedroom has a colour TV, direct-dial telephone and tea- and coffee-making facilities. All are individually furnished to a high standard, many with splendid sea views. Not only has Orestone Manor been ranked highest in Torbay by the AA (1993), it is also the only

hotel there to be awarded 2 AA Rosettes (1993) for cuisine. An imaginative menu always includes a vegetarian option. To accommodate its growing reputation for fine food, the non-smoking restaurant has been extended and fully refurbished. There are five golf courses within 7 miles, as well as sailing, horse-riding, tennis, squash and sailboarding. Dartmoor and many National Trust properties are nearby. Phone for details of special low-season breaks and Christmas packages. **Directions:** About 3 miles north of Torquay on B3199 (formerly A379) coast road towards Teignmouth. Price guide: Single £35–£75; double/twin £80–£130.

THE OSBORNE

MEADFOOT BEACH, TORQUAY, DEVON TQ1 2LL
TEL: 0803 213311 FAX: 0803 296788

The combination of Mediterranean chic and the much-loved Devon landscape has a special appeal which is reflected at The Osborne. The hotel is the centrepiece of an elegant Regency crescent in Meadfoot, a quiet location within easy reach of the centre of Torquay. Known as a 'country house by the sea', the hotel offers the friendly ambience of a country home complemented by the superior standards of service and comfort expected of a hotel on the English Riviera. Most of the 23 bedrooms have breathtaking views and are decorated in pastel shades. Overlooking the sea, Langtry's acclaimed award winning restaurant provides fine English cooking and tempting regional specialities, while Raffles Bar/Brasserie has a menu available throughout the day. Guests may relax in the attractive 5-acre gardens and make use of indoor and outdoor swimming pools, tennis court and putting green – all without leaving the grounds. Sailing, archery, clay pigeon shooting and golf can be arranged. Devon is a county of infinite variety, with its fine coastline, bustling harbours, tranquil lanes, sleepy villages and the wilds of Dartmoor. The Osborne is ideally placed to enjoy all these attractions. **Directions:** The hotel is in Meadfoot, to the east of Torquay. Price guide: Single £43–£67; double/twin £86–£134; suite £134–£158.

THE SWAN HOTEL

THE PANTILES, ROYAL TUNBRIDGE WELLS, KENT TN2 5TD
TEL: 0892 541450/527590 FAX: 0892 541465

At the heart of The Pantiles, the historic centre of Royal Tunbridge Wells, lies The Swan Hotel, an immaculately refurbished 17th-century town house. The medicinal waters, discovered by Lord North in 1606, can still be sampled in this ancient part of the town. Tunbridge Wells rapidly became a destination for the aristocracy and for 26 years the social scene was dominated by Beau Nash, the rake of 18th-century society. Bright and cheerful, The Swan is a pleasant town-centre hotel, with friendly staff offering attentive service. Each of the bedrooms is individually designed and appointed. Guests may choose to dine in the elegant Kendals Restaurant or enjoy a light meal or snack in the lively Pantiles Bar. The Kendal Suite, named after the original 17th-century coffee house which stood on the site, is an ideal setting for a banquet or an informal party. The adjacent boardroom and four additional syndicate rooms are well equipped with private facilities and a range of audio-visual aids to cater for executive meetings. **Directions:** Tunbridge Wells is on the A26. The hotel fronts the junction with Major Yorks Road, and has alternative (pedestrian) access direct from The Pantiles. Price guide: Single £64.60; double/twin £80–£110.

LORDS OF THE MANOR HOTEL

UPPER SLAUGHTER, NR BOURTON-ON-THE-WATER, CHELTENHAM, GLOUCESTERSHIRE GL54 2JD
TEL: 04518 20243 FAX: 04518 20696 TELEX: 83147 VIA OR G

Situated in the heart of the Cotswolds, on the outskirts of one of England's most unspoiled and picturesque villages, stands the Lords of the Manor Hotel. Built in the 17th century of honeyed Cotswold stone, the house enjoys splendid views over the surrounding meadows, stream and parkland. For generations the house was the home of the Witts family, who historically had been rectors of the parish. It is from these origins that the hotel derives its distinctive name. Charming, walled gardens provide a secluded retreat at the rear of the house. Each bedroom bears the maiden name of one of the ladies who married into the Witts family: each room is individually and imaginatively decorated with traditional chintz and period furniture. The reception rooms are magnificently furnished with fine antiques, paintings, traditional fabrics and masses of fresh flowers. Log fires blaze in cold weather. The heart of this English country house is its dining room, where truly memorable dishes are created from the finest local ingredients. Nearby are Blenheim Palace, Warwick Castle, the Roman antiquities at Bath and Shakespeare country. **Directions:** Upper Slaughter is 2 miles west of the A429 between Stow-on-the-Wold and Bourton-on-the-Water. Price guide: Single £85; double/twin £105–£185.

THE LAKE ISLE

16 HIGH STREET EAST, UPPINGHAM, RUTLAND, LEICESTERSHIRE LE15 9PZ
TEL: 0572 822951 FAX: 0572 822951

This small, personally run restaurant and town house hotel is situated in the centre of the pretty market town of Uppingham, dominated by its famous public school and only 6 miles from Rutland Water. The entrance to the 18th-century hotel is approached via a quiet yard hung with flowering baskets. There is also a small walled garden where guests can relax. In the bedrooms, all named after the wine regions of France, guests will find fresh fruit, home-made biscuits and a decanter of sherry. All en suite, the bedrooms vary in size and character from the first floor rooms with large windows to the cosy, cottage style of those on the second floor. Under the guidance of chef-patron David

Whitfield, the restaurant is gaining a considerable reputation, offering small, weekly-changing menus using fresh ingredients from as far afield as Paris and Scotland. The extensive list of over 300 wines ranges from regional labels to clarets from the '50s and '60s, about 100 of which are half bottles. Many special events are held throughout the year such as the 'Wine Dinners', enabling guests to appreciate fully this unique cellar. Burghley House, Rockingham Castle and Belvoir Castle are within a short drive. **Directions:** The hotel is on the High Street and is reached on foot via Reeves Yard and by car via Queen Street. Price guide: Single £45–£50; double/twin £60–£70; suite £70–£80.

THE SPRINGS HOTEL

NORTH STOKE, WALLINGFORD, OXFORDSHIRE OX10 6BE
TEL: 0491 836687 FAX: 0491 836877

In the heart of the Thames Valley The Springs Hotel is equally perfect for a quiet holiday or a secluded business meeting. Sheltered in 30 acres of wooded grounds, the hotel overlooks the spring-fed lake from which it takes its name. In the panelled reception lounge, traditional furnishings and a glowing log fire complete a friendly atmosphere. The bedrooms offer every comfort, down to ice cubes and bathrobes. Two of the suites have Jacuzzi baths and many of the bedrooms have balconies for summer relaxation. Overlooking the gardens is the oak-panelled cocktail bar. The candle-lit restaurant faces the floodlit lake, the habitat of swans, wild ducks and kingfishers. International cooking of a high quality defines the menu and guests may dine *alfresco* during the warmer months. Leisure facilities include the swimming pool, a putting green, sauna bath and touring bicycles. Oxford and Windsor are nearby and the hotel is convenient for many sporting events, including racing at Newbury and Ascot and the Royal Henley Regatta. **Directions:** From the M40, take exit 6 onto the B4009, through Watlington to Benson; turn left onto A4074 towards Reading at roundabout. After 1/2 mile go right back onto B4009. The hotel is 1/2 mile further, on the right-hand side. Price guide: Single £80; double/twin £110–£140; suite £150.

HANBURY MANOR

WARE, HERTFORDSHIRE SG12 0SD
TEL: 0920 487722 FAX: 0920 487692

A quite exceptional hotel, Hanbury Manor combines palatial grandeur with the most up-to-date amenities. Designed in 1890 in a Jacobean style, the many impressive features include elaborately moulded ceilings, carved wood panelling, leaded windows, chandeliers, portraits and huge tapestries. These create an elegant and comfortable environment. The three dining rooms vary in style from the formal Zodiac Restaurant to the relaxed Vardon Restaurant. All the cuisine is under the inspired guidance of Albert Roux of Le Gavroche. The health club includes an indoor swimming pool, Jacuzzi, squash courts, fully equipped gymnasium, crèche, sauna and steam baths. Professional treatments include herbal wraps, aromatherapy, mineral baths and massage, while specialists can advise on a personal fitness programme. There is an 18-hole golf course *par excellence* designed by Jack Nicklaus II. Outdoor pursuits which can be arranged include shooting, archery, horse-riding and hot-air ballooning. Ten rooms offer versatile business meetings facilities, including fax, photocopying, secretarial services and full professional support. New award of 4 AA Rosettes for cuisine 1991 & 1992. Stansted Airport is 16 miles away. **Directions:** On the A10 25 miles north of London and 32 miles south of Cambridge. Price guide: Single: £98–£200; double/twin £108–£210; suite £225–£350.

               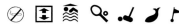   

Exclusive HOTELS UK · SMALL LUXURY HOTELS OF THE WORLD

BISHOPSTROW HOUSE

BISHOPSTROW, WARMINSTER, WILTSHIRE BA12 9HH
TEL: 0985 212312 FAX: 0985 216769 TELEX: 444829

Built by John Pinch of Bath in 1817, Bishopstrow House offers its visitors the grace of a Georgian mansion together with all the benefits of modern facilities. Displayed in the finely proportioned public rooms is an impressive collection of antiques, 19th-century oil paintings and Persian carpets. Bedrooms feature canopied beds, festoon draperies and in some cases, private safes. Grandly furnished suites are available with luxurious bathrooms which have large, circular baths fitted with Jacuzzi whirlpools. The emphasis is on light, imaginative cooking in the modern style, with English and French dishes prepared by Chris Suter, winner of the 1990 Young Chef of the Year Award. A wide selection of carefully chosen wine is kept in the vaulted cellars. Guests may use the sauna and solaria, an indoor floodlit tennis court, perhaps followed by a leisurely swim in the heated pool, which is housed in an elegant, marble-pillared room. There is access to fishing within the hotel grounds, on the banks of the River Wylye. Longleat House, the beautiful gardens and arboretum of Stourhead, Bath and Shaftesbury are close at hand. Less than 1 mile away is the West Wiltshire Golf Course. **Directions:** Bishopstrow House is just south-east of Warminster on the B3414. Price guide: Single £75; double/twin £110–£175.

THE GLEBE AT BARFORD

CHURCH STREET, BARFORD, WARWICKSHIRE CV35 8BS
TEL: 0926 624218 FAX: 0926 624625

The Glebe at Barford was built in the 1820s as a rectory to the Church of St Peter, which stands next to the hotel gardens. Each of the 41 bedrooms has been tastefully decorated with soft, pastel fabrics and features either a coronet-style bed, a tented ceiling or a four-poster bed. The en suite bathrooms are all attractively finished with golden fittings and Italian marble floors. Pre-dinner drinks can be enjoyed in either the spacious lounge bar or the stylish cocktail bar with its flowing drapes and elegant seating. Overlooking the croquet lawn, the Cedars Conservatory Restaurant is the setting for dinner, where a wide selection of imaginatively prepared English and continental dishes are available. The showpiece of Glades Leisure Club is the beautiful heated swimming pool, fitted with the latest hydro swim jets and incorporating a massage spa pool. In addition, guests have free use of the sauna, steam room and trimnasium. The Bentley Suite can be tailored to suit conferences, weddings and dinners, while the Directors Suite is a smaller executive-style meeting room. Stratford-upon-Avon, Leamington Spa, Warwick Castle, Birmingham and the Cotswolds are all accessible from The Glebe. **Directions:** From junction 15, M40 take A429 to Barford. At roundabout turn into Church Street. Price guide: Single £60–£90; double/twin £95–£140.

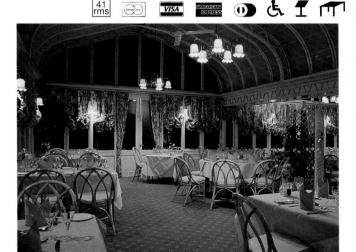

WOOD HALL

LINTON, NR WETHERBY, WEST YORKSHIRE LS22 4JA
TEL: 0937 587271 FAX: 0937 584353

Built of stone from the estate, Wood Hall is an elegant Georgian house overlooking the River Wharfe. Its grounds, over 100 acres in all, are approached along a private drive that winds through a sweep of parkland. The sumptuously furnished drawing room and the oak-panelled bar, with its gentleman's club atmosphere, lead off the grand entrance hall. Superb floral displays, gleaming chandeliers and immaculately designed interiors hint at the careful attention that has been lavished on Wood Hall. Gastronomes will relish the excellent à la carte menu, which combines contemporary Anglo-French style with attractive presentation. The mile-long private stretch of the Wharfe offers up trout and barbel to the keen angler, while miles of walks and jogging paths encompass the estate. There is a leisure club including a swimming pool, spa bath, steam room, gymnasium, solarium and treatment salon. York, Harrogate, Leeds, the Dales and Harewood House are only a short distance away. **Directions:** From Wetherby, take the A661 towards Harrogate. Take turning for Sicklinghall and Linton, then left for Linton and Wood Hall. Turn right opposite the Windmill public house; hotel is 1½ miles further on. Price guide: Single £83–£128; double/twin £93–£143; suite £250.

OATLANDS PARK HOTEL

146 OATLANDS DRIVE, WEYBRIDGE, SURREY KT13 9HB
TEL: 0932 847242 FAX: 0932 842252

Records of the Oatlands estate show that Elizabeth I and the Stuart kings spent time in residence in the original buildings. The present mansion dates from the late-18th century and became a hotel in 1856: famous guests included Émile Zola, Anthony Trollope and Edward Lear. The hotel stands in acres of parkland overlooking Broadwater Lake, with easy access to Heathrow, Gatwick and central London. Although it caters for the modern traveller, the hotel's historic character is evident throughout. The accommodation ranges from superior rooms to large de luxe rooms and suites. The elegant, high-ceilinged Broadwater Restaurant is the setting for creative à la carte menus with dishes to suit all tastes. A traditional roast is served every Sunday lunchtime. The professional conference team, five meeting rooms and up-to-date facilities make Oatlands Park a popular function venue. Theme evenings, such as Henry VIII banquets, are a speciality. Many sporting and leisure activities can be arranged, including golf, archery and shooting. Reductions at weekends. **Directions:** From M25 junction 11, follow signs to Weybridge. Follow A317 through Weybridge High Street into Monument Hill to mini-roundabout. Turn left into Oatlands Drive; hotel is 50 yards on left. Price guide: Single £97–£108; double/twin £128–£143; suite £153. Special Break rate: Single £45; double/twin £60–£70.

WOODHAYES COUNTRY HOUSE HOTEL

WHIMPLE, NR EXETER, DEVON EX5 2TD
TEL: 0404 822237

Woodhayes is a small, Georgian country-house hotel on the edge of the village of Whimple, in the heart of Somerset's cider-apple country. Although it's off the beaten track, the A30 and M5 are easily accessible. The house stands in 4 acres of park-like gardens, where guests can enjoy a game of croquet or tennis or simply sit and gaze at the backdrop of apple orchard and grazing sheep. A fine portico leads to the large, bright entrance hall. There are two comfortably furnished lounges, one of them leading to the snug bar. The 10 spacious bedrooms are all en suite with direct dial telephones, TV and radio. French doors lead onto a sun terrace from the beautifully proportioned dining room, which has a well-deserved reputation for fine food and has received accolades from all the major food guides. The menus change daily and feature dishes using only fresh seasonal produce. There are some lovely walks to be found down the nearby narrow lanes and the Devon coast is 11 miles away. The city of Exeter, which dates from Roman times, is just a few miles away, and Exmoor and Dartmoor National Parks, with their abundance of wildlife and dramatic scenery, are within easy reach. **Directions:** Whimple lies just off the A30, between Exeter and Honiton. Price guide: Single £70; double/twin £90.

THE OLD HOUSE

THE SQUARE, WICKHAM, HAMPSHIRE PO17 5JG
TEL: 0329 833049 FAX: 0329 833672

This beautiful early Georgian house is a Grade II listed building, preserved for its architectural interest – as is the whole of the village square in Wickham on which it stands. Perhaps the first house in the village to be built in the new style of the early 18th century, it originally belonged to one Roger Clare, a local carrier. Under the personal supervision of Richard and Annie Skipwith, owners since 1970, the hotel has been skilfully converted from a private residence and has many interesting features. Fine panelling in the more typically Georgian rooms on the ground and first floors contrasts with the beamed bedrooms on the upper floors, once the servants' quarters. All rooms have period furniture, much of which is original. The bar has a provincial French atmosphere and is open only to restaurant and hotel guests. The restaurant, occupying what was once the outhouse and stables, specialises in French regional cuisine and the fixed-price menu, using only ingredients of the highest quality, changes weekly. The cellar offers an interesting selection of wines. A private dining room is available for up to 14 people or for small meetings. Winchester, the New Forest and Portsmouth are all within easy reach. **Directions:** The hotel is situated on the market square in Wickham, at the junction of B2177 and A32, 3 miles from the M27. Price guide: Single from £70; double/twin £85.

     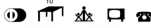

WILLINGTON HALL HOTEL

WILLINGTON, NR TARPORLEY, CHESHIRE CW6 0NB
TEL: 0829 52321 FAX: 0829 52596

Built by Cheshire landowner Charles Tomkinson, Willington Hall was converted into a hotel by one of his descendants in 1977. Set in 17 acres of woods and parkland, the hotel affords wonderful views across the Cheshire countryside towards the Welsh mountains. There are both formally landscaped and 'wild' gardens, which create a beautiful backdrop for the handsome architectural proportions of the house. The hotel is a comfortable and friendly retreat for those seeking peace and seclusion. Under the personal supervision of Ross Pigot, Willington Hall has acquired a good reputation with local people for its extensive bar meals and à la carte restaurant, along with friendly and attentive service. The menus offer traditional English cooking, with dishes such as roast duckling with black cherry sauce. It is an ideal location for visiting the Roman city of Chester, Tatton Park, Beeston Castle and Oulton Park racetrack. North Wales is easily accessible from Willington Hall. The hotel is closed on Christmas Day. **Directions:** Take the A51 from Tarporley to Chester and turn right at the Bull's Head public house at Clotton. Willington Hall Hotel is 1 mile ahead on the left. Price guide: Single £44–£54; double/twin £80.

THE STANNEYLANDS HOTEL

STANNEYLANDS ROAD, WILMSLOW, CHESHIRE SK9 4EY
TEL: 0625 525225 FAX: 0625 537282

Privately owned and managed by Gordon Beech, Stanneylands is a handsome country house set in several acres of impressive gardens with an unusual collection of trees and shrubs. Some of the bedrooms offer lovely views over the gardens while others overlook the undulating Cheshire countryside. A sense of quiet luxury prevails in the reception rooms, where classical decor and comfortable furnishings create a relaxing ambience. In the restaurant, contemporary English cooking is prepared to a very high standard both in terms of composition and presentation, while live occasional music adds to the atmosphere. In addition, a private oak-panelled dining room can accommodate up to 50 people, while a larger suite is available for conferences and personal celebrations. The Stanneylands Hotel is conveniently located for tours of the rolling Cheshire plain or the more rugged Peak District, as well as the bustling market towns and notable industrial heritage of the area. Special corporate and weekend rates are available. **Directions:** Three miles from Manchester International Airport, Stanneylands is on a minor road which runs from the B5166 at Styal to the A34 between Wilmslow and Handforth. Bear right on this road to find the hotel just after crossing the River Dean. Price guide: Single £79; double/twin £85–£120.

BEECHLEAS

17 POOLE ROAD, WIMBORNE MINSTER, DORSET BH21 1QA
TEL: 0202 841684

Beechleas is a delightful, Georgian Grade II listed town house hotel. It has been carefully restored and offers guests comfortable accommodation in tastefully furnished bedrooms of quality, all with en suite bathrooms. The hotel has been awarded two Red Stars by the AA and one Rosette for its restaurant. It takes just 5 minutes to walk into the centre of Wimborne Minster, a historic market town with an interesting twin-tower church built on the site of its old Saxon Abbey during the 12th and 13th centuries. There are many National Trust properties within easy reach, including Kingston Lacy House, Badbury Rings and Corfe Castle. Why not take a sailing trip from Poole Harbour, go fishing or play golf on one of the many local courses, perhaps take a drive to Bournemouth on the south coast (just 20 minutes away), then explore the New Forest or the Purbeck Hills? Return to dine in the charming restaurant, cosy in winter with open log fires, light and airy in the summer, overlooking the pretty walled garden. The menu is carefully prepared daily, using only the finest fresh ingredients and, where possible, natural produce, backed up by a fine wine list. Closed January. **Directions:** From London, take M3, M27 and then B3073 to Wimborne. Price guide: Single £60–£80; double/twin £80–£100.

LAINSTON HOUSE HOTEL

SPARSHOLT, WINCHESTER, HAMPSHIRE SO21 2LT
TEL: 0962 863588 FAX: 0962 72672

The fascinating history of Lainston House is well documented, some of its land having been recorded in the *Domesday Book* of 1087. Set in 63 acres of superb downland countryside, this graceful William and Mary country house has been sympathetically restored to create a beautiful hotel. From the individually designed bedrooms to the main reception rooms, elegant and comfortable furnishings are the hallmark of Lainston House. Freshly prepared food, attentive service and views over the lawn make the restaurant one of the most popular in Hampshire. Facilities are available for small meetings in the Mountbatten Room or larger functions in the recently converted 17th century Dawley Barn. The charming grounds hold many surprises – a 12th century chapel, reputedly haunted by the legendary Elizabeth Chudleigh, an 18th century herb garden and a dovecote. Historic Winchester is only 2 miles south, while Romsey Abbey, Salisbury and the New Forest are a short drive away. Other local activities include riding, country walking and good trout fishing on the River Test at nearby Stockbridge. **Directions:** Lainston House is well signposted off the A272 Winchester–Stockbridge road, at Sparsholt 2½ miles from Winchester. Price guide: Single from £95; double/twin from £120–£225; suite from £240

        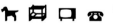

GILPIN LODGE

CROOK ROAD, WINDERMERE, CUMBRIA LA23 3NE
TEL: 05394 88818 FREEPHONE: 0800 269460 FAX: 05394 88058

Gilpin Lodge is a small, family-run country-house hotel and restaurant in 20 acres of woodlands and moors 2 miles from Lake Windermere. A profusion of flower arrangements, picture-lined walls, antique furniture and log fires in winter are all part of John and Christine Cunliffe's perception of hospitality. Their aim is to provide relaxation in charming surroundings. The bedrooms all have en suite bathrooms and every comfort. Some have four-poster beds and one a whirlpool bath. The food earned 2 Rosettes from the AA – which speaks for itself. It is recommended in all the leading guides. Service in the elegant dining room is attentive but unpretentious. There is an extensive wine list to suit all tastes and pockets. The beautiful gardens are the perfect place in which to muse while savouring the lakeland scenery. Windermere golf course is $1/2$ mile away. There's almost every kind of outdoor activity imaginable. This is Wordsworth and Beatrix Potter country and nearby there are several stately homes, gardens and castles. Gilpin Lodge is ETB 4 Crowns Highly Commended and in 1993 won the AA Best Newcomer Award for the North of England. Dinner inclusive rates available. **Directions:** M6 exit 36. A591 Kendal bypass then B5284 to Crook (12 miles from M6). Price guide: Single £45–£65; double/twin £70–£120.

HOLBECK GHYLL COUNTRY HOUSE HOTEL

HOLBECK LANE, WINDERMERE, CUMBRIA LA23 1LU
TEL: 05394 32375 FAX: 05394 34743

For a short or long visit to the Lake District, Holbeck Ghyll is ideal. The saying goes that all the best sites for building a house in England were taken long before the days of the motor car. Holbeck Ghyll has one such prime position. It was built in the early days of the 19th century and is superbly located overlooking Lake Windermere and Langdale Fells. Today this luxury hotel has an outstanding reputation and it is managed personally and expertly by its resident proprietors, David and Patricia Nicholson. As well as being awarded the RAC Blue Ribbon and AA Red Stars, they were among an élite who won an AA Courtesy and Care Award in 1991 for total consideration of their guests. All visitors are made to feel welcome as soon as they step into the entrance hall. As is traditional in many country homes, the bedrooms vary in size, yet all are en suite with comfortable furnishings. The oak-panelled restaurant is a delightful setting for memorable dining and meals are classically prepared, with focus on flavours and presentation, while an extensive wine list reflects quality and variety. The hotel has a billiard room and putting green. **Directions:** M6 junction 36, then A591 through Windermere towards Ambleside. Go past Brockhole Visitors Centre, then after $1/2$ mile turn right into Holbeck Lane (signed Troutbeck). Hotel is $1/2$ mile on left. Price guide (including dinner): Single £90; double/twin £110–£190.

LANGDALE CHASE

WINDERMERE, CUMBRIA LA23 1LW
TEL: 05394 32201 FAX: 05394 32604

Langdale Chase stands in 5 acres of grounds on the shores of Lake Windermere, with panoramic views over England's largest lake to the Langdale Pikes beyond. The Langdale Chase rose was named after the hotel to mark its centenary. Visitors will receive good hospitality in this well-run country home, which is splendidly decorated with oak panelling, fine oil paintings and ornate, carved fireplaces. A magnificent staircase leads to the well-appointed bedrooms, many overlooking the lake. One unique bedroom is sited over the lakeside boathouse, where the traveller may be lulled to sleep by the gently lapping waters below. For the energetic, there is a choice of water-skiing, bathing or sailing from the hotel jetty, or perhaps simply rowing a boat on the lake. Guests have free access to the facilities of the adjacent leisure centre. The Lake District also offers plenty of opportunities for pony-trekking, fell-walking and rock-climbing. This beautiful area was an inspiration for Wordsworth, Ruskin and Beatrix Potter, whose homes can be visited locally. **Directions:** Situated on the A591, 3 miles north of Windermere, 2 miles south of Ambleside. Price guide: Single from £40–£70; double/twin from £80–£110; suite £150.

LINTHWAITE HOUSE HOTEL

CROOK ROAD, BOWNESS-ON-WINDERMERE, CUMBRIA LA23 3JA
TEL: 05394 88600 FAX: 05394 88601

Situated in 14 acres of gardens and woods in the heart of the Lake Distict, Linthwaite House overlooks Lake Windermere and Belle Island, with Claiffe Heights and Coniston Old Man beyond. Here, guests will find themselves amid spectacular scenery, yet only a short drive from the motorway network. The hotel combines stylish originality with the best of traditional English hospitality. The superbly decorated bedrooms, all ensuite, offer glorious views. The comfortable lounge is the perfect place to unwind and there is a fire on winter evenings. In the restaurant, excellent cuisine features the best of fresh, local produce, accompanied by a fine selection of wines. Within the hotel grounds, there is a 9-hole putting green and par 3 practice green. Fly fishermen can fish for brown trout in the hotel tarn. Guests have complimentary use of a private swimming pool and lesiure club nearby, while fell walks begin at the hotel's front door. The area around Linthwaite abounds with places of interest: this is Beatrix Potter and Wordsworth country, and there is much to interest the visitor. **Directions:** From the M6 junction 36 follow Kendal by-pass (A590) for 8 miles. Take B5284 Crook Road for 6 miles. 1 mile beyond Windermere Golf Club, Linthwaite House is signposted on left. Price guide: Single £65–£90; double/twin £86–£120; suite £130.

SIR CHRISTOPHER WREN'S HOUSE

THAMES STREET, WINDSOR, BERKSHIRE SL4 1PX
TEL: 0753 861354 FAX: 0753 860172

Situated close to Windsor Castle, Eton College, Ascot and Henley, Sir Christopher Wren's House is perfectly located for sightseeing and enjoying two of the major events on the English social calendar. This elegant town house is tucked away beside the River Thames and Eton Bridge. Designed, built and lived in by Sir Christopher Wren in 1676, the house possesses the quiet dignity and charm of that era, furnished in period style with fine antiques. More recent additions have respected the original nature of the house. Guests have a choice of spacious older rooms or more modern, compact rooms. All are well appointed, several with four-poster beds. (Sir Christopher Wren's bedroom is particularly comfortable!) The 17th century drawing room, complete with alabaster fireplace, is the perfect place to enjoy afternoon tea or apéritifs. In the elegant Orangerie Restaurant and Cocktail Lounge, overlooking the Thames, superb lunches and dinners are served. Just 10 minutes from Heathrow, the hotel has five fully equipped meeting rooms – a popular choice for conferences and seminars. The extensive range of function suites, terrace garden and riverside setting also make the hotel a picturesque venue for wedding receptions. **Directions:** On the riverside in Windsor beside Eton Bridge. Price guide: Single £49.50–£89; double/twin £69–£99.

OAKLEY COURT

WINDSOR ROAD, WATER OAKLEY, NR WINDSOR, BERKSHIRE SL4 5UR
TEL: 0628 74141 FAX: 0628 37011 TELEX: 849958

The turreted towers of Oakley Court rise majestically over the banks of the Thames, where this handsome mansion has stood since 1859. The waterside location enables the hotel to offer a unique range of boating facilities, from a champagne picnic hamper for two on a chauffeured punt to a gastronomic feast for 100 on a steamboat. The hotel's grandeur is quite awe-inspiring. Restored to their original splendour, the entrance hall, library and drawing room feature elaborate plasterwork, fresh flowers and elegant furnishings. An antique billiard table in the games room is kept in pristine condition. All of the bedrooms have views over the river or the 35-acre gardens. Gourmet cuisine is prepared by a skilled team, under acclaimed chef Murdo MacSween, and is served with finesse in the candle-lit Oakleaf Restaurant, or choose Boaters for lighter, less formal dining. Private dining can be arranged in the superbly equipped conference and banqueting suites. Activities organised for corporate parties may include archery, go-karting or wine tasting. There is a 9-hole par 3 golf course on site and $^3/_4$ mile of exclusive fishing rights on the Thames. Windsor Castle, Eton and Ascot are nearby, and Heathrow is 20 minutes' drive. **Directions:** Situated just off the A308, between Windsor and Maidenhead. Price guide: Single £125–£245; double/twin £145–£375.

THE OLD VICARAGE COUNTRY HOUSE HOTEL

CHURCH ROAD, WITHERSLACK, NR GRANGE-OVER-SANDS, CUMBRIA LA11 6RS
TEL: 05395 52381 FAX: 05395 52373

Cradled in a vale of green beneath Yewbarrow fell, this delightful Georgian period country vicarage, now a comfortable hotel, has been described as "God's little acre". Set in a peaceful and unspoilt part of the Lake District National Park, this family owned hotel, surrounded by beautiful gardens, offers a relaxed and friendly atmosphere. The en suite bedrooms are furnished with antiques, bric-à-brac and Victorian wine and medicine bottles discovered in the garden. Overlooking private woodland, The Orchard House offers luxury accommodation; one room with a four-poster, the others with a private terrace. Excellent food complemented by an award-winning wine list is served by candle-light in the Victorian stlye dining room. The menu features many Lakeland specialities. Top culinary awards and recommendations include: ETB 4 Crowns Highly Commended, Good Hotel Guide – Hospitality Award, Restaurant of the Year 1992 Lancanshire Life Magazine, and AA Rosette & Red Star. Egon Ronay British Cheeseboard of the Year Award 1993. All weather tennis court, National Trust properties and Lake Windermere 10 minutes away. **Directions:** From M6 junction 36, follow A590 to Barrow. After 6 miles turn into Witherslack, then first left after phone box. Bargain Breaks and dinner inclusive options. Price guide: Single £49–£79; double/twin £78–£138.

LANGLEY HOUSE HOTEL

LANGLEY MARSH, WIVELISCOMBE, SOMERSET TA4 2UF
TEL: 0984 623318 FAX: 0984 624573

Langley House is a 16th century retreat set in four acres of beautifully kept gardens on the edge of the pretty Somerset town of Wiveliscombe. Modifications in Georgian times have invested this small, cosy hotel with a unique period charm, which explains its enduring popularity among visitors. Owners Peter and Anne Wilson have excelled in making Langley House a relaxed and comfortable place to stay. The eight bedrooms, all en suite, are individually decorated, with direct-dial telephone, TV and radio. Most have peaceful garden views and personal touches throughout include fresh flowers and mineral water, books and hot-water bottles. Discreet good taste has been exercised in furnishing the public rooms with pastel sofas, traditional rugs, china and glass, antiques and paintings. (Langley House won the Wedgwood/British Tourist Authority Interior Design Award for 1989.) In the beamed restaurant, Peter Wilson serves critically acclaimed cuisine, prepared from fresh, local produce. The wine list boasts some 140 wines. Places of interest include the Brendon Hills, Exmoor, and famous gardens Knightshayes, Stourhead and Hestercombe. **Directions:** Wiveliscombe is 10 miles from Taunton on B3227. Langley House is half a mile north, signposted Langley Marsh. Price guide: Single £62–£68.50; double/twin £79–£104.50.

THE OLD VICARAGE HOTEL

WORFIELD, BRIDGNORTH, SHROPSHIRE WV15 5JZ
TEL: 07464 497 FAX: 07464 552

Standing in 2 acres of mature grounds on the edge of Worfield, The Old Vicarage Hotel offers its visitors an opportunity to enjoy a peaceful retreat in the Shropshire countryside. Structurally, this red-brick building has been little altered since its days as a turn-of-the-century parsonage. However, the restoration of the Edwardian conservatory and subtle refurbishment of the interior have created an exceptionally comfortable country house hotel. The bedrooms are luxuriously furnished in Victorian and Edwardian styles in keeping with the period features. The four Coach House rooms offer the chance to relax in complete luxury, with one ground floor suite specially adapted for disabled guests.

An imaginative menu features the best of local produce with an award winning range of British cheeses including many regional specialities. Over 200 fine wines are kept in the award winning cellar. Local attractions include the world-famous Ironbridge Gorge museum complex, the Severn Valley preserved steam railway and the splendour of the border towns and villages. Half-price golf is available at Worfield Golf Club. Two-day breaks available from £55 per person per day (includes Passport Tickets to Ironbridge Gorge museums). **Directions:** Eight miles west of Wolverhampton, 1 mile off A454, 8 miles south of junction 4 of M54. Price guide: Single £63.50–£74.50; double/twin £85–£100.

SECKFORD HALL

WOODBRIDGE, SUFFOLK IP13 6NU
TEL: 0394 385678 FAX: 0394 380610

Seckford Hall dates from 1530 and it is said that Elizabeth I once held court here. The hall has lost none of its Tudor grandeur. Furnished as a private house with many fine period pieces, the panelled rooms, beamed ceilings, carved doors and great stone fireplaces are displayed against the splendour of English oak. Local delicacies such as the house speciality, lobster, feature on the à la carte menu. The original minstrels gallery can be viewed in the banqueting hall, which is now a conference and function suite designed in keeping with the general style. The Courtyard area was converted from a giant Tudor tithe barn, dairy and coach house. It now incorporates ten charming cottage-style suites and a modern leisure complex, which includes a heated swimming pool, exercise machines, solarium and spa bath. The hotel is set in 34 acres of tranquil parkland with sweeping lawns and a willow-fringed lake, and guests may stroll about the grounds or simply relax in the attractive terrace garden. There is a 18-hole golf course on a pay and play basis, where equipment can be hired. A walk along the riverside will take the visitor to picturesque Woodbridge, with its tide mill, antiques shops, yacht harbours and quaint old streets. Constable country and the Suffolk coast are nearby. **Directions:** Remain on the A12 Woodbridge bypass until you see the blue-and-white hotel sign. Price guide: Single £75–£95; double/twin £90–£135.

PETWOOD HOUSE HOTEL

STIXWOULD ROAD, WOODHALL SPA, LINCOLNSHIRE LN10 6QF
TEL: 0526 352411 FAX: 0526 353473

Petwood House Hotel was built at the turn of the century by Lady Weigall, the daughter of furniture stores magnate Sir Blundell Maple. It is reputed that the Maple craftsmen created much of Petwood's superb oak panelling and wood carving. King George V and his son (later to become George VI) were regular visitors here, attending many tennis parties on the lawns. During the Second World War the Royal Air Force requisitioned the building and in 1943 several squadrons, including the famous 617 'Dambusters' Squadron, turned it into their Officers' Mess. Nowadays it is a fine hotel, set in 30 acres of secluded gardens and mature woodland. Offering the elegance of a period country house, the continuity of tradition prevails throughout. The en suite bedrooms are spacious and comfortably appointed. The restaurant serves the best of English, French and Continental cuisine, complemented by a well-stocked cellar of wines, ports and liqueurs. Residents can use a nearby leisure club, including an 18-hole golf course, swimming pool and gymnasium. Petwood House is an ideal venue for conferences, banquets and receptions for up to 200 – there is a choice of function suites, and a marquee can be set up on the lawn. **Directions:** From Lincoln, take the B1188 left onto B1189 (Metheringham), then left onto B1191 to Woodhall Spa. Price guide: Single £69.70; double/twin £81.

THE FEATHERS HOTEL

MARKET STREET, WOODSTOCK, OXFORDSHIRE OX20 1SX
TEL: 0993 812291 FAX: 0993 813158

The Feathers is a privately owned and run country house hotel, situated in the centre of Woodstock, a few miles from Oxford. Woodstock is one England's most attractive country towns, constructed mostly from Cotswold stone and with buildings dating from the 12th century. The hotel, built in the 17th century, was originally four separate houses. Antiques, log fires and traditional English furnishings lend character and charm. There are only 17 bedrooms, each one individual. All have private bathrooms and showers. Public rooms, including the drawing room and study, are intimate and comfortable. The small garden is a delightful setting for a light lunch or afternoon tea and guests can enjoy a drink in the cosy courtyard bar, which has an open fire in winter. The antique-panelled restaurant is internationally renowned for its fine cuisine, complemented by a high standard of service. The menu changes daily and offers a wide variety of dishes, using the finest local ingredients. Blenheim Palace, seat of the Duke of Marlborough and birthplace of Sir Winston Churchill, is just around the corner. The Cotswolds and the dreaming spires of Oxford are a short distance away. **Directions:** From London leave M40 at junction 8; from Birmingham leave at junction 9. Take A44 and follow signs to Woodstock. The hotel is on the left. Price guide: Single £75; double/twin £90–£138; suite £170.

WATERSMEET HOTEL

MORTEHOE, WOOLACOMBE, DEVON EX34 7EB
TEL: 0271 870333 FAX: 0271 870890

In a superb setting on the National Trust's North Atlantic coastline, Watersmeet Hotel commands dramatic views across Woolacombe Bay past Hartland Point to Lundy Island. Private steps lead directly from the hotel garden to the beach below. Resident owners Brian and Pat Wheeldon ensure that Watersmeet exudes the comfortable luxury of a country house. Attractive décor and floral fabrics in soft colours create a summery impression. The main bedrooms overlook the sea and visitors can fall asleep to the sound of lapping waves. Coffee, lunch and afternoon tea can be taken in the lounge, on the terrace or by the pool. Each evening the candles flicker in the Pavilion Restaurant and as the sun sets across the sea, guests can savour traditional English and continental dishes with a good choice of wines. That the hotel has been awarded an AA Rosette for cuisine and all three RAC Merit awards for excellent hospitality, restaurant and comfort is indicative of its high standards. Locally, visitors can enjoy surfing, bathing, riding, bracing walks along coastal paths and exploring North Devon and Exmoor. Closed December to January. **Directions:** From Barnstaple follow A361 signed Ilfracombe for 8 miles. Turn left at roundabout and follow signs to Mortehoe. Price guide (including dinner): Single £55–£85; double/twin £90–£180.

WOOLACOMBE BAY HOTEL

SOUTH STREET, WOOLACOMBE, DEVON EX34 7BN
TEL: 0271 870388 FAX: 0271 870613

Woolacombe Bay Hotel stands in 6 acres of grounds, leading to 3 miles of golden sand. Built by the Victorians, the hotel has an air of luxury, style and comfort. There is a good range of well-equipped, en suite bedrooms, offering facilities such as satellite TV, baby-listening and, in some of the speciality rooms, spa baths. Traditional English and French dishes are offered in the dining room. Superb recreational amenities on site include unlimited free access to tennis, squash, indoor and outdoor pools, billiards, bowls, croquet, dancing and films, a health suite with steam room, solarium, sauna, spa bath with heated benches and high impulse shower. Chartered power-boating, massage, pheasant and clay pigeon shooting and riding can be arranged, and preferential rates are offered for golf at the Saunton Golf Club. However, being energetic is not a requirement for enjoying the qualities of Woolacombe Bay. Many of its regulars choose simply to relax in the grand public rooms and in the grounds, which extend to the rolling surf of the magnificent bay. A drive along the coastal route in either direction will guarantee splendid views. Exmoor's beautiful Doone Valley is an hour away by car. ETB 5 Crowns. Closed January. **Directions:** At centre of village, off main Barnstaple–Ilfracombe road. Price guide (including dinner): Single £60–£107; double/twin £120–£214.

BILBROUGH MANOR

BILBROUGH, YORK, NORTH YORKSHIRE YO2 3PH
TEL: 0937 834002 FAX: 0937 834724

This gracious manor house is situated on the edge of the conservation village of Bilbrough, just five miles from the centre of York. Since they acquired it in 1986, owners Colin and Susan Bell have transformed the manor from a private house into a comfortable hotel, with all the elements of the *Upstairs Downstairs* portrayal of service, comfort and fine food – including a butler! The 12 bedrooms are all individual in character with bathrooms en suite, colour television and direct dial telephone. Oak panelling, beautiful fireplaces with open fires in winter and comfortable furniture are features of the public rooms. In the formal dining room, New Classical French dishes are prepared by a team of young chefs, headed by Andrew Pressley. The restaurant is managed by Antonio Esteve. Extensive gardens, where you can relax or play croquet on the lawn, and 100 acres of farmland and woodland surround the Manor. There are views to the Vale of York and Ilkley Moor beyond. Riding can be arranged locally and there are racecourses at York, Doncaster and Ripon. Also within reach are the Yorkshire Dales, Castle Howard, Whitby and Scarborough. Closed at Christmas. **Directions:** From A64 at Bilbrough (west of York), turn opposite the Happy Eater, then take first left to the Manor. Price guide: Single £77; double/twin £85–£150.

THE GRANGE HOTEL

CLIFTON, YORK, NORTH YORKSHIRE YO3 6AA
TEL: 0904 644744 FAX: 0904 612453

Set near the ancient city walls, 4 minutes' walk from the famous Minster, this sophisticated Regency town house has been carefully restored and its spacious rooms richly decorated. Beautiful stone-flagged floors in the corridors of The Grange lead to the classically styled reception rooms. The flower-filled Morning Room is welcoming, with its blazing log fire and deep sofas, and double doors between the panelled library and drawing room can be opened up to create a dignified venue for parties, wedding receptions or business entertaining. Prints, flowers and English chintz in the bedrooms reflect the proprietor's careful attention to detail. Utilising skills acquired at London's Le Gavroche, chef Cara Baird has established a reputation at the Ivy Restaurant for first-class gastronomy, incorporating the best in French and country house cooking. Light gourmet meals are served in The Brasserie which is open until after the theatre closes in the evening. For conferences, a computer, fax and telex are available as well as secretarial services. Brimming with history, York's list of attractions includes the National Railway Museum, the Jorvik Viking Centre and the medieval Shambles. **Directions:** The Grange Hotel is on the A19 York–Thirsk road, $^1/_2$ mile from the centre on the left. Price guide: Single £85; double/twin £98–£140.

MIDDLETHORPE HALL

BISHOPTHORPE ROAD, YORK YO2 1QB
TEL: 0904 641241 FAX: 0904 620176

Middlethorpe Hall is a delightful William III house, built in 1699 for Thomas Barlow, a wealthy merchant, and was for a time the home of Lady Mary Wortley Montagu, the 18th-century diarist. The house has been immaculately restored by Historic House Hotels who have decorated and furnished it to its original elegance and style. There are beautifully designed bedrooms and suites in the main house and in the adjacent classical courtyard. The restaurant offers the best in contemporary English cooking with an imaginative menu and a carefully chosen wine list. Middlethorpe stands in 26 acres of parkland where guests can wander and enjoy the walled garden, the white garden, the lake and the original ha ha's. The hotel overlooks York Racecourse – known as the 'Ascot of the North' – and the medieval city of York with its fascinating museums, restored streets and world-famous Minster is only 2 miles away. From Middlethorpe you can visit Yorkshire's famous country houses, like Castle Howard, Beningbrough and Harewood, the ruined Abbeys of Fountains and Rievaulx and explore the magnificent Yorkshire Moors. Helmsley, Whitby and Scarborough are nearby. **Directions:** Take A64 (T) off A1 (T) near Tadcaster, follow signs to York West, then smaller signs to Bishopthorpe. Price guide: Single £83–£99; double/twin £135–£170; suite from £170–£195.

MOUNT ROYALE HOTEL

THE MOUNT, YORK, YORKSHIRE YO2 2DA
TEL: 0904 628856 FAX: 0904 611171 TELEX: 57414

Two elegant William IV houses have been restored to their former glory to create the Mount Royale Hotel, which is personally run by resident proprietors Richard and Christine Oxtoby and their family. Comfortable bedrooms are furnished with imagination, all in an individual style. Each of the garden rooms opens onto the garden and has its own verandah. Downstairs, the public rooms are filled with interesting items of antique furniture, *objets d'art* and gilt-framed paintings. To the rear of the building, overlooking the gardens, is the restaurant, where guests can enjoy the best of traditional English cooking and French cuisine. Amenities include a snooker room with a full-sized table, steam room, sauna, solarium and trimnasium. With a delightful English garden and heated outdoor pool, the one acre grounds are a peaceful haven just minutes from York's centre. York is a historic and well-preserved city, famous for its Minster and medieval streets. Also within walking distance is York racecourse, where the flat-racing season runs from May to October. Lovers of the great outdoors will find the Yorkshire Dales and North York Moors a 45-minute drive away. Small dogs by arrangement only. Closed 23-31 December.
Directions: From A64, turn onto the A1036 signposted York. Go past racecourse; hotel is on right before traffic lights. Price guide: Single £75–£80; double/twin £85–£110; suites £110.

     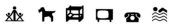

For hotel location, see maps on pages 458–464

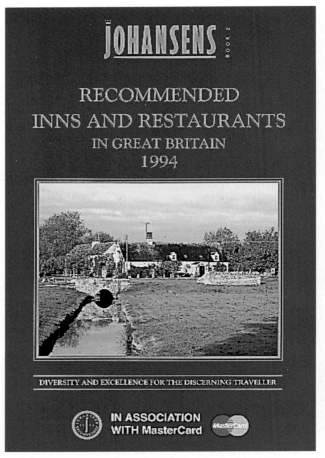

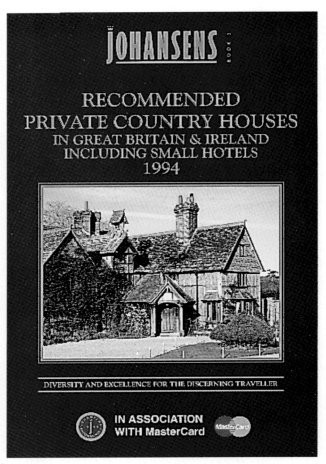

Johansens Recommended Inns and Restaurants in Great Britain is a popular publication and the 1994 edition contains over 150 establishments. The majority of properties offer value for money accommodation, good cooking, fine wines and ales; all offer a very warm welcome to travellers. Many are splendid old coaching inns retaining features from bygone eras, situated adjacent to village greens or nestling deep in unspoiled countryside. These establishments provide ideal locations for those seeking a relaxing weekend away or short break. Price £8.95

This guide features over 180 privately owned country houses and small owner managed hotels, each unique and many of significant historical interest. Picturesque surroundings, well tended gardens and an intimate atmosphere are their hallmarks. Most establishments have just a few guest bedrooms. In some, guests dine en-famille - all offer attractive accommodation and the genuine warmth of convivial hosts into whose home you are stepping. Stay in Johansens Recommended country houses and discover some of Britain's finest heritage. Price £8.95

Copies may be obtained from most Johansens recommended establishments, good bookshops or direct from the publishers.*

*See order coupon at the back of this guide.

Johansens Recommended Hotels in

Wales

ABERGAVENNY (Walterstone)

In association
with MasterCard MasterCard

ALLT-YR-YNYS HOTEL

WALTERSTONE, HEREFORDSHIRE HR2 0DU
TEL: 0873 890307 FAX: 0873 890539

Allt-yr-Ynys straddles the border that runs between England and Wales – with rural Herefordshire on one side and the Black Mountains on the other. The original manor house on this site belonged to the estate of Robert Cecil, a Knight of the Court during the reign of King Henry II; however, the buildings that comprise today's hotel date from 1550. Many of the authentic features have been preserved, typically the moulded ceilings, oak panelling and massive oak beams. The bedrooms, some of which are situated in the converted outbuildings, have been beautifully appointed to complement their period character. Delicious British cooking features on the menu, and the chef can also prepare 'special dishes for special occasions' to cater for private functions of up to 60 people. In the bar, adjacent to the Jacuzzi and indoor heated pool, there is an ancient, horse-powered cider press. An undercover clay pigeon range is in the grounds, with all equipment – shotguns, cartridges and tuition. There are four golf courses within the vicinity. **Directions:** Midway between Abergavenny and Hereford, turn off A465 by Pandy Inn. Turn right at Green Park Barn crossroads as signposted to Walterstone. Price guide: Single £55; double/twin £85.

328

PORTH TOCYN COUNTRY HOUSE HOTEL

ABERSOCH, PWLLHELI, GWYNEDD LL53 7BU
TEL: 0758 713303 FAX: 0758 713538

Porth Tocyn is a friendly, family-owned hotel offering country charm and good food in a beautiful location. Situated in 25 acres of gardens and pasture, the house enjoys glorious views across Cardigan Bay to Snowdonia. In the 45 years that the Fletcher-Brewer family have owned the hotel, they have concentrated their efforts into creating a comfortable, attractive hotel without the stuffiness associated with some establishments. Children of all ages are welcomed: there are family bedrooms, a small children's sitting room, and high tea is provided for the younger ones every evening. However, this is very much a place where adults can relax. First-class home cooking has long been the cornerstone of Porth Tocyn's reputation. Focusing on the quality of each dish, dinner is a short-choice, five-course affair followed by coffee and home-made petits fours. The menu is changed completely each day. A dinner-party atmosphere brings a sense of occasion to the evening. Lunch is more informal and may be taken in the garden or by the pool. A variety of water sports and riding can be arranged locally, while the heritage coastline makes for ideal clifftop walks. Closed November to Easter. **Directions:** From Abersoch go 2¹/₂ miles, through Sarn Bach and Bwlchtocyn. 'Gwesty/Hotel' signs lead to Porth Tocyn. Price guide: Single £44.50; double/twin £58–£90.

CONRAH COUNTRY HOUSE HOTEL

RHYDGALED, CHANCERY, ABERYSTWYTH, DYFED SY23 4DF
TEL: 0970 617941 FAX: 0970 624546

One of Wales' much-loved country house hotels, the Conrah is tucked away at the end of a rhododendron-lined drive, only minutes from the spectacular rocky cliffs and sandy bays of the Cambrian coast. Set in 22 acres of rolling grounds, the Conrah's magnificent aspect affords views as far north as the Cader Idris mountain range. Afternoon tea and Welsh cakes or pre-dinner drinks can be taken at leisure in the drawing room or quiet writing room, furnished for comfort with plump chintz armchairs. Antiques, fresh flowers and books add to the relaxed country style. The cuisine is a marriage of classical and nouvelle forms, with fresh salmon and game among the specialities. An extensive daily menu is provided for vegetarians. Resident proprietors John and Patricia Heading extend a warm invitation for a real 'taste of Wales', combined with old-fashioned, high standards of service. For recreation, guests may enjoy a game of table-tennis in the summer house or enjoy a walk around the gardens and the Conrah fields, where sheep and donkeys graze. Country pursuits such as pony-trekking, sea-fishing and birdwatching are available locally, while the university town of Aberystwyth is only 3 miles away. Closed Christmas. **Directions:** The Conrah lies 3 miles south of Aberystwyth on the A487. Price guide: Single £56; double/twin £79–£99.

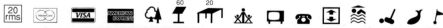

TREARDDUR BAY HOTEL

LON ISALLT, TREADDUR BAY, HOYLHEAD, ANGLESEY
TEL: 0407 860301 FAX: 0407 861181

This coastal hotel enjoys a magnificent location on the Anglesey coast, overlooking Trearddur Bay and close to a medieval chapel dedicated to the nun St Brigid. An extensive refurbishment programme in recent years has given the hotel a completely new look. Many of the spacious bedrooms, all of which are en suite, have panoramic views over the bay. All are furnished to a high standard. There are also nine studio suites, including one with four-poster bed. The comfortable lounge is the perfect place to relax and read the papers over morning coffee or afternoon tea. Before dinner, enjoy an apéritif in one of the hotel bars. Superb views apart, the hotel restaurant enjoys a reputation for excellent food – including locally caught fish and seafood – complemented by fine wines. Table d'hôte and à la carte menus offer a good choice of dishes. For those who find the Irish Sea too bracing, the hotel has an indoor pool. The beach is just a short walk away and there is an 18-hole golf course nearby. Anglesey is a haven for watersports enthusiasts and birdwatchers. Places of interest include Beaumaris Castle and the Celtic burial mound at Bryn Celi Ddu. Snowdonia is a little further afield. **Directions:** From Bangor, take A5 to Valley crossroads. Turn left onto B4545 for 3 miles, then turn left at garage. Hotel is 350 yards on right. Price guide: Single £65-£90; double/twin £92-£100; studio suite £112.

PALÉ HALL

LLANDDERFEL, BALA, GWYNEDD LL23 7PS
TEL: 06783 285 FAX: 06783 220

Palé Hall is an elegant 19th century residence which was built in 1870 for a certain Mr Henry Robertson. This Scottish gentleman (and engineer) instructed his architects to spare no expense in the construction of Palé Hall. The sumptuous end result was to attract many a notable guest, among them Queen Victoria, who pronounced the place enchanting – and stayed. Over 200 years later, Palé Hall is still a luxurious retreat, refurbished and restored with care and attention to offer the visitor the last word in comfortable and tranquil accommodation. All 17 bedrooms have beautiful views over the gardens. Some of them still have open fireplaces; all have been individually designed and furnished –

facilities include colour TV, direct-dial telephones, trouser press plus other thoughtful extras. Among the fine period features in the building is the hand-painted domed ceiling in the boudoir, where guests can relax in no-smoking surroundings. The Corwen Bar centres around a bar top constructed from the marble fireplaces salvaged from the bedrooms and is the perfect place for drinks before dinner. Facilities available locally include walking, fishing, sailing, surfing, golf and shooting the rapids down the River Tryweryn. **Directions:** Palé Hotel is situated just off the B4401 Corwen to Bala road 4-5 miles from Llandrillo. Price guide: Single £85–£95; double/twin £120–£135; suite £160.

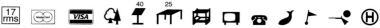

BONTDDU HALL

BONTDDU, NR BARMOUTH, GWYNEDD LL40 2SU
TEL: 0341 49661 FAX: 0341 49284

Set in 14 acres of landscaped gardens with mixed woodland and a rhododendron forest, Gothic-styled Bontddu Hall commands a lofty position overlooking the Mawddach Estuary in Snowdonia National Park. Built in 1873 as a country mansion for the aunt of Neville Chamberlain, the hotel is reminiscent of the Victorian era and was frequented by several Prime Ministers during the days of the British Empire. The reception rooms are richly decorated in a fashion that complements the grandeur of the high, corniced ceilings and ornate, marble fireplaces. As well as the comfortable bedrooms in the main building, a number of suites are available in the Lodge, each with a private balcony facing the mountains.

Regional and classical cuisine are served in the Garden Restaurant. Lunch and afternoon teas can be taken on the sun terrace. Hill walking, climbing, pony-trekking, surfing, sail-boarding, skin-diving and bowling are available in the locality. Bontddu also has a gold mine. A tour of the area could include a trip on the famous narrow-gauge railways, or a visit to one of the many interesting castles, such as Harlech or Penrhyn. Closed November to Easter. **Directions:** Situated midway between Dolgellau and Barmouth on the A469. Price guide: Single £62.50; double/twin £90–£115; suite £165.

LLANGOED HALL

LLYSWEN, BRECON, POWYS, WALES LD3 0YP
TEL: 0874 754525 FAX: 0874 754545

The history of Llangoed Hall dates back to 560 AD when it is thought to have been the site of the first Welsh Parliament. Inspired by this legend, the architect Sir Clough Williams-Ellis, transformed the Jacobean mansion he found here in 1914 into an Edwardian country house. Situated deep in a valley of the River Wye, surrounded by a walled garden, the hotel commands breathtaking views of the Black Mountains and Brecon Beacons beyond. The rooms are warm and welcoming, furnished with antiques and oriental rugs and, on the walls, an outstanding collection of paintings acquired by the owner, Sir Bernard Ashley. Head Chef Mark Salter makes eating at Llangoed one of the principal reasons for visiting. Classic but light, his menus represent the very best of modern cuisine, complemented by a cellar of more than 300 wines. Tennis and croquet are available on site, and nearby there is golf, fishing, riding, shooting, and some of the best mountain walking and gliding in Britain. For expeditions, there are the Wye Valley, Hay-on-Wye and its bookshops, the border castles, Hereford and Leominster. Children over 8 are welcome. The hotel is a member of Welsh Rarebits and Small Luxury Hotels of the World. **Directions:** The hotel is 9 miles west of Hay, 11 miles north of Brecon on the A470. Price guide: Single £95; double/twin £130–£185; suite £185–£275.

PETERSTONE COURT

LLANHAMLACH, BRECON, POWYS LD3 7YB
TEL: 0874 86387 FAX: 0874 86376

Set in a tiny village on the eastern edge of the mysterious Brecon Beacons National Park, Peterstone is a carefully restored Georgian manor, swathed in history which can bed traced back to the time of William the Conqueror. It was voted the best new hotel in Wales by the AA in 1992 and amongst a string of awards collected merits from the RAC and the Welsh Tourist Board. There are just 12 guest bedrooms at the court, 8 beautifully proportioned period style rooms in the main house, and 4 split level rooms in the former stable and have all the things you expect and many you don't, such as tape players, video players and a welcoming decanter of sherry. Intimate parties and special occasions can be accommodated in one of the two small private rooms. The surrounding countryside has an abundance of walks, one of which starts at the end of the hotels drive and goes along the river and the canal back into Brecon. Alternatively, or perhaps even, after all the walking, there is in the hotels basement a fully equipped leisure suite, with gymnasium, sauna, solarium and Jacuzzi. In the grounds is an outdoor heated pool, croquet and putting. **Directions:** Peterstone Court is located in the village of Llanhamlach, on the A40, 3 miles east of Brecon. Price guide: Single £72.50–£85; double/twin £85–£105; suite £125. Short breaks available all year round.

SEIONT MANOR HOTEL

LLANRUG, CAERNARVON, GWYNEDD LL55 2AQ
TEL: 0286 673366 FAX: 0286 672840

Set in 150 acres of parkland amid the majestic scenery of Snowdonia, Seiont Manor has been stylishly remodelled from original rustic buildings to create a unique luxury hotel offering guests every comfort. The oak-panelled bar and library, with its collection of leather-bound volumes, provide the perfect environment for relaxing with a drink before dinner. For lovers of good food, the excellent restaurant, overlooking the hotel's lake and grounds, serves classic French cuisine as well as superb local dishes, all prepared from the finest ingredients. Each of the 28 bedrooms, with furnishings from around the world, is comfortable and spacious and has en suite facilities. The hotel is an ideal venue for conferences, functions and meetings of up to 120 people. A heated pool housed in the Victorian-style 'chapel' takes pride of place among the leisure facilities, which also include a sauna, solarium, multi-gym, aromatherapy and reflexology treatments. Mountain bikes and a jogging track are available for guests' use and there is fishing for salmon and trout in the river. Caernarvon golf course, with its stunning views over the Menai Straits, is nearby, as are the Snowdonia National Park, Ffestiniog Mountain Railway and Caernarvon Castle. **Directions:** 3 miles from Caernarvon on the A4086. Price guide: Single £72.50; double/twin £96–£124.

EGERTON GREY COUNTRY HOUSE HOTEL

PORTHKERRY, NR CARDIFF, SOUTH GLAMORGAN CF62 3BZ
TEL: 0446 711666 FAX: 0446 711690

A distinguished former rectory dating from the early-19th century, Egerton Grey is tucked away in 7 acres of gardens in a secluded, wooded valley in the Vale of Glamorgan. Visitors can enjoy glorious views towards Porthkerry Park and the sea beyond. The interior design complements the architectural features of the house. The Edwardian drawing room has intricate plaster mouldings, chandeliers, an open fireplace and oil paintings. A quiet library overlooks the garden. All of the immaculately presented bedrooms are extremely comfortable, and several have Victorian baths and brasswork. Original Cuban mahogany panelling and candle-lit tables create an air of intimacy in the main restaurant. Private dinner parties can be accommodated in the oak-panelled dining room. High-quality English dishes are presented with finesse on bone china, and wine is served in Welsh Royal Crystal glasses. Riding and sailing can be arranged and there is a pitch-and-putt course a short stroll away. Dyffryn House, Castle Coch and Cardiff Castle are nearby. **Directions:** From M4 junction 33, take A4050; follow airport signs for 10 miles. Take the A4226 towards Porthkerry; after 400 yards turn into the lane between two thatched cottages and hotel is at end of lane. Price guide: Single £69.50–£95; double/twin £85–£120.

 # NEW HOUSE COUNTRY HOTEL

THORNHILL, CARDIFF CF4 5UA
TEL: 0222 520280 FAX: 0222 520324

Situated on the edge of Cardiff in 11 acres of parkland, New House Country Hotel is sheltered by trees on the southern slope of Caerphilly Mountain and affords views across the Vale of Glamorgan towards the Severn Estuary. A stylish 18th century mansion, New House forms the nucleus of a prestigious country hotel project. Antique furniture, oil paintings, attractive fabrics and crystal chandeliers set the tone of the interiors. The bedrooms have been appointed to evoke the style of 18th century England and Wales with reproduction furniture in the classic designs of Chippendale, Sheraton and Hepplewhite. Five spacious bedrooms are housed within the main building while the others are housed in a newer addition. Whether for a quiet dinner à deux, family Sunday lunch or a large gathering, the cooking, complemented by an extensive wine list, is contemporary and lively. The function rooms range from the Wyndham Suite, which can accommodate a banquet, wedding reception or conference, to a library which is ideal for small board meetings. The Welsh Folk Museum at St Fagans, Duffryn Gardens, the Maritime Museum, the National Museum of Wales and the Welsh National Opera Company are all nearby. **Directions:** On the A469 Cardiff–Caerphilly road, 4 miles north of Cardiff. Price guide: Single £55; double/twin £70; suites from £80.

SOUGHTON HALL COUNTRY HOUSE HOTEL

NORTHOP, NR MOLD, CLWYD CH7 6AB
TEL: 0352 840811 FAX: 0352 840382

Built as a bishop's palace in 1714, Soughton Hall is set in 150 acres of parkland and is approached via a spectacular avenue of lime trees. The 12 luxurious bedrooms are decorated with the emphasis on comfort. Antique furniture, baroque marble fireplaces, French tapestries and Persian carpets adorn a house of unique history and architecture. The hotel is regularly frequented by the famous and was proud to be host in 1992 to King Juan Carlos and Queen Sophia of Spain during their visit to Merseyside for the Grand Parade of the Tall Ships. The personal welcome of the Rodenhurst family – 'Our guests arrive as customers and leave as friends' – and attentive service ensure a memorable stay. The hotel is also ideal for exclusive business use, with a boardroom that is second to none. A chauffeur-driven visit, including dinner, to an informal restaurant in farm buildings converted to a museum and craft centre and hosted by Simon Rodenhurst is an option available in a special three-day package. From the hotel, excursions can be made into North Wales and historic Chester. An exclusive, full-colour guide to selected holiday drives in the area is provided. **Directions:** From the M56 take the A55 towards North Wales, then the A5119 to Northop. Cross the traffic lights; the hall is 1 mile along the road on the left. Price guide: Single £80; double/twin £100–£140.

BERTHLWYD HALL HOTEL

LLECHWEDD, NR CONWY, GWYNEDD LL32 8DQ
TEL: 0492 592409 FAX: 0492 572290

One mile from historic Conwy and in sight of its famous castle, is Berthlwyd Hall Hotel, a charming Victorian manor surrounded by the unblemished country byways and woodlands of the picturesque Conwy Valley. Many of the Victorian characteristics have been preserved, such as the splendid oak panelling in the entrance hall, a wide staircase sweeping up to an impressive galleried landing, elaborately carved fireplaces and stained-glass windows. Each of the bedrooms has been individually styled and comfortably appointed. Resident proprietors Brian and Joanna Griffin spent some years in the Périgord region of south-west France, renowned for its gastronomic heritage and the inspiration for their popular award winning restaurant, 'Truffles'. The 140-year-old wine press, which they brought back from Bordeaux, evokes a Gallic atmosphere appropriate for the imaginative menu of French dishes and a wine list of good clarets and regional vintages. Snacks are served in the bar where there is a small games room. From Berthlwyd Hall the majestic peaks of Snowdonia, the Welsh coast and Anglesey can be explored, while Bodnant Gardens are nearby. **Directions:** Entering Conwy over the bridge on the A55, into the centre, turn left into Sychnant Pass, after 1 mile look for the sign on the left. Price guide: Single £42.50; double/twin £50–£95.

TYDDYN LLAN COUNTRY HOUSE HOTEL

LLANDRILLO, NR CORWEN, CLWYD LL21 0ST
TEL: 049084 264 FAX: 049084 264

Tyddyn Llan is an elegant Georgian country house situated amid breathtaking scenery in the Vale of Edeyrnion. Owned and run by Peter and Bridget Kindred, the hotel is a quiet oasis in an area of outstanding natural beauty at the foot of the Berwyn Mountains. There are 10 bedrooms, all individual in style and elegantly furnished with antiques and period furniture. Each enjoys views of the gardens and the mountains beyond and has a bathroom en suite. The hotel is proud of the reputation it has established for the quality of the food served in the restaurant. Inventive and frequently changing menus feature dishes using fresh local ingredients and herbs from the kitchen garden. A carefully selected wine list complements the cuisine. In the gardens, guests may enjoy a game of croquet and tea is served on fine days. The hotel has rights to 4 miles of fly-fishing on the River Dee. Keen walkers can trace the ancient Roman road, Ffordd Gam Elin, which traverses the Berwyn Mountains. Here, naturalists will find many different species of birds and wild flowers. Tyddyn Llan is well placed to explore nearby Snowdonia, and the Roman city of Chester is only 35 miles away. **Directions:** Llandrillo is midway between Corwen and Bala on the B4401, 4 miles from the A5 at Corwen. Price guide: Single £54–£58; double/twin £84–£92.

COED-Y-MWSTWR HOTEL

COYCHURCH, NEAR BRIDGEND, MID GLAMORGAN CF35 6AE
TEL: 0656 860621 FAX: 0656 863122

Coed-y-Mwstwr is a country mansion of Victorian origin set in 17 acres of mature woodland, which is also home to an abundance of wildlife – kestrels, woodpeckers and buzzards all nest here, with foxes, rabbits and badgers never far away. Much thought has gone into ensuring that the décor and furnishings are in keeping with the style of the house. High ceilings, chandeliers and large fireplaces feature in the elegant public rooms. The 23 luxurious bedrooms all have en suite facilities and wonderful views. The elegant oak-panelled restaurant enjoys a good reputation locally and offers a blend of traditional and modern cuisine, with both table d'hôte and à la carte menus with 2 AA Rosettes. The wine list has more than 250 wines. Private functions for up to 150 people may be held in the Hendre Suite. In addition, there are two private dining rooms. A heated outdoor swimming pool, all-weather tennis court and snooker room are available for guests' use. For golfers, Royal Porthcawl and Southerndown courses are 10 minutes' drive from the hotel. The beautiful Gower and Pembrokeshire coastline and Brecon Beacons National Park are within easy reach. Open all year. **Directions:** Leave M4 at junction 35, take A473 towards Bridgend for 1 mile, turn right into Coychurch. At filling station turn right and follow signs uphill. Price guide: Single £75; double/twin £90; suite £140.

BRON EIFION COUNTRY HOUSE HOTEL

CRICCIETH, GWYNEDD LL52 0SA
TEL: 0766 522385 FAX: 0766 522003

The location of Bron Eifion makes many guests keen to return time after time. It is gloriously situated close to the Snowdonia National Park and less than a mile from the shores of Cardigan Bay. Built as a residence for the slate master, John Greaves, this Victorian house has several notable features. Extensive carved panelling can be seen throughout the reception rooms, and the minstrels gallery, in pitch and Oregon pine, has been preserved in perfect condition. In the conservatory dining room, table d'hôte and à la carte menus offer innovative cuisine, supported by a good wine list. The 19 bedrooms all have either private bath or shower facilities, and de luxe and family rooms are also available.

A series of interlocking, thematic gardens, stone-walled terraces and paths for pleasant strolls can be found in the 5-acre grounds. Sightseeing attractions nearby include Porthmadog and Portmeirion, the Ffestiniog Railway and Caernarfon Castle. Aside from having its own castle, Criccieth is well known as the birthplace of Lloyd George. As a designated area of outstanding natural beauty, the Lleyn Peninsula has plenty to explore.
Directions: The hotel is on the A497, just on the outskirts of the town, on the road to Pwllheli. Price guide: Single £45–£53; double/twin £70–£86.

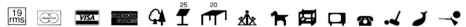

GLIFFAES COUNTRY HOUSE HOTEL

CRICKHOWELL, POWYS NP8 1RH
TEL: 0874 730371 FAX: 0874 730463

Visitors may be surprised to discover a hotel featuring distinctive Italianate architecture tucked midway between the Brecon Beacons and the Black Mountains. Gliffaes Country House Hotel is poised 150 feet above the River Usk and commands glorious views of the surrounding hills and valley. The elegantly furnished, Regency-style drawing room leads into a glass-fronted sun room and on to the terrace, from which guests may enjoy the magnificent scenery. In addition to a panelled lounge, there is a billiard room with a full-sized table. An informal atmosphere prevails in the dining room, where a good choice of attractively presented dishes is offered. A specific attraction for many visitors is the abundance of good fishing. The Gliffaes fishery includes every type of water, from slow-flowing flats to fast-running rapids, on $2\frac{1}{2}$ miles of the River Usk, renowned for its wild brown trout and salmon fishing. For still-water fishing, there are eight well-stocked reservoirs in the area. The 29-acre hotel grounds have rare trees and shrubs as well as lawns for putting and croquet. Hang-gliding, caving and trekking can be arranged nearby. Closed 31 December to mid-February. **Directions:** Gliffaes is signposted from the A40, $2\frac{1}{2}$ miles west of Crickhowell. Price guide: Single £31–£39; double/twin £62–£92.

HOTEL MAES-Y-NEUADD

TALSARNAU, NR HARLECH, GWYNEDD LL47 6YA
TEL: 0766 780200 FAX: 0766 780211

This part-14th century house, built of granite and slate, is cradled by 8 acres of landscaped mountainside. This much-loved hotel has been run by the Horsfall and Slatter families since 1981. Peace and tranquillity are all-pervasive, whether relaxing in the pretty, beamed lounge or reclining in a leather chesterfield in the bar while enjoying an apéritif. Talented chefs create delicious English and Welsh dishes using fresh produce such as lamb, fish and a variety of Welsh farmhouse cheeses, along with vegetables and herbs from the kitchen garden. As an alternative dining venue for special occasions and parties, dinner can be provided on the world famous Festiniog railway (minimum 30 persons). Also the hotel produces its own oils and vinegars which are stylishly presented for resale. Spring and autumn brochures available. The bedrooms vary in style, from early beams and dormers to later Georgian elegance with full-length windows. Hotel residents are offered preferential green fees at Royal St David's Golf Course, 3 miles away. Nearby attractions include the Italianate village of Portmeirion, slate caverns, beautiful beaches, Snowdonia, Edward I's castle at Harlech and the Festiniog railway. USA toll-free reservations: 1-800 635 3602. **Directions:** Hotel is 3$\frac{1}{2}$ miles north of Harlech, off the B4573, signposted at the end of the lane. Price guide (including dinner): Single £68; double/twin £151–£192.

LAKE VYRNWY HOTEL

LAKE VYRNWY, LLANWDDYN, MONTGOMERYSHIRE SY10 0LY
TEL: 069173 692 FAX: 069173 259

The Lake Vyrnwy Hotel occupies a unique position high on the hillsides of the Berwyn Mountains and commands awe-inspiring views of the mountains, lake and moorland of the 24,000-acre Vyrnwy Estate. Built in 1890 when the lake was created, the hotel was, and still is, intended very much as a country house and sporting retreat for all country lovers. Each of the 38 bedrooms is individually decorated and furnished, many with antiques, and some have special features such as private suites, balconies, four-posters and Jacuzzis. The award-winning restaurant often features produce from the hotel's market garden, and everything from the marmalade at breakfast to the bread and petits fours at dinner is created in the kitchens. The hotel also owns the sole sporting rights on 24,000 acres of land, together with sole fishing rights on the 5-mile-long lake providing excellent fishing. Other pursuits available include sailing, archery, cycling, walking trails, tennis, four-wheel driving and birdwatching. Peace and tranquillity reign, and those who are looking simply to relax in beautiful surroundings will not be disappointed. **Directions:** From Shrewsbury take the A458 to Welshpool, then turn right onto B4393 just after Ford (signposted to Lake Vyrnwy 28 miles). Price guide: Single £58; double/twin from £75; suite £118.

THE FALCONDALE HOTEL

LAMPETER, DYFED SA48 7RX
TEL: 0570 422910 FAX: 0570 423559

Situated at the head of a sheltered, forested valley, The Falcondale Hotel stands in 14 acres of rhododendron plantation and ornamental woodland. This Italianate mansion was developed around 1859 by John Batasby Harford, whose extensive travels in Italy influenced his redesign of the property. Re-opened as a country house hotel in 1980, The Falcondale Hotel has been tastefully refurbished throughout by resident owners Stephen and Christine Smith. Furnished in the style of Louis XIV, the South Lounge houses a cocktail bar, where log fires glowing in winter make for a convivial atmosphere. Bedrooms are decorated in a classic style and fitted to a high standard with all the essential facilities. Soft candle-light in the restaurant makes dining a special occasion, with an extensive menu offering a varied choice. Visitors are welcomed at this family home with warmth, and friendly, efficient service can be expected. On the south lawn there is an 18-hole putting green; a 10-acre lake nearby offers coarse fishing; and further afield, pony-trekking can be enjoyed through the Cambrian foothills. The hotel is minutes from the university market town of Lampeter and makes a good base for exploring south-west Wales. **Directions:** A few minutes' drive from Lampeter on the A475 Cardigan road. Price guide: Single £55; double/twin £75.

Bodysgallen Hall

LLANDUDNO, GWYNEDD LL30 1RS
TEL: 0492 584466 FAX: 0492 582519

Bodysgallen Hall, owned and restored by Historic House Hotels, lies at the end of a winding drive in 200 acres of wooded parkland and beautiful formal gardens. Magnificent views encompass the sweep of the Snowdonia range of mountains, and the hotel looks down on the imposing medieval castle at Conwy. This Grade I listed house was built mainly in the 17th century, but the earliest feature is a 13th century tower, reached by a narrow winding staircase, once used as a lookout for soldiers serving the English kings of Conwy and now a safe place from which to admire the views. The hotel has 19 spacious bedrooms in the house and nine delightful cottage suites in the grounds. Two of the finest rooms in the house are the large oak-panelled entrance hall and the first floor drawing room, both with splendid fireplaces and mullioned windows. Head chef is Mair Lewis, one of the few women head chefs in a top hotel, who produces superb dishes using fresh local ingredients. The hotel is ideally place for visiting the many historic castles and stately homes in North Wales and admiring the splendid mountain scenery. **Directions:** On the A470 1 mile from the intersection with the A55. Llandudno is a mile further on the A470. Price guide: Single £89–£112; double/twin £122–£169; suite £164.

ST TUDNO HOTEL

PROMENADE, LLANDUDNO, GWYNEDD LL30 2LP
TEL: 0492 874411 FAX: 0492 860407

Undoubtedly one of the most delightful small hotels to be found on the coast of Britain, St Tudno Hotel which won the *1992 Johansens Hotel of the Year Award for Excellence* certainly offers a very special experience. The hotel, which has been elegantly and lovingly furnished with meticulous attention to detail, offers a particularly warm welcome from owners, Martin and Janette Bland, and their caring and friendly staff. Each beautifully co-ordinated bedroom has been individually designed with many thoughtful extras provided to ensure guests' comfort. The bar lounge and sitting room, which overlook the sea, have an air of Victorian charm. Regarded as one of Wales' leading restaurants,

the air-conditioned Garden Room has won two AA Rosettes for its excellent cuisine. This AA Red Star hotel has won a host of other awards, including *Best Seaside Resort Hotel in Great Britain*, national winner of the AA's *Warmest Welcome Award* and even an accolade for having the *Best Hotel Loos in Britain!* St Tudno is ideally situated for visits to Snowdonia, Conwy and Caernarfon Castles, Bodnant Gardens and Anglesey. Golf, riding, swimming and dry-slope skiing and tobogganing can be enjoyed locally. **Directions:** On the promenade opposite the pier entrance and gardens. Price guide: Single £52.50; double/twin £70–£120.

  # THE LAKE COUNTRY HOUSE

LLANGAMMARCH WELLS, POWYS LD4 4BS
TEL: 05912 202 FAX: 05912 457

The Lake Hotel is hidden away in 50 acres of grounds, with sweeping lawns, thick woodlands, rhododendron-lined pathways and riverside walks. The spacious reception hall and drawing room are enhanced by cosy log fires and antique furniture. Spectacular views of the surrounding countryside are offered by many of the comfortable, well-designed bedrooms. The hotel presents excellent food from a menu that is changed daily. Award winning hotel with 2 AA Rosettes for food. Meals are served in the elegant dining room and complemented by one of the finest wine lists in Wales. This is a fisherman's paradise – the hotel's own lake is well stocked with trout, or alternatively fish for salmon in the nearby Rivers Wye and Irfon. The Lake Hotel is renowned among birdwatchers, with 94 species of bird having been recorded here. For an exhilarating appreciation of the Welsh scenery, hacking and pony-trekking can be arranged. There are scenic drives in all directions, particularly towards the Brecon Beacons and Wye Valley. With a large billiard room in the hotel and a 6-hole practice golf course, there is no lack of recreational activity here. AA and RAC 3 Stars and Merit Award. **Directions:** From the A483, follow signs to Llangammarch Wells and then to the hotel. Price guide: Single £65–£85; double/twin £98.50; suite from £120.

YNYSHIR HALL

EGLWYSFACH, MACHYNLLETH, POWYS SY20 8TA
TEL: 0654 781209 FAX: 0654 781366

Once owned by Queen Victoria, Ynyshir Hall is a captivating Georgian manor house that perfectly blends modern comfort and old-world elegance. Its 12 acres of picturesque, landscaped gardens are set alongside the Dovey Estuary, one of Wales' most outstanding areas of natural beauty and surrounded by the Ynyshir Bird Reserve. Hosts Rob and Joan Reen offer guests a warm welcome and ensure a personal service, the hallmark of a good family-run hotel. Period furniture and opulent fabrics enhance the eight charming bedrooms. The suites are particularly luxurious and, along with a four-poster room and ground floor room, are popular with many guests. The interiors are exquisitely furnished throughout with comfortable sofas, antiques, contemporary colour schemes, oriental rugs and many original paintings. These works of art are the creation of Rob, an established and acclaimed artist. Local seafood, game, and vegetables from the kitchen garden are used to create superb English, French and Welsh dishes. Dogs by prior arrangement. **Directions:** Off the main road between Aberystwyth and Machynlleth. Price guide: Single £65–£95; double/twin £90–£110; suite £120–£130.

THE CROWN AT WHITEBROOK

WHITEBROOK, MONMOUTH, GWENT NP5 4TX
TEL: 0600 860254 FAX: 0600 860607

A romantic auberge nestling deep in the Wye Valley, a designated area of outstanding natural beauty, The Crown is ideally situated for those seeking peace and tranquillity. Located in the wooded Whitebrook Valley on the fringe of Tintern Forest and only 1 mile from the River Wye, this is a place where guests can enjoy spectacular scenery. Roger and Sandra Bates offer their visitors a genuinely friendly welcome. Guests can relax in the cosy lounge and bar areas or in the Manor Room, with its ash furniture, hand-made locally. Sandra Bates' cooking earned the Gwent Restaurant of the Year Award 1991 from Taste of Wales, as well as recommendations from other guides. Dishes include maize-fed chicken served in a cream, lime and tarragon sauce with a crab mousse, followed by a choice of delicious home-made puddings and a selection of British farm cheeses. Most dietary requirements can be catered for as all food is freshly cooked to order. There is an extensive wine list. Tintern Abbey, Chepstow Castle and the Brecon Beacons National Park are nearby. **Directions:** Whitebrook is situated between the A466 and the B4293 approximately 5 miles south of Monmouth. Price guide: Single £48–£55; double/twin £76–£90.

 # THE CELTIC MANOR HOTEL

COLDRA WOODS, NEWPORT, GWENT NP6 2YA
TEL: 0633 413000 FAX: 0633 412910

Consistently acknowledged as one of the finest hotels in Wales, this refurbished Victorian manor house is set in its own 300-acre estate of mature parkland. Spacious rooms are elegantly furnished with comfort in mind – a lounge for relaxation, two bars and a splendid terrace. There are two fine restaurants – The Patio, located in the picturesque conservatory, and Hedley's. Although they differ in style, both benefit from the culinary skills of reigning Welsh Chef of the Year Trefor Jones and his award-winning junior chef. Careful design has ensured that recent extensions are in keeping with the original style. A full range of banqueting and conference facilities caters for all requirements.

Sports enthusiasts will enjoy the good recreational and leisure facilities available on site and in the locality. On the estate, an ancient woodland walk winds through Coldra Wood, with its rare flora and fauna. Special activity weekends can be arranged for parties, including murder mysteries and hot-air ballooning. Of interest nearby are Tintern Abbey, the Wye Valley and the castles at Chepstow and Caerphilly. **Directions:** Leave M4 at junction 24; hotel is 400 yards along the A48 towards Newport on the right-hand side. Price guide: Single £85–£100; double/twin £99–£150; suite £150–£165.

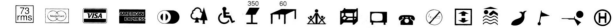

THE COURT HOTEL & RESTAURANT

LAMPHEY, NR TENBY, PEMBROKE, PEMBROKESHIRE SA71 5NT
TEL: 0646 672273 FAX: 0646 672480

Relax and – if you want to – shape up at The Court Hotel, which has an indoor heated swimming pool, sauna, solarium and gymnasium. If you prefer to play in open waters, the hotel provides yacht and boat hire on a daily basis and nearby Milford Haven Waterway offers a range of other water-borne activities. The hotel has special arrangements for golf at nearby Tenby Golf Club, or try sea, coarse or fly-fishing, riding, tennis or squash – all are available locally. For ramblers, the 180-mile Pembrokeshire Coast Footpath is not to be missed. Bargains may be found in the local craft and antiques shops, or discover history at Caldey Island Monastery, St David's Cathedral and the 13th-century Bishop's Palace at Lamphey. Alternatively, just unwind in the seclusion of the hotel's extensive gardens or conservatory and enjoy being cossetted and waited upon. Choose from the daily country house menu or dine à la carte in the elegant restaurant. Seafood is a speciality, with Llawhaden trout a particular favourite. All the bedrooms are individually furnished. There is no extra charge for children up to 16 sharing a room with their parents. Call the conference and meeting services division for details of business facilities. **Directions:** A477 from Carmarthen. Left at Milton village for Lamphey. Price guide: Single £59–£69; double/twin £79–£99; suite £89–£129. **Special rates for 2 days or more D.B.B.**

THE HOTEL PORTMEIRION

PORTMEIRION, GWYNEDD LL48 6ET
TEL: 0766 770228 FAX: 0766 771331

Portmeirion is a magical, private Italianate village, designed by the renowned architect Sir Clough Williams-Ellis, which was started in 1925 and completed in the 1970s. It enjoyed a celebrated clientele from the start – writers such as George Bernard Shaw, H G Wells, Bertrand Russell and Noel Coward were habitués. It is set in 120 acres of beautiful gardens and woodland, including 2 miles of tranquil sandy beaches, and provides accommodation for visitors either in the village or in the main hotel. The Hotel Portmeirion, originally a mansion house, has been sensitively restored, retaining striking features from the period, such as the Victorian Mirror Room. The bedrooms are furnished to the highest standards, 14 rooms being in the hotel and 21 rooms and suits in the village while the restaurant offers the best French and British cooking, the seasonal menu relying on fresh, locally produced ingredients. AA C & Care award. Swimming and tennis are available within the grounds as well as golf at Porthmadog (with complimentary green fees), and sailing is close at hand. The Ffestiniog and Snowdon mountain railways, slate caverns and Bodnant Gardens are nearby. Conference facilities can accommodate up to 100 people. Closed 9th January to 4th February. **Directions:** Portmeirion lies off the A487 between Penrhyndeudrath and Porthmadog. Price guide: Single £57–£102; double/twin £67–£112; suite £96–£146.

In association with MasterCard

WARPOOL COURT HOTEL

ST DAVID'S, PEMBROKESHIRE SA62 6BN
TEL: 0437 720300 FAX: 0437 720676

Originally built as St David's Cathedral Choir School in the 1860s, Warpool Court enjoys spectacular scenery at the heart of the Pembrokeshire National Park, with views over the coast and St Bride's Bay to the islands beyond. First converted to a hotel 30 years ago, the Court has undergone extensive refurbishments during the last 10 years. All 25 comfortably furnished bedrooms have en suite bathrooms and some have glorious sea views. The hotel restaurant enjoys a splendid reputation. Imaginative table d'hôte and à la carte menus offer a wide selection of modern and traditional dishes. Local produce, including Welsh lamb and beef, is used whenever possible, with crab, lobster, sewin and sea bass caught just off the coast. Salmon and mackerel are smoked on the premises and a variety of herbs are grown. The hotel gardens are ideal for a peaceful stroll or an after-dinner drink on a summer's evening. There is a covered heated swimming pool and all-weather tennis court in the grounds. A path from the hotel leads straight onto the Pembrokeshire Coastal Path, with its rich variety of wildlife and spectacular scenery. Boating and watersports are available locally. St David's Peninsula offers a wealth of history and natural beauty and has inspired many famous artists. **Directions:** The hotel is signposted from St David's town centre. Price guide: Single £40–£65; double/twin £64–£130.

FAIRYHILL

REYNOLDSTON, GOWER, NR SWANSEA, WEST GLAMORGAN SA3 1BS
TEL: 0792 390139 FAX: 0792 391358

An 18th century mansion, Fairyhill is set in 24 acres of glorious wooded parkland, and a $\frac{1}{2}$ mile of trout stream winds through its grounds. Fairyhill lies at the heart of the Gower peninsula, Britain's first designated area of outstanding natural beauty. Originally a family home, Fairyhill has a delightfully uncommercial, unpretentious atmosphere to it. The owners complement this informality with first-class hospitality and attention to detail: all 11 double bedrooms have been decorated and furnished individually, and each has an en suite bathroom. The restaurant, one of the most coveted in South Wales, is loved for its excellent cuisine. Fairyhill is recommended in the Good Hotel Guide. There are conference facilities for up to 50, in the boardroom or the spacious conference room. Some of Britain's finest beaches fringe the Gower coastline, and activities include hill-walking, hang-gliding, wind-surfing and pony-trekking. **Directions:** Exit junction 47 off M4. Follow Swansea signs. After 1 mile turn right at roundabout and follow signs for Gower and Gowerton. Turn right at Gowerton lights and continue for 12 miles. Fairyhill is on the left. Price guide: Single £65–£75; double/twin £75–£85.

NORTON HOUSE HOTEL AND RESTAURANT

NORTON ROAD, MUMBLES, SWANSEA SA3 5TQ
TEL: 0792 404891 FAX: 0792 403210

This elegant Georgian hotel, set in well-kept gardens only a few hundred yards from the seashore of Swansea Bay, provides a comfortable and peaceful base from which to explore the countryside of South Wales. Resident proprietors Jan and John Power have earned a reputation for offering attentive, friendly service. The bedrooms all have private amenities and four of the more spacious rooms have four-poster beds. The restaurant overlooks the terrace and gardens. Starters include bara lawr, a puff-pastry shell filled with cockles, laverbread and smoked bacon, followed by main-course dishes such as stiw cig oen, a rich Welsh-lamb stew served with buttered vegetables and herb dumplings. Golf and riding can be arranged locally. The hotel has conference facilities for up to 20 people. The unspoiled Gower Peninsula is nearby, with its wide sandy bays and rugged cliffs. Mumbles village is only a short walk away, while the city of Swansea is alive with galleries, theatres, a good shopping centre, its famous market and the maritime quarter. **Directions:** From London, leave the M4 at junction 42. After Briton Ferry Bridge take A483 to Swansea, then A4067 alongside Swansea Bay. A mile beyond the Mumbles sign, the hotel is signposted on the right-hand side. Price guide: Single £55–£65; double/twin £65–£80.

PENALLY ABBEY

PENALLY, TENBY, PEMBROKESHIRE SA70 7PY
TEL: 0834 843033 FAX: 0834 844714

Penally Abbey, a beautiful, Gothic-style mansion, offers comfort and hospitality in a secluded setting by the sea. Standing in 5 acres of gardens and woodland on the edge of Pembrokeshire National Park, the hotel overlooks Carmarthen Bay and Caldey Island. The bedrooms in the main building and in the adjoining coach house are well furnished, many with four-poster beds. The emphasis is on relaxation – enjoy a late breakfast and dine at leisure. Fresh seasonal delicacies are offered in the candle-lit restaurant, with its chandeliers and colonnades. Guests can enjoy a game in the snooker room or relax in the elegant sunlit lounge, overlooking the terrace and gardens. In the grounds there is a wishing well and a ruined chapel – the last surviving link with the hotel's monastic past. Water-skiing, surfing, sailing, riding and parascending are available nearby. Sandy bays and rugged cliffs are features of this coastline, making it ideal for exhilarating walks or simply building sandcastles on the beach. As its rates include the cost of dinner, this friendly hotel offers splendid value for money. **Directions:** Penally Abbey is situated adjacent to the church on Penally village green. Price guide (including dinner): Single £80; double/twin £128–£140.

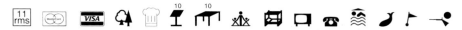

TYNYCORNEL HOTEL

TAL-Y-LLYN, TYWYN, GWYNEDD LL36 9AJ
TEL: 0654 782288 FAX: 0654 782679

Situated in the magnificent Snowdonia National Park, Tynycornel Hotel overlooks its own 222-acre lake, whose waters reflect the grandeur of Cader Idris. Originally constructed as a farmhouse in the 16th century, the hotel has been extensively and sensitively refurbished so that none of the original ambience has been lost. The spacious lounge has views over the lake, with comfortable furniture, fine antiques and original prints and a blazing fire in winter. The 15 pretty bedrooms enjoy lakeside or garden views, with bathrooms en suite. There is a cosy bar. The restaurant offers a high standard of cuisine and the set-price menu changes daily. Within the grounds there is a sauna,

solarium, and heated outdoor swimming pool against a beautiful mountain backdrop. Tynycornel is an angler's paradise – wild brown trout, salmon and sea trout fishing are readily available – and the hotel is equipped with 8 petrol-powered boats and provides tackle hire, freezing facilities and a drying room. The stunning landscape offers many opportunities for those interested in birdwatching, walking and photography. Snowdonia and mid-Wales are steeped in history and a wide variety of leisure pursuits can be enjoyed. **Directions:** Tal-y-Llyn is signposted from the main A487 Machynlleth-Dolgellau road. The hotel is on the lake shore. Price guide: Single £45; double/twin £90; suite £120.

THE CWRT BLEDDYN HOTEL

LLANGYBI, NEAR USK, GWENT, SOUTH WALES NP5 1PG
TEL: 0633 49521 FAX: 0633 49220

Set in 17 acres of wooded grounds, this 14th century manor house, not far from the Roman town of Caerleon, is the perfect location from which to explore the Wye Valley and Forest of Dean. The hotel is a fine example of the traditional and the modern under one roof. Carved panelling and huge fireplaces in the lounge lend an air of classic country-house comfort. The 36 en suite bedrooms are spacious and offer guests every amenity, and most have wonderful views over the surrounding countryside. Cwrt Bleddyn's restaurant is renowned for its French-influenced cuisine, with both à la carte and table d'hôte menus. There is a good choice of vegetarian dishes. Light meals are also served in the hotel's country club. Here, extensive leisure facilities include an indoor heated swimming pool, sauna, solarium, steam room and beauty salon. Alternatively, guests may just wish to stroll and relax in the grounds. Nearby is the local beauty spot of Llandegfedd, with its 434-acre reservoir. The hotel is open all year round. Private dining/function rooms are available. **Directions:** From Cardiff/Bristol, leave M4 at junction 25. Hotel is 3 miles north of Caerleon on the road to Usk. From the Midlands, take M5, then A40 to Monmouth. Turn off A449, through Usk, over stone bridge, then left towards Caerleon for 4 miles. Price guide: Single £85; double/twin £115.

Settle down to enjoy a real Scottish Classic

Filled with character and all the flavour of the highlands, Walkers shortbread has been a traditional favourite since Joseph Walker first opened his bakery in the village of Aberlour in 1898.

Baked to the original family recipe, Walkers shortbread contains only the finest ingredients, with not an artificial flavouring, colouring or additive in sight – just natural goodness and the unmistakable taste of pure, creamery butter.

In its distinctive tartan packaging, no other shortbread looks or tastes like Walkers. So take a Scottish classic off the shelf and savour the flavour of the highlands.

The world's classic pure butter shortbread

 Walkers Shortbread Ltd, Aberlour-on-Spey, Scotland AB38 9PD. Telephone: 0340 871555 Fax: 0340 871355

Johansens Recommended Hotels in

Scotland

THAINSTONE HOUSE HOTEL AND COUNTRY CLUB

INVERURIE, ABERDEENSHIRE AB51 5NT
TEL: 0467 621643 FAX: 0467 625084

Sitting resplendent in 40 acres of lush meadowland, Thainstone House opened in summer 1992 to offer the best in private and corporate hospitality. With its range of modern facilities and comfortable classical style, its environment is one where tradition and innovation live in perfect harmony. Couples, families and individuals alike are invited to indulge themselves in this luxuriously appointed, 19th-century Palladian mansion. High-ceilinged rooms with deep cornices, columns and neo-classical relief are decorated with antique furnishings and fine fabrics, wood and plasterwork. The culinary team includes Bill Gibb, 1990 World Championship silver medal winner, and Edward Donovan, 1990 Junior Chef of the Year UK. Their marvellous cooking can be enjoyed in Simpson's Restaurant. There is a splendid Roman-style indoor swimming pool and a host of leisure facilities. Opportunities for golf, shooting, fishing, pony-trekking and hill-walking abound. The hotel stands at the start of the famous Castle and Whisky trails. Flexible conference and banqueting facilities are available. **Directions:** Take A96 north from Aberdeen (14 miles). Turn left at Thainstone roundabout; hotel is 2 miles south of Inverurie. Price guide: Single £75; double/twin £95; suite £125.

FARLEYER HOUSE HOTEL

ABERFELDY, PERTHSHIRE PH15 2JE
TEL: 0887 820332 FAX: 0887 829430

Farleyer House stands amid mature woodland overlooking the Tay Valley. The restaurant won the *Good Food Guide* Tayside Restaurant of the Year 1990 award for its wonderful cuisine. It is also the holder of two AA Rosettes, and is highly praised in the most prestigious food guides. A more relaxed and informal meal may be enjoyed in the new Scottish Bistro where the blackboard menu offers an outstanding choice. The house has a lengthy history, dating back to the 16th century. It has 'a warm luxurious feel with soft-pile carpets, full-bodied drapes, clusters of paintings and scattered '*objets d'art*'. The 30 acres of woodland and parkland in which Farleyer House stands are popular with grouse shooters. Deer-stalking, fishing, riding, sailing and water sports can be arranged and there is a 6-hole practice golf course in the grounds. The central location makes this hotel with its two Red Stars a perfect base for touring the countryside and historic towns of Scotland. Dogs are accommodated separately from the main house and strictly by prior arrangement. **Directions:** Drive through Weem on the B846 past Castle Menzies and Farleyer is on the Kinloch–Rannoch road. Price guide: Single £40–£60; double/twin £70–£90.

SUMMER ISLES HOTEL

ACHILTIBUIE, ROSS-SHIRE IV26 2YG
TEL: 085482 282 FAX: 085482 251

The awe-inspiring wilderness of sea, mountains and islands is the setting for this unique hotel. It has been personally run for many years by proprietors Mark and Geraldine Irvine, and the atmosphere is relaxed and unstuffy – visitors unwind easily and soon find themselves among friends. So therapeutic is the combination of good food, comfortable accommodation and splendid surroundings that many guests return year after year. Nearly everything served in the restaurant is home-produced or caught locally. There are scallops, lobsters, langoustines, halibut, turbot, salmon and venison, along with home-made breads and pastries. Access to fresh ingredients allows award-winning chef Chris Firth-Bernard to produce superb menus – he strives for perfection with every course. Dinner is served at 8pm. After breakfast, Mark and Geraldine are happy to talk to guests about fishing, birdwatching, sailing around the islands to see the seal colonies or exploring on foot. It is advisable to bring sensible outdoor clothing. Open from Easter to mid-October. **Directions:** Ten miles north of Ullapool, turn along the twisting single-track road that skirts Lochs Lurgain, Badagyle and Oscaig under the eye of Stac Polly. Achiltibuie is 15 miles further; hotel is just past post office. Price guide: Single £40–£55; double/twin £60–£85.

INVERCRERAN COUNTRY HOUSE HOTEL

GLEN CRERAN, APPIN, ARGYLL PA38 4BJ
TEL: 063 173 414 FAX: 063 173 532

The outstanding setting of Invercreran House is one of the many reasons for its popularity. Surrounded by mountains, it stands in 25 secluded acres of shrub gardens and woodland, overlooking the mature trees and meadows of Glen Creran. Guests can stroll through the grounds towards the River Creran. Viewed from the outside, it is surprising to discover that the hotel has only nine guest bedrooms. The interiors, reception rooms and bedrooms alike are spacious. In the large lounge there is a free-standing fireplace where logs burn beneath a copper canopy. The Kersley family are involved in all aspects of the day-to-day running of the house. Their son Tony, the master chef, prepares delicious dishes that emphasise the full flavour of fresh Scottish game, fish, vegetables and soft fruits. Meals are served in the semi-circular, marble-floored dining room. Invercreran House is well positioned for touring the Western Highlands, offering easy access to Oban, Fort William and Glencoe. Closed November to early March. **Directions:** Hotel is off the A828 Oban–Fort William road, 14 miles north of Connel Bridge, 18 miles south of Ballachulish Bridge. Travelling to Invercreran at the head of Loch Creran, stay on the minor road going north east into Glen Creran; hotel is 3/4 mile on left. Price guide: Single £54; double/twin £88–£120.

     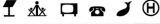

DARROCH LEARG HOTEL

BRAEMAR ROAD, BALLATER, ABERDEENSHIRE AB35 5UX
TEL: 03397 55443 FAX: 03397 55443

Built in 1888 as a fashionable country residence, Darroch Learg lies in 4 acres of leafy grounds and gardens high above the Ballater Golf course, the River Dee and the Balmoral Estate, on the slopes of the Craigendarroch. A hotel of some 50 years' standing, the building was formerly used as a shooting lodge, and clay-pigeon and game shooting count today among the activities available to visitors to this fine Scottish retreat. The hotel comprises two 19th century country residences: Darroch Learg and Oakhall (the latter a turreted baronial mansion) both noted for their architectural flourishes. In the public rooms, an understated elegance is created from polished natural pine, select furnishings and crackling log fires on chilly nights. The bright, colourful bedrooms have been newly and individually decorated, with all modern conveniences. Guests are invited to unwind in the non-smoking drawing room (or adjacent smoke room) before choosing delicious food from chef Robert MacPherson's imaginative and widely-renowned menu in the dining room (and conservatory) which splendidly overlooks the Glen Muick hills. The wealth of outdoor activities on offer includes walking, riding, mountain-biking, loch and river fishing, gliding, paragliding and skiing. **Directions:** At the western edge of Ballater on the A93. Price guide: Single £40; double/twin £70–£90.

RAEMOIR HOUSE HOTEL

BANCHORY, KINCARDINESHIRE AB31 4ED
TEL: 03302 4884 FAX: 03302 2171 TELEX: 73315

Raemoir House is delightfully situated in an estate of 3,500 acres, sheltered from the northerly winds by the Hill of Fare, which rises some 1,500 feet behind the house. The main part of this elegant mansion dates from the 18th century, and to the rear the 16th-century Ha'Hoose is listed for its special architectural interest. An extremely friendly greeting is extended to guests during their stay in this family-run hotel, with its fine views of the surrounding countryside. The house is tastefully furnished with antiques and many of the rooms have valuable wall tapestries. In addition to the attractive bedrooms in the main building, charming self-catering apartments are situated in the converted coach house and stables. Good Scottish and international cooking, prepared to a high standard, is served in the dining room. Fishing, shooting and stalking on the estate can be arranged. A compact 9-hole pitch-and-putt golf course is available on site, or 18-hole golf can be played at Banchory. Guests can tone up in the exercise room with its sauna, multi-gym, bike and rowing machine. There are numerous castles to visit nearby, such as Balmoral and Crathes. **Directions:** Raemoir House Hotel is on the A980 Raemoir road from Banchory. Price guide: Single £52.50–£79; double/twin £115–£128.

ARISAIG HOUSE

BEASDALE, BY ARISAIG, INVERNESS-SHIRE PH39 4NR
TEL: 068 75 622 FAX: 068 75 626

Princely redwoods rising above the sudden abundance of Arisaig's oak and rhododendron declare your journey done: now it is time to relax and enjoy the hospitality offered by your hosts, the Smither family. Natural light floods into the house, streaming through tall windows into the inner hall to warm the oak staircase and cast a gleam across polished furniture. The chef's epicurean offerings – supported by a lineage of fine château bottlings – give promise of the restoration of body and soul. Comprising game in season, crisp local vegetables, fruits de mer and pâtisserie baked daily, the cuisine is always a gastronomic delight. High above the ponticum and crinodendrons, the 13 spacious bedrooms afford a magnificent vista of mountains, sea and ever-changing sky. On some days, the clink of billiard balls or the clunk of croquet from the beautiful grounds are the only sounds to thread their way across the rustle of a turning page. On other days guests are hard to find, taking trips on ferries to Skye and the Inner Hebrides or discovering the landscape that has barely changed since Bonnie Prince Charlie's passage through these parts many years ago. Closed early November to mid-March. Arisaig House is a Relais et Châteaux member. **Directions:** Three miles from Arisaig village on the A830 Mallaig road. Price guide : Single £65; double/twin £130–£215.

13 rms | MasterCard | VISA | AMERICAN EXPRESS | ⌂ | 🏕 12 | ⚔ 10 | 🖵 | ☎ | 🏌 | 🦢 | → | Ⓗ

DALMUNZIE HOUSE

SPITTAL O'GLENSHEE, BLAIRGOWRIE, PERTHSHIRE PH10 7QG
TEL: 0250 885224 FAX: 0250 885225

Dalmunzie House is beautifully tucked away high in the Scottish Highlands, 18 miles north of Blairgowrie and 15 miles south of Braemar. Standing in its own mountainous 6,000-acre sporting estate, it is run by Simon and Alexandra Winton. Guests come to enjoy the relaxed family atmosphere which, together with unobtrusive service and attention, ensures a comfortable stay. The bedrooms are individual in character, some with antiques, others romantically set in the turrets of the house, all tastefully decorated. Delicately cooked traditional Scottish fare is created from local ingredients fresh from the hills and lochs. The menu changes daily and dishes are served in the dining room, accompanied by wines from the well-stocked cellar. Among the sporting activities available on site are golf (the 9-hole course is the highest in Britain) and shooting for grouse, ptarmigan and black game. Other country pursuits include river and loch fishing and stalking for red deer. Pony-trekking can be organised locally. Glenshee Ski Centre is 6 miles away: it offers cross-country and downhill skiing. Closer to home, the hotel games room provides more sedate pastimes for all the family. Closed early November to 28 December. **Directions:** Dalmunzie is on the A93 at the Spittal O'Glenshee, south of Braemar. Price guide: Single £45–£51; double/twin £67–£83.

KINLOCH HOUSE HOTEL

BY BLAIRGOWRIE, PERTHSHIRE PH10 6SG
TEL: 0250 884237 FAX: 0250 884333

Built in 1840, Kinloch House is an elegant example of a Scottish country home. Set in 25 acres of wooded parkland grazed by Highland cattle, it offers panoramic views to the south, over Marlee Loch to the Sidlaw Hills beyond. It has a grand galleried hall with an ornate glass ceiling and fine paintings and antiques in the reception rooms. A carefully incorporated extension echoes the original style, with oak panelling and ornate friezes. Chef Bill McNicoll has built a reputation for good Scottish fare – lamb, fish, shellfish, wildfowl and game are all available in season. Choices from the menu such as sautéed breast of woodcock or roast partridge complemented by an extensive wine list. The cocktail bar, which stocks over 140 malt whiskies, is adjacent to the conservatory and is a focal point of the hotel. David and Sarah Shentall offer a warm welcome to all the guests, whether they come simply to enjoy the beauty of the area, or to take advantage of the local pursuits of golf, hill walking, fishing and shooting. For the sightseer, Glamis Castle, Scone Palace and Blair Castle are among the area's attractions. 2 AA Rosettes. Winner 1992 Scotlands Commended STB "Best Dining Experience". Closed at Christmas. **Directions:** The hotel is 3 miles west of Blairgowrie, off the A923 Dunkeld road. Price guide (including dinner): Single £72.95; double/twin £144.90–£177.45.

BORTHWICK CASTLE

BORTHWICK, NORTH MIDDLETON, MIDLOTHIAN EH23 4QY
TEL: 0875 820514 FAX: 0875 821702 TELEX: 72422

Sir Walter Scott described this illustrious castle, built in 1430, as 'the finest example of a twin-tower keep'. Nestling in a valley 12 miles south of Edinburgh, its massive towers rise 110 feet to dominate the hamlet of Borthwick. Once the refuge of Mary, Queen of Scots, and the Earl of Bothwell, and later besieged by Oliver Cromwell, its medieval ambience has been maintained. The art of the 15th-century stonemasons is an impressive backdrop for the heraldic trappings, swords, tapestries and gleaming suits of armour that decorate the interiors. Guests dine by candlelight in the Great Hall, with its magnificent 40-foot Gothic arch, minstrels gallery and enormous hooded fireplace.

The castle offers modern British cuisine with a bias to Scottish fayre and is equally suited to intimate dinners as it is to glittering banquets. The 10 bedchambers, including 4 with four-poster beds, are all different in décor, but all offer en suite facilities and are in keeping with their historic surroundings. There is access to some 45,000 acres of land, including prime salmon and trout beats and shooting facilities. Riding and golf can also be arranged. Closed December, January and February. **Directions:** 12 miles south of Edinburgh on the A7. At North Middleton, follow signs for Borthwick. A private road then leads to the castle. Price guide: Single £80–£150; double/twin £95–£165.

ROMAN CAMP HOTEL

CALLANDER, PERTHSHIRE FK17 8BG
TEL: 0877 30003 FAX: 0877 31533

Roman Camp Hotel, originally built in 1625 as a hunting lodge for the Dukes of Perth, takes its name from a nearby Roman encampment. Reminiscent of a French château, the hotel's turrets house myriad period features, including a tiny chapel, linenfold wood panelling and ornate moulded ceilings. Set on the banks of the River Teith, the hotel is surrounded by 20 acres of superb grounds including a listed walled garden where herbs and flowers are grown for the hotel. The public rooms, drawing room, sun lounge and library are characterised by grand proportions, antique furnishings and fine views over the river and gardens. The bedrooms are individually and tastefully furnished. A richly painted ceiling, depicting traditional Scottish designs, is a unique feature of the restaurant, where the thoughtfully compiled menu is complemented by an extensive wine list. Guests are welcome to fish free of charge on the private stretch of the river, while all around are plenty of interesting walks. Within easy reach are the Trossachs, Doune Motor Museum and Aberfoyle. Dogs are welcome by prior arrangement. **Directions:** Approaching Callander on the A84, the entrance to the hotel is between two cottages in Callander's main street. Price guide: Single £70; double/twin from £90–£125; suite £145.

CRAIGELLACHIE HOTEL

CRAIGELLACHIE, BANFFSHIRE AB38 9SR
TEL: 0340 881204 FAX: 0340 881253

Overlooking the River Spey, with direct access to the Speyside Walk, Craigellachie Hotel is located in the centre of Scotland's famous Malt Whisky and Castle Trails, in one of the most picturesque villages in Moray. This Victorian hotel opened in 1893 and has recently undergone a meticulous restoration to incorporate all the amenities of a first-class hotel while retaining the charm and elegance of a Scottish country house. Many of the 30 individually designed bedrooms overlook the River Spey and several have a view of the local landmark, Thomas Telford's slender iron bridge. The hotel's Ben Aigan Restaurant has firmly established a good reputation for its innovative treatment of traditional Scottish recipes. Only fresh local produce is used in the preparation of dishes, which are always beautifully presented and accompanied by an extensive wine list. After dinner, guests can choose from a wide selection of local malt whiskies. Craigellachie specialises in personalised packages including traditional Scottish Christmas and New Year events. Sporting holidays can include golf with private tuition, salmon and trout fishing, deer stalking, game shooting, falconry and pony-trekking. There is also a sauna & solaruim and an old-fashioned games room. **Directions:** Just off the A95 between Grantown-on-Spey (24 miles) and Elgin (12 miles). Price guide: Single £53–£78.50; double/twin £87–£153.

BARON'S CRAIG HOTEL

ROCKCLIFFE BY DALBEATTIE, KIRKCUDBRIGHTSHIRE DG5 4QF
TEL: 055663 225 FAX: 055663 328

Baron's Craig Hotel stands in wooded country overlooking Solway and Rough Firth, a tidal inlet biting deep into tree-covered and heathered hills. Thanks to the mild climate, the 12-acre grounds are ablaze with colour throughout much of the holiday season, especially in May, when masses of rhododendrons are in bloom. An imposing granite edifice, Baron's Craig was built in 1880 and harmoniously extended more recently to provide several new rooms. Most of the 27 comfortable bedrooms have en suite facilities; all have colour TV, video, radio, direct-dial telephone and baby-listening service. The original character of the building has been retained, with furnishings chosen to complement the period style. Excellent international cooking is augmented by a comprehensive wine list. Only three minutes from the hotel is a safe beach for swimming, while there is abundant scope for golf, fishing, boating, sailing and walking nearby. Among the local attractions are Castle Douglas, New Abbey, Glen Trool and Kirkcudbright. The new owner, Alberto Capaccioli, offers a warm welcome to all guests. Closed from November to Easter. **Directions:** Rockcliffe is a small village just off the A710 south of Dalbeattie. Price guide: (including bed and breakfast) Single £30–£40; double/twin £32–£45.

CROMLIX HOUSE

KINBUCK, DUNBLANE, PERTHSHIRE FK15 9JT
TEL: 0786 822125 FAX: 0786 825450

The Cromlix estate of some 5,000 acres in the heart of Perthshire is a relaxing retreat. Built as a family home in 1874, much of the house remains unchanged including many fine antiques acquired over the generations. Proprietors David and Ailsa Assenti (previously nominated for excellence at Ballathie) are proud of their tradition of country house hospitality. The individually designed bedrooms and spacious suites have recently been redecorated with period fabrics to enhance the character and fine furniture whilst retaining the essential feeling of a much loved home. Unpretentious, relaxing and most welcoming. The spacious public rooms have open fires. In the restaurant, the finest local produce is used, including game from the estate, lamb and locally caught salmon. Cromlix is an ideal venue for small conferences and business meetings, and there is a small chapel – the perfect setting for weddings. Extensive sporting and leisure facilities include trout and salmon fishing and game shooting in season. Challenging golf courses within easy reach include Rosemount, Carnoustie and St Andrews. The location is ideal for touring the Southern Highlands, with Edinburgh and Glasgow only an hour away. **Directions:** Cromlix House lies 4 miles north of Dunblane, north of Kinbuck on B8033 and 4 miles south of Braco. Price guide: Single £95; double/twin £130; suite £180.

ENMORE HOTEL

MARINE PARADE, KIRN, DUNOON, ARGYLL PA23 8HH
TEL: 0369 2230 FAX: 0369 2148

Known by some as the jewel on the Clyde, the waterfront town of Dunoon is often regarded as the gateway to the Western Highlands. Enmore Hotel is an attractive house, built in 1785 as a summer retreat for a wealthy cotton merchant. It has since been fully restored by owners David and Angela Wilson. Pretty country wallpaper and bright fabrics characterise the bedrooms, with fluffy towelling robes and flowers among the extras. One of the bedrooms has a water bed and an invigorating whirlpool bath and another has a four-poster bed with a Jacuzzi. In the restaurant, the emphasis is very much on the use of fresh, local produce to create traditional Scottish dishes. Typical choices may include Arbroath smokies, haggis soup, kippers or steak served in a Drambuie and cream sauce. Chef-patron David Wilson offers a five-course table d'hôte menu each evening. Two international-standard squash courts are available; guests can improve their game by watching themselves on the video playback. Dunoon is well equipped with recreational amenities, including bowling, tennis, sailing and a championship golf course. **Directions:** Kirn is on the A815, north-west of Dunoon (A885). Price guide: Single £35–£45; double/twin £78–£110.

CHANNINGS

SOUTH LEARMONTH GARDENS, EDINBURGH EH4 1EZ
TEL: 031-315 2226 FAX: 031-332 9631

Channings is located on a quiet cobbled street only 10 minutes' walk from the centre of Edinburgh, with easy access to the host of shops on Princes Street and the timeless grandeur of Edinburgh Castle. Formerly five Edwardian town houses, the original features have been restored with flair and consideration and the atmosphere is like an exclusive country club. Guests can relax in one of the lounges with a coffee or afternoon tea. For those who like to browse, the hotel has an interesting collection of antique prints, furniture, objets d'art, periodicals and books. The Brasserie offers varied menus from a light lunch to full evening meals. Seven ground floor suites provide versatile accommodation for corporate requirements, small seminars and presentations, while both the Kingsleigh Suite and oak-panelled library make an ideal venue for cocktail parties and private dinners. At the rear of the hotel is a terraced, patio garden. Special weekend breaks are available throughout the year and offer good value. Closed for Christmas. **Directions:** Go north-west from Queensferry Street, over Dean Bridge on to Queensferry Road. Take third turning on right down South Learmonth Avenue, turn right at end into South Learmonth Gardens. Price guide: Single £90; double/twin £125.

THE HOWARD

32-36 GREAT KING STREET, EDINBURGH EH3 6QH
TEL: 031-557 3500 FAX: 031-557 6515

Since its conversion from private residence to hotel, The Howard has been sumptuously appointed throughout and offers a service to match the surroundings. The character of this Georgian town house prevails. The 16 bedrooms, including two suites, are beautifully furnished with antiques, while the drawing room centres on an elaborate crystal chandelier. The restaurant, Number 36, seats up to 50 people for business and private lunches, offering top Scottish cuisine, with a classical inspiration. Importantly in this busy city, car-parking at The Howard is free for diners as well as guests in the private car park immediately next to the hotel. Two meeting rooms, the Oval Room and the Cumberland Room, can accommodate 12-30 guests, and business visitors may like to note a special deal with BA: Heathrow –Edinburgh return flight, bed and breakfast, for less than the price of a standard scheduled flight. The Howard is an integral part of the largest classified historical monument in Britain: Edinburgh's New Town. It is an ideal base from which to explore Edinburgh's cultural heritage. **Directions:** Take the third road on the left off Princes Street into Frederick Street. Go right into George Street, left into Hanover Street. At third set of lights, right into Great King Street. Hotel is on left. Price guide: Single £110–140; double £180; suite £255.

JOHNSTOUNBURN HOUSE

HUMBIE, NR EDINBURGH, EAST LOTHIAN EH36 5PL
TEL: 0875 33696 FAX: 0875 33626
As from January 1994 Tel: 0875 833696 Fax: 0875 833626

Dating from 1625, Johnstounburn House stands at the foot of the Lammermuir Hills, only 15 miles south of Edinburgh. Set amid lawns and parklands in a private estate, its grounds feature imposing yew hedges, an orchard, a patio rose garden and a herbaceons walled garden. Upon entering the house, guests will sense the depth of Scottish heritage preserved here. Refurbishments have enhanced the historical features while enabling guests to enjoy modern comforts. Of the 20 well-appointed bedrooms, 11 are in the house and nine in the tastefully converted coach house. There is a spacious cedar-panelled lounge where an open fire will warm you on chilly days. In the 18th-century, pine-panelled dining room, chef Bryan Thom prepares sumptuous fare from the finest Scottish produce. In the grounds guests can enjoy clay pigeon shooting, riding or fish in the trout-filled loch. Rough shooting and stalking can be arranged. There are also all-terrain vehicles which guests may drive over the Johnstoun 'burn' and through the fields. Muirfield and Gullane are among 15 golf courses nearby. Tantallon Castle, Abbotsford and Traquair House are a short drive away. **Directions:** From Edinburgh take A68 through Dalkeith and Pathhead to Fala. Turn left through Fala 1½ miles to T-junction; the hotel is on your right. Price guide: Single £95; double/twin £130; suite £155.

THE NORTON HOUSE HOTEL

INGLISTON, EDINBURGH EH28 8LX
TEL: 031-333 1275 FAX: 031-333 5305

This Victorian mansion, dating back to 1861, is now part of the Virgin Group. Situated in 55 acres of mature parkland, Norton House combines modern comforts with elegance. The 47 en suite bedrooms are bright and spacious, with many facilities, including a video channel. Influenced by the best Scottish and French traditions, the menu offers a balanced choice. Moments away, through leafy woodlands, a former stable block has been converted into a tavern, where drinks and snacks are available to families and friends. Set in a walled garden, it is an ideal venue for the barbecues which are a regular feature in the summer months. The Patio, Veranda and Usher Room lend a sense of occasion to small gatherings, while the Linlithgow Suite can cater for large-scale events such as banquets, weddings and conferences. Norton House is 1 mile from Edinburgh Airport and 6 miles from the city centre, making it a convenient base from which to explore the Trossachs, Borders and Lothians. Dogs accommodated by request. Special weekend rate, enquires welcome. **Directions:** From Edinburgh take A8 past airport and hotel is 1/2 mile on left. From Glasgow, follow M8 to its close, take the first exit off the roundabout following signs for Ratho, then turn left at the top of the hill. Price guide: Single £98–£115; double/twin £110–£140; suite £160.

THE ROYAL TERRACE

18 ROYAL TERRACE, EDINBURGH EH7 5AQ
TEL: 031-557 3222 FAX: 031-557 5334

The Royal Terrace Hotel, set in an old-world, cobblestoned road, is a beautiful and distinctive hotel, fashioned – as the name suggests – from a terrace of Georgian houses built to celebrate King George IV's visit to the city in 1822. Behind a façade inset with elegantly proportioned windows, the Royal Terrace is a sumptuous, yet warm and hospitable place to stay – beautifully furnished, with every facility on offer. The professionally staffed Leisure Club houses an indoor pool, Jacuzzi, sauna, steam room and solarium; the gardens are well landscaped – a peaceful retreat with fountains softly splashing and even a meditation temple. The management and staff are attentive yet discreet – chef Stuart Nichols' first-class cuisine is served in the Peacock Restaurant (or guests may choose to eat in the Conservatory overlooking the gardens). The Peacock Bar, stocking over 20 brands of fine malt whiskies, is a calm corner in which to meet friends or colleagues. The lounge and reception are likewise plushly furnished. Bedrooms are extravagantly carpeted and curtained, many with marble bathrooms, chandeliers and sofas just made for sinking into after a day spent exploring Edinburgh city centre, 8 minutes' walk away. **Directions:** travel down Princes Street. Left into Leith Street/Leith Walk. Right into Royal Terrace. Price guide: Single £98–£110; double/twin £135–£150; suite £185.

Mansion House Hotel

THE HAUGH, ELGIN, MORAY IV30 1AW
TEL: 0343 548811 FAX: 0343 547916

Overlooking the quietly flowing River Lossie stands this former baronial mansion, built in the mid-19th century. There are many beautiful trees in the grounds, including a copper beech tree dating back to the reign of Charles I. Carefully restored by its resident owners, this fine Victorian building offers first-class hotel facilities, including an indoor pool with gymnasium, Jacuzzi and sauna, as well as a new snooker room. The tastefully decorated public rooms are well furnished and the comfortably appointed bedrooms offer a choice of four-poster beds, family rooms and suites. Leading onto the riverside lawn is the ballroom, an attractive venue for private parties, dinner dances and other entertainment. The creative menu offers a range of original dishes, prepared with a high degree of culinary flair. Fish, chicken, lamb, beef and game are accompanied by a well-chosen wine list of over 100 bins, from vintage French labels to younger New World wines. Snacks and light meals are available from the bistro bar, The Dip Inn. Visitors to the Moray area can enjoy walks, visit castles and take part in a variety of country pursuits. The Whisky Trail is nearby, as is the historic town of Elgin itself. **Directions:** In Elgin, turn off the main A96 road into Haugh Road. The hotel is at the end of this road by the river. Price guide: Single £75; double/twin £110–£150.

CALLY PALACE HOTEL

GATEHOUSE OF FLEET, DUMFRIES & GALLOWAY DG7 2DL
TEL: 0557 814341 FAX: 0557 814522

Set in over 100 acres of forest and parkland, this 18th-century country house has been restored to its former glory by the McMillan family, the proprietors since 1981. On entering the hotel, guests will initially be impressed by the grand scale of the interior. Two huge marble pillars support the original moulded ceiling of the entrance hall. All the public rooms have ornate ceilings, original marble fireplaces and fine reproduction furniture. Combine these with good, traditional Scottish cooking and you have a hotel *par excellence*. The 55 en suite bedrooms have been individually decorated. Some are suites with a separate sitting room; others are large enough to accommodate a three-piece suite comfortably. An indoor leisure complex includes a swimming pool, Jacuzzi, saunas and solaria. In the grounds, there is an all-weather tennis court, a putting green, croquet, and a loch for fishing or boating. The hotel has its own 18-hole golf course situated around a loch and mature woodlands. Special weekend and over-60s breaks are available out of season. Closed January and February.

Directions: Sixty miles west of Carlisle, 1-1 1/2 miles from Gatehouse of Fleet junction on the main A75 road. Price guide: Including dinner: Single £70; double/twin £104–£140.

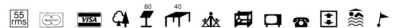

GLASGOW (Stewarton)

In association
with MasterCard **MasterCard**

CHAPELTOUN HOUSE

STEWARTON, AYRSHIRE KA3 3ED
TEL: 05604 82696 FAX: 05604 85100

Two brothers, Colin and Graeme McKenzie, run this friendly hotel with a personal, informal touch. The house was built to be the family home for a wealthy Scots industrialist and his young English wife. To celebrate this match, a romantic theme of thistles and roses was incorporated into the ornate plasterwork and masonry. A welcoming atmosphere is felt immediately on arrival in the spacious, oak-panelled hall, with its crackling log fire. There are splendid dining rooms and bedrooms with views across the gardens to the river. The two adjoining dining rooms are elegantly furnished with polished oak tables and tapestry chairs, while the cuisine is held in high regard. The hotel's hospitality has been acknowledged by the Scottish Tourist Board (4 Crowns, Highly Commended) and numerous travel guides. Landmarks within a 30-minute drive include the Burrell Collection, Royal Troon and the fascinating collections at Dean Castle, while there are ferries to Arran and Cumbrae. Culzean Castle and Burns country are less than an hour's drive away. Dogs by arrangement. **Directions:** The hotel is 18 miles south of Glasgow and 30 minutes from Glasgow Airport, off the Stewarton–Irvine road (B769). Go through Stewarton on the A735, take the second right after the viaduct onto B769. Hotel is 2 miles on. Price guide: Single £69–£84; double/twin £95–£129.

GLEDDOCH HOUSE

LANGBANK, RENFREWSHIRE PA14 6YE
TEL: 047554 711 FAX: 047554 201

Once the home of a Glasgow shipping baron, Gleddoch House stands in 360 acres, in a magnificent position with dramatic views across the River Clyde to Loch Lomond and the hills beyond. The hotel's public rooms have been recently renovated and there is a new sitting room. From the morning room and conservatory there are spectacular views over the Clyde estuary and Gleddoch estate. Fires are lit every morning in the three open fireplaces. The individually appointed bedrooms all have en suite facilities and some have four-poster beds. For business guests, more spacious executive-style rooms are available with writing desks. The Garden restaurant is renowned for its award-winning modern Scottish cuisine, enhanced by a list of more than 300 wines. Guests may use the Gleddoch Golf and Country Club adjacent to the hotel. On the estate, activities include clay pigeon shooting, archery, falconry and off-road driving, all of which can be tailored for corporate packages. The all-weather Gleddoch Equestrian Centre caters for riders of all levels. The hotel is 10 minutes from Glasgow Airport, and 20 minutes from the city centre. **Directions:** M8 towards Greenock; take B789 Langbank/ Houston exit. Follow signs to left and then right after $^{1}/_{2}$ mile; hotel is on left. Price guide: Single £90–£105; double/twin £130–£170; suite £170.

GLENBORRODALE CASTLE

GLENBORRODALE, ACHARACLE, ARGYLL PH36 4JP
TEL: O97 24 266 FAX: 097 24 224

Poised on the northern shores of Loch Sunart, overlooking the Isle of Mull, is Glenborrodale Castle, a magnificent château built at the turn of the century by a Victorian mining magnate. One of Scotland's finest castle hotels, it occupies about 1,000 acres and has been carefully restored by international entrepreneur, Peter de Savary. The furnishings are suitably stately, with well-chosen antiques, paintings and tapestries, indicative of the dignified sense of luxury which characterises this hotel. Local salmon, trout, shellfish and game all feature prominently on the menus, whether the choice be a light lunch or a five-course dinner. A possible topic of debate over the meal may be deciding which of the numerous leisure activities to undertake the following day. In addition to putting, snooker, clay pigeon shooting and sailing facilities on-site, there is a solarium, gymnasium and resident beautician and masseuse. A trip to Mull can be made on the Kilchorn–Tobermory ferry or a picnic taken to the secluded beach of Sanna. For guests who want to arrive in style, a helicopter service or a chauffeured limousine can be arranged. Closed 31 October to Easter. **Directions:** Take the A82 to Glasgow, 8 miles before Fort William turn left at Corran Ferry and follow signs to Glenborrodale via Strontian and Salen. Price guide: Single £105; double/twin £160–£260.

CULLODEN HOUSE HOTEL

INVERNESS, INVERNESS-SHIRE IV1 2NZ
TEL: 0463 790461 FAX: 0463 792181

Culloden House is a handsome Georgian mansion with a centuries-old tradition of hospitality. Among its famous visitors was Bonnie Prince Charlie, who fought his last battle by the park walls. The house stands in 40 acres of elegant lawns and parkland, where wild deer occasionally roam. Proprietors Ian and Marjory McKenzie have a high reputation with guests from all over the world. Thorough refurbishments of the décor and furnishings have enhanced the magnificent interiors. A good choice of accommodation is offered – from en suite single rooms to a four-poster double, or room with Jacuzzi – with the assurance that all rooms are appointed to the highest standards. New no-smoking suites are situated near the walled garden. In the Adam Dining Room, guests can savour superb cuisine prepared by acclaimed chef Michael Simpson, who trained at the Gleneagles Hotel and Hamburg Congress Centre. Business lunches, celebrations and functions can be held in the private dining room. Boat trips to Loch Ness can be arranged, while nearby are Cawdor Castle, the Clava Cairns burial ground and Culloden battlefield. From the hotel, numerous routes lead into the glens. **Directions:** Take the A96 road and turn as signed to Culloden. Turn again at little white church. Price guide: Single £110–£150; double/twin £150–£190; suite £190.

23 rms   40   20   10

KINGSMILLS HOTEL

CULCABOCK ROAD, INVERNESS, INVERNESS-SHIRE IV2 3LP
TEL: 0463 237166 FAX: 0463 225208 TELEX: 75566

Built in 1785, this historic hotel has been extended to offer comfort and elegance. It is only a mile from the town centre, in 3 acres of sleepy gardens, adjacent to Inverness Golf Course. There is a choice of attractively appointed bedrooms, all with modern amenities. In addition to the standard rooms, as pictured below, there are seven beautifully furnished suite-style rooms, also family rooms with bunk beds and six self-catering villas. The Leisure Club incorporates a large heated swimming pool, spa bath, steam cabin, sauna, sunbeds, mini-gym and pitch-and-putt. Hairdressing facilities are also provided. Throughout the year exceptionally good value is offered by special breaks which include local seasonal attractions. Golf, fishing, skiing, riding and pony-trekking can all be enjoyed nearby and, if required, arranged as part of an activity holiday. Christmas, Easter and New Year packages are also available. The Kingsmills Hotel is well placed for visiting the Highlands, Loch Ness, the Whisky Trail, Culloden battlefield and Cawdor Castle. USA representative – Thomas McFerran, telephone toll free: 800-215 443 7990.
Directions: Turn left off A9 signposted Kingsmills and Culcabock. Turn right at first roundabout, left at the second and hotel is on left just past golf course. Price guide: Single £80–£82; double/twin £97.50–£125.

MONTGREENAN MANSION HOUSE HOTEL

MONTGREENAN ESTATE, KILWINNING, AYRSHIRE KA13 7QZ
TEL: 0294 57733 FAX: 0294 85397

Set in 48 acres of wooded gardens, Montgreenan commands views towards Ailsa Craig and the Arran Hills, which make a spectacular sight at sunset. The history of the estate dates back to 1310, and the present mansion house was built in 1817 by Dr Robert Glasgow. The original features, including marble and brass fireplaces, decorative ceilings and plasterwork, have been retained. A family home until 1980, the hotel has a friendly atmosphere. The bedrooms are well appointed with antique and reproduction furniture and one of the bedrooms has a Jacuzzi bath. The elegant dining room, with burgundy-and-gold tapestried chairs, is the setting for dinner. Gourmet cooking features fresh Scottish salmon, lobster, oysters, game and Ayrshire beef. To accompany your meal, choose from 200 fine vintages. Glasgow and Prestwick Airport are only 30 minutes' drive away. Whatever the occasion, there are good facilities for conferences and entertaining. In addition to the 5-hole golf course on site, over 30 courses, including those at Royal Troon and Turnberry, are within 45 minutes' drive. Special rates available. **Directions:** 19 miles south of Glasgow, 4 miles north of Irvine. From Irvine take A736 towards Glasgow for 4 miles. Turn left at Torranyard Inn; hotel entrance is 2 minutes from there. Price guide: Single £60–£70; double/twin £80–£133.

In association with MasterCard · MasterCard

ISLE OF ERISKA

LEDAIG, BY OBAN, ARGYLL PA37 1SD
TEL: 0631 72371 FAX: 0631 72531

The island of Eriska lies off Scotland's rugged west coast, steeped in tradition (it derives its name from Erik the Red, who led the Norse invasions through the area in the 10th century). Eriska has been inhabited since the Bronze Age; the stern, imposing granite hotel itself dates back to 1884, when it was designed by architect Hippolyte Blanc to withstand the austerity of its locality. Argyll's only 5 Crown De Luxe hotel, Eriska is easily reached from the mainland by private vehicle bridge. Its family proprietors, who have run it for 20 years, are fully committed to the care and welfare of their guests. Bedrooms, each with private bathroom, are mostly spacious and all have been recently renovated.

Comfortable furnishings and atmosphere characterise the public rooms; here log fires and oak panels induce relaxation and conversation before an evening meal of Scottish cuisine, prepared from fresh and homegrown produce, and served in the candle-lit dining room by friendly attentive staff. Outdoor pursuits include clay pigeon shooting, water-skiing and windsurfing, plus pony-trekking or hiking around the island in search of flora and fauna. **Directions:** A85 towards Oban. At Connel proceed by bridge on A828 (to Fort William) for 4 miles, to north of Benderloch. Follow signs to Isle of Eriska. Price guide: Single: £110–£135; double/twin £150–£185.

UIG HOTEL

UIG, ISLE OF SKYE IV51 9YE
TEL: 0470 42205 FAX: 0470 42308

Grace Graham and her son David Taylor welcome guests to their hotel, set on the northern peninsula of the mystical Isle of Skye, where the golden eagle soars overhead and the once-familiar call of the corncrake can still be heard. The hotel is set in 3 acres of grounds on a hillside overlooking Uig Bay. Grace is responsible for the comfortable furnishings and decoration, which include a collection of watercolours and etchings by well-known artists. David ensures the smooth day-to-day running of the hotel and the good home cooking. Skye, nearly 70 miles long, is a wildlife haven of bays, moors and glens. Uig is the departure point for the Hebridean Ferry to the Outer Hebrides, North and South Uist,

Harris and Lewis. The hotel has its own pony-trekking using sturdy, good natured Highland ponies. From time to time Bridge Congresses and Garden and Wild Life tours are organised, details on request. In the west, near Dunvegan Castle, the ancestral seat of the MacLeods, are beautiful white coral beaches. The nearby town of Portree has a heated swimming pool, squash and tennis courts. There is a 9-hole golf course at Sconser. Closed mid-October to 1st April. Dogs accommodated by arrangement. **Directions:** Approaching Uig from Portree, the hotel is on the right, beside a white church. Price guide: Single £34; double/twin £68–£80.

EDNAM HOUSE HOTEL

BRIDGE STREET, KELSO, ROXBURGHSHIRE TD5 7HT
TEL: 0573 24168 FAX: 0573 226319

Overlooking the River Tweed, in 3 acres of gardens, Ednam House is one of the region's finest examples of Georgian architecture. This undulating, pastoral countryside was immortalised by Sir Walter Scott. Ednam House has been owned and managed by the Brooks family for over 60 years, spanning four generations. Although the grandiose splendour may seem formal, the warm, easy-going atmosphere is all-pervasive. The dining room, lounges and bars are comfortably furnished and command scenic views of the river and grounds. The bedrooms, 11 single and 21 double, are all well equipped. In the spacious dining room, the accent is on traditional cooking, with hot dishes, cold meats and home-made soups featured on the daily table d'hôte menu. A selection of interesting and reasonably priced wines is available. Ednam House is extremely popular with fishermen, the Borders being renowned for salmon and trout. Other field sports such as stalking, hunting and shooting can be arranged locally, as can riding, curling and bowls. Local landmarks include the abbeys of Dryburgh, Melrose, Jedburgh and Kelso. Closed Christmas and New Year. **Directions:** From the south, reach Kelso via A698; from the north, via A68. Hotel is just off market square by the river. Price guide: Single £42; double/twin £60–£84.

SUNLAWS HOUSE HOTEL

KELSO, ROXBURGHSHIRE TD5 8JZ
TEL: 0573 450331 FAX: 0573 450611

Converted by the owner, the Duke of Roxburghe, into a luxury hotel of charm and character, Sunlaws House is situated in hundreds of acres of rolling grounds on the bank of the Teviot. There are 22 bedrooms which, like the spacious reception rooms, are furnished with care and elegance. The menu, which is changed daily, reflects the hotel's position at the source of some of Britain's finest fish, meat and game – salmon and trout from the waters of the Tweed, or grouse, pheasant and venison from the Roxburghe estate – complemented with wines from the Duke's own cellar. A fine selection of whiskies is offered in the Library Bar, with its log fire and leather-bound tomes. A full sporting programme can be arranged, including fly and coarse fishing, and falconry. The shooting school offers tuition in game and clay shooting. Cultural interest is also well served, with seven great country houses within easy reach. No stay would be complete without a visit to one of the many woollen mills to see tartans being made. The Christmas and New Year breaks are very popular. Member of Scotland's Heritage Hotels, Scotland's Commended Country Hotels and Inns. **Directions:** The hotel is at Heiton, just off the A698 Kelso–Jedburgh road. Price guide: Single £85; double/twin £128–£135; suite £155.

WILD HAGGIS

ARDSHEAL HOUSE

KENTALLEN OF APPIN, ARGYLL PA38 4BX
TEL: 0631 74227 FAX: 0631 74342

Ardsheal House is set high on a peninsula, commanding wonderful views of Loch Linnhe and the mountains of Morvern. The house is approached along a private drive that borders the loch and winds through ancient woodland. Set in 900 acres of hills, woods, gardens and shore front, this historic manor, built in 1760, has a charming, country house atmosphere. A friendly welcome is extended to all guests by resident proprietors Robert and Jane Taylor. The interiors are cosy and decorative, with polished oak panelling and open fires on chilly evenings. In the conservatory dining room, memorable dishes delight the eye and please the palate. Fresh seafood, prime local meat and game, herbs and fruit from the hotel garden and home-made jellies, preserves and seasoned vinegars form the basis for innovative cooking. Dinner may be accompanied by a selection from the excellent wine list. Ardsheal House is open daily for lunch and dinner: non-residents are welcome. Antique furniture and bright fabrics are to be found in all the en suite bedrooms. Using the hotel as a base, guests can visit islands, castles, lochs and glens or enjoy splendid walks in every direction. Closed 3 weeks in January. **Directions:** Hotel is on the A828 4 miles south of Ballachulish Bridge on the way to Oban. Price guide (including dinner): Single £85; double/twin £128–£180. Special reduced winter rates, also at Christmas and New Year.

KILDRUMMY CASTLE HOTEL

KILDRUMMY, BY ALFORD, ABERDEENSHIRE AB33 8RA
TEL: 09755 71288 FAX: 09755 71345

Set in the heart of Donside adjacent to the renowned Kildrummy Castle Gardens, and overlooking the ruins of the original 13th century castle from which it takes its name, Kildrummy Castle Hotel offers a rare opportunity to enjoy the style and elegance of a bygone era combined with all the modern comforts of a first-class hotel. Recent improvements have not detracted from the turn-of-the century interior, featuring the original wall tapestries and oak-panelled walls and high ceilings. The bedrooms, some with four-poster beds, all have en suite bathrooms. All have been refurbished recently to a high standard. In the restaurant, chef Kenneth White prepares menus using fresh, local produce – fish and shellfish from the Moray Firth, local game and, of course, Aberdeen Angus beef. Kildrummy Castle is ideally located for touring Royal Deeside and Balmoral, the Spey Valley, Aberdeen and Inverness, while the surrounding Grampian region has more castles than any other part of Scotland – 8 of the National Trust for Scotland's finest properties are within an hour's drive of the hotel. Also within an hour's drive are more than 20 golf courses. Visitors to the region can discover the 'Scotch Whisky Trail' and enjoy a tour of some of Scotland's most famous distilleries. **Directions:** Off the A97 Ballater/Huntly road, 35 miles west of Aberdeen. Price guide: Single £65; double/twin £110–£130.

THE KINLOCHBERVIE HOTEL

KINLOCHBERVIE, BY LAIRG, SUTHERLAND IV27 4RP
TEL: 0971 521275 FAX: 0971 521438

Set against the awesome beauty and solitude of the Atlantic coastline is The Kinlochbervie Hotel. Situated just below Cape Wrath – the turning point for the Viking longships – this enigmatic, far north-western corner of Scotland is steeped in legend and folklore. Situated in the fishing port of Kinlochbervie, the hotel is owned by Rex and Kate Neame, who, with their helpful and enthusiastic staff, guarantee that guests enjoy their stay. The lounges and bars are comfortably relaxed and the atmosphere is always warm and cosy – even during the wildest winter storms. The dining room imparts exactly the right ambience in which to savour the delights of The Kinlochbervie kitchens and expertly managed cellars. Delicious fish and seafood dishes figure prominently on the menus, as the daily arrival of deep-sea trawlers to the local market ensures a plentiful source of fresh shellfish, monkfish, turbot and sole – to name a few. Ornithologists and naturalists will revel in the abundance of wildlife and the diversity of flora and fauna. Britain's highest cliffs are nearby and the pre-Cambrian rock formations are among the world's oldest. Pony-trekking, golf, fly and sea-fishing and sea-diving can be arranged. Advance notice is advisable. Closed 1 November to 1 March. **Directions:** Fifty miles from Lairg; B851 via A838. Price guide (including dinner): Single £75; double/twin £136.

MANOR PARK HOTEL

SKELMORLIE, AYRSHIRE PA17 5HE
TEL: 0475 520832 FAX: 0475 520832

Manor Park Hotel stands in 15 acres of carefully tended lawns, shrubberies, water gardens and woodland, where guests can stroll. It is a convenient base from which to explore the fine scenery around the Firth of Clyde and its islands. The hotel was built in 1840, and although all modern amenities have been added, the sense that this is a gracious old country house remains. Original features like imposing portals, log fires and an oak staircase have been preserved. Residents are always fascinated to learn that Winston Churchill and General Eisenhower convened at the house to plan the D-Day landings. Indeed, guests can now stay in the Cowal Suite, the room in which the historic meeting took place. All the bedrooms have fine views over the garden and many face the Firth of Clyde, mountains and lochs. A good menu includes traditional dishes alongside Scottish specialities. For the dedicated malt lover, there are over 190 whiskies to try. The nearby resort of Largs offers water sports, yachting, boating, fishing and golf. Ferry services to Argyll, Bute, the Cumbraes and Arran are a short drive away, as is Burns country. Conference facilities are available and the hotel is open for Christmas and New Year parties. **Directions:** Hotel is off the A78, 3 miles north of Largs Pier. Price guide: Single £50–£80; double/twin £65–£115.

CAMERON HOUSE

LOCH LOMOND, ALEXANDRIA, DUNBARTONSHIRE G83 8QZ
TEL: 0389 55565 FAX: 0389 59522

The splendour and location of this impressive baronial house has lured many famous visitors, from Dr Johnson and the Empress Eugénie to Sir Winston Churchill. Standing in 100 acres of green lawns and wooded glades leading down to the shores of Loch Lomond, Cameron House offers luxurious accommodation and superlative recreational amenities. The indoor leisure club includes squash, badminton and aerobic facilities, four beauty treatment rooms, a games room with three full-size snooker tables and a well-equipped gymnasium. For children there is a games room, toddlers' pool, créche and, during the school holidays, a children's club. Outside, another sporting world unfolds, with professional tennis coaching, 9-hole golf, clay pigeon shooting, archery, off-road driving, sailing, cruising and wind-surfing available. Each of the bedrooms and the five opulent suites is furnished in soft colours that complement the beautiful views from the windows. Guests can dine in the intimate Georgian Room or the Brasserie overlooking the loch. The conference, banqueting and function facilities are second to none and Glasgow, with its museums, art galleries and theatres, is less than 30 minutes' drive away. **Directions:** Cameron House is on the southern banks of Loch Lomond, via the A82 from Glasgow. Price guide: Single £125–£135; double/twin £150–£160; suite £225–£295.

KIRROUGHTREE HOTEL

NEWTON STEWART, WIGTOWNSHIRE DG8 6AN
TEL: 0671 2141 FAX: 0671 2425

Situated in the foothills of the Cairnsmore of Fleet, on the edge of Galloway Forest Park, Kirroughtree Hotel stands in 8 acres of landscaped gardens, where guests can relax and linger over the spectacular views. This striking mansion was built by the Heron family in 1719 and the rococo furnishings of the oak-panelled lounge reflect the style of that period. From the lounge rises the original staircase, from which Robert Burns often recited his poems. Each bedroom is well furnished – guests may choose to spend the night in one of the hotel's spacious 'draped canopy suites'. Many guests are attracted by Kirroughtree's culinary reputation – only the finest produce is used to produce meals of

originality and finesse. There are two intimate dining rooms: the red room for smokers and the blue for non-smokers. This is a good venue for small conferences. Pitch-and-putt, lawn tennis and croquet can be enjoyed in the grounds. Residents can play golf on the many local courses and from this year use of our sister hotels new exclusive 18-hole course at Gate house of Fleet. Trout and salmon fishing can be arranged nearby, as can rough shooting and deer stalking during the season. STB 5 Crowns Highly Commended. Closed 3 January to mid-February. **Directions:** The hotel is signposted 1 mile outside Newton Stewart on the A75. Price guide: Single £80; double/twin £125–£170; suite £170.

M V HEBRIDEAN PRINCESS

THE ELEGANT WAY TO CRUISE THE WESTERN HIGHLANDS AND ISLANDS OF SCOTLAND. TEL: 0756 701338 FAX: 0756 701455

M V Hebridean Princess was originally designed to carry 600 passengers on inter-island journeys. Following a £3 million refit she now provides luxurious 3, 4, 5, 7 and 14-night 'Country House Hotel' cruises for up to 50 guests. From her home port of Oban, she sails around the whole of Scotland's magnificent Western Highlands and Islands, including Orkney and St Kilda. Often, two visits ashore are made each day and, as destinations can be as remote as they are stunning, the ship's small boats are used for these visits. Castles and gardens are included in various itineraries. Nights are usually spent anchored in a secluded loch or sheltered bay. A real escape: no traffic, no crowds! The brigade of chefs prepares Scottish fare guaranteed to delight and, with a crew ratio of 36 to just 50 guests, there is more than a touch of a bygone era! Twin- and double-bedded accommodation is available, as well as single staterooms. Four staterooms have private balconies outside and there is one large suite. As passengers embark at Oban, special travel arrangements can be made from London and other areas. Cruises operate from March to late October. For a full brochure telephone: 0756 701338 or write to Jacqueline Groves, Hebridean Island Cruises Ltd, Acorn Park, Skipton, North Yorkshire BD23 2UE. Price guide, inclusive of meals and excursions ashore: £250 per person per day.

KNIPOCH HOTEL

BY OBAN, ARGYLL PA34 4QT
TEL: 08526 251 FAX: 08526 249

Six miles south of Oban lies Knipoch, an elegant Georgian building set halfway along the shore of Loch Feochan, an arm of the sea stretching 4 miles inland. Wildlife is abundant in this area – rare birds of prey, deer and otters can often be seen. The hotel is owned and personally run by the Craig family, who go out of their way to ensure that their guests enjoy their stay. All the bedrooms are fully equipped and offer splendid views either of the loch or the surrounding hills. High standards of cooking are proudly maintained here. The daily menu features many Scottish specialities, prepared with imaginative flair. Not only is the choice of wines extensive – there are over 350 labels – but the list is informative, too: guests are given a copy to peruse at leisure rather than to scan hurriedly before ordering. In addition, the bar stocks a wide range of malt whiskies. Sporting activities available locally include fishing, sailing, yachting, golf, tennis, pony-trekking and skiing. A traditional Scottish event, the Oban Highland Games, is particularly renowned for its solo piping competition. The Knipoch Hotel makes a good base from which to visit the Western Isles and explore the spectacular scenery of the area. Closed mid-November to mid-February. **Directions:** On the A816, 6 miles south of Oban. Price guide: Single £60–£80; double/twin £120–£130.

CRINGLETIE HOUSE HOTEL

PEEBLES EH45 8PL
TEL: 0721 730233 FAX: 0721 730244

This distinguished mansion, turreted in the Scottish baronial style, stands in 28 acres of beautifully maintained gardens and woodland. Designed by Scottish architect David Bryce, Cringletie was built in 1861 for the Wolfe Murray family, one of whom – Colonel Alexander Murray – accepted the surrender of Quebec after General Wolfe was killed. All of the bedrooms have fine views and many have been redesigned with attractively co-ordinated curtains and furnishings. The splendid panelled lounge has an impressive carved oak and marble fireplace, a painted ceiling and many oil portraits. The imaginative cooking, prepared with flair, attracts consistently good reports. The range and quality of fruit and vegetables grown in the 2-acre walled garden make this the only Scottish garden recommended in Geraldene Holt's *The Gourmet Garden*, which includes some of Britain's most distinguished hotels. On-site facilities include a new hard tennis court, croquet lawn and putting green. Golf can be played at Peebles and fishing is available by permit on the River Tweed. Aside from visits to Edinburgh, Cringletie is a good base from which to discover the rich historic and cultural heritage of the Borders. Closed 3 January to 12 March. **Directions:** The hotel is on the A703 Peebles–Edinburgh road, about 2 miles from Peebles. Price guide: Single £50; double/twin £90.

For hotel location, see maps on pages 458–464

BALLATHIE HOUSE HOTEL

KINCLAVEN BY STANLEY, NR PERTH, PERTHSHIRE PH1 4QN
TEL: 0250 883268 FAX: 0250 883396

Set in an estate overlooking the River Tay, Ballathie House Hotel offers Scottish hospitality in a house of character and distinction. Dating from 1850, this mansion has a French baronial façade and handsome interiors. Overlooking lawns which incline to the riverside, the drawing room is an ideal place to relax with coffee and the papers, or to enjoy a malt whisky after dinner. The premier bedrooms are large and elegant, while the standard rooms are designed in a cosy, cottage style. On the ground floor there are several bedrooms suitable for guests with disabilities. Local ingredients such as Tay salmon, Scottish beef, seafoods and piquant soft fruits are used by chef Kevin McGillivray to create menus catering for all tastes. The hotel has been awarded two AA Rosettes for its food. Activities available on the estate include trout and salmon fishing and clay pigeon shooting. The Sporting Lodge adjacent to the main house is designed to accommodate sporting parties. The area has many good golf courses. Perth, Blairgowrie and Edinburgh are within an hour's drive. STB 4 Crowns De Luxe. Dogs in certain rooms only.
Directions: From A93 at Beech Hedges, signposted for Kinclaven and Ballathie, or off the A9, 2 miles north of Perth through Stanley. Price guide: Single £60–£75; double/twin £90–£160.

PARKLANDS HOTEL & RESTAURANT

ST LEONARD'S BANK, PERTH, PERTHSHIRE PH2 8EB
TEL: 0738 22451 FAX: 0738 22046

The Parklands Country Hotel and Restaurant, which overlooks Perth's South Inch Park, has benefited from an extensive programme of improvements. The hotel, with its classic lines, was formerly the home of John Pullar, who was Lord Provost of the City of Perth from 1867 to 1873. The 14 bedrooms all have en suite facilities and are immaculate. Each has been individually decorated to high standards under the personal supervision of proprietor Pat Deeson. In the main restaurant the accent is on light, traditional Scottish food. A full choice of à la carte and table d'hôte meals is available at both lunchtime and dinner. The boardroom opens off the hotel's entrance and overlooks the hotel gardens. It is a perfect venue for small private lunches or dinners or for business meetings and seminars, and has a large mahogany table and all the latest audio-visual equipment. **Directions:** From the M90 head towards the station; Parklands is on the left at the end of the park. Price guide: Single £80; double/twin £90.

THE FOUR SEASONS HOTEL

ST FILLANS, PERTHSHIRE PH6 2NF
TEL & FAX: 0764 685333

The charming village of St Fillans is surrounded by beautiful Highland scenery, yet both Glasgow and Edinburgh are within 1½ hours' drive. The Four Seasons' airy public rooms and most of the spacious bedrooms command glorious views over Loch Earn, 'the jewel in the crown of Perthshire lochs'. Six chalets on the wooded hillside behind the hotel offer total privacy. Each accommodates three adults or a family of four; there is car access to the door in most cases. The Scott family and staff take pleasure in the company of their guests, and are always on hand, be it to offer a suggestion for a day's outing or to advise on the choice of wine. Chef Andrew Scott and his team prepare imaginative meals, making use of fresh, Scottish produce, with an emphasis on game and seafood. The menu is changed daily and guests' preferences are considered, with individually prepared dishes to please the adventurous diner, as well as those with more conventional tastes. The hotel has its own jetty and the area is ideal for water sports and hill walking. Also, guests can explore by car on the easy roads which link picturesque villages or the narrow tracks which entice travellers through peaceful glens. Callander is a 30-minute drive. Closed December to February. **Directions:** St Fillans is 13 miles from Crieff on the A85. Price guide: Double/twin £60–£80.

STONEFIELD CASTLE HOTEL

TARBERT, LOCH FYNE, ARGYLL PA29 6YJ
TEL: 0880 820836 FAX: 0880 820929

This 19th-century castle, with spectacular views over Loch Fyne, stands in 60 acres of wooded grounds, 2 miles from the fishing village of Tarbert. A former Campbell home, the chateau-style hotel offers comfort and historic charm and remains under the personal direction of Alistair Campbell of Bowfield. The traditional Scottish menu features local produce including prawns, salmon, venison, game and herring. The gardens are renowned for their exotic shrubs, Himalayan rhododendrons and azaleas, and have been made more accessible by the construction of interesting walkways. All the bedrooms have en suite facilities, and those in the main building overlooking the loch have recently been refurbished. Facilities include a library, bar, sauna, solarium, deep-water yacht moorings, sea and loch fishing. Clay pigeon shooting for groups of up to 40 can be arranged on site, with tuition and equipment supplied. There is riding nearby, and five golf courses within 40 miles of the hotel. Ferry trips to Arran, Islay, Gigha, Mull and Iona are ever popular. Helicopter travel from Glasgow (30 minutes) can be arranged. STB 4 Crowns Commended. USA bookings: Toll free 800-247-7268 (Ex NJ)/201-768-5505 (NJ only). **Directions:** From Lochgilphead take Tarbert road south; 10 miles further to Stonefield Castle. Price guide: (including dinner, bed and breakfast) £45–£75 p.p.

WESTERN ISLES HOTEL

TOBERMORY, ISLE OF MULL, ARGYLL PA75 6PR
TEL: 0688 2012 FAX: 0688 2297

Poised above Tobermory Harbour, the Western Isles Hotel combines friendly hospitality with breathtaking views over an ever-changing vista of mountain and sea. An appetite sharpened by the fresh sea air is certain to be sated in the elegant restaurant, with its spectacular outlook over the Sound of Mull. Special diets and vegetarians are well catered for with some notice. The lounge has an atmosphere of grace and comfort, while the conservatory is delightful on scented summer evenings. The bedrooms are spacious, with two rooms reserved for non-smokers. Guests can commune with nature amid Mull's wilderness or enjoy exhilarating outdoor sports. Off Mull's coast is the holy island of Iona, while Fingal's Cave can be seen on Staffa. Special rates for Easter, Christmas and New Year. If bringing a dog, please say when booking and bring a basket/bed for it. **Directions:** Travelling to Mull is so pleasurable that it should be considered part of the holiday. On booking, contact ferry operators Caledonian MacBrayne, The Pier, Gourock; or ring 0631 62285 and book the Oban–Craignure ferry (40 minutes). There is an hourly Lochaline–Fishnish ferry. Oban is on the A82/A85 from Glasgow (2 hours) or the A85 from Perth. At Craignure, turn right off ferry; Tobermory is 40 minutes' drive. A warm welcome awaits! Price guide: Single £30–£55; double/twin £60–£110.

LOCH TORRIDON HOTEL

BY ACHNASHEEN, WESTER-ROSS IV22 2EY
TEL: 0445 791242 FAX: 0445 791296

Loch Torridon Hotel is gloriously situated at the foot of wooded mountains beside the loch which gives it its name. The hotel was built as a shooting lodge for the first Earl of Lovelace in 1887. The 58-acre estate contains formal gardens, mature trees and the shores of the loch. David and Geraldine Gregory, formerly of the Kinlochbervie Hotel, acquired the hotel in March 1992. They brought with them an excellent reputation for their brand of Highland hospitality and good cooking. A phased upgrading of the property has been completed to enhance the impact of the interiors and provide every comfort. Geraldine's cooking requires no such improvement – she is renowned for her inventive use of the finest local ingredients. She has been joined recently by Timothy Morris from Kinnaird House, and together they make a formidable team. The hotel has been chosen as the Best New Three Star Hotel in Scotland by the AA Inspector for 1993 and awarded two Rosettes for its food. Dinner is served between 7.15pm and 8.30pm. A starter of home-made Scotch broth or spinach roulade with prawns and cream could be followed by roast saddle of hare with caramelized onion tart or seafood kebab with tomato sauce and saffron rice. **Directions:** Ten miles from Kinlochewe on the A896. Price guide: Single £45–£110; double/twin £70–£160.

LOCHGREEN HOUSE

MONKTONHILL ROAD, SOUTHWOODS, TROON, AYRSHIRE KA10 7EN
TEL: 0292 313343 FAX: 0292 318661

Built in 1905 by a Glasgow lawyer, Lochgreen House stands in 16 acres of gardens in the heart of Ayeshire's Burns Country. The home of several notable families over the years, Lochgreen has been fully restored to create a de luxe country house hotel. Oak panelling features strongly throughout, the finest examples being in the magnificent entrance hall and the main restaurant. The ambience and general pace of life in the house are what make Lochgreen such a special place to visit. There are seven superb en suite bedrooms and an elegant family cottage suite, each individually designed and decorated with views over the secluded countryside, Royal Troon Golf Course and the Firth of Clyde.

Lochgreen has two contrasting dining rooms, the grand, oak-panelled restaurant and the Conservatory. Other rooms are available for private dinner parties, weddings and meetings. Lochgreen is owned by Bill and Catherine Costley, and as the first Scottish Gold Medal winner in the International Food Olympics, Bill Costley ensures that the standard of cuisine is excellent with such a focus on flavour and presentation. Ten championship golf courses are within easy reach as is many country park and sandy beaches for the family to enjoy. **Directions:** South of Troon, just off the coastal Troon–Ayr road, 1 mile north of Prestwick Airport on the B749. Price guide: Single £89; double/twin £99.

PIERSLAND HOUSE HOTEL

15 CRAIGEND ROAD, TROON, AYRSHIRE KA10 6HD
TEL: 0292 314747 FAX: 0292 315613

This historic listed house, built for the grandson of Johnnie Walker, founder of the Scottish whisky firm, is as attractive inside as out. All the public rooms are spacious and inviting, with original features such as oak panelling and a frieze of Jacobean embroidery. Retaining their original charm, the bedrooms are formally decorated in a period style with soft colourings. Afternoon cream teas are served on the verandah, an airy sun-lounge opening on to beautiful gardens. The 4-acre grounds include immaculate lawns, a Japanese water garden and a croquet lawn. Guests can enjoy classically prepared gourmet dishes and Continental-style cooking in the warm, intimate atmosphere of the restaurant. The wine list is compiled from labels supplied by one of Scotland's oldest-established wine firms. For golfers, Royal Troon is across the road, and Turnberry and Old Prestwick are nearby. Ayr, the birthplace of Robert Burns, Kilmarnock and Irvine are a short drive away and Culzean Castle, the seat of the Kennedy clan, is 19 miles away. Glasgow, Stirling and Edinburgh are easily accessible, as are Loch Lomond, the Trossachs and the isles of the Firth of Clyde. **Directions:** The hotel is on the B749, just beside Royal Troon Golf Club. Price guide: Single £56–£85; double/twin £89–£115.

KNOCKIE LODGE HOTEL

WHITEBRIDGE, INVERNESS-SHIRE, IV1 2UP
TEL: 0456 486276 FAX: 0456 486389

Built originally as a shooting lodge in 1789, Knockie Lodge stands not far from Loch Ness, 25 miles south of Inverness, in an area of outstanding natural beauty and total peace and quiet. It is now very much the home of Ian and Brenda Milward. With its 10 spotlessly clean bedrooms, each comfortably and individually furnished, its drawing and dining rooms filled with antique furniture and family paintings, the billiard room and, of course, superb food prepared from a wide range of local produce, guests at Knockie Lodge can be assured of a real welcome and a very relaxed and hospitable atmosphere. For the brown trout fly-fisherman, there is excellent fishing on two lochs close to the house. It is also possible to cast for salmon on Loch Ness or, by arrangement, in the local salmon rivers. Other activities on offer locally include deerstalking in the autumn, bird-watching, sailing, ponytrekking and hill-walking. Knockie Lodge Hotel prides itself on its deserved awards: the AA 2 Red Stars, and the STB 3 Crowns deLuxe. The hotel is open from the end of April until the end of October and welcomes children aged ten and above. Those wishing to reserve from the USA can telephone 1-800-635 3603. **Directions:** Knockie Lodge Hotel is situated 8 miles north of Fort Augustus on the B862. Price guide (including dinner, bed and breakfast): Single: £75; double/twin: £125–£190.

Complete peace of mind for the traveller...

... because no matter where you travel, help is always at hand with MasterCard®. Our extensive range of emergency services are available through any one of over 2,000 Thomas Cook owned, representative and franchise locations worldwide. So visit your nearest office to:

- Report a lost or stolen card.

- Request an emergency replacement card, available within 2 working days.

- Make emergency communications by phone, fax or telex.

- Request airline re-routing, re-ticketing and re-validation.

- Plan future trips and make reservations.

So with MasterCard and Thomas Cook, you can relax and enjoy your stay - no matter what.

Ask your bank for further details.

ADARE MANOR

ADARE, CO LIMERICK
TEL: 061 396566 FAX: 061 396124

Nestling in 840 acres of rolling countryside and gardens, Adare Manor is an architectural gem, a proud reminder of the Earls of Dunraven who once resided here. The magnificent public rooms range from the cosy library to the majestic Long Gallery – the venue for banquets and conferences. The purpose-built conference suite and boardroom are ideal for smaller gatherings. International and the best of Irish cuisine from Limerick is served in the beautiful dining room, with its views over the parterre and River Maigue. Afternoon tea is served in the elegant drawing room. To round off a relaxing day, guests will find a delightful retreat in one of the 64 sumptuously furnished bedrooms with en suite marble bathrooms. Country pursuits, including fishing, archery, clay pigeon shooting and riding, are offered on the estate. The leisure centre includes a heated indoor pool, sauna and gymnasium. A driving range is available for golfers. From UK phone 010 353 61 396566. **Directions:** Adare Manor is 30 minutes from Shannon Airport, adjacent to Adare village. Price guide: Per room IR£110–IR£265.

For hotel location, see maps on pages 458–464

GLENLO ABBEY

BUSHYPARK, CO GALWAY, IRELAND
TEL: 353 091 26666 FAX: 353 091 27800

Situated some 3 miles from the city of Galway on Ireland's west coast, Glenlo Abbey, built in 1740, was formerly the ancestral home of the Ffrench and Blake families, two of Galway's 14 great tribes who ruled over the city for centuries. The current owners, John and Peggy Bourke, have taken great care in their restoration of Glenlo Abbey, transforming it into a magnificent hotel and conference centre. Spaciousness and tranquillity are the key notes in the accommodation at Glenlo Abbey, reflecting the very essence of Irish hospitality. The public rooms feature solid antique furniture and a beautiful collection of Irish art, in keeping with the character of the surroundings. All bedrooms have marbled en suite bathrooms and many have scenic views over Lough Corrib. Guests may relax over cocktails in the Kentfield or in the Oak Cellar Bar, before dining in the Ffrench Room restaurant. Here, fine Irish and international cuisine is served in an atmosphere reflecting the gracious living of the past. Glenlo Abbey offers a choice of conference rooms. The gentle slopes around the Glenlo Abbey reveal a challenging golf course. Tours through Connemara and fishing for trout and salmon on Lough Corrib can be arranged. **Directions:** The hotel is about 3 miles north of Galway on the road to Moycullen. Price guide: Single IR£65–IR£80; double/twin IR£96–IR£115; suite IR£175–IR£350.

NUREMORE HOTEL

CARRICKMACROSS, CO MONAGHAN, IRELAND
TEL: 042 61438 FAX: 042 61853

Set in 200 acres of glorious countryside on the fringe of Carrickmacross, the Nuremore Hotel has been extensively renovated. It offers guests all-round enjoyment, a vast array of activities and facilities and all that is best in a first-class country hotel. The bedrooms are well appointed and attractively designed to create a generous sense of personal space. Lunch and dinner menus, served in a spacious and elegant dining room, emphasise classic European cooking, with French and Irish dishes featured alongside. For sport, fitness and relaxation, guests are spoiled for choice by the range of amenities. A major feature is the championship-length, par 73, 18-hole golf course designed by Eddie Hackett to present an exciting challenge to beginners and experts alike. Maurice Cassidy has been appointed as resident professional and is on hand to give tuition. The leisure club has a superb indoor pool, modern gymnasium, squash and tennis courts, sauna, steam room and whirlpool bath. Meetings, conferences and seminars held here are guaranteed a professional support service. Dublin is 90 minutes' drive away, while Drogheda and Dundalk are nearby for shopping. From the UK phone 010 353 42 61438. **Directions:** The hotel is on the main N2 road between Dublin and Monaghan. Price guide: Single IR£75–£90; double/twin IR£105–£130.

ASHFORD CASTLE

CONG, CO MAYO
TEL: 092 46003 FAX: 092 46260

On the beautiful shores of Lough Corrib lies Ashford Castle – an Irish legend where time seems to stand still. Parts of the original 13th-century castle were incorporated into the magnificent edifice built by Lord Ardilaun in the 19th century. Lofty panelled ceilings, knights in armour, weathered battlements, rich furnishings, crystal chandeliers, oil paintings and *objets d'art* set the tone of the gracious halls and luxurious rooms. The 83 lavishly appointed guest rooms and suites all have superb bathrooms and a full range of amenities. Guests may dine in either of two acclaimed restaurants and enjoy gourmet cuisine that specialises in the prawns, salmon, lamb, steaks and game for which the region is famous. Standing amid acres of romantic gardens, forests and walks, Ashford Castle offers a full range of country sports. Salmon and trout fishing on Lough Corrib, clay pigeon shooting and 9-hole golf are among the activities available to residents. Ashford is also an ideal base for touring the nearby historic, scenic and absorbing sights of the west of Ireland. Ashford Castle is a Relais et Châteaux member. From UK phone 010 353 92 46003. **Directions:** Twenty-eight miles north of Galway on the shore of Lough Corrib, on the left when entering the village of Cong. Price guide from: IR£138–IR£235 (single, twin or double occupancy).

RENVYLE HOUSE HOTEL

CONNEMARA, CO GALWAY
TEL: 095 43511 FAX: 095 43515

Renvyle Hotel has occupied its rugged, romantic position on Ireland's west coast for over four centuries. Set between mountains and sea on the unspoilt coast of Connemara, this hardy, beautiful building with its superlative views over the surrounding countryside is just an hours drive from Galway or Sligo. Originally constructed in 1541, Renvyle has been an established hotel for many years, witnessing in that time a procession of luminaries through its doors – among them Augustus John, Lady Gregory, Yeats and Churchill, drawn no doubt by an atmosphere as warm and convivial then as it is today. Renvyle now welcomes visitors with turf fires glowing in public areas, wood-beamed interiors and comfortable, relaxed furnishings in the easy rooms. The bedrooms are comfortably appointed and all have been refurbished in the past two years. In the dining room, meals from a constantly-changing menu are served with emphasis on local fish and Renvyle lamb. In the grounds activities include tennis, croquet, riding, bowls and golf. Beyond the hotel, there are walks in the heather-clad hills, or swimming and sunbathing on empty beaches. **Directions:** On the N39 from Galway turn right at recess, take the Letterfrack turning to Tully Cross and Renvyle is signposted. Price guide: Single £21–£41; double/twin £42–£82.

       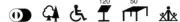   

THE HIBERNIAN HOTEL

EASTMORELAND PLACE, BALLSBRIDGE, DUBLIN 4
TEL: 01668 7666 FAX: 01660 2655

Tucked away in bustling downtown Dublin, the Hibernian Hotel is a magnificent architectural feat constructed just before the turn of the century in the commercial heart of the city. Refurbished and reopened last year as a grand 30-bedroom townhouse hotel, The Hibernian now prides itself on the elegance, style and warmth of service it can offer visitors to this vibrant metropolis: a unique blend of modern ease and bygone atmosphere. David Butt, the general manager, is ably assisted by a professional team who ensure that the needs of both business and holiday guests are met quickly and efficiently. Luxury prevails at The Hibernian in soft furnishings, rich fabrics and deep upholstery; in each of the 30 individually designed bedrooms and suites, en suite bathrooms with a full range of toiletries are standard, as are fax/modem points, drinks facilities, individually controlled thermostats and and hairstyling appliances. In the restaurant, the luncheon and à la carte menus offer the full gamut of gastronomic dishes, from locally caught, artfully interpreted seafood to modern cuisine classics and fine wines to accompany them. The hotel makes an ideal base from which to explore the city. **Directions:** Turn right from Mespil road into Baggot Street Upper, then left into Eastmoreland Place; The Hibernian is at the end on the left. Price guide: Single £85; double/twin £135 ;suite £135.

MARLFIELD HOUSE HOTEL

GOREY, CO WEXFORD
TEL: 055 21124 FAX: 055 21572 TELEX: 80757

Staying at Marlfield House is a memorable experience. Set in 34 acres of woodland and gardens, this former residence of the Earl of Courtown, built in 1820, preserves the Regency lifestyle in all its graciousness. It is recognised as one of the finest country houses in Ireland, and is supervised by the welcoming host/proprietors, Raymond and Mary Bowe. The suites all have period fireplaces where open fires blaze in the cooler weather, and have been built in a traditional, very grand style. All the bedroom furniture is of the Regency period and the roomy beds are draped with ruffled, sumptuous fabrics. The bathrooms are made of highly polished marble and have large freestanding bathtubs. There is a luxurious drawing room, an impressive curved Richard Turner conservatory, and an opulent dining room. The hotel's gastronomic delights have earned it numerous awards. Located 2 miles from fine beaches, the hotel is central to many touring high points: Powerscourt Demesne, Mount Usher Gardens and the Devil's Glen. When phoning from the British mainland dial 010 353 55 21124. Closed December and January. **Directions:** On the Gorey–Courtown road, just over a mile east of Gorey. Price guide: Single from £IR65; double/twin IR£114–IR£135; suite from IR£165.

In association with MasterCard

SHEEN FALLS LODGE

KENMARE, CO KERRY
TEL: 064 41600 FAX: 064 41386

Sheen Falls stands on the former seat of the Earl of Kerry, overlooking the falls of the Sheen River where it tumbles dramatically into the head of the tidal estuary. Amid the breathtaking beauty of south-west Kerry, this luxurious hotel is surrounded by 300 acres of lawns, gardens, verdant pastures and lofty forests. An exquisitely restored hotel, Sheen Falls continues a tradition of elegance and comfort allied with impeccable personal service. Marble bathrooms, pastel décor and soft furnishings grace the spacious bedrooms. Highly regarded cuisine is served in La Cascade restaurant, with a choice of over 400 wines. Particularly popular with sporting enthusiasts, the Sheen Falls Estate can arrange for golf at the nearby Kenmare course, salmon fishing along 15 miles of the Sheen River, riding and clay pigeon shooting. Additional amenities include a fully equipped leisure centre, a billiard room and an exquisite, mahogany-panelled library with over 1,200 volumes. The conference centre offers sophisticated presentation equipment to meet modern business needs. Closed January. From UK phone 010 353 64 41600. **Directions:** Hotel is 1 mile outside Kenmare. Follow the Glengarriff road, take first turn on left and hotel is ¹/₂ mile further on left. Price guide: Single IR£155–£175; double/twin IR£190–£295; suite IR£295–£350.

AGHADOE HEIGHTS HOTEL

AGHADOE, KILLARNEY, CO KERRY
TEL: 064 31766 FAX: 064 31345 TELEX: 73942

In the heart of beautiful County Kerry overlooking stunning panoramic views of the lakes and mountains of Killarney, stands the Aghadoe Heights Hotel, sister hotel to Fredrick's of Maidenhead. It reflects owner Fredrick Losel's influence: rich tapestries, crystal chandeliers, paintings and antiques. Much attention has been given to the bedrooms. The furniture is of mahogany, ash or cherry wood, with soft drapes and deep carpets. Excellent cuisine and fine wines are served in the rooftop restaurant. Chef Robin Suter uses the freshest local ingredients to create innovative dishes. Three function rooms offer good conference facilities. A new leisure club includes an indoor pool, Jacuzzi, sauna, plunge pool, solarium, fitness room and now by appointment a massage and beauty treatment service in the hotel. Aghadoe Heights is a good departure point for tours of Kerry or for playing south-west Ireland's premier golf courses, such as Killarney, Waterville and Ballybunion. The hotel has its own stretch of river for salmon fishing and there is also a tennis court within the 8-acre gardens. Pony-trekking, lake and sea fishing are also offered locally. From the UK phone 010 353 64 31766. **Directions:** The hotel is 10 miles south of Kerry Airport, 3 miles north of Killarney. It is situated off the N22 Tralee road. Price guide: Single IR£72–IR£100; double/twin IR£105–IR£145; suite IR£150–IR£195.

DROMOLAND CASTLE

NEWMARKET-ON-FERGUS, SHANNON AREA, CO CLARE
TEL: 061 368144 FAX: 061 363355 TELEX: 70654

Dromoland Castle, just 8 miles from Shannon Airport, is one of the most famous baronial castles in Ireland, dating from the 16th century. Dromoland was the ancestral seat of the O'Briens, direct descendants of Irish King Brian Boru. Priceless reminders of its past are everywhere: in the splendid wood and stone carvings, magnificent panelling, oil paintings and romantic gardens. The 73 en suite guest rooms and suites are all beautifully furnished. Stately halls and an elegant dining room are all part of the Dromoland experience. The new Dromoland International Centre is one of Europe's most comprehensive conference venues, hosting groups of up to 450. Classical cuisine is prepared by award-winning chef Jean Baptiste Molinari. Dromoland was named Best Restaurant in Ireland by Egon Ronay in 1991 and by the RAC in 1992. Fishing, 18-hole golf and boating are all available on the estate, while activities nearby include riding, shooting and golf on some of Ireland's foremost courses. The castle is an ideal base from which to explore this breathtakingly beautiful area. Dromoland Castle is a Relais et Châteaux member. From UK phone 010 353 61 368144. **Directions:** Take the N18 to Newmarket-on-Fergus, go 2 miles beyond the village and hotel entrance is on the right-hand side. Price guide from: IR£138–IR£235 (single, twin or double occupancy).

KELLY'S STRAND HOTEL

ROSSLARE, CO. WEXFORD, IRELAND
TEL: 053 32114 FAX: 053 32222

Situated beside the long, sandy beach at Rosslare, Kelly's Strand is very much a family hotel, now managed by the fourth generation of Kellys. With a firm reputation as one of Ireland's finest hotels, based on a consistently high standard of service, Kelly's extends a warm welcome to its guests, many of whom return year after year. The public rooms are tastefully decorated and feature a collection of carefully selected paintings. The Carmen Bar, with its soft lighting and grand piano, is the perfect venue for pre-dinner drinks. All bedrooms have been refurbished and extended in the last 2 years and have en suite facilities. The hotel restaurant is highly regarded for its superb cuisine, served with great attention to detail. An extensive wine list includes individual estate wines imported directly from France. Children are catered for with special menus and mealtimes. For exercise and relaxation, guests have the use of the hotel's new Aqua Club, with 2 swimming pools and a range of water and health facilities including hydro massage, 'swimming lounge', plunge pool and hot tub. There is also a beauty salon. Keen golfers are well served with courses at Rosslare and Wexford, which has an excellent shopping centre. Places of interest nearby include the Irish National Heritage Park at Ferrycarrig. **Directions:** Follow signs to Rosslare. Price guide: Single IR£38–IR£45; double/twin IR£76–IR£82.

HUNTER'S HOTEL

NEWRATH BRIDGE, RATHNEW, CO WICKLOW
TEL: 0404 40106 FAX: 0404 40338

Hunter's Hotel, one of Ireland's oldest coaching inns, has been established for over 200 years, since the days of post horses and carriages. Run by the same family for five generations, the hotel has built up a strong tradition based on good food, comfortable surroundings and unique, old-world charm. Set in one of Ireland's most beautiful counties, the hotel stands in gardens bordering the River Vartry. All the rooms retain the character of bygone days, with antique furniture, open fires, fresh flowers and polished brass. Most of the 18 attractive bedrooms overlook the gardens. In 1806 John Carr, traveller and author of *The Stranger in Ireland*, wrote: 'Here [Bray] we took a fresh chaise and proceeded to Newry Bridge where we found an old but comfortable inn. This spot we made our headquarters and strongly recommended them to every future Wicklow wanderer.' When these words were written, John Hunter, a direct ancestor of the present owners – the Gelletlie family – was in charge. Today Hunter's Hotel continues to be recommended by leading international guides, as it upholds the tradition of providing good hospitality for travellers. Dogs by arrangement. From the UK phone 010 353 404 40106. **Directions:** Take N11 to Rathnew; turn left just before the village on Dublin side. Price guide: Single IR£37.50–£40.50; double/twin IR£70–£80.

TINAKILLY HOUSE HOTEL

RATHNEW, WICKLOW, CO WICKLOW
TEL: 0404 69274 FAX: 0404 67806

Less than an hours drive from Dublin stands Tinakilly House, set on seven acres of beautifully landscaped gardens overlooking the Irish Sea. Tinakilly was built by Captain Halpin, the man who, as Commander of the *Great Eastern*, laid the transatlantic telegraph cables in the 1860s. Tinakilly is now a luxury country house and restaurant, where owners William and Bee Power create a house-party atmosphere for guests. The bedrooms, including three suites, are a perfect blend of Victorian splendour and modern comfort. Superb country house cooking is complemented by an excellent wine cellar. Open all year round, Tinakilly offers special short break packages to take advantage of the many wonderful gardens, touring, sporting and historic attractions nearby. Tinakilly is ideal for business functions: four meeting rooms, modern equipment and the highest possible standards of professional service, ensure the success of every occasion. A corporate activity brochure, which suggests a variety of country sporting pursuits and evening entertainment is available. From the UK phone 010 353 404 69274. **Directions:** Take the N11 from Dublin to Rathnew village. The hotel is on the left-hand side as you come out of the village. Price guide: Single IR£75–IR£80; double/twin IR£100–IR£140; suite IR£170.

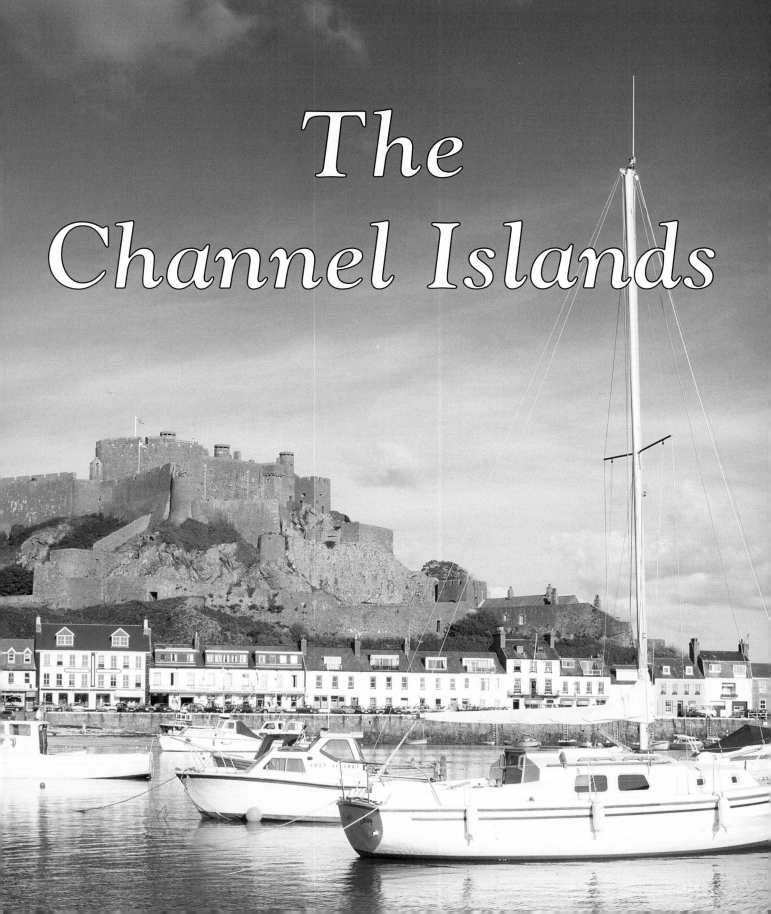

Johansens Recommended Hotels in
The Channel Islands

LA GRANDE MARE HOTEL

VAZON BAY, CASTEL, GUERNSEY, CHANNEL ISLANDS
TEL: 0481 56576 FAX: 0481 56532

One hour by air from London – and 10 minutes by road on arrival – brings the visitor to the select La Grande Mare Hotel, set in over 100 acres of private grounds on the idyllic west coast of Guernsey. Just 15 minutes away from the hubbub of St Peter Port, La Grande Mare is a place of peace and tranquillity, the home of award-winning cuisine, and close by the sandy bays and the breezy cliff tops, that characterise this spectacular stretch of coast. Run by the Vermeulen family, La Grande Mare has been tastefully furnished throughout, with exotic rugs and pieces of genuine Bretagne furniture. Bedrooms – suites, self-contained apartments, even exclusive penthouse suites – offer visitors spacious, fully appointed accommodation, with satellite TV and baby-minding. Some have locally crafted four-poster beds; self-contained apartments have their own kitchens. Guests will enjoy dining in the Les Routiers and RAC-recommended restaurant, which combines local and home-grown produce to create a menu of distinction, complemented by a fine wine list personally selected by the Hotel Director. Leisure facilities include golf, coarse fishing, croquet and basketball, windsurfing, jogging and sailing. Directions: La Grande Mare overlooks Vazon Bay on the west coast of the island. Price guide: Single from £84; double/twin from £99 suite from £145.

OLD GOVERNMENT HOUSE HOTEL

ANN'S PLACE, ST PETER PORT, GUERNSEY GY1 4AZ
TEL: 0481 724921 FAX: 0481 724429

Affectionately known as OGH, the hotel was, from the mid-18th century, the official residence of Guernsey's governors and it is inextricably bound to the island through history and tradition. Constantly modernised since 1858 when it became a hotel, it offers modern amenities and comforts while retaining an ambience of the past. The OGH can justly claim not only one of Guernsey's finest restaurants but also one of its most favoured settings, with views over Herm, Sark and Jethou. Upon entering the hotel, guests will note that the time-honoured standards of courtesy, discretion and impeccable personal attention are held in the highest regard. Awarded 5 Crowns by Guernsey Tourism, the accommodation is very comfortable and attractive throughout. Many of the bedrooms overlook the sea. There is regular dancing in the Centenary Bar and in Scarlett's night-club, which is situated in the soundproofed basement. Its central position makes OGH an ideal venue for business and social gatherings of all kinds. The hotel is close to the town centre, with its shops, harbour, marina and the 12th-century Castle Cornet. Executive breaks are available October–March and a fully inclusive Christmas programme is offered. **Directions:** The OGH is situated in the centre of St Peter Port. Price guide: Single £25–£54; double/twin £50–£126; suite £138.

ST PIERRE PARK HOTEL

ROHAIS, ST PETER PORT, GUERNSEY, CHANNEL ISLANDS GY1 1FD
TEL: 0481 728282 (FREEPHONE 0800 373321) FAX: 0481 712041

A splendid 5 Crown hotel, St Pierre Park is situated on the outskirts of St Peter Port. Set in 45 acres of quiet, mature parkland, the estate has its own lake and fountain as well as a superb range of recreational facilities. These include a challenging 9-hole par 3 golf course, designed by Tony Jacklin, and a driving range. The health and leisure centre comprises an indoor heated pool, gymnasium, saunas, solarium, Jacuzzi, steam rooms and a hair and beauty salon. A snooker room, trim trail with exercise stations and a shop can also be found within the hotel complex. Families will welcome the children's play area and the baby-listening service. Guests may dine in either of the hotel's restaurants. Gourmet cuisine is offered in one of Guernsey's finest French restaurants, the Victor Hugo. Brasserie-style meals, ice-creams and refreshments are served throughout the day at the Café Renoir. With its French influence and varied coastline, Guernsey has much to offer. The St Pierre Park Hotel is an ideal choice for a business function, short break, sporting or family holiday. **Directions:** The hotel is centrally situated, only 15 minutes' drive from the airport and 5 minutes' drive from St Peter Port, Guernsey's main town. Take the Rohais road westbound out of St Peter Port. Price guide: Single £75; double/twin £130; suite £165.

THE ATLANTIC HOTEL

LA MOYE, ST BRELADE, JERSEY JE3 8HE
TEL: 0534 44101 FAX: 0534 44102

Only 7 miles from the town of St Helier and 10 minutes from the airport, the four-star luxury modern Atlantic Hotel enjoys a premier location, in its own extensive grounds, overlooking the massive sandy sweep of St Ouen's Bay. For a hotel of its size, The Atlantic manages to retain an intimate continental atmosphere that sets it apart from Jersey's more traditional hotels, and draws guests back year after year. Privately owned and supervised, the hotel is managed by Mario Dugini, ably assisted by a professional team who ensure its smooth running. All 50 bedrooms have been appointed to meet the most exacting international standards. Furniture is 18th century inspired, beautiful and comfortable, with co-ordinating accessories. There is also the choice of staying in the Garden Studios and the two luxury suites. In the award-winning restaurant, impeccable standards of cuisine and wine are maintained by chef Anselmo Teruggi, who conjures up appetising table d'hôte and traditional à la carte menus. Guests seeking to work up an appetite (or work off a meal) have free access to the extensive health and leisure facilities in the Palm Club or the outdoor pool, or may alternatively walk on the beach, go riding, or play golf on the adjoining course. **Directions:** off a private drive off the A13 at La Pulente, 2 miles from the airport. Price guide: Single £75; double/twin £110; suite £175.

CHATEAU LA CHAIRE

ROZEL BAY, JERSEY
TEL: 0534 863354 FAX: 0534 865137

This beautiful, serene Victorian house is situated on the north-east coast of Jersey, only a short distance from the beach. Château La Chaire is set in 7 acres of terraced grounds in the picturesque Rozel Valley, one of the most tranquil and peaceful places on the island. Each of the 14 luxurious en suite bedrooms has been elegantly appointed with much careful attention to detail, such as fresh fruit, mineral water, bathrobes and fresh flowers. All the bedrooms are individual in style and decor, with spa baths fitted in seven of them. The intimate oak-panelled La Chaire restaurant and extended conservatory have rated for many years among Jersey's top gourmet establishments. Haute cuisine is complemented by a choice of fine wines. Guests can relax in the immaculately restored Rococo Lounge or enjoy an apéritif in the panelled bar. Less than an hour by air from the UK mainland, Jersey has a distinctly Continental and cosmopolitan character, as well as beaches, scenery and many places of historical interest. Special packages are available on request. **Directions:** Château La Chaire is signposted off the main coastal road to Rozel Bay, 6 miles north east of St Helier. Price guide: Single £57–£100; double/twin £82–£120; suites £150–£180.

LONGUEVILLE MANOR

ST SAVIOUR, JERSEY
TEL: 0534 25501 FAX: 0534 31613

Three generations of the Lewis family have welcomed guests to Longueville Manor for 40 years or so. For their endeavours, they were named the 1991 Egon Ronay Hotel of the Year. Set in 15 acres at the foot of its private wooded valley, the manor has stood here since the 13th century. Nowadays, in the comfort of exquisitely decorated rooms and surrounded by beautiful floral displays, fine antique furnishings and elegant fabrics, guests are pampered by attentive staff. The ancient, oak-panelled dining room sports an array of silver trophies awarded for excellent cuisine. Many of the fruits, vegetables, herbs and flowers are grown in the walled kitchen gardens, which include hothouses to provide fresh produce that would otherwise be out of season. Wines from all over the world are stocked in the expertly managed cellars. Each bedroom is individually decorated with flair and imagination – separate sitting areas have books, magazines, flowers and fresh fruit. By the heated swimming pool, a bar and service area offer a special alfresco menu in the summer months. Beyond this, a stream trickles down a hillside into a lake, with black swans and mandarin ducks completing the picture. Longueville Manor is a Relais et Châteaux hotel. **Directions:** On A3, 1 mile from St Helier. Price guide: Single from £110; double/twin £140; suite £250.

POTTER & MOORE · Gilchrist & Soames
LONDON

Potter & Moore and Gilchrist & Soames,
both traditional manufacturers of luxury toiletries, offer to the
select and discerning hotelier a wide variety of
high quality bath products.

The perfect touch to the perfect stay.

POTTER & MOORE. GILCHRIST & SOAMES. TELEPHONE: 0733 281000. FAX: 0733 281028

The following establishments can be found described in full in the *Johansens Recommended Inns and Restaurants in Great Britain 1994*. For their map locations see pages 458–464.

There are three guides in the Johansens series - *Johansens Recommended Hotels in Great Britain and Ireland*, *Johansens Recommended Inns and Restaurants in Great Britain* and *Johansens Recommended Private Country Houses and Small Hotels in Great Britain and Ireland*.

An order form can be found at the back of this guide or copies may be obtained from Johansens establishments, good bookshops or direct from the publishers by calling the credit card orderline free on **0800 269397**.

Appleby-In-Westmorland
The Royal Oak Inn
Bongate
Appleby-In-Westmorland
Cumbria CA16 6UN
07683 51463

Basingstoke (Odiham)
The George Hotel
Basingstoke
High Street
Basingstoke
Hampshire RG25 1LP
0256 70208

Arundel (Crossbush)
Howards Hotel
Crossbush
Arundel
West Sussex BN18 9PQ
0903 882655

Beckington (Nr Bath)
The Woolpack Inn
Beckington
Nr Bath
Somerset BA3 6SP
0373 831244

Ashford-In-The-Water
Ashford Hotel
1 Church Street
Ashford-In-The-Water
Bakewell,
Derbyshire DE45 1QB
0629 812725

Belbroughton
Freshmans Restaurant
Church Hill
Belbroughton
Near Stowbridge
Gloucester DY9 0DT
0562 730467

Askrigg
The Kings Arms Hotel And
Restaurant
Market Place,
Askrigg Wensleydale,
North Yorkshire DL8 3HQ
0969 50258

Belford
Blue Bell Hotel
Belford Market Place
Belford
Northumberland NE70 7NE
0668 213543

Badby (near Daventry)
The Windmill Inn Hotel
Main Street
Badby,
Nr Daventry,
Northants NN11 6AN
0327 702363

Brendon (Exmoor)
Stag Hunters Hotel
Brendon
Lynton
Devon EX35 1PS
05987 222

Bainbridge
Rose And Crown Hotel
Bainbridge
Wensleydale
North Yorkshire DL8 3EE
0969 50225

Bridport
Manor Hotel
West Bexington
Dorset DT2 9DF
0308 89761/785

Banbury (Deddington)
The Holcombe Hotel
High Street
Deddington
Oxfordshire OX5 4SL
0869 38274

Brighton (Lancing)
Sussex Pad Hotel
Lancing
Sussex BN15 0RH
0273 454647

Barnstaple (Croyde)
Kittiwell House Hotel And
Restaurant
Croyde
Devon EX33 1PG
0271 890247

Broadway
Collin House Hotel
Collin Lane
Broadway
Hereford & Worcester WR12 7PB
0386 858354

Burford
The Lamb Inn
Sheep Street
Burford
Oxon OX18 4LR
0993 823155

Calver, Nr Bakewell
The Chequers Inn
Froggatt Edge
Nr Calver
Derbyshire S30 1ZB
0433 630231

Camborne
Tyacks Hotel
27 Commercial Street
Camborne
Cornwall TR14 8LD
0209 612424

Cambridge
Panos Hotel and Restaurant
154-156 Hills Road
Cambridge
Cambridgeshire CB2 2PB
0223 212958

Carlisle (Faugh)
The String Of Horses Inn
Faugh
Heads Nook
Carlisle
Cumbria CA4 9EG
0228 70297

Castle Ashby (Northampton)
The Falcon Hotel and Restaurant
Castle Ashby
Northampton
Northamptonshire NN7 1LF
0604 696200

Castleton
Ye Olde Nags Head
Cross Street
Castleton
Derbyshire S30 2WH
0433 620248

Cheltenham (Birdlip)
Kingshead House Restaurant
Birdlip
Gloucestershire GL4 8JH
0452 862299

Cheltenham (Colesbourne)
The Colesbourne Inn
Colesbourne
Nr Cheltenham
Gloucester GL53 9NP
0242 870376

Chichester
The White Horse At Chilgrove
Chilgrove
Nr Chichester
West Sussex PO18 9HX
024359 219

Chipping Camden
The Noel Arms
Chipping Camden
Gloucestershire GL55 6AT
0386 840317

Chipping Camden
Seymour House Hotel & Restaurant
High Street
Chipping Campden
Gloucestershire GL55 6AH
0386 840429

Cirencester (Ewen)
Wild Duck Inn
Drakes Island
Ewen
Nr Cirencester
Gloucestershire GL7 6B4
0285 770310

Cleobury Mortimer
The Talbot Hotel
The High Street
Cleobury Mortimer
Nr Kidderminster
Worcestershire DY14 8QJ
0299 270036

Cleobury Mortimer
The Crown At Hopton
Hopton Waters
Cleobury Mortimer
Nr Kidderminster
Worcestershire DY14 0NB
0299 270372

Cleobury Mortimer
The Redfern Hotel
Cleobury Mortimer
Shropshire DY14 8AA
0299 270395

Crewkerne (North Perrott)
The Manor Arms
North Perrott
Nr Crewkerne
Somerset TA18 7SG
0460 72901

Dartmouth
The Royal Castle Hotel
11 The Quay
Dartmouth
Devon TQ6 9PS
0803 833033

Doddiscombleigh
The Nobody Inn
Doddiscombeleigh
Nr Exeter
Devon EX6 7PS
0647 52394

Dronfield (Sheffield)
Manor House Hotel & Restaurant
Dronfield
High Street
Old Dronfield
Derbyshire S18 6PY
0246 413971

Dulverton (Exebridge)
The Anchor Inn
Exebridge
Nr Dulverton
Somerset TA22 9AZ
0398 23433

East Witton
The Blue Lion
East Witton
Nr Leyburn
North Yorkshire DL8 4SN
0969 24273

Egton
The Wheatsheaf Inn
Egton
Nr Whitby
North Yorkshire YO21 1TZ
0947 85271

Evershot
The Acorn Inn Hotel
Fore Street
Evershot
Dorset DT2 0JW
0935 83228

Exeter (Trusham)
The Cridford Inn
Trusham
Nr Newton Abbot
Devon TQ13 0NR
0626 853694

Exford (Exmoor)
The Exmoor White Horse Inn
Exford
W Somerset TA24 7PY
064 383 229

Fairford
Bull Hotel
Market Place
Fairford
Gloucestershire GL7 4AA
0285 712535

Falmouth (Constantine)
Trengilly Wartha Country Inn
Nancenoy
Constantine
Falmouth
Cornwall TR11 5RP
0326 40332

Ford (Nr Bath)
The White Hart
Ford
Chippenham
Wiltshire SN14 8LP
0249 782213

Goathland
Mallyan Spout Hote
Goathland
Whitby
North Yorkshire YO22 5AN
0947 86206

Goldaming
The Inn On The Lake
Ockford Road
Godalming
Surrey GU7 1RH
0483 415575

Goring-On-Thames
Leatherne Bottel Riverside Inn
  And The Bridleway
Goring On Thames
Berkshire RG8 0HS
0491 872667

Grantham (Oasby)
Houblon Arms
Oasby
Grantham
Lincolnshire NG32 3NB
05295 215

Great Dunmow
The Starr
Market Place
Great Dunmow
Essex CM16 1AX
0371 874321

Greta Bridge
The Morritt Arms Hotel
Greta Bridge
Nr Barnard Castle
Durham DL12 9SE
0833 27232

Guildford (Hurtmore)
Squirrels Restaurant And
  Country House
Hurtmore
New Godalming
Surrey GU7 2RN
0483 860223

Handcross
The Chequers At Slaugham
Slaugham
Nr Handcross
West Sussex RH17 6AQ
0444 400239

Hatherleigh
The George Hotel
Market Street
Hatherleigh
Devon
0837 810454

Haworth
Old White Lion Hotel
Haworth
Keighley
West Yorkshire BD22 8DU
0535 642313

Hay-On-Wye
Rhydspence Inn
Rhydspence
Whitney-On-Wye
Nr Hay-On-Wye
Hereford & Worcester HR3 6EU
0497 831262

Hay-On-Wye (Brewardine)
Red Lion Hotel
Bredwardine
Herefordshire HR3 6BU
09817 303

Hayfield (Birch Vale)
The Waltzing Weasel
New Mills Road
Birch Vale
Derbyshire SK12 5BT
0663 743402

Henley (Ibstone)
Fox Country Hotel
Ibstone
Near High Wycombe
Buckinghamshire HP14 3GG
0491 638289

Hereford
The Green Man Inn
Fownhope
Nr Hereford
Hereford & WorcesterHR1 4PE
0432 860243

Isles Of Scilly (Tresco)
The New Inn,
Tresco
Isles Of Scilly TR24 0QQ
0720 22844

Kingsbury (Nr Sutton Coldfield)
Marston Farm Hotel
Bodymoor Heath
Sutton Coldfield
Warwickshire B76 9JD
0827 872133

Kingsclere
The Swan Hotel
Swan Street
Kingsclere
Nr Newbury
Berkshire RG15 8PP
0635 298314

Kirkby Lonsdale
Whoop Hall Inn
Burrow With Burrow
Kirkby Lonsdale
Carnforth
Lancashire LA6 2HP
05242 71284

Kirkby Lonsdale (Casterton)
The Pheasant Inn
Casterton
Kirkby Lonsdale
Cumbria LA6 2RX
05242 71230

Kirkbymoorside
The George & Dragon
Kirkbymoorside
Market Place
Kirkbymoorside
North Yorkshire YO6 6AA
0751 31637

Knutsford
La Belle Epoque
60 King Street
Knutsford
Cheshire WA16 6DT
0565 633060

Lavenham
The Angel
Market Place
Lavenham
Suffolk
0787 247388

Ledbury
The Feathers Hotel
Ledbury High Street
Ledbury
Hereford & Worcester HR8 1DS
0531 635266

Long Melford
Countrymen Restaurant At
 The Black Lion
The Green
Long Melford
Suffolk CO10 9DN
0787 312356

Longframlington
The Granby Inn
Front Street
Longframlington
Morpeth
Northumberland NE65 8DP
0665 570228

Lutterworth
The Greyhound
Market Street
Lutterworth
Leicestershire LE17 4EJ
0455 553307

Lynmouth
The Rising Sun Hotel
Harbourside
Lynmouth
Devon EX38 6EQ
0598 53223

Maidstone (Ringlestone)
Ringlestone Inn
Harrietsham
Nr Maidstone
Kent ME17 1NY
0622 859900

Maidstone (Warren Street)
The Harrow At Warren Street
Warren Street
New Lenham
Kent ME17 2ED
0622 858727

Malmsbury
The Horse & Groom Inn
Charlton
Nr Malmsbury
Wiltshire SN16 9DL
0666 823904

Malton
The Green Man
Market Street
Malton
North Yorkshire YO17 0LY
0653 600370

Malvern
The Colwall Park Hotel
Colwall
Malvern
Hereford & Worcester WR13 6QG
0684 40206

Market Harborough
The Sun Inn
Marston Trussel
Market Harborough
Leicestershire LE16 7TY
0858 465531

Milton-Under-Wychwood
Hillborough Hotel & Restaurant
The Green
Milton-Under-Wychwood
Oxfordshire OX7 6JH
0993 830501

Montacute
The Kings Arms Inn Hotel
Montacute
Somerset TA15 6UU
0935 822513

Newby Bridge
The Swan Hotel
Newby Bridge
Newby Bridge
Nr Ulverston
Cumbria LA12 8MB
05395 31681

Newton Abbott (Kingskerswell)
The Barn Owl Inn
Aller Mills
Kingkerswell
Newton Abbot
Devon TQ12 5AN
0803 872130

North Newnton
The Woodbridge Inn
North Newnton
Nr Pewsey
Wiltshire SN9 6JZ
0980 630266

Nottingham
Hotel Des Clos
Old Lenton Lane
Nottingham
Nottinghamshire NG7 2SA
0602 866566

Nottingham
Walton's
North Lodge
2 North Road
The Park
Nottinghamshire NG7 1AG
0602 475215

Okehampton (South Zeal)
The Oxenham Arms
South Zeal
Nr Okehampton
Devon EX20 2JT
0837 840244

Onneley
The Wheatsheaf Inn At Onneley
Barhill Road
Onneley
Staffordshire CW3 9QF
0782 751581

Oxford (Middleton Stoney)
The Jersey Arms
Middleton Stoney
Oxfordshire OX6 8SE
086989 234

Padstow
The Old Custom House Inn
South Quay
Padstow
Cornwall PL28 8ED
0841 532359

Pelynt (nr Looe)
Jubilee Inn
Pelynt
Nr Looe
Cornwall PL13 2JZ
0503 220312

Petworth (Sutton)
The White Horse Inn
Sutton
Nr Pulborough
West Sussex RH20 1PS
07987 221

Pickering
The White Swan
The Market Place
Pickering
North Yorkshire YO18 7AA
0751 72288

Port Gaverne
Port Gaverne Hotel
Port Gaverne
Nr Port Isaac
North Cornwall PL29 3SQ
0208 880244

Porthleven, Nr Helston
The Harbour Inn
Commercial Road
Porthleven
Nr Helston
Cornwall TR13 9JD
0326 573876

Preston (Goosnargh)
Ye Horns Inn
Goosnargh
Nr Preston
Lancashire PR3 27Y
0772 865230

Quorn
Quorn Grange
Wood Lane
Quorn
Leics LE12 8DB
0509 412167

Seavington St Mary, Nr Ilminster
The Pheasant Hotel
Ilminster
Seavington St Mary
Nr Ilminster
Somerset TA19 0QH
0460 40502

Ramsey
The George At Ramsey
High Street
Ramsey
Huntingdon
Cambridgeshire PE17 1AA
0487 815264

Sheringham
The Pheasant Hotel
The Coast Road
Kelling
Nr Holt
Norfolk NR25 7EG
0263 70382

Ringwood
The Struan Hotel And Restaurant
Horton Road
Ashley Heath
Nr Ringwood
Hampshire BH24 2EG
0425 473553

Shipton-under-Wychwood
The Shaven Crown Hotel
High Street
Shipton-under-Wychwood
Oxfordshire OX7 6RA
0993 830330

Rosedale Abbey
The Milburn Arms Hotel
Rosedale Abbey
Pickering
North Yorkshire
YO18 8RA
07515 312

Shipton-under-Wychwood
The Lamb Inn
Shipton-Under-Wychwood
Oxfordshire OX7 6DQ
0993 830465

Ross-On-Wye
The New Inn
St Owen's Cross
Hereford
Herefordshire HR2 8LQ
0989 87 274

Southport (Formby)
Treetops Country House Restaurant
Southport Old Road
Formby
Nr Southport
Merseyside L37 0AB
0704 879651

St Austell
The White Hart Hotel
Church Street
St Austell
Cornwall PL25 4AT
0726 72100

Southwold
The Crown Hotel
The High Street
Southwold
Suffolk IP18 6DP
0502 722275

St Ives (Hollywell)
The Old Ferry Boat Inn
Holywell
St Ives
Huntingdon
Cambridgeshire PE17 3TG
0480 463227

Stamford (Stretton)
Ram Jam Inn
Great North Road
Stretton
Oakham, Rutland
Leicestershire LE15 7QX
0780 410776

St Mawes
The Rising Sun
The Square
St Mawes
Cornwall TR2 5DJ
0326 27023

Stilton
The Bell Inn
Great North Road
Stilton
Peterborough
Cambridgeshire PE7 3RA
0733 241066

Saddleworth (Delph)
The Old Bell Inn Hotel
Huddersfield Road
Delph
Saddleworth
Lancashire OL3 SE6
0457 876597

Stow-on-the-Wold
The Royalist
Digbeth Street
Stow-on-the-Wold
Gloucestershire GL54 1BN
0451 830670

Scarborough (East Ayton)
East Ayton Lodge Country Hotel
Moor Lane
Forge Valley
East Ayton
Scarborough, North Yorkshire
0723 864227

Stow-on-the-Wold (Blockley)
The Crown Inn & Hotel
High Street
Blockley
Nr Moreton-In-Marsh
Gloucestershire GL56 9EX
0386 700245

Stow-on-the-Wold
The Kingshead Inn And Restaurant
The Green
Bledington
Nr Kingham
Oxfordshire OX7 6HD
0608 658365

Tunbridge Wells
Royal Wells Inn
Mount Ephraim
Tunbridge Wells
Kent TN4 8BE
0892 511188

Stratford-upon-Avon
The Blue Boar Inn
Temple Grafton
Alcester
Warwickshire B49 6NRE
0789 750010

Upton-upon-Severn, Nr Malvern
White Lion Hotel
High Street
Upton-upon-Severn
Worcestershire WR8 0HJ
0684 592551

Stratford-upon-Avon
(Chipping Norton)
The Crown & Cushion Hotel
Chipping Norton
Oxfordshire OX7 5AD
0608 642533

Wasdale
The Wasdale Head Inn
Wasdale Head
Nr Gosforth
Cumbria CA20 1EX
09467 26229

Telford (Norton)
The Hundred House Hotel
Bridgnorth Road
Norton
Nr Shifnal, Telford
Shropshire TF11 9EE
095 271 353

Waterhouses, nr Ashbourne
The Old Beams Restaurant
 With Rooms
Waterhouses
Staffordshire ST10 3TW
0538 308254

Thame, Nr Oxford
Thatchers Hotel & Restaurant
29/30 Lower High Street
Thame
Nr Oxford
Oxfordshire OX9 2AA
084 421 2146

Wensleydale (West Witton)
The Wensleydale Heifer
West Witton
Wensleydale
North Yorkshire DL8 4LS
0969 22322

Thelbridge
Thelbridge Cross Inn
Thelbridge
Nr Witheridge
Devon EX17 4SQ
0884 860316

Weobley
Ye Olde Salutation Inn
Market Pitch
Weobley
Herefordshire HR4 8SJ
0544 318443

Thornham (Norfolk)
The Lifeboat Inn
Ship Lane
Thornham
Hunstanton
Norfolk PE36 6LT
0485 526236

Westerham
The Kings Arms
Westerham
Kent TN16 1AN
0959 562990

Thorpe Market
Green Farm Restaurant And Hotel
North Walsham Road
Thorpe Market
Norfolk NR11 8TH
0263 833602

Whitewell
The Inn At Whitewell
Forest Of Bowland
Clitheroe
Lancashire BB7 3AT
0200 448222

Totnes (Staverton)
The Sea Trout Inn
Staverton
Nr Totnes
Devon TQ9 6PA
0803 762274

Winchester
Wykeham Arms
75 Kingsgate Street
Winchester
Hampshire SO23 9PG
0962 853834

Troutbeck, nr Windermere
The Mortal Man Hotel
Troutbeck
Nr Windermere
Cumbria LA23 1PL
05394 33193

Winsford
The Royal Oak Inn
Winsford
Exmoor National Park
Somerset TA24 7JE
064385 455

Withypool
The Royal Oak Inn
Exmoor National Park
Withypool
Somerset TA24 7QP
064 383 506/7

Wroxham
The Barton Angler Country Inn
Irstead Road
Neatishead
Nr Wroxham
Norfolk NR12 8YD
0692 630740

Yattendon
The Royal Oak Hotel
Yattendon
Newbury
Berkshire RG16 0UF
0635 201325

York (Copmanthorpe)
The Duke Of Connaught Hotel
Copmanthorpe Grange
Copmanthorpe
York
North Yorkshire YO2 3TN
0904 744318

WALES

Chepstow
Castle View Hotel
16 Bridge Street
Chepstow
Gwent NP6 5E2
0291 620349

Llanarmon DC
The West Arms Hotel
Llanarmon Dc
"Nr Llangollen
Clwyd LL20 7LD
0691 76665

Llandeilo (Rhosmaen)
The Plough Inn
Rhosmaen
Llandeilo
Dyfed SA19 6NP
0558 823431

Welshpool (Berriew)
The Lion Hotel And Restaurant
Berriew
Nr Welshpool
Powys SY21 8PQ
0686 640452

SCOTLAND

Banchory (Royal Deeside)
Potarch Hotel
By Banchory
Royal Deeside
Kincardineshire AB3 4BD
03398 84339

Beauly
Lovat Arms Hotel
Beauly
Inverness-Shire IV4 7BS
0463 782313

Edinburgh (Dalkeith)
The Sun Inn
Lothianbridge
Nr Dalkeith
Mid Lothian EH22 4TR
031 663 2456

Fort William
Moorings Hotel
Banavie
Fort William
Inverness-Shire PH33 7LY
0397 772797

Glendevon
Tormaukin Hotel
Glendevon
By Dollar
Perthshire FK14 7JY
0259 781252

Isle Of Skye
Isle Ornsay Hotel
Eilean Iarmain
Isle Of Skye
Scotland IV43 8QR
047 13332

Kilfinan
Kilfinan Hotel
Nr Tignabruaich
Argyllshire PA21 2AP
070082 201

Kilmelford
Cuilfail Hotel
Kilmelford
Nr Oban
Argyll PA34 4XA
085 22274

Tarbert
The Columba Hotel
East Pier Road
Tarbert
Loch Fyne
Argyllshire PA29 6UF
0880 820808

The following establishments can be found described in full in the *Johansens Recommended Private Country Houses and Small Hotels in Great Britain and Ireland 1994*. For their map locations see pages 458–464.

There are three guides in the Johansens series - *Johansens Recommended Hotels in Great Britain and Ireland*, *Johansens Recommended Inns and Restaurants in Great Britain* and *Johansens Recommended Private Country Houses and Small Hotels in Great Britain and Ireland*.

An order form can be found at the back of this guide or copies may be obtained from Johansens establishments, good bookshops or direct from the publishers by calling the credit card orderline free on **0800 269397**.

Allendale
Bishop Field Cottage
Allendale
Hexham
Northumberland NE47 9EJ
0434 683248

Allendale (weekley let)
Bishop Field Cottage
Allendale
Hexham
Northumberland NE47 9EJ
0434 683248

Ambleside
Laurel Villa
Lake Road
Ambleside
Cumbria LA22 0DB
05394 33240

Atherstone
Chapel House
Friars Gate
Atherstone
Warwickshire CV9 1EY
0827 718949

Bakewell
Croft Country House Hotel
Great Longstone
Bakewell
Derbyshire DE45 1TF
0629 640278

Bamburgh
Waren House Hotel
Waren Mill
Belford
Northumberland NE70 7EE
066 84 581

Banbury
Easington House
50 Oxford Road
Banbury
Oxfordshire OX16 9AN
0295 270181

Bath
The Bath Tasburgh Hotel
Warminster Road
Bathampton
Bath
Avon BA2 6SH
0225 425096

Bath
Bloomfield House
146 Bloomfield Road
Bath
Avon BA2 2AS
0225 420105

Bath
Eagle House
Church Street
Bathford
Bath
Avon BA1 7RS
0225 859946

Bath
Newbridge House
Kelson Road
Bath BA1 3QH
0225 446676

Bath
Oakhill Manor
Oakhill
Nr Bath
Somerset BA3 5AW
0749 840977

Bath
Paradise House
Holloway
Bath
Avon BA2 4PX
0225 317723

Bath (Branford-on-Avon)
Widbrook Grange
Trowbridge Road
Bradford-on-Avon
Wiltshire BA15 1UH
0225 864750

Belper (Shottle)
Dannah Farm Country Guest House
Bowmans Lane
Shottle
Nr Belper
Derbyshire DE5 2DR
0773 550273/630

Biggin-by-Hartington
Biggin Hall
Biggin-by-Hartington
Buxton
Derbyshire SK17 0DH
0298 84451

Blawith
Appletree Holme Farm
Blawith
Nr Ulverston
South Lakes
Cumbria LA12 8EL
0229 885618

Buttermere
Pickett Howe
Brackenthwaite
Buttermere Valley
Cumbria CA13 9UY
0900 85444

Bolton-by-Bowland
Harrop Fold
Bolton By Bowland
Clitheroe
Lancashire BBY 4PY
0200 447600

Buxton
Coningsby
6 Macclesfield Road
Buxton
Derbyshire SK17 9AH
0298 26735

Bridgnorth
Cross Lane House Hotel
Astley Abbots
Bridgnorth
Shropshire WV16 4SJ
0746 764887

Calne
Chilvester Hill House
Calne
Wiltshire SH11 0LP
0249 813981

Bristol (Hutton)
Hutton Court
Church Lane
Hutton
Nr Weston Super Mare
Avon BS24 9SN
0934 814343

Cambridge (Melbourne)
Melbourne Bury
Melbourne
Nr Royston
Hertfordshire SG3 6DE
0763 261151

Broadway
Leason House
Laverton Meadows
Broadway
Worcestershire WR12 7NA
0386 73526

Carlisle (Crosby-on-Eden)
Crosby Lodge Country House Hotel
High Crosby
Crosby-on-Eden
Carisle
Cumbria CA6 4QZ
0228 573618

Bromyard (Tedstone Delamere)
Tedstsone Court
Tedstone Delamere
Bromyard
Herefordshire HR7 4PS
0886 21814

Cartmel
Aynsome Manor Hotel
Cartmel
Nr Grange-over-Sands
Cumbria LA11 6HH
05395 36653

Bryher (Isles Of Scilly)
Hell Bay Hotel
Bryher
Isles Of Scilly TR23 0PR
0720 22947

Castle Hedingham
The Old School House
St James Street
Castle Hedingham
Essex CO9 3EW
0787 61370

Burley, nr Ringwood
Toad Hall
The Cross
Burley
New Forest
Hampshire BH24 2AB
0425 403448

Cawsand, nr Plymouth
Polhawn Fort
Rame
Torpoint
Cornwall PL10 1LL
0752 822864

Bury St Edmunds
12 Angel Hill
12 Angel Hill
Bury St Edmunds
Suffolk IP33 1UZ
0284 704085

Charing (Charing Heath)
Tram Hatch
Charing Heath
Nr Ashford
Kent TN27 0BN
0233 713373

Bury St Edmunds
Bradfield House
Bradfield Combust
Bury St Edmunds
Suffolk IP30 OL3
0284 386301

Cheltenham (Withington)
Halewell
Halewell Close
Withington
Nr Cheltenham
Gloucestershire GL54 4BN
0242 890238

Chester (Huxley)
Higher Huxley Hall
Huxley
Chester CH3 9BZ
0829 781484

Diss (Gissing)
The Old Rectory
Gissing
Diss
Norfolk IP22 3XB
0379 77575

**Chipping Campden
(Broad Campden)**
Malt House
Broad Campden
Chipping Campden
Gloucestershire GL55 6UU
0386 840295

Diss (Palgrave)
The Malt House
Denmark Hill
Palgrave
Nr Diss
Norfolk IP22 1AE
0379 642107

Chobham
Knaphill Manor
Carthouse Lane
Woking
Surrey GU21 4XT
0276 857962

Dorchester
Yalbury Cottage
Lower Bockhampton
Dorchester
Dorset DT2 8PZ
0305 262382

Clovelly (Horn's Cross)
Foxdown Manor
Horn's Cross
Nr Clovelly
Devon EX39 5PJ
0237 451325

Dorchester (Maiden Newton)
Maiden Newton House
Maiden Newton
Nr Dorchester
Dorset DT2 0AA
0300 320336

Combe Martin (Berrynarbor)
Bessemer Thatch
Berrynarbor
Nr Combe Martin
North Devon EX34 9SE
0271 882296

Dover (West Cliffe)
Wallett's Court
West Cliffe
St Margarets-at-Cliffe
Dover
Kent CT15 6EW
0304 852424

Crayke (York)
Halfway House
Crayke
Yorkshire YO6 4TJ
0347 822614

Doveridge (Nr Uttoxeter)
The Beeches Farmhouse
Waldley
Doveridge
Derbyshire
DE6 5LR
0889 590288

Dartmoor (Leusdon)
Leusdon Lodge Hotel
Leusdon
Poundsgate
Nr Ashburton
Devon TQ13 7PE
0364 3304

Ellesmere
Stanwardine House
Cockshutt
Nr Ellesmere
Shropshire
0939 270534

Dartmoor (Two Bridges)
Prince Hall Hotel
Two Bridges
Yelverton
Devon PL20 6SA
0822 890403

Ely (Stuntney)
Forge Cottage
Lower Road
Stuntney
Ely
Cambridge CB7 5TN
0831 833932

Diss
Chippenhall Hall
Fressingfield
Eye
Suffolk IP21 5TD
037986 8180

Etchingham
King Johns Lodge
Sheppstreet Lane
Etchingham
East Sussex TN19 7AZ
0580819 232

Diss
Salisbury House
Victoria Road
Diss
Norfolk IP22 3JG
0379 644738

Evershot
Rectory House
Fore Street
Evershot
Dorset DT2 0JN
093583 273

Exeter (Dunchideock)
The Lord Haldon Hotel
Dunchideock
Nr Exeter
Devon EX6 7YF
0392 832483

Heacham
Holly Lodge
Lynn Road
Heacham
Norfolk PE31 7HY
0485 70790

Framlingham (Tannington)
Tannington Hall
Tannington
Woodbridge
Suffolk IP13 7NH
0728 628226

Holmfirth
Holme Castle Country House
Holme Village
Nr Holmfirth
West Yorkshire HG7 1QG
0484 686764
CHOUS12/08/93

Gatwick (Horley)
Langshott Manor
Langshott
Horley
Surrey RH6 9LN
0293 786680

Hunstanton (Sedgeford)
Sedgeford Hall
Sedgeford
Nr Hunstanton
Norfolk PE36 5LT
0485 70902

Glossop
The Wind in the Willows
Level
Glossop
Derbyshire SK13 9PT
0457 868001

Isle Of Wight (Bonchurch)
Madeira Hall
Trinity Road
Bonchurch
Ventnor
Isle Of Wight PO38 1NS
0983 852624

Goathland
Whitfield House Hotel
Darmholm
Goathland
North Yorkshire YO22 5LA
0947 86215

Jervaulx
Jervaulx Hall
Jervaulx
Nr Masham
Ripon
North Yorkshire HG4 4PH
0677 460235

Grantham
Barkston House
Harkston
Grantham
Linconshire NG32 2NH
0400 50555

Keswick (Lake Thirlmere)
Dale Head Hall
Thirlmere
Keswick
Cumbria CA12 4TN
07687 72478

Hampton Court
Chase Lodge
10 Park Road
Hampton Wick
Kingston-upon-Thames
Surrey KT1 4AS
081 943 1862

Keswick (Newlands)
Swinside Lodge Hotel
Grange Road
Newlands
Keswick
Cumbria CA12 8UE
07687 72948

Harrogate
The White House
10 Park Parade
Harrogate
North Yorkshire HG1 5AH
0423 501388

Keswick-On-Derwent-Water
The Grange Country House Hotel
Manor Brow
Keswick-On-Derwent-Water
Cumbria CA12 4BA
07687 72500

Hawes
Rookhurst Georgian
Country House Hotel
West End
Gayle
Hawes, North Yorkshire DL8 3RT
0969 667454

Kinston Bagpuize
Fallowfields
Southmoor
Kinston Bagpuize
Oxford OX13 5BH
0865 820416

Haytor
The Bel Alp House
Haytor
Nr Bovey Tracey
Devon TQ13 9XX
0364 661217

Ladock (nr Truro)
Bissick Old Mill
Ladock
Nr Truro
Cornwall TR2 4PG
0726 882 557

Lastingham
Lastingham Grange
Lastingham
Nr Kirkbymoorside
York
North Yorkshire YO6 6TH
0751 417345

Louth
Birdsong Country House Hotel
Little Cawthorpe
Louth
Lincolnshire LN11 8NT
0507 480717

Ledbury (Bromsberrow Heath)
Grove House
Bromsberrow Heath
Nr Ledbury
Herefordshire HR8 1PE
0531 650584

Lowick Bridge
Bridgefield House
Lowick Bridge
Nr Ulverston
Cumbria LA12 8DA
0229 885239

Leicester (Newtown Linford)
The Johnscliffe Hotel &
Old John Restaurants
Main Street
Newton Linford
Leicestershire LE6 0AF
0530 242228

Ludlow (Diddlebury)
Delbury Hall
Diddlebury
Craven Arms
Shropshire SY7 9DH
058476 267

Leominster
Lower Bache
Kimbolton
Nr Leominster
Herefordshire HR6 0ER
0568 87304

Luton (Little Offley)
Little Offley
Hitchin
Hertfordshire SG5 3BU
0462 768243

Leominster (Eyton)
The Marsh Country Hotel
Eyton
Nr Leominster
Herefordshire HR6 0AG
0568 613952

Lydford (Vale Down)
Moor View Hotel
Vale Down
Lydford
Devon EX20 4BB
082 282220

Lifton (Sprytown)
The Thatched Cottage
Country Hotel
Sprytown
Lifton
Devon PL16 0AY
0566 784224

Maidstone (Boughton Chelsea)
Tanyard
Wierton Hill
Boughton
Monchelsea
Kent ME17 4JT
0622 744705

Lincoln
Minster Lodge Hotel
3 Church Lane
Lincoln
Lincolnshire LN2 1QS
0522 513220

Malpas
Broughton House
Threapwood
Malpas
Cheshire SY14 7AU
0948 770610

Liskeard (St Keyne)
The Old Rectory Country Hotel
St Keyne
Duloe Road
St Keyne
Cornwall PL14 4RL
0579 342617

Malton
Newstead Grange
Norton
Malton
North Yorkshire YO17 9PJ
0653 692502

London (Enfield)
Oak Lodge Hotel
Village Road
Bush Hill Park
Enfield EN1 2EU
081 360 7082

Malvern
Old Parsonage Farm
Hanely Castle
Worcester WR8 0BU
0684 310124

Looe (Talland Bay)
Allhays Country House
Talland Bay
Looe
Cornwall PL13 2JB
0503 72434

Manaton (Dartmoor)
Barracott
Manaton
Newton Abbot
Devon TQ13 9XA
0647 22312

Market Harborough (Medbourne)
The Old Rectory
Medbourne
Market Harborough
Leicestershire LE16 8DZ
085 883 330

Marlborough
The Old Vicarage
Marlborough Burbage
Nr Marlborough
Wiltshire SN8 3AG
0672 810495

Middleham
The Millers House Hotel
Market Place
Middleham
Wensleydale
North Yorkshire DL8 4NR
0969 22630

Minehead
The Beacon Country House
Beacon Road
Minehead
Somerset TA24 5SD
0643 703476

Morchard Bishop
Wigham
Morchard Bishop
Nr Crediton
Devon EX17 6RJ
0363 877350

Moreton-in-Marsh (Blockley)
Lower Brook House
Blockley
Moreton-in-Marsh
Gloucestershire GL56 9DS
0386 700286

Morston, Nr Blackeney
Morston Hall
Morston
Holt
Norfolk NR25 7AA
0263 741041

Needham Market, Nr Ipswich
Pipps Ford
Norwich Road
Needham Market
Ipswich
Suffolk IP6 8LJ
044 979 208

New Romney (Littlestone)
Romney Bay House
Coast Road
Littlestone
New Romney
Kent TN28 8QY
0679 64747

Oxhill
Nolands Farm & Country Restaurant
Oxhill
Warwickshire CV35 0RJ
0926 640309

Porthleven, nr Helston
Tye Rock Hotel
Loe Bar Road
Porthleven
Cornwall TR13 9EW
0326 572695

Redditch
The Old Rectory
Ipsley Lane
Redditch
Hereford & Worcester B98 0AP
0527 23000

Ross-on-Wye (Kilcot)
Orchard House
Astoningham Road
Kilcot
Gloucestershire GL18 1NP
0989 82417

Ross-on-Wye
Glewstone Court
Nr Ross-on-Wye
Herefordshire HR9 6AW
0989 84367

Ross-on-Wye (weekly Let)
Wye Lea
Bridstow
Ross-on-Wye
Herefordshire HR9 6PZ
0989 62880

Ross-on-Wye (Yatton)
Rock's Place
Yatton
Ross-on-Wye
Hertfordshire HR9 7RD
053 184 218

Rye
Little Orchard House
West Street
Rye
East Sussex TN31 7ES
0797 223831

Simonsbath (Exmoor)
Simonsbath House Hotel
Simonsbath
Exmoor
Somerset TA24 7SH
064383 259

Sissinghurst (Biddenden)
Vine Farm
Waterman Quarter
Headcorn
Kent TN27 9VV
0622 890203

Slaidburn
Parrock Head
Woodhouse Lane
Slaidburnroe
Nr Clitheroe
Lancashire BB7 3AH
02006 614

South Molton
Marsh Hall Country House Hotel
South Molton
Devon EX36 3HQ
0769 572666

South Petherton
Oaklands House
8 Palmer Street
South Petherton
Somerset TA13 5DB
0460 40272

St Agnes (Mithian)
Rose-In-Vale Country House Hotel
Mithian
St Agnes
Cornwall TR5 0QD
0787 552202

St Ives (Trink)
The Countryman At Trink
Old Coach Road
St Ives
Cornwall TR26 3JQ
0736 797571

Sway, Nr Lymington
The Tower
Barrows Lane
Sway
Hampshire SO41 6DE
0590 682117

Taunton (Churchstanton)
Burnworthy Manor
Churchstanton
Taunton
Somerset TA3 7DR
0823 60588

Tenterden (Wittersham)
Budds House
Isle Of Oxney
Wittersham
Kent TN30 7EL
0797 270204

Tewkesbury
Upper Court
Kemerton
Nr Tewkesbury
Gloucestershire GL20 7HY
0386 89351

Thornton Watlass (Wensleydale)
The Old Rectory
Thornton Watlass
Masham
North Yorkshire HG4 4AH
0677 423456

Tintagel (Trenale)
Trebrea Lodge
Trenale
Tintagel
Cornwall PL34 0HR
0840 770410

Totnes (Harbertonford)
The Old Mill Country House
Harbertonford
Nr Totnes
South Devon TQ9 7SW
0803 732349

Uckfield
Hooke Hall
High Street
Uckfield
East Sussex TN22 1EN
0825 761578

Ullingswick
The Steppes
Ulllingswick
Nr Hereford
Hereford NR1 3JG
0432 820424

Wells (Wookey Hole)
Glencot House
Glencot Lane
Wookey Hole
Wells
Somerset BA5 1BH
0749 77160

Whitby (Dunsley)
Dunsley Hall
Dunsley
Whitby
North Yorkshire YO21 3TL
0947 83437

Willaton (Vellow)
Curdon Mill
Lower Vellow
Willaton
Nr Taunton
Somerset TA4 4LS
0984 56522

Windermere
Braemount House
Sunny Bank Road
Windermere
Cumbria LA23 2EM
05394 45967

Windermere
Quarry Garth Country House Hotel
Windermere
The Lake District
Cumbria LA23 1LF
05394 88282

Woodbridge (Otley)
Otley House
Helmingham Road
Otley
Suffolk IP6 9NR
0473 890253

York
4 South Parade
York
North Yorkshire YO2 2BA
0904 628229

WALES

Abergavenny
Llanwenarth House
Govilon
Abergavenny
Gwent NP7 9SF
0873 830289

**Abergavenny
(Llanfihangel Crucorney)**
Penyclawdd Court
Llanfihangel Crucorney
Nr Abergavenny
Gwent
0873 890719

Betws-Y-Coed
Tan-Y-Foel
Capel Garmon
Nr Betws-Y-Coed
Gwynedd LL26 0RE
0690 710507

Brecon (Felindre)
Old Gwernyfed Country Manor
Felindre
Three Cocks
Brecon
Powys LD3 0SU
0497 847376

Conwy
The Old Rectory
Conwy
Llanwrst Road
Llansanffraid Glan Conwy
Gwynedd LL28 5LF
0492 580611

Criccieth
Myndd Ednyfed
  Country House Hotel
Caernarfon Road
Criccieth
Gwynedd LL52 0PH
0766 523269

Dolgellau (Bontddu)
Borthwnog Hall Country
  House & Restaurant
Bontddu
Dolgellau
Gwynedd LL40 2TT
0341 49271

Dolgellau (Ganllwyd)
Dolmelynllyn Hall Hotel
Ganllwyd
Dolgellau
Gwynedd LL40 2HP
0341 40273

Fishguard
Plas Glyn-Y-Mel
Lower Town
Fishguard
Dyfed SA65 9LY
0348 872296

Fishguard (Welsh Hook)
Stone Hall
Welsh Hook
Haverford
WestPembrokeshire
Dyfed SA62 5NS
0348 840212

Llandovery
Glanrannell Park Hotel
Crugybar
Llanwrda
Dyfed SA19 85A
0558 685230

Llanfyllin
Bodfach Hall Country House Hotel
Llanfyllin
Powys SY22 5HS
0691 648272

Llanwrtyd Wells
Cwmirfon Lodge
Llanwrtyd Wells
Powys LD5 4TN
05913 217

Mold
Tower
Off Nercwys Road
Mold
Clwyd CH7 4ED
0352 700220

Tenby (Waterwynch Bay)
Waterwynch House Hotel
Waterwynch Bay
Tenby
Pembrokeshire
Dyfed SA70 8TJ
0834 842464

Tintern
Parva Farmhouse
Tintern
Chepstow
Gwent NP6 6SQ
0291 689411

SCOTLAND

Aviemore
Courrour House Hotel
Inverdruie
Inverness-Shire PH22 1QH0
479 810220

Ballater (Royal Deeside)
Balgonie Country House
Braemar Place
Ballater
Royal Deeside
Grampian AB35 5RP
03397 55482

Blairgowrie
Altamount House Hotel
Coupar Angus Road
Blairgowrie
Perthshire PH10 6JN
0250 873512

Cardross (Dunbartonshire)
Kirkton House
Cardress
Dunbartonshire
0389 841951

Dunfermline (Cleish)
Nivingston House
Cleish
Kinross-Shire KY13 7LS
0577 850216

Dunoon
Ardfillayne Hotel
West Bay
Dunoon
Argyll
Argyllshire PA23 7QJ
0369 2267

Fintry (Stirlingshire)
Culcreuch Castle Hotel
Fintry
Loch Lomond
Stirling & Trossachs
Stirlingshire
036 086 228

Forres
Knockomie Hotel
Grantown Road
Forres
Morray IV36 0SG
0309 673146

Grantown-on-Spey
Culdearn House
Woodlands Terrace
Grantown-on-Spey
Moray
Morayshire PH26 3JU
0479 2106

Haddington
Brown's Hotel
West Road
Haddington EH41 3RD
062082 2254

Inchbae (By Ullapool)
Inchbae Lodge Hotel
By GarveRoss-Shire IV23 2PH
09975 269

Innerleithen, nr Peebles
Traquair House
Innerleithen
Peebleshire
0896 830323

Isle Of Harris
Ardvourlie Castle
Aird A Mhulaidh
Isle Of Harris PA85 3AB
0859 23073

Isle Of Mull
Druimnacroish Country House Hotel
Druimnacroish
DervaigIsle Of Mull
Argyllshire
06884 274

Killiecrankie
TheKilliecrankie Hotel
Killiecrankie
By Pitlochry
Perthshire PH16 5LG
0796 473220

Loch Lochy, By Spean Bridge
Corriegour Lodge Hotel
Loch Lochy
By Spean Bridge
Inverness-Shire PH34 4EB
0397 712685

Oban
The Manor House
Gallanach Road
Oban
Scotland PA34 4LS
0631 62087

Oban
Dungallan Country House
Gallanach Road
Oban
Argyll PA34 4PD
0631 63799

Pitlochry
Craigmhor Lodge
27 West Moulin Road
Pitlochry PH16 5EF
0796 472123

Pitlochry
Dunfallandy House
Logierait Road
Pitlochry
Perthshire PH16 5NA
0796 472648

Port Of Menteith
The Lake Hotel
Port Of Menteith
Perthshire FK8 3RA
08775 258

Strath Brora
Sciberscross Lodge
Strath Brora
Rogart
Sutherland IV28 3YQ
0408641 246

Strathpeffer
Contin House
Contin Strathpeffer
Ross-Shire IV14 9EB
0997 421920

Wicklow Town, Co Wicklow
The Old Rectory
Wicklow
Co Wicklow
0404 67048

IRELAND

CHANNEL ISLANDS

Bantry
Bantry House
Bantry
Co Cork
027 50047

Castel
Les Embruns Hotel
Route De La Margion
Vazon Bay
Castel
Guernsey
0481 64834

Caragh Lake
Ard Na Sidhe
Killarney
Killorglin
Co Kerry
0666 9105

St Peters Port
Midhurst House
Candie Road
St Peter Port
Guernsey
0481 724391

Enniscorthy Co Wexford
Ballinkeele House
Ballymurn
Enniscorthy
Co Wexford
05338105

St Helier
Almorah Hotel
One Almorah Crescent
Lower Kings Cliff
La Pouque Lay
St Helier, Jersey JE2 3GU
0534 21648

Riverstown, Co Sligo
Coopershill House
Riverstown
Co Sligo
071 65108

St Peter
Greenhill Country Hotel
St Peter's Valley
Jersey JE3 7EL
0534 481042

Straffan, Co Kildaire
Barberstown Castle
Straffan
Co Kildaire
016288157

Sark
Stocks
Sark Island Hotel
Sark
0481 832001

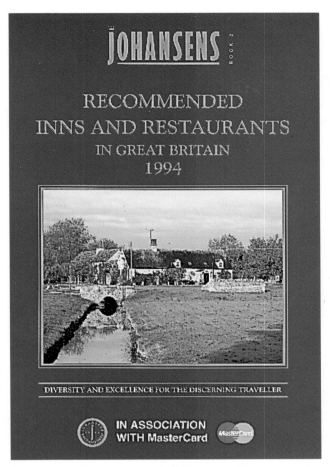

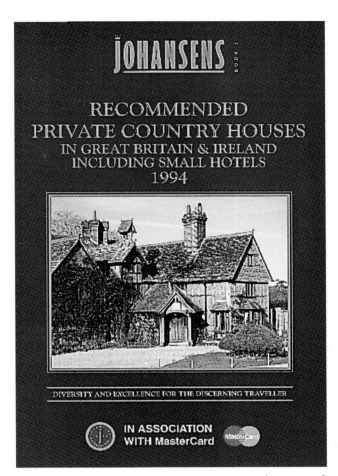

Johansens Recommended Inns and Restaurants in Great Britain is a popular publication and the 1994 edition contains over 150 establishments. The majority of properties offer value for money accommodation, good cooking, fine wines and ales; all offer a very warm welcome to travellers. Many are splendid old coaching inns retaining features from bygone eras, situated adjacent to village greens or nestling deep in unspoiled countryside. These establishments provide ideal locations for those seeking a relaxing weekend away or short break. Price £8.95

This guide features over 180 privately owned country houses and small owner managed hotels, each unique and many of significant historical interest. Picturesque surroundings, well tended gardens and an intimate atmosphere are their hallmarks. Most establishments have just a few guest bedrooms. In some, guests dine en-famille - all offer attractive accommodation and the genuine warmth of convivial hosts into whose home you are stepping. Stay in Johansens Recommended country houses and discover some of Britain's finest heritage. Price £8.95

*Copies may be obtained from most Johansens recommended establishments, good bookshops or direct from the publishers.**

*See order coupon at the back of this guide.

CHAMPAGNE POMMERY
REIMS·FRANCE

ENJOY

the

ELEGANCE

of

CHAMPAGNE

POMMERY

Sole UK Agents
Teltscher Brothers Ltd
Imperial Way
Southampton
Hampshire SO1 0RB

Tel: 0703 312000
Fax: 0703 311111

No matter where you are, cash is always at hand...

...from Austria to Venezuela, whenever you need cash in the local currency you can rely on the MasterCard®/CIRRUS® ATM Network. With over 135,000 cash machines in 49 countries and territories worldwide, your cash is always at hand.

Simply match the symbols on your card and cash machine and tap in the same personal identification number you use at home.

And remember, when you use your MasterCard or CIRRUS card for cash, you'll receive an excellent foreign exchange rate. So no matter where you are, trust MasterCard and CIRRUS for cash at the touch of a button.

OFFICIAL CARD
WorldCupUSA**94**™

Ask your bank for further details.

JOHANSENS RECOMMENDED HOTEL
JOHANSENS RECOMMENDED INN OR RESTAURANT
JOHANSENS RECOMMENDED PRIVATE COUNTRY HOUSE

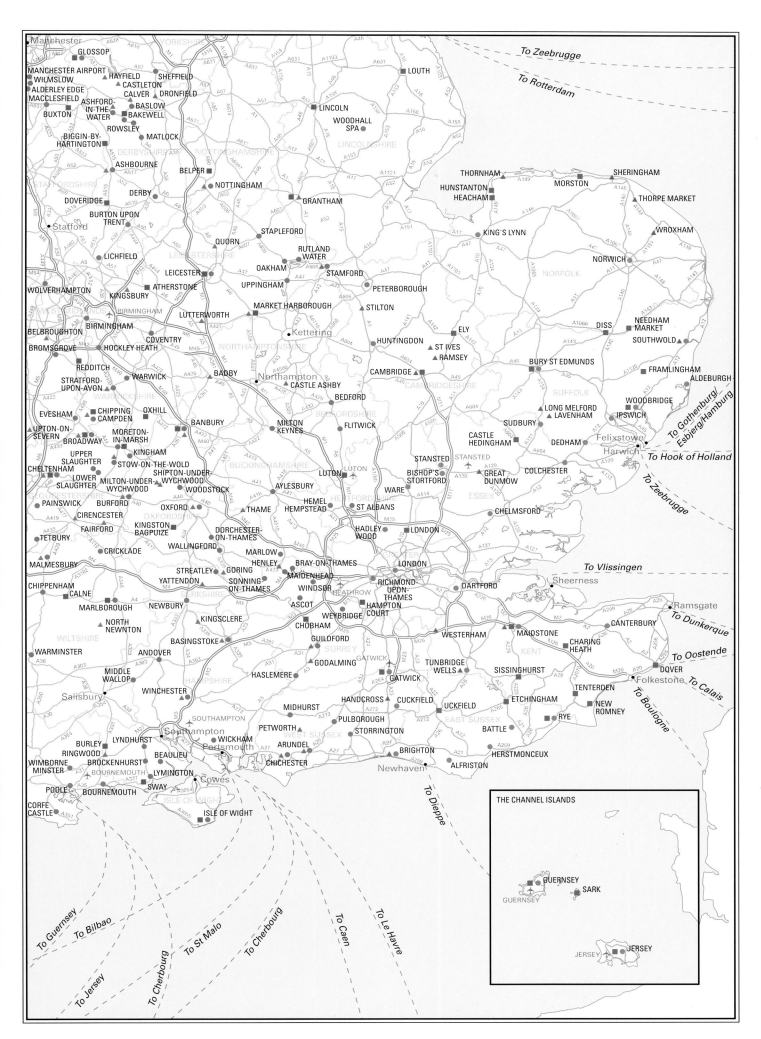

THE CHANNEL ISLANDS

GUERNSEY
GUERNSEY
SARK
JERSEY
JERSEY

To Zeebrugge
To Rotterdam
To Gothenburg/Esbjerg/Hamburg
To Hook of Holland
To Zeebrugge
To Vlissingen
To Dunkerque
To Oostende
To Calais
To Boulogne
To Dieppe
To Guernsey
To Bilbao
To Jersey
To Cherbourg
To St Malo
To Cherbourg
To Caen
To Le Havre

© Lovell Johns Ltd, Oxford

459

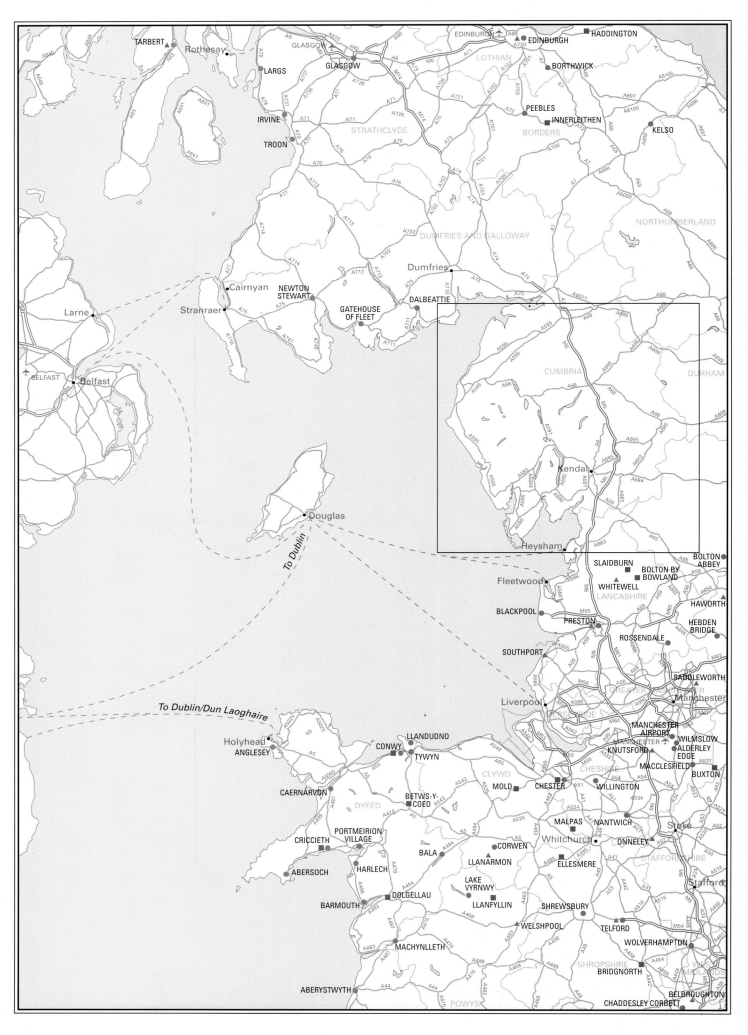

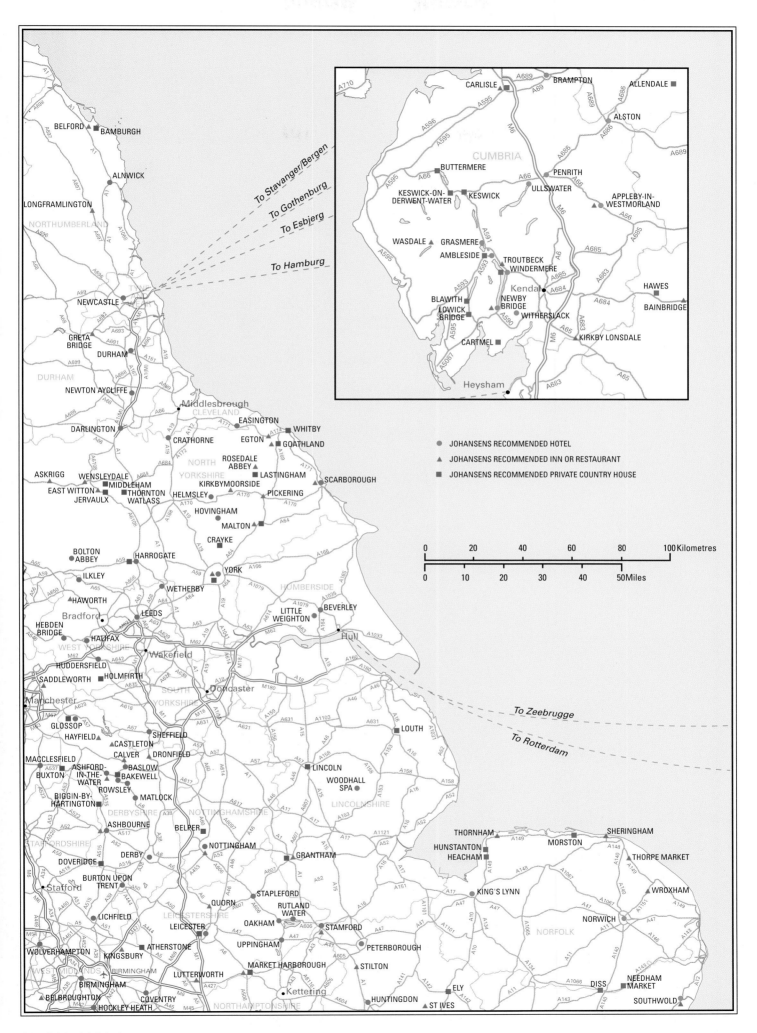

JOHANSENS RECOMMENDED HOTEL
JOHANSENS RECOMMENDED INN OR RESTAURANT
JOHANSENS RECOMMENDED PRIVATE COUNTRY HOUSE

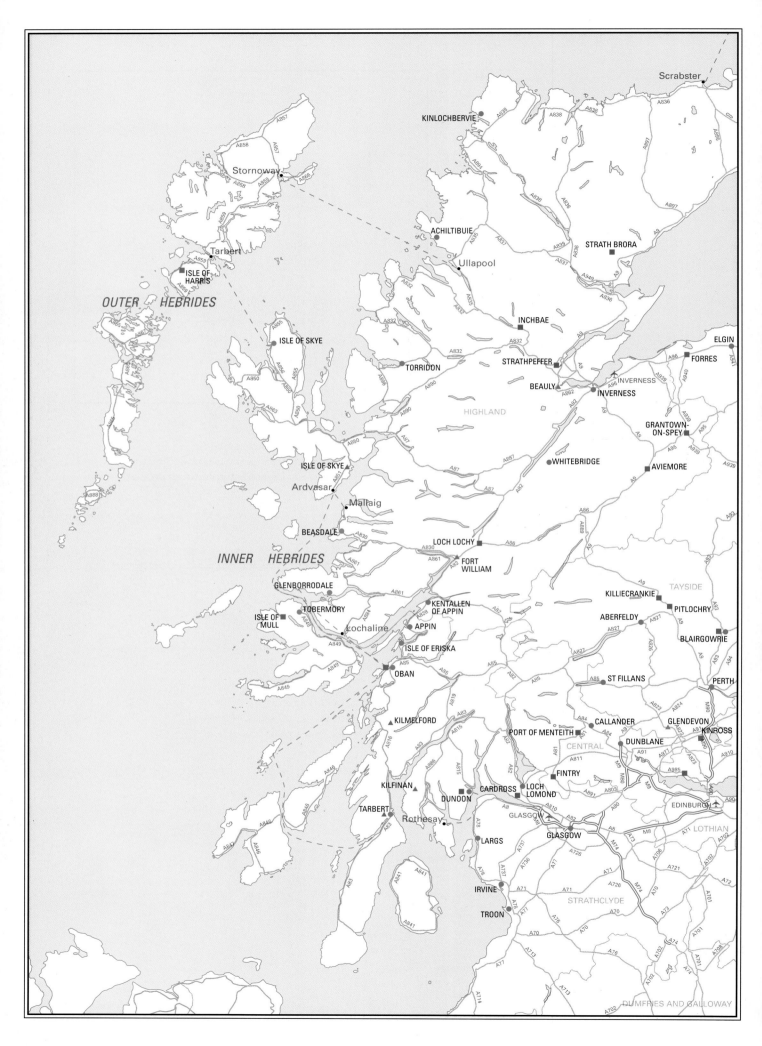

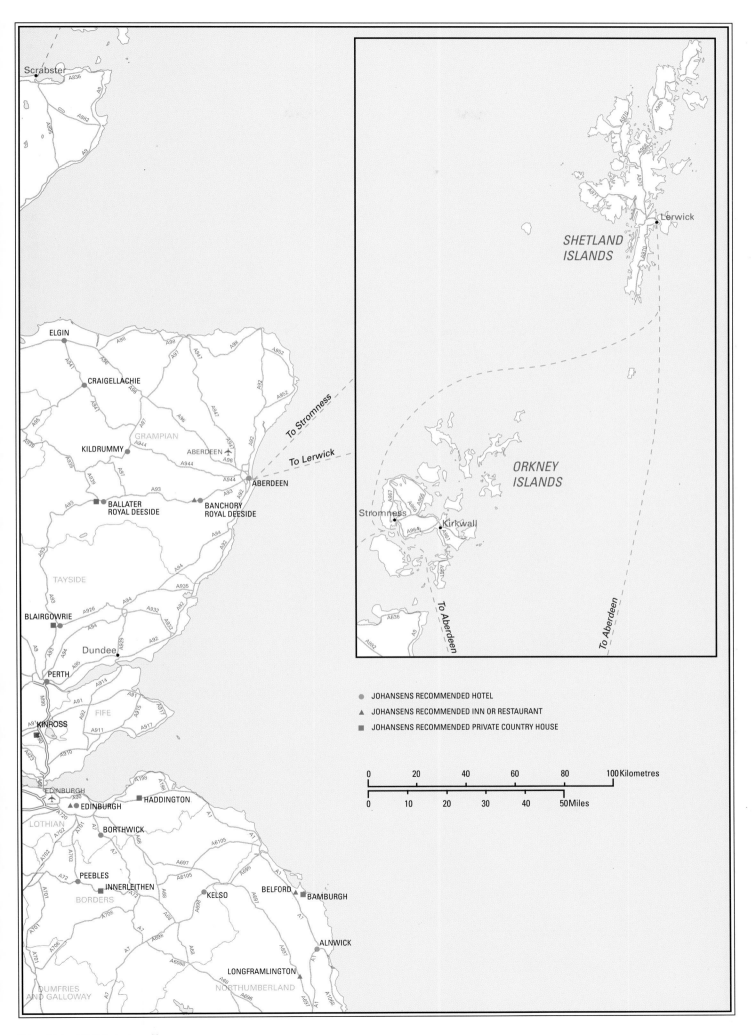

Scrabster

ELGIN
CRAIGELLACHIE

GRAMPIAN

KILDRUMMY
ABERDEEN ✈

BALLATER
ROYAL DEESIDE
BANCHORY
ROYAL DEESIDE

ABERDEEN

To Stromness
To Lerwick

TAYSIDE

BLAIRGOWRIE

Dundee

PERTH

FIFE

KINROSS

EDINBURGH ✈
EDINBURGH
HADDINGTON

LOTHIAN

BORTHWICK

PEEBLES
INNERLEITHEN
KELSO
BELFORD
BAMBURGH

BORDERS

ALNWICK

DUMFRIES
AND GALLOWAY

LONGFRAMLINGTON

NORTHUMBERLAND

SHETLAND
ISLANDS

Lerwick

ORKNEY
ISLANDS

Stromness
Kirkwall

To Aberdeen

To Aberdeen

● JOHANSENS RECOMMENDED HOTEL
▲ JOHANSENS RECOMMENDED INN OR RESTAURANT
■ JOHANSENS RECOMMENDED PRIVATE COUNTRY HOUSE

0	20	40	60	80	100 Kilometres

0	10	20	30	40	50 Miles

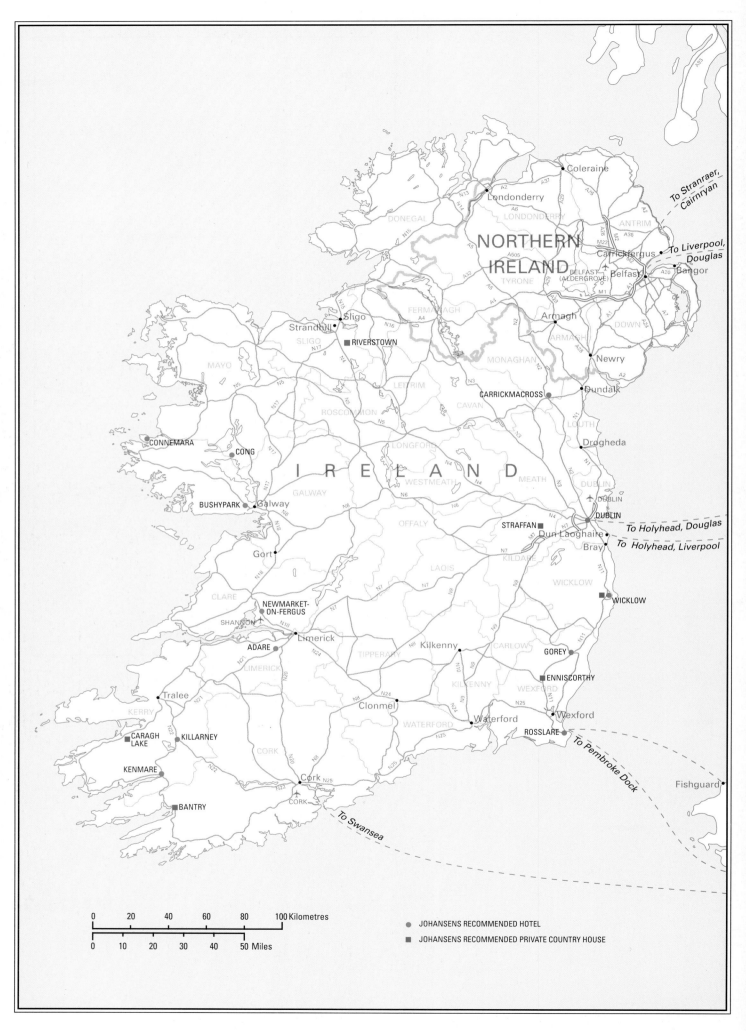

NORTHERN IRELAND

To Stranraer, Cairnryan

To Liverpool, Douglas

Coleraine

Londonderry

LONDONDERRY

ANTRIM

Carrickfergus

DONEGAL

TYRONE

BELFAST (ALDERGROVE)

Belfast

Bangor

FERMANAGH

Armagh

DOWN

Sligo

Strandhill

RIVERSTOWN

SLIGO

LEITRIM

MONAGHAN

ARMAGH

Newry

MAYO

ROSCOMMON

CAVAN

CARRICKMACROSS

Dundalk

LONGFORD

LOUTH

CONNEMARA

CONG

Drogheda

I R E L A N D

WESTMEATH

MEATH

BUSHYPARK

Galway

GALWAY

OFFALY

DUBLIN

DUBLIN

STRAFFAN

Gort

Dun Laoghaire

To Holyhead, Douglas

To Holyhead, Liverpool

Bray

KILDARE

CLARE

LAOIS

WICKLOW

NEWMARKET-ON-FERGUS

WICKLOW

SHANNON

Limerick

ADARE

Kilkenny

CARLOW

GOREY

LIMERICK

TIPPERARY

KILKENNY

ENNISCORTHY

Tralee

WEXFORD

KERRY

Clonmel

Waterford

Wexford

CARAGH LAKE

Killarney

WATERFORD

ROSSLARE

CORK

To Pembroke Dock

KENMARE

Cork

Fishguard

BANTRY

CORK

To Swansea

| 0 | 20 | 40 | 60 | 80 | 100 Kilometres |

| 0 | 10 | 20 | 30 | 40 | 50 Miles |

● JOHANSENS RECOMMENDED HOTEL

■ JOHANSENS RECOMMENDED PRIVATE COUNTRY HOUSE

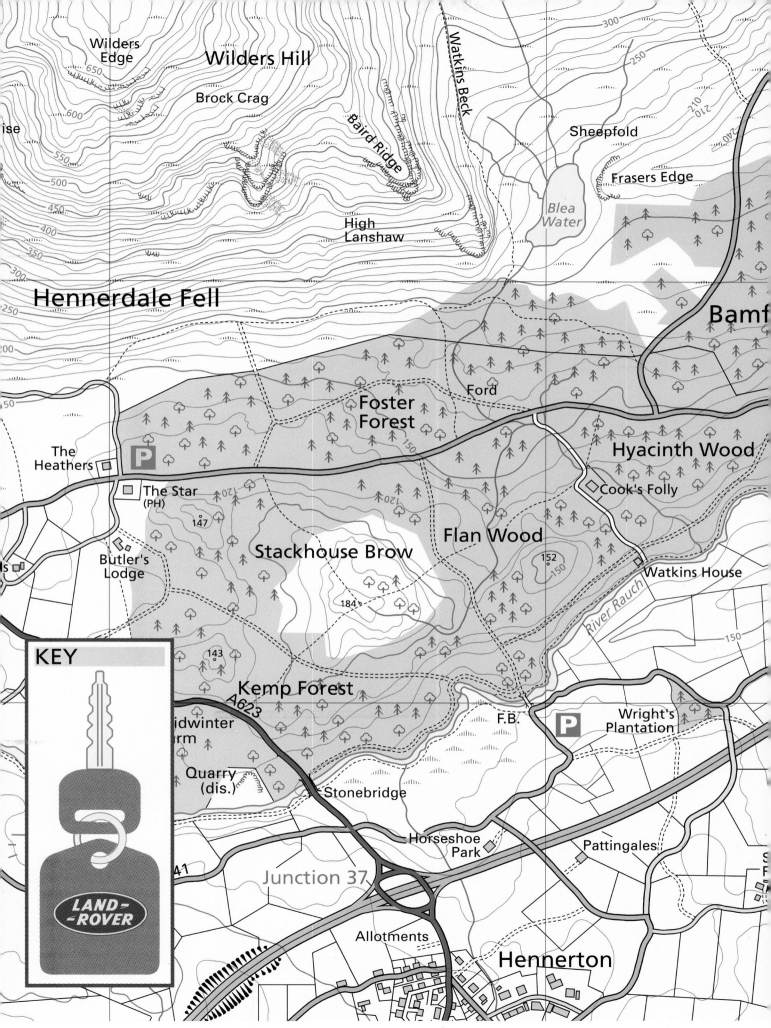

DEFENDER, DISCOVERY, RANGE ROVER. THE BEST 4x4's x FAR.

LAND ROVER ENCOURAGES RESPONSIBLE OFF-ROAD DRIVING. LAND ROVER, LODE LANE, SOLIHULL, ENGLAND B92 8NW.

To enable you to use your 1994 Johansens Recommended Hotels Guide more effectively, the following seven pages of indexes contain a wealth of useful information about the hotels featured in the Guide. As well as listing the hotels alphabetically and by county, the indexes also show at a glance which hotels offer certain specialised facilities.

The indexes are listed as follows:

- Alphabetically by region
- By county
- With a heated indoor swimming pool
- With a golf course on site
- With a golf course nearby
- With shooting arranged
- With salmon or trout fishing on site
- With health/fitness facilities
- With childcare facilities
- With conference facilities for 250 delegates or more

- Nominations for Johansens Awards for Excellence
- Relais et Châteaux members
- Small Luxury Hotels of the World members
- Pride of Britain members
- Exclusive Hotels members
- Taste of Wales members
- Welsh Gold Collection members
- Index of advertisers

1994 Johansens Recommended Hotels listed alphabetically by region

1994 Johansens Recommended Hotels by county

ENGLAND

469

Hotels with a heated indoor swimming pool

Swimming pools at these hotels are open all year round

Hotels with golf

Hotels with golf on site

PLAY THE ROLE OF HOTEL INSPECTOR!

At the back of this book you will notice a quantity of Guest Survey Forms. If you have had an enjoyable stay at one of our recommended hotels, or alternatively you have been in some way dissapointed, please complete one of these forms and send it to us FREEPOST.

These reports essentially complement the assessments made by our team of professional inspectors, continually monitoring the standards of hospitality in every establishment in our guides.

Guest Survey reports also have an important influence on the selection of nominations for our annual awards for excellence.

'Diversity and excellence for the discerning traveller'.

GUEST SURVEY REPORT

To: Johansens, FREEPOST (CB264),
Astley House, 33 Notting Hill Gate,
Notting Hill, London W11 3BR

Name and location of hotel: ....

Name and address of guest: ....

....Date of visit: ....

Please tick one box in each category below:	Excellent	Good	Acceptable	Disappointing	Poor
Bedrooms					
Public Rooms					
Restaurant/Cuisine					
Service					
Welcome/Friendliness					
Value For Money					

PLEASE return your Guest Survey Report form!

Establishment(s) you would like to see in a Johansens guide:
Name: ....
Address or location: ....
❏ Please add my name to your mailing list to receive privileged Johansens information

Your own Johansens 'inspection' gives reliability to our guides and assists in the selection of Award Nominations

✂ ···

GUEST SURVEY REPORT

To: Johansens, FREEPOST (CB264),
Astley House, 33 Notting Hill Gate,
Notting Hill, London W11 3BR

Name and location of hotel: ....

Name and address of guest: ....

....Date of visit: ....

Please tick one box in each category below:	Excellent	Good	Acceptable	Disappointing	Poor
Bedrooms					
Public Rooms					
Restaurant/Cuisine					
Service					
Welcome/Friendliness					
Value For Money					

PLEASE return your Guest Survey Report form!

Establishment(s) you would like to see in a Johansens guide:
Name: ....
Address or location: ....
❏ Please add my name to your mailing list to receive privileged Johansens information

Your own Johansens 'inspection' gives reliability to our guides and assists in the selection of Award Nominations

✂ ···

GUEST SURVEY REPORT

To: Johansens, FREEPOST (CB264),
Astley House, 33 Notting Hill Gate,
Notting Hill, London W11 3BR

Name and location of hotel: ....

Name and address of guest: ....

....Date of visit: ....

Please tick one box in each category below:	Excellent	Good	Acceptable	Disappointing	Poor
Bedrooms					
Public Rooms					
Restaurant/Cuisine					
Service					
Welcome/Friendliness					
Value For Money					

PLEASE return your Guest Survey Report form!

Establishment(s) you would like to see in a Johansens guide:
Name: ....
Address or location: ....
❏ Please add my name to your mailing list to receive privileged Johansens information

Your own Johansens 'inspection' gives reliability to our guides and assists in the selection of Award Nominations

Order Coupon

To order Johansens guides, simply indicate which publications you require by putting the quantity(ies) in the boxes provided. Choose you preferred method of payment and return this coupon (NO STAMP REQUIRED). You may also place your order using FREEPHONE 0800 269397 or by fax on 071 792 0824.

❏ I enclose a cheque for £........................ payable to Biblios PDS Ltd (Johansens book distributor).
❏ I enclose my order on company letterheading, please invoice me. (UK companies only)
❏ Please debit my credit/charge card account (please tick)
❏ MASTERCARD/ACCESS ❏ VISA ❏ DINERS ❏ AMEX

Card Number ....

Signature...Expiry Date...........................
Name (Mr/Mrs/Miss) ....
Address..
....
....Postcode ....

(We aim to despatch your order with 10 days, but please allow 28 days for delivery)

Occasionally we may allow reputable organisations to write to you with offers which may interest you. If you prefer not to hear from them, tick this box ❏

CALL THE JOHANSENS CREDIT CARD ORDER SERVICE FREE ☎ **0800 269397**

save £10	WHEN YOU BUY A SET OF ALL THREE JOHANSENS GUIDES	PRICE	QTY	TOTAL
		£31.80		
	Boxed set of Johansens guides including slip case 1 30000 701 J	£35.00		
	Johansens Recommended Hotels in Great Britain & Ireland 1994 1 85324 750 2	£19.90		
	Johansens Recommended Inns & Restaurants in Great Britain 1994 1 85324 752 9	£10.95		
	Johansens Recommended Private Country Houses in Great Britain & Ireland 1994 1 85342 753 7	£10.95		

ALL PRICES INCLUDE HANDLING AND UK POSTAGE ONLY
REST OF EUROPE ADD: 1 copy £2.50; 2 or more £6.50.
OUTSIDE EUROPE (surface mail) ADD: 1 copy £3.50; 2 or more £7.50 (allow 40 days for delivery).
AIR MAIL ADD: 1 copy £14.00; 2 or more £17.00.

6J7 TOTAL

PRICES VALID UNTIL 31/12/94

Post free to:
JOHANSENS, FREEPOST (CB264), HORSHAM, WEST SUSSEX RH13 8ZA

Order Coupon

To order Johansens guides, simply indicate which publications you require by putting the quantity(ies) in the boxes provided. Choose you preferred method of payment and return this coupon (NO STAMP REQUIRED). You may also place your order using FREEPHONE 0800 269397 or by fax on 071 792 0824.

❏ I enclose a cheque for £........................ payable to Biblios PDS Ltd (Johansens book distributor).
❏ I enclose my order on company letterheading, please invoice me. (UK companies only)
❏ Please debit my credit/charge card account (please tick)
❏ MASTERCARD/ACCESS ❏ VISA ❏ DINERS ❏ AMEX

Card Number ....

Signature...Expiry Date...........................
Name (Mr/Mrs/Miss) ....
Address..
....
....Postcode ....

(We aim to despatch your order with 10 days, but please allow 28 days for delivery)

Occasionally we may allow reputable organisations to write to you with offers which may interest you. If you prefer not to hear from them, tick this box ❏

CALL THE JOHANSENS CREDIT CARD ORDER SERVICE FREE  ☎ **0800 269397**

save £10	WHEN YOU BUY A SET OF ALL THREE JOHANSENS GUIDES	PRICE	QTY	TOTAL
		£31.80		
	Boxed set of Johansens guides including slip case 1 30000 701 J	£35.00		
	Johansens Recommended Hotels in Great Britain & Ireland 1994 1 85324 750 2	£19.90		
	Johansens Recommended Inns & Restaurants in Great Britain 1994 1 85324 752 9	£10.95		
	Johansens Recommended Private Country Houses in Great Britain & Ireland 1994 1 85342 753 7	£10.95		

ALL PRICES INCLUDE HANDLING AND UK POSTAGE ONLY
REST OF EUROPE ADD: 1 copy £2.50; 2 or more £6.50.
OUTSIDE EUROPE (surface mail) ADD: 1 copy £3.50; 2 or more £7.50 (allow 40 days for delivery).
AIR MAIL ADD: 1 copy £14.00; 2 or more £17.00.

6J7 TOTAL

PRICES VALID UNTIL 31/12/94

Post free to:
JOHANSENS, FREEPOST (CB264), HORSHAM, WEST SUSSEX RH13 8ZA

Order Coupon

To order Johansens guides, simply indicate which publications you require by putting the quantity(ies) in the boxes provided. Choose you preferred method of payment and return this coupon (NO STAMP REQUIRED). You may also place your order using FREEPHONE 0800 269397 or by fax on 071 792 0824.

❏ I enclose a cheque for £........................ payable to Biblios PDS Ltd (Johansens book distributor).
❏ I enclose my order on company letterheading, please invoice me. (UK companies only)
❏ Please debit my credit/charge card account (please tick)
❏ MASTERCARD/ACCESS ❏ VISA ❏ DINERS ❏ AMEX

Card Number ....

Signature...Expiry Date...........................
Name (Mr/Mrs/Miss) ....
Address..
....
....Postcode ....

(We aim to despatch your order with 10 days, but please allow 28 days for delivery)

Occasionally we may allow reputable organisations to write to you with offers which may interest you. If you prefer not to hear from them, tick this box ❏

CALL THE JOHANSENS CREDIT CARD ORDER SERVICE FREE ☎ **0800 269397**

save £10	WHEN YOU BUY A SET OF ALL THREE JOHANSENS GUIDES	PRICE	QTY	TOTAL
		£31.80		
	Boxed set of Johansens guides including slip case 1 30000 701 J	£35.00		
	Johansens Recommended Hotels in Great Britain & Ireland 1994 1 85324 750 2	£19.90		
	Johansens Recommended Inns & Restaurants in Great Britain 1994 1 85324 752 9	£10.95		
	Johansens Recommended Private Country Houses in Great Britain & Ireland 1994 1 85342 753 7	£10.95		

ALL PRICES INCLUDE HANDLING AND UK POSTAGE ONLY
REST OF EUROPE ADD: 1 copy £2.50; 2 or more £6.50.
OUTSIDE EUROPE (surface mail) ADD: 1 copy £3.50; 2 or more £7.50 (allow 40 days for delivery).
AIR MAIL ADD: 1 copy £14.00; 2 or more £17.00.

6J7 TOTAL

PRICES VALID UNTIL 31/12/94

Post free to:
JOHANSENS, FREEPOST (CB264), HORSHAM, WEST SUSSEX RH13 8ZA

GUEST SURVEY REPORT

To: Johansens, FREEPOST (CB264), Astley House, 33 Notting Hill Gate, Notting Hill, London W11 3BR

Name and location of hotel: ....

Name and address of guest: ....

....Date of visit: ....

Please tick one box in each category below:	Excellent	Good	Acceptable	Disappointing	Poor
Bedrooms					
Public Rooms					
Restaurant/Cuisine					
Service					
Welcome/Friendliness					
Value For Money					

PLEASE return your Guest Survey Report form!

Establishment(s) you would like to see in a Johansens guide:
Name: ....
Address or location: ....
❏ Please add my name to your mailing list to receive privileged Johansens information

Your own Johansens 'inspection' gives reliability to our guides and assists in the selection of Award Nominations

✂ ....

GUEST SURVEY REPORT

To: Johansens, FREEPOST (CB264), Astley House, 33 Notting Hill Gate, Notting Hill, London W11 3BR

Name and location of hotel: ....

Name and address of guest: ....

....Date of visit: ....

Please tick one box in each category below:	Excellent	Good	Acceptable	Disappointing	Poor
Bedrooms					
Public Rooms					
Restaurant/Cuisine					
Service					
Welcome/Friendliness					
Value For Money					

PLEASE return your Guest Survey Report form!

Establishment(s) you would like to see in a Johansens guide:
Name: ....
Address or location: ....
❏ Please add my name to your mailing list to receive privileged Johansens information

Your own Johansens 'inspection' gives reliability to our guides and assists in the selection of Award Nominations

✂ ....

GUEST SURVEY REPORT

To: Johansens, FREEPOST (CB264), Astley House, 33 Notting Hill Gate, Notting Hill, London W11 3BR

Name and location of hotel: ....

Name and address of guest: ....

....Date of visit: ....

Please tick one box in each category below:	Excellent	Good	Acceptable	Disappointing	Poor
Bedrooms					
Public Rooms					
Restaurant/Cuisine					
Service					
Welcome/Friendliness					
Value For Money					

PLEASE return your Guest Survey Report form!

Establishment(s) you would like to see in a Johansens guide:
Name: ....
Address or location: ....
❏ Please add my name to your mailing list to receive privileged Johansens information

Your own Johansens 'inspection' gives reliability to our guides and assists in the selection of Award Nominations

Order Coupon

To order Johansens guides, simply indicate which publications you require by putting the quantity(ies) in the boxes provided. Choose you preferred method of payment and return this coupon (NO STAMP REQUIRED). You may also place your order using FREEPHONE 0800 269397 or by fax on 071 792 0824.

❑ I enclose a cheque for £......................... payable to Biblios PDS Ltd (Johansens book distributor).
❑ I enclose my order on company letterheading, please invoice me. (UK companies only)
❑ Please debit my credit/charge card account (please tick)
❑ MASTERCARD/ACCESS ❑ VISA ❑ DINERS ❑ AMEX

Card Number ....

Signature...Expiry Date...............................
Name (Mr/Mrs/Miss) ....
Address...
....
....Postcode ....

(We aim to despatch your order with 10 days, but please allow 28 days for delivery)

Occasionally we may allow reputable organisations to write to you with offers which may interest you. If you prefer not to hear from them, tick this box ❑

CALL THE JOHANSENS CREDIT CARD ORDER SERVICE FREE ☎ **0800 269397**

save £10	WHEN YOU BUY A SET OF ALL THREE JOHANSENS GUIDES	PRICE	QTY	TOTAL
		£31.80		
	Boxed set of Johansens guides including slip case 1 30000 701 J	£35.00		
	Johansens Recommended Hotels in Great Britain & Ireland 1994 1 85324 750 2	£19.90		
	Johansens Recommended Inns & Restaurants in Great Britain 1994 1 85324 752 9	£10.95		
	Johansens Recommended Private Country Houses in Great Britain & Ireland 1994 1 85342 753 7	£10.95		

ALL PRICES INCLUDE HANDLING AND UK POSTAGE ONLY
REST OF EUROPE ADD: 1 copy £2.50; 2 or more £6.50.
OUTSIDE EUROPE (surface mail) ADD: 1 copy £3.50; 2 or more £7.50 (allow 40 days for delivery).
AIR MAIL ADD: 1 copy £14.00; 2 or more £17.00.

6J7   TOTAL

PRICES VALID UNTIL 31/12/94

Post free to:
JOHANSENS, FREEPOST (CB264), HORSHAM, WEST SUSSEX RH13 8ZA

Order Coupon

To order Johansens guides, simply indicate which publications you require by putting the quantity(ies) in the boxes provided. Choose you preferred method of payment and return this coupon (NO STAMP REQUIRED). You may also place your order using FREEPHONE 0800 269397 or by fax on 071 792 0824.

❑ I enclose a cheque for £......................... payable to Biblios PDS Ltd (Johansens book distributor).
❑ I enclose my order on company letterheading, please invoice me. (UK companies only)
❑ Please debit my credit/charge card account (please tick)
❑ MASTERCARD/ACCESS ❑ VISA ❑ DINERS ❑ AMEX

Card Number ....

Signature...Expiry Date...............................
Name (Mr/Mrs/Miss) ....
Address...
....
....Postcode ....

(We aim to despatch your order with 10 days, but please allow 28 days for delivery)

Occasionally we may allow reputable organisations to write to you with offers which may interest you. If you prefer not to hear from them, tick this box ❑

CALL THE JOHANSENS CREDIT CARD ORDER SERVICE FREE ☎ **0800 269397**

save £10	WHEN YOU BUY A SET OF ALL THREE JOHANSENS GUIDES	PRICE	QTY	TOTAL
		£31.80		
	Boxed set of Johansens guides including slip case 1 30000 701 J	£35.00		
	Johansens Recommended Hotels in Great Britain & Ireland 1994 1 85324 750 2	£19.90		
	Johansens Recommended Inns & Restaurants in Great Britain 1994 1 85324 752 9	£10.95		
	Johansens Recommended Private Country Houses in Great Britain & Ireland 1994 1 85342 753 7	£10.95		

ALL PRICES INCLUDE HANDLING AND UK POSTAGE ONLY
REST OF EUROPE ADD: 1 copy £2.50; 2 or more £6.50.
OUTSIDE EUROPE (surface mail) ADD: 1 copy £3.50; 2 or more £7.50 (allow 40 days for delivery).
AIR MAIL ADD: 1 copy £14.00; 2 or more £17.00.

6J7   TOTAL

PRICES VALID UNTIL 31/12/94

Post free to:
JOHANSENS, FREEPOST (CB264), HORSHAM, WEST SUSSEX RH13 8ZA

Order Coupon

To order Johansens guides, simply indicate which publications you require by putting the quantity(ies) in the boxes provided. Choose you preferred method of payment and return this coupon (NO STAMP REQUIRED). You may also place your order using FREEPHONE 0800 269397 or by fax on 071 792 0824.

❑ I enclose a cheque for £......................... payable to Biblios PDS Ltd (Johansens book distributor).
❑ I enclose my order on company letterheading, please invoice me. (UK companies only)
❑ Please debit my credit/charge card account (please tick)
❑ MASTERCARD/ACCESS ❑ VISA ❑ DINERS ❑ AMEX

Card Number ....

Signature...Expiry Date...............................
Name (Mr/Mrs/Miss) ....
Address...
....
....Postcode ....

(We aim to despatch your order with 10 days, but please allow 28 days for delivery)

Occasionally we may allow reputable organisations to write to you with offers which may interest you. If you prefer not to hear from them, tick this box ❑

CALL THE JOHANSENS CREDIT CARD ORDER SERVICE FREE ☎ **0800 269397**

save £10	WHEN YOU BUY A SET OF ALL THREE JOHANSENS GUIDES	PRICE	QTY	TOTAL
		£31.80		
	Boxed set of Johansens guides including slip case 1 30000 701 J	£35.00		
	Johansens Recommended Hotels in Great Britain & Ireland 1994 1 85324 750 2	£19.90		
	Johansens Recommended Inns & Restaurants in Great Britain 1994 1 85324 752 9	£10.95		
	Johansens Recommended Private Country Houses in Great Britain & Ireland 1994 1 85342 753 7	£10.95		

ALL PRICES INCLUDE HANDLING AND UK POSTAGE ONLY
REST OF EUROPE ADD: 1 copy £2.50; 2 or more £6.50.
OUTSIDE EUROPE (surface mail) ADD: 1 copy £3.50; 2 or more £7.50 (allow 40 days for delivery).
AIR MAIL ADD: 1 copy £14.00; 2 or more £17.00.

6J7   TOTAL

PRICES VALID UNTIL 31/12/94

Post free to:
JOHANSENS, FREEPOST (CB264), HORSHAM, WEST SUSSEX RH13 8ZA

GUEST SURVEY REPORT

To: Johansens, FREEPOST (CB264), Astley House, 33 Notting Hill Gate, **Notting Hill, London W11 3BR**

Name and location of hotel: ....

Name and address of guest: ....

....Date of visit: ....

Please tick one box in each category below:	Excellent	Good	Acceptable	Disappointing	Poor
Bedrooms					
Public Rooms					
Restaurant/Cuisine					
Service					
Welcome/Friendliness					
Value For Money					

PLEASE return your Guest Survey Report form!

Establishment(s) you would like to see in a Johansens guide:
Name: ....
Address or location: ....
❏ Please add my name to your mailing list to receive privileged Johansens information

Your own Johansens 'inspection' gives reliability to our guides and assists in the selection of Award Nominations

GUEST SURVEY REPORT

To: Johansens, FREEPOST (CB264), Astley House, 33 Notting Hill Gate, **Notting Hill, London W11 3BR**

Name and location of hotel: ....

Name and address of guest: ....

....Date of visit: ....

Please tick one box in each category below:	Excellent	Good	Acceptable	Disappointing	Poor
Bedrooms					
Public Rooms					
Restaurant/Cuisine					
Service					
Welcome/Friendliness					
Value For Money					

PLEASE return your Guest Survey Report form!

Establishment(s) you would like to see in a Johansens guide:
Name: ....
Address or location: ....
❏ Please add my name to your mailing list to receive privileged Johansens information

Your own Johansens 'inspection' gives reliability to our guides and assists in the selection of Award Nominations

GUEST SURVEY REPORT

To: Johansens, FREEPOST (CB264), Astley House, 33 Notting Hill Gate, **Notting Hill, London W11 3BR**

Name and location of hotel: ....

Name and address of guest: ....

....Date of visit: ....

Please tick one box in each category below:	Excellent	Good	Acceptable	Disappointing	Poor
Bedrooms					
Public Rooms					
Restaurant/Cuisine					
Service					
Welcome/Friendliness					
Value For Money					

PLEASE return your Guest Survey Report form!

Establishment(s) you would like to see in a Johansens guide:
Name: ....
Address or location: ....
❏ Please add my name to your mailing list to receive privileged Johansens information

Your own Johansens 'inspection' gives reliability to our guides and assists in the selection of Award Nominations

Order Coupon

To order Johansens guides, simply indicate which publications you require by putting the quantity(ies) in the boxes provided. Choose you preferred method of payment and return this coupon (NO STAMP REQUIRED). You may also place your order using FREEPHONE 0800 269397 or by fax on 071 792 0824.

❑ I enclose a cheque for £......................... payable to Biblios PDS Ltd (Johansens book distributor).

❑ I enclose my order on company letterheading, please invoice me. (UK companies only)

❑ Please debit my credit/charge card account (please tick)

❑ MASTERCARD/ACCESS ❑ VISA ❑ DINERS ❑ AMEX

Card Number ....

Signature..Expiry Date......................

Name (Mr/Mrs/Miss) ....

Address...

....

....Postcode ....

(We aim to despatch your order with 10 days, but please allow 28 days for delivery)

Occasionally we may allow reputable organisations to write to you with offers which may interest you. If you prefer not to hear from them, tick this box ❑

CALL THE JOHANSENS CREDIT CARD ORDER SERVICE FREE ☎ **0800 269397**

save £10	WHEN YOU BUY A SET OF ALL THREE JOHANSENS GUIDES	PRICE	QTY	TOTAL
		£31.80		
	Boxed set of Johansens guides including slip case 1 30000 701 J	£35.00		
	Johansens Recommended Hotels in Great Britain & Ireland 1994 1 85324 750 2	£19.90		
	Johansens Recommended Inns & Restaurants in Great Britain 1994 1 85324 752 9	£10.95		
	Johansens Recommended Private Country Houses in Great Britain & Ireland 1994 1 85342 753 7	£10.95		

ALL PRICES INCLUDE HANDLING AND UK POSTAGE ONLY
REST OF EUROPE ADD: 1 copy £2.50; 2 or more £6.50.
OUTSIDE EUROPE (surface mail) ADD: 1 copy £3.50; 2 or more £7.50 (allow 40 days for delivery).
AIR MAIL ADD: 1 copy £14.00; 2 or more £17.00.

6J7 TOTAL

PRICES VALID UNTIL 31/12/94

Post free to:
JOHANSENS, FREEPOST (CB264), HORSHAM, WEST SUSSEX RH13 8ZA

Order Coupon

To order Johansens guides, simply indicate which publications you require by putting the quantity(ies) in the boxes provided. Choose you preferred method of payment and return this coupon (NO STAMP REQUIRED). You may also place your order using FREEPHONE 0800 269397 or by fax on 071 792 0824.

❑ I enclose a cheque for £......................... payable to Biblios PDS Ltd (Johansens book distributor).

❑ I enclose my order on company letterheading, please invoice me. (UK companies only)

❑ Please debit my credit/charge card account (please tick)

❑ MASTERCARD/ACCESS ❑ VISA ❑ DINERS ❑ AMEX

Card Number ....

Signature..Expiry Date......................

Name (Mr/Mrs/Miss) ....

Address...

....

....Postcode ....

(We aim to despatch your order with 10 days, but please allow 28 days for delivery)

Occasionally we may allow reputable organisations to write to you with offers which may interest you. If you prefer not to hear from them, tick this box ❑

CALL THE JOHANSENS CREDIT CARD ORDER SERVICE FREE ☎ **0800 269397**

save £10	WHEN YOU BUY A SET OF ALL THREE JOHANSENS GUIDES	PRICE	QTY	TOTAL
		£31.80		
	Boxed set of Johansens guides including slip case 1 30000 701 J	£35.00		
	Johansens Recommended Hotels in Great Britain & Ireland 1994 1 85324 750 2	£19.90		
	Johansens Recommended Inns & Restaurants in Great Britain 1994 1 85324 752 9	£10.95		
	Johansens Recommended Private Country Houses in Great Britain & Ireland 1994 1 85342 753 7	£10.95		

ALL PRICES INCLUDE HANDLING AND UK POSTAGE ONLY
REST OF EUROPE ADD: 1 copy £2.50; 2 or more £6.50.
OUTSIDE EUROPE (surface mail) ADD: 1 copy £3.50; 2 or more £7.50 (allow 40 days for delivery).
AIR MAIL ADD: 1 copy £14.00; 2 or more £17.00.

6J7 TOTAL

PRICES VALID UNTIL 31/12/94

Post free to:
JOHANSENS, FREEPOST (CB264), HORSHAM, WEST SUSSEX RH13 8ZA

Order Coupon

To order Johansens guides, simply indicate which publications you require by putting the quantity(ies) in the boxes provided. Choose you preferred method of payment and return this coupon (NO STAMP REQUIRED). You may also place your order using FREEPHONE 0800 269397 or by fax on 071 792 0824.

❑ I enclose a cheque for £......................... payable to Biblios PDS Ltd (Johansens book distributor).

❑ I enclose my order on company letterheading, please invoice me. (UK companies only)

❑ Please debit my credit/charge card account (please tick)

❑ MASTERCARD/ACCESS ❑ VISA ❑ DINERS ❑ AMEX

Card Number ....

Signature..Expiry Date......................

Name (Mr/Mrs/Miss) ....

Address...

....

....Postcode ....

(We aim to despatch your order with 10 days, but please allow 28 days for delivery)

Occasionally we may allow reputable organisations to write to you with offers which may interest you. If you prefer not to hear from them, tick this box ❑

CALL THE JOHANSENS CREDIT CARD ORDER SERVICE FREE ☎ **0800 269397**

save £10	WHEN YOU BUY A SET OF ALL THREE JOHANSENS GUIDES	PRICE	QTY	TOTAL
		£31.80		
	Boxed set of Johansens guides including slip case 1 30000 701 J	£35.00		
	Johansens Recommended Hotels in Great Britain & Ireland 1994 1 85324 750 2	£19.90		
	Johansens Recommended Inns & Restaurants in Great Britain 1994 1 85324 752 9	£10.95		
	Johansens Recommended Private Country Houses in Great Britain & Ireland 1994 1 85342 753 7	£10.95		

ALL PRICES INCLUDE HANDLING AND UK POSTAGE ONLY
REST OF EUROPE ADD: 1 copy £2.50; 2 or more £6.50.
OUTSIDE EUROPE (surface mail) ADD: 1 copy £3.50; 2 or more £7.50 (allow 40 days for delivery).
AIR MAIL ADD: 1 copy £14.00; 2 or more £17.00.

6J7 TOTAL

PRICES VALID UNTIL 31/12/94

Post free to:
JOHANSENS, FREEPOST (CB264), HORSHAM, WEST SUSSEX RH13 8ZA

£50 VI-SPRING
VOUCHER

This voucher entitles you to claim £50 against your purchase of a new Vi-Spring bed

See reverse for full terms and conditions of this offer

£50 VI-SPRING
VOUCHER

This voucher entitles you to claim £50 against your purchase of a new Vi-Spring bed

See reverse for full terms and conditions of this offer

£50 VI-SPRING
VOUCHER

This voucher entitles you to claim £50 against your purchase of a new Vi-Spring bed

See reverse for full terms and conditions of this offer

TERMS AND CONDITIONS OF OFFER

1. This voucher is only exchangeable against a new Vi-Spring bed at *point of purchase* from participating Vi-Spring stockists.

2. Full participating stockist list available from Vi-Spring Marketing Department. Telephone 0752 366311.

3. It is non-exchangeable for cash in whole or in part.

4. Valid until 31 December 1994.

5. Only one voucher per bed.

6. This is a manufacturers offer and is in addition to any retailer's sale or promotion.

JVS1

TERMS AND CONDITIONS OF OFFER

1. This voucher is only exchangeable against a new Vi-Spring bed at *point of purchase* from participating Vi-Spring stockists.

2. Full participating stockist list available from Vi-Spring Marketing Department. Telephone 0752 366311.

3. It is non-exchangeable for cash in whole or in part.

4. Valid until 31 December 1994.

5. Only one voucher per bed.

6. This is a manufacturers offer and is in addition to any retailer's sale or promotion.

JVS1

TERMS AND CONDITIONS OF OFFER

1. This voucher is only exchangeable against a new Vi-Spring bed at *point of purchase* from participating Vi-Spring stockists.

2. Full participating stockist list available from Vi-Spring Marketing Department. Telephone 0752 366311.

3. It is non-exchangeable for cash in whole or in part.

4. Valid until 31 December 1994.

5. Only one voucher per bed.

6. This is a manufacturers offer and is in addition to any retailer's sale or promotion.

JVS1